Special Dedication to Jeremy Hope

While this book was in the editing stages, Jeremy Hope was diagnosed with a severe illness. In September 2011 he passed away. Jeremy was an inspirational leader for the Beyond Budgeting Round Table and a dear friend, colleague, and mentor. He was a prolific writer who always remained open to the people and the world around him. He was a great guy to learn from, to share ideas with, and to work with on changing the way the world is led and managed.

In our time together, Jeremy and I worked with some great thought leaders and some equally big egos. Fortunately, Jeremy always retained a common touch. He had time for everyone and a love of life that was infectious. He focused on the big things in life and tried to make the world a better place. His legacy lives on in his writing. I hope our readers learn from his many insights.

—Steve Player

Don't Blame the Tools—It's How You Use Them
By Jeremy Hope

A range of tools and techniques has emerged over the past decade,
Designed to solve many of the problems that traditional management
    made.
Advocates of these tools claim they can be powerful and effective,
What they mean is that tools should be more interconnected.
But systems designers have to change their view,
Instead of dictating and directing what people do.
They need to rethink how the system works,
From the outside in and from the customer first.

The major problem with most best practices and tools
Such as scorecards, benchmarks, plans, and other management jewels
Is that they are used as additional management controls
Within the traditional hierarchy with top-down roles.
The satisfaction scores struggle to strive
To get over three or four out of five,
Yet we spend millions on these tools each year
With patchy results and little cheer.

The problem is that many people are bemused
By a management model too often misused.
Attempts to improve the system are neutralized and lose their resistance
By the powerful antibodies of the command and control system.
Thus, if any proposed actions threaten those norms
The corporate immune system will ring the alarms.
That is why there is often such a gulf in clarity
Between the reefs and the rocks of rhetoric and reality.

It is interesting to note what one user said
When the budget was removed from around her head,
"The balanced scorecard has been 'turbo-charged'"
Was written in letters bold and enlarged.
Empower and adapt are the words we'd choose
With more flexible models and multiple views.
More diversity is what we're aiming for
Different ways of thinking that open the door.

BEYOND PERFORMANCE MANAGEMENT

Why, When, and How to Use
40 Tools *and* **Best Practices** *for*
Superior Business Performance

BEYOND
PERFORMANCE
MANAGEMENT

Jeremy Hope and Steve Player

HARVARD BUSINESS REVIEW PRESS
BOSTON, MASSACHUSETTS

Library of Congress Cataloging-in-Publication Data

Hope, Jeremy.
Beyond performance management : why, when, and how to use 40 tools and best practices for superior business performance / Jeremy Hope and Steve Player.
    p. cm.
  ISBN 978-1-4221-4195-3 (alk. paper)
  1. Organizational effectiveness—Measurement.   2. Performance—Management.
3. Total quality management.   I. Player, Steve, 1958- II. Title.
  HD58.9.H67 2011
  658.3'14—dc23

                                                    2011018739

This book is dedicated to the pioneer companies and

visionary leaders who were brave enough to try new approaches,

even when the path was not clear;

and to our families and friends who encourage us, enable our pursuits,

and whose love we hold so dear.

We thank you and hope this book helps others find their way.

Contents

Preface

Can you really "manage" performance? The conundrum is in the question and is at the core of this book. In a traditional command-and-control management model, managers indeed aim to set clear goals, lay out strategic themes, and then march the organization toward the execution of the goals. And, you might say, there is nothing wrong with that.

This approach has been the standard for decades. But while it might have worked well in the past, there are few people today who believe it is the right way forward. They recognize that in an increasingly uncertain and turbulent world, businesses need more flexibility in their planning and decision-making processes. This means always monitoring and adapting to changes in markets, customers, products, and business models. *Innovation* and *adaptation* are the key words.

But we also need to think about what the words mean. They are not command-and-control words. We cannot command innovation and adaptation. We can enable and encourage and inspire and even lead. But we can't command someone to be creative or adaptive. People must have other intangible performance drivers that get them out of bed each morning and fire them with ambition and creativity. In other words, we need to move beyond traditional performance management.

The changes in how we are starting to think about management have deep implications for how we lead, plan, and perform. They also help us to rethink how we use all the tools and practices that have been an accepted part of management life and work for years. Most have been conceived and born in the command-and-control model. They are either owned by senior management teams or executed down the hierarchical lines of the business. Many are project driven from the corporate center. For these reasons, many have lost their effectiveness, and some are falling by the wayside.

But these tools and practices also represent a deep, invaluable repository of knowledge. We need to reexamine and represent them for a new management age. We need to preserve and, in some cases, repackage the wisdom.

That is the aim of this book.

INTRODUCTION

Over the past twenty-five years, leaders in both private and public sectors have spent billions of dollars implementing a range of management tools and practices in their efforts to improve performance. But the evidence of success on the ground is thin. In 1995, Harvard professor John Kotter published research indicating that only 30 percent of change programs succeed; in 2008, a McKinsey & Company survey came up with exactly the same percentage.[1] It seems that change initiatives have continued to have minimal impact. Why is it that tools such as the balanced scorecard, benchmarking, and customer relationship management, which the management consulting industry trumpeted so loudly, have not had the impact their sponsors proclaimed? Many of the answers lie in ineffective leadership, lack of commitment, and poor implementation. But other, less obvious answers relate to how managers implement and use tools and practices.

Most tools and practices suffer from poor practice. And having absorbed huge amounts of management time and expense, companies abandon many tools as the consultants move out and the internal project champions move on. Abortive tools and systems are a major source of management frustration, added complexity, and wasted time and cost. Too many organizations rush into buying and implementing tools without first considering the fundamental question: which problem are we trying to solve? Framing and answering this question would avoid many expensive mistakes. Peter Drucker put it this way: "I was taught that you make a diagnosis before you operate. And nine times out of ten, when you make the diagnosis, you don't operate."[2]

We have spent the past fifteen years examining the management practices of many large organizations. We have written many books, articles, and case reports and conducted numerous interviews, trying to make sense of what works and what doesn't. Our conclusion is that in an increasingly turbulent world, companies can best use tools and practices to engage and empower frontline teams (who work in the "value zone" between the organization and the customer), rather than to command and control them. In other words, organizations that base their management models on "empower and adapt" rather than command and control have greater long-term success. The reasons are not hard to find. Management models based on empower and adapt operate with less bureaucracy (smaller back offices), fewer people (self-managed teams), and fewer top-down controls (information is integrated in the work). The result is lower costs, more flexibility, and more satisfied employees, customers, and shareholders.

The purpose of this book is to critically review a wide range of management tools and practices and provide a number of guidelines that will help leaders select the right ones, implement them in the right way, and gain maximum value from their use.

Selection of tools and practices

According to a recent survey of twenty-five management tools and practices containing 1,430 responses from a range of organizations across every industry and region of the world, the average global usage is 34 percent, though among large companies (over $2 billion), the usage rises to 40 percent.[3] The highest regional user is North America (51 percent), with Asia-Pacific second (35 percent), Europe third (34 percent), and Latin America fourth (25 percent). However, these figures increase dramatically when respondents were asked what tools they expect to use over the next few years. Some tools are consistently popular. Benchmarking (76 percent), strategic planning (67 percent), and mission statements (65 percent), for example, have remained in the top-five throughout the period.[4]

Our focus will be on forty tools and practices—those that typically represent a major change initiative and significant capital investment. We will examine these tools and practices through five perspectives of what is often known as "performance management": strategic planning, shareholder and customer value, lean cost management, performance measurement, and performance evaluation.

Different organizations and many consultants use alternative terms to describe these tools and practices. In most cases, the success criteria and implementation insights—the primary focus of the reviews—are similar, if not exactly the same.

There are of course hundreds of management tools and practices to select from. So why have we chosen these and not others? One reason is the focus on performance management that also reflects our own experiences. Another is to bring to your attention new ideas that are having an impact. Of course, we also have limited time and space to communicate our key points, so the size and scope of the text are limiting factors.

Scope of reviews

All surveys show consistent levels of dissatisfaction with management tools. In a recent 2009 Bain survey, only one tool, strategic planning, had a composite score of over 4 out of 5. The top six by usage—benchmarking, strategic planning, mission statements, customer relationship management, outsourcing, and the balanced scorecard—all have dismal satisfaction scores that ranged from 3.7 to 4 out of 5. (Satisfaction scores are not linear.[5] Many years ago, research found that customers scoring a 5 were six times more likely to repurchase than those who scored a 4.[6]). The average satisfaction score was 3.6, with almost no variation across regions.[7] These results provide strong evidence that most tools are either badly chosen or poorly implemented. They also show that major efforts at implementation produce better results than limited efforts.

Each of our reviews contains the following sections:

- **What is this practice and how effective is it?** This section looks at why the practice exists and what it is supposed to do. It briefly examines the practice's evolution as well as strengths and weaknesses.
- **What is the performance potential of this practice?** This section sets out some aims and benefits that you can gain from using this practice.
- **What actions do you need to take to maximize the potential of this practice?** In this section, we will suggest reasons why the tool or practice is not delivering on its promise and implementation insights that will help you to decide whether to invest and how to extract the maximum value from your investment.
- **Further reading.** We provide a short reading list if you want to know more.

Generic success factors

All advocates of tools and practices claim powerful results *if implemented in the right way.* What they mean is if the business case is clearly articulated, the culture of the organization is supportive and its leaders are committed. These are big "ifs." Listed next are some of the most common success factors. They apply to all the tools we review, and hence they *will not necessarily be repeated within each review.*

- **Examine the evidence.** Every tool and practice has strengths and weaknesses. According to a Bain survey, success requires understanding the full effects—and side effects—of each tool or practice and then creatively combining the right ones in the right ways at the right time. Bain advises users to look at the research, to talk to other users, and not to accept hyperbole and simplistic solutions.[8]

Context for reviews

While we hope these reviews will inform you about whether or not to invest in implementation efforts and, if you have already invested, how to extract more value, they are *not* intended to be a "how to" guide to implementation (build a case for change, get senior executive commitment, set up a project team, set goals and milestones, build a road map, and so forth). The history, leadership, culture, and readiness for change in every organization are different, so there cannot be a standard implementation approach for any of these tools and practices. Our focus is on *why these tools do or don't work and what can be done to create more value.*

Our reviews are intended to be *objective* rather than the usual sycophantic articles or papers you read in journals or on Web sites, often written or sponsored by consultants. But we hope they are skeptical rather than cynical. Above all, they do not necessarily support conventional wisdom.

We assume that in choosing a particular practice, you are generally aiming to make your organization more *adaptive* (respond rapidly to unpredictable change), *leaner* (operate with fewer costs), more *innovative* (encourage more creativity and organic growth), and more *ethical* (encourage the right behavior). We also assume that to achieve these aims, the organization needs to be more decentralized and its people more empowered and engaged. These are key assumptions that in some cases radically affect how to implement and use the tools and practices.

- **Make a clear and compelling business case.** Managers need to carefully think through an objective business case before investing in any tool or practice. How will it add value? Does it meet customer needs? Does it build distinctive capabilities? Does it support strategic objectives? What are the hidden side effects and costs? How long will it take to implement? Who is accountable? You need to answer these and other questions before going ahead.
- **Obtain C-level sponsorship.** We can express one of the key change-management conundrums as follows: "You can't expect to sustain top executive support without producing consistent bottom-line results, yet consistent results aren't likely without sustained top executive support." Getting the CEO, CFO, CIO, or COO behind the project can improve its chances significantly. Line managers will be more likely to engage positively if they believe that the change project has the backing of respected senior people.

- **Make a total commitment.** Surveys indicate a strong correlation between *total commitment* to a tool or practice and levels of satisfaction. Take six sigma. The Bain survey indicates that this tool is ranked first for satisfaction when used as part of a major initiative, but falls to twenty-fourth when used on a limited basis.[9] In other words, low-level experimentation without the backing of the leadership team and without the resources to maintain a long-term program is more than likely to end in disappointment.
- **Involve key people in the implementation process.** A successful implementation should involve the people that the tool will affect. If they are alienated, they will see the tool as just another top-down control system and fail to engage in the process. Reporting progress is also important. One way to keep people engaged is to show results graphically on intranets and bulletin boards.
- **Communicate continuously.** Effective communication is essential to the success of any project. This means keeping aims and objectives simple and straightforward, ensuring that key leaders give consistent messages and that their behavior is aligned with these messages.
- **Be patient.** Implementing most tools and practices fully can take many years to realize the benefits, yet many leaders expect bottom-line results in a fraction of that time.

How to use this book

We would be delighted if you were to read this book cover to cover and soak up the hundreds of insights and recommendations that we provide. However, we suspect that most people will use it more as a reference guide to help them learn and improve their performance within their particular areas of interest. The reading lists and notes should help.

Conclusions

Many of the tools and practices we review in this book have been around for years, and the accumulated knowledge of what works and what doesn't is quite extensive. But companies select too many on the basis of "flavor of the month" decisions or use them to fix a particular problem; for example, using the balanced scorecard to fix the strategy problem or rolling forecasts to fix the budgeting problem. This approach is wrong. Performance management is not comprised of a number of disconnected pieces that can be separately improved. It is a holistic model within which all the moving parts need to combine and connect to execute the organization's strategy in a seamless and coherent way.

If we've learned anything over the past fifteen years, it's that big top-down change programs don't work that well. Leaders first need to understand their own organizations. What works for them? And how does change happen? All our experience as management educators tells us that change has to come from within. The people affected have to be involved. Many of the best ideas for change are already in the heads of people working in the organization. They just need releasing. Taking a list of best practices from somewhere else and parachuting them into some poorly performing system or unit is not the right way. But to unleash the knowledge and energy within the organization needs something else. It needs real *insights*. Just one or two fresh ideas can be the catalyst to real progress and sustainable change. That's all most educators can hope to achieve. That's what this book is about.

Part I

Strategic Planning

1

MISSION STATEMENTS

What is this practice and how effective is it?

Mission statements have become popular in recent years as managers look to build a high-performance culture. The trouble is that most focus on lofty goals and meaningless words rather than inspiring people with a compelling "reason for being" and core values that build their emotional commitment. Consequently, despite the time and effort involved, people end up ignoring most of them. We will look at how the best organizations deal with these problems and inspire their people.

Alternative names and related topics: corporate governance; business ethics; emotional commitment

How an organization defines its purpose and defines and articulates its goals influences how its people think, behave, and act in any given situation. Many organizations have focused their purpose and goals on making money or maximizing shareholder value rather than building great businesses and satisfying stakeholders, including employees, customers, and the wider community. The shareholder value model is rooted in traditional economic thinking. The model assumes that individuals are self-interested, rational decision makers driven by economic goals, and that economic relationships—with employees, suppliers, customers, and external partners—are governed by binding contracts. In the industrial age, most people didn't need to understand their company's purpose; they simply did what was specified on their job descriptions and what their bosses told them to do.

In this model, the senior executive officers are agents of the owners, who act as stewards for the owners' capital and are hired and paid to invest it wisely and grow its value over successive years. If they succeed, they are well rewarded, but if they fail, their jobs are on the line. Most large corporations

Businesses and great relationships
"Businesses that are most profitable and are able to sustain profits in the long run are actually those that build great relationships with customers, employees and suppliers. On the other hand, businesses that are most profit-oriented, like Enron, Bear Stearns and Lehman Brothers, are not in the long run profitable because they are pulled apart by the greed of their own employees."—John Kay, business economist
Source: Vivek Kaul, "Profit Can't Be Primary Goal of Business," *DNA India*, June 19, 2010, www.dnaindia.com/opinion/interview_profit-can-t-be-primary-goal-of-business_1398327.

have mission statements filled with words such as "shareholder value," "customer service," and "product quality." And of course every chairman's report pays homage to the firm's employees, who are usually "the company's greatest assets." But despite pandering to other stakeholders, most executive teams know that it is increasing shareholder value that will keep them in their jobs.

But is the explicit pursuit of shareholder value the best way to actually achieve it? Not according to British economist John Kay. He believes that great organizations are not exclusively profit oriented.

Take the case of ICI, Britain's leading industrial company for most of the twentieth century. Its original purpose was about the responsible application of chemistry to business. The company began in dyes and explosives and then moved into new chemical businesses like fertilizers, petrochemicals, and finally into pharmaceuticals, all in the pursuit of applying chemistry to business in different ways as the needs of the wider economy changed. But in the 1990s, the company very explicitly abandoned that kind of goal in favor of shareholder value. Leaders disposed of many of their traditional businesses and bought a range of new ones, and paid too much for the businesses they bought. The company declined rapidly and disappeared altogether in 2007 (the business was sold to the Dutch company, Akzo Nobel). So not only did the responsible application of chemistry create a better business than did the attempts at increasing value; it also created more shareholder value. "So it's a process of adapting, a very loose general idea, to changing particular circumstances over time," noted Kay.[1]

When Citicorp merged with Travelers in 1999 to create the sprawling bank conglomerate Citigroup, the joint CEOs held a press conference. John Reed, Citicorp's CEO, declared, "The model I have is of a global consumer company that really helps the middle class with something they haven't been served well by historically. That's my vision. That's my dream." His joint-CEO, Travelers' Sandy Weill, rapidly interjected, "My goal is increasing shareholder value." Reed and his old-fashioned, oblique way of running a business was sidelined. Just a few years later, Citi was in trouble and Weill was forced out; within a decade, Citigroup was forced into the arms of the U.S. government.[2]

What these stories tell us is that by pandering to rapacious shareholders, firms are not just trying to come up with the results too quickly. They're actually pursuing the wrong goal. It's not just about numbers and targets and synergies. It's about great products, happy customers, and loyal staff. As Kay says, no one will be buried with the epitaph, "He maximized shareholder value."[3]

But in recent years, the assumptions underpinning this model have started to unravel. Other stakeholders have started to flex their muscles. For example, in knowledge-based organizations—that is, just about every company other than some traditional manufacturers—employees are claiming that their interests should come before shareholders. They say they have more at risk; it is harder and more expensive to change jobs than to move capital around. Customers also want more influence as they demand more choice, lower prices, and better service; otherwise, they will take their business elsewhere. And local communities demand that corporations consider their interests and protect local jobs and the environment.

Paul Polman, chief executive of Unilever, has added his voice to the growing number of business leaders who argue that shareholder value is a misguided and potentially harmful goal for companies to pursue. He said shareholders had benefited as a result of his concentration on customers: "I drive this business model by focusing on the consumer and customer in a responsible way . . . and I know that shareholder value can come."[4]

We are also living through a sea change in how society and governments view commercial organizations and the values they espouse. Over the past ten

---

Shareholder value

In a recent interview, legendary leader and former CEO of General Electric, Jack Welch, stated, "Shareholder value is the dumbest idea in the world." He added, "Shareholder value is a result, not a strategy . . . Your main constituencies are your employees, your customers and your products."[a]

[a] Michael Skapinker, "Replacing the 'Dumbest Idea in the World,'" *Financial Times*, April 10, 2010, www.ft.com/cms/s/0/98e020d0-4664-11df-9713-00144feab49a.html.

A noble purpose at Whole Foods

The CEO of organic foods retailer Whole Foods, John Mackey, is a devout believer in each business having a noble purpose. "It's not that there's anything wrong with making money," notes Mackey. "It's one of the important things that business contributes to society. But it's not the sole reason that businesses exist. Just like every other profession, business serves society. They produce goods and services that make people's lives better. Doctors heal the sick. Teachers educate people. Architects design buildings. Lawyers promote justice. Whole Foods puts food on people's tables and we improve people's health. And we provide jobs. And we provide capital through profits that spur improvements in the world. And we're good citizens in our communities, and we take our citizenship very seriously at Whole Foods."[a]

[a] John Mackey, "Creating the High Trust Organization," Whole Foods Market CEO Blog, March 9, 2010, http://www2.wholefoodsmarket.com/blogs/jmackey/2010/03/09/creating-the-high-trust-organization.

---

years, bad news from the corporate sector has dominated the headlines as organizations such as Enron, WorldCom, Tyco, HealthSouth, Adelphia, Global Crossing, Xerox, Lehman Brothers, Fannie Mae, Citigroup, AIG, Royal Bank of Scotland, and HBOS have all become notorious for the wrong reasons. Greed, corruption, and fraud, often at the highest levels—and all in the pursuit of short-term shareholder value—have ensured their places in the governance hall of shame. You can be sure that all these organizations had carefully crafted mission statements with all the right words on them. But their actions spoke louder than their words.

Clearly, defining an organization's purpose in terms above and beyond shareholder value really matters in the long run. Only if employees have a crystal-clear understanding of business purpose, boundaries, goals, ethics, values, and performance standards will they be able to make decisions with speed, confidence, and consistency. But such clarity rarely exists in organizations today. All too often mission and values statements are too bland to convey deep meaning. Employees end up ignoring them.

A noble purpose and clear, inviolate values have never been more important. We have witnessed many examples of senior executives abusing fair values and acting in their own self-interests. The message this sends to employees is disturbing. Why should employees act in the interests of the organization when senior executives do not? This leads to a slippery slope toward unethical behavior and, ultimately, fraudulent action. We need more leaders like Herb Kelleher, former CEO of Southwest Airlines, who once said: "The more people will devote themselves to your cause on a voluntary basis, a willing basis, the fewer hierarchs and control mechanisms you need. We're not looking for blind obedience. We're looking for people who on their own initiative want to be doing what they're doing because they consider it to be a worthy objective."[5]

What is the performance potential of this practice?

- **To recruit the "right" people.** There is little doubt that establishing a clear purpose and a set of inviolate values is a critical step in recruiting the right people, who naturally fit with your culture and values.[6]
- **To build a high-performance culture.** You want people to believe in the organization's purpose and values and work together as a team. With a clear social purpose, employees have a reason for coming to work every day that transcends shareholder value. This purpose helps to build a high-performance culture that encourages ambition, creativity, and sharing.
- **To provide a framework for coherent decision making across the company.** In a fast-changing world, organizations increasingly depend on the passion and creativity of their employees to provide innovative products and high-quality service. These can no longer be mandated from the corporate center. Clear and inviolate values set the boundaries for innovation, decision making, and management behavior.
- **To build emotional commitment.** Most people go to work each day to earn their monthly paycheck. If you want people to volunteer their passion and creativity, you need to inspire them with a purpose above and beyond profit. To witness the power of a clear purpose and how it can inspire and motivate people to raise their game, you only have to look at the nonprofit or voluntary sector. Major charities attract and retain very talented people, who work incredibly hard for modest rewards.

What actions do you need to take to maximize the potential of this practice?

ACTIONS TO AVOID

- ✖ **Avoid framing your mission (either explicitly or implicitly) in terms of profit or shareholder value.** The words on the mission statement won't matter if the actions of senior executives and influential employees are all geared to making short-term gains. Companies can boost profits and share prices by closing plants or selling parts of the business, but they undermine long-term value creation. Over the past few years, we have seen the "get rich quick" macho managers and salespeople drive greed and unethical behavior in the finance sector. Shareholder value is a reasonable measure of management performance over the medium term, but it represents a dysfunctional purpose and a lousy target.

✖ **Avoid the "fund manager" approach.** Try this test: How would your board members react if they discovered that there was more shareholder value available if the organization was broken apart and sold off in pieces? How would this view square with the words on the mission statement? Some boards see their organizations as no more than a portfolio of businesses to buy and sell, rather like football players. The role of the fund manager usurps the role of the CEO and, in some cases, the CFO. Sunbeam's CEO, "Chainsaw" Al Dunlap, became a crusader for shareholder value as he closed down factories and cut product lines. In his view, businesses didn't need to grow or satisfy customers; they only needed to unlock underperforming assets. But his status soon turned from hero to villain as it dawned on shareholders that his actions ended up destroying value as employees and customers voted with their feet and their orders, respectively.

✖ **Avoid mission statements that lack meaning or inspiration.** In *The Mission Statement Book*, Jeffrey Abrahams reviewed 301 corporate mission statements from the top U.S. companies and noted that the words mission statement writers most frequently used were: service (230 times), customers (211), quality (194), value (183), employees (157), growth (118), environment (117), profit (114), shareholders (114), leader (104), and best (102). The word *exciting* appears three times, and the words *conscience* and *joy* twice each.[7] Making statements too bland, such as, "We will strive to provide the highest return to shareholders and offer the highest-quality products and services, while achieving the highest customer loyalty and the highest employee satisfaction," is unlikely to grab anyone in the gut. Compare it with Google's mission—"to organize the world's information and make it universally accessible and useful."[8]

✖ **Be wary of bogus rationality.** John Kay believes that leaders have too much faith in rational decision making—for example, the alignment of mission, objectives, strategy, and tactics. "The world in which we are pretending to make decisions through a kind of formal, spelled-out process, is really not the reality," Kay says. "Bogus rationality," he notes, "is probably best described as the kind of rationality that says, this is the way we are going to make decisions in a world in which we think we know much more than we (actually) do and believe we have much more control over it than we (actually) do. It is a process which has the appearance of rationality but in the end it doesn't. It isn't rational."[9]

✖ **Stop sending messages (e.g., through performance evaluations) that say that profits come before values.** If you don't make clear that there will be severe consequences if people don't abide by the company's values and ethics, few people will take them seriously.

ACTIONS TO TAKE

✓ **Frame your mission in terms of supporting society's needs or improving the environment.** Leaders need to articulate a purpose above and beyond profit or shareholder value and more in terms of the organization's clear social purpose, such as saving lives, improving the environment, or supporting society's needs. According to Mackey, the single most important requirement for the creation of higher levels of trust for any organization is to discover or rediscover its higher purpose. Why does the organization exist? What is it trying to accomplish? What core values will inspire it and create greater trust from all of its stakeholders?[10] The aim for any organization should be to grow, improve, and endure over time through a strong belief in its people's ability to learn and adapt. But organizations know that if they do not make sufficient profit or satisfy shareholders, they will not survive over the long term. Profit, or better still, free cash flow, is the oxygen of corporate life, but, just as breathing is to human life, profit should not be its primary purpose.

✓ **Communicate purpose and values to all employees in every possible way.** Just agreeing and writing about values is insufficient. You must also communicate in every possible way, including in handbooks, Web sites, seminars, and so on. At Southwest Airlines, values include profitability, low cost, family, fun, love, hard work, individuality, ownership, legendary service, egalitarianism, common sense, good judgment, simplicity, and altruism. Whether in a memo, newsletter, training program, ad campaign, or awards ceremony, there are multiple ways that guiding values and other key messages spread around the organization. At Southwest, employees have internalized these messages so they know instinctively what the right action is in any given situation.

✓ **Create a shared vision.** Being forward looking—envisioning exciting possibilities and enlisting others in a shared view of the future—is the attribute that most distinguishes leaders from nonleaders, according to researchers James Kouzes and Barry Posner.

✓ **Recruit and develop the right people.** Even the most carefully crafted mission statements will have little meaning if you recruit the wrong people. The right people are those who fit well with the values and culture of the business and, even more crucially, are able to take responsibility and use their intuition and judgment. Xerox's chief scientist, John Seely

Too many leaders think they are visionaries

According to James Kouzes and Barry Posner, too many leaders have reached the unfortunate conclusion that they as individuals must be visionaries. With leadership development experts urging them along, they've taken to posing as emissaries from the future, delivering the news of how their markets and organizations will be transformed. The research is clear on this point, as Kouzes and Posner explain: "This is not what constituents want. Yes, leaders must ask, 'What's new? What's next? What's better?'—but they can't present answers that are only theirs. Constituents want visions of the future that reflect their own aspirations. They want to hear how their dreams will come true and their hopes will be fulfilled."

Kouzes and Posner draw their conclusion from their analysis of nearly 1 million responses to a leadership assessment program, "The Leadership Practices Inventory." The data tells us that what leaders struggle with most is communicating an image of the future that draws others in—that speaks to what others see and feel. As counterintuitive as it might seem, the best way to lead people into the future is to connect with them deeply in the present. The only visions that take hold are shared visions—and you will create them only when you listen very, very closely to others, appreciate their hopes, and attend to their needs. The best leaders are able to bring their people into the future because they engage in the oldest form of research: they observe the human condition.[a]

[a] James M. Kouzes and Barry Z. Posner, "To Lead, Create a Shared Vision," *Harvard Business Review*, January 2009, 20–21.

Brown, explains why this is becoming even more important in the Internet age. "On the Web," he notes, "most information does not have an institutional warranty behind it, which really means that you have to learn to exercise much more judgment . . . Thus we are creating a medium that takes us right back to the 1700s and to what enabled our democracy to exist, because democracy requires a deliberate populace that is capable of making judgments."[11] Southwest Airlines' policy is to "hire for attitude and train for skills."[12] This message encapsulates what it means to recruit the right people, who need to be able to analyze and interpret information and take responsibility for decisions.

✓ **Walk the talk of purpose and values.** Mackey believes that a higher purpose doesn't matter if the leadership doesn't understand it and seek to serve it. The various stakeholders of an organization, especially employees and customers, look to the leadership to "walk the talk"—to serve its purpose and mission and to lead by example. The CEO and other senior leadership must embody the higher purpose.[13] Understanding how an organization recognizes and rewards people and spends its money will tell you much about its values. If it rewards and promotes managers who will do anything to meet their numbers (the Enron culture), then getting people to work together in teams will be hard to achieve. If it spends money on limousines, lavish head offices, and executive perks (the WorldCom culture), then asking people to increase their efforts will likely fall on deaf ears. If it pays large bonuses to only a few senior people (as most investment bankers did), then it will find it hard to manage risk and hold a strong, ethical line. Operating teams across the organization need standards and guidelines within which they can function and make decisions that are consistent and coherent with the company's strategy and direction. That's why statements of purpose and values need to exist not just on paper but also in all employees' hearts and minds.

✓ **Make core values a top agenda item at executive meetings.** Despite his best efforts at BP, former CEO Tony Hayward struggled to make health, safety, and the environment the company's highest priority because BP was desperate to please its investors. One company that did succeed was aluminum producer Alcoa. When CEO Paul O'Neill arrived in 1987, he decided to make health and safety the company's highest priority—one that he would address in top-level meetings ahead of profit. So embedded has this objective become that Alcoa now reports its lost-workday accident rate to all employees and stakeholders in real time. The rate hovers near 0.2—significantly better than the national average for all manufacturers of 2.2.[14]

✓ **Make values a core part of management evaluation and rewards.** Communicating clear values is necessary but often insufficient to make people take notice. Inviolate values are the new "fixed reference points" in a fast-changing world. There must be no gray areas. The right, ethical decision always wins. The seminal moment came in Jack Welch's transformation of General Electric in the 1980s and 90s when he dismissed the managers who made their financial targets but failed to live up to GE's values.[15]

✓ **Clearly set out codes of conduct.** How are some professionals able to lie, cheat, or steal, and not feel guilty about it? In light of the banking industry's collapse, understanding what motivates people to bend the rules is critical for those in positions of oversight. The authors of one study conducted four experiments with students, designed to measure their willingness to commit dishonest acts. In one scenario, the participants had a

---

Rethinking rewards at BP

BP's new CEO, Bob Dudley, was quick to distance himself from the problems at BP following the 2010 disaster in the Gulf of Mexico. One of his first significant announcements was to change the bonus formula: staff bonuses for the fourth quarter would be based *solely* on how employees performed in terms of safety and risk management. He commented, "We are taking this step in order to be absolutely clear that safety, compliance and operational risk management is BP's number one priority, well ahead of all other priorities."[a]

[a] Sylvia Pfeifer, "BP Links Bonuses to Safety Performance," *Financial Times*, October 18, 2010, www.ft.com/cms/s/ca170960-dadf-11df-a5bb-00144feabdc0,dwp_uuid=2592a208-a4fb-11dd-b4f5-000077b07658,print=yes.html.

---

chance to pocket more money than they were owed, and could shred the documents related to their "crime." Those who took the opportunity to cheat justified their dishonest deeds by disengaging morally and claiming to "forget" the rules. But participants who were asked to read an honor code beforehand were significantly less likely to behave unethically, suggesting that making employees adhere to an established code of conduct increases their awareness of moral stringency. Reinforcing such rules also ensures a greater adherence to ethical behavior; the authors found that participants were more willing to bend the rules and claim they didn't realize what they had done when the rules were not clearly presented and when they were questioned after they committed the dishonest act.[16]

✓ **Make performance a marathon rather than a sprint.** How leaders perceive their time in office matters. If they see it as essentially brief, with the objective of maximizing short-term shareholder value without considering the long-term survival of the business, they are more likely to want to take "bet the farm"–type risks to accelerate performance improvements. On the other hand, if they see their time as a way to hand off a stronger company to the next management generation, they will be more inclined to build the organization steadily over time.

Conclusions

To succeed in today's fast-changing business environment, leaders must clarify and communicate the organization's purpose and provide and support a set of inviolate corporate values. Great leaders live the purpose and values day in and day out, spreading the message, and inspiring other leaders across the organization.

FURTHER READING

Collins, James C., and Jerry I. Porras. "Building Your Company's Vision." *Harvard Business Review*, September–October 1996, 65–77.

Collins, James C., and Jerry I. Porras. *Built to Last: Successful Habits of Visionary Companies.* New York: HarperBusiness, 1997.

Haeckel, Stephan. *Adaptive Enterprise: Creating and Leading Sense-and-Respond Organizations.* Boston: Harvard Business School Press, 1999.

Kay, John. *Obliquity*. London: Profile Books, 2010.

Kotter, John P. "Leading Change: Why Transformation Efforts Fail." *Harvard Business Review*, March–April 1995, 59–67.

Kotter, John P., and James L. Heskett. *Corporate Culture and Performance*. New York: Free Press, 1992.

Krattenmaker, Tom. "Write a Mission Statement That Your Company Is Willing to Live." *Harvard Management Communication Letter*, March 2002.

2

STRATEGIC PLANNING

What is this practice and how effective is it?

Strategic planning is a process for determining medium- or long-term goals and how the organization will reach them. Done well, the process should stimulate imaginative or breakthrough thinking and enable the organization to adapt to change. But for most, the planning process is bureaucratic and regimented and driven by the accounting calendar rather than changes in the market. We will examine how leaders overcome these problems and use the planning process to adapt, improve, and endure over extended periods.

Alternative names and related topics: innovation; growth strategies; scenario and contingency planning

In the days when competitors' actions were more predictable and suppliers held sway over customers, firms could plan years ahead with reasonable confidence. The successful companies of the industrial age such as General Motors and IBM were expert planners and, given that their customers had few choices, they could execute these plans efficiently. Planners were important people. In 1973, IBM had three thousand planners, and its "annual" planning process approached an eighteen-month cycle.[1]

In his 1962 landmark book *Strategy and Structure*, Alfred Chandler explained the adoption of the multidivisional organization structure by fifty of the largest companies in America. His detailed examination of four pioneers of that revolutionary structural form led him to develop his highly influential strategy and structure thesis. His central conclusion was that companies driven by market growth and technological change to develop greater diversity in their products and markets were able to manage their new strategies efficiently only if they adopted a multidivisional organizational structure—the so-called M-form.[2]

The M-form model coalesced around the central theme of command and control. And it worked well when the pace of change was incremental, growth was constrained by access to capital, strategy and product life cycles were lengthy, customers had limited choice, and leaders could manage their earnings to meet market expectations. Since the 1920s, most large organizations also adopted the same make-and-sell business model designed to execute their strategies. In this model, managers first decided which products to make, how much to produce, and then used all their marketing muscle to persuade customers to buy their output. They also developed performance management processes to support this planning model.

MOST (mission, objectives, strategy, tactics) is an acronym describing this step-by-step process. The mission statement that senior executives agreed on was translated into the strategic plan by the planners and handed down the hierarchy to operational managers who prepared their budgets. Once these were accepted, all that the company demanded was adherence to the plan. The head office did not like surprises. Control reports were constantly fed back up the line, and should they show that performance was veering off track, the head office would issue new directives (see figure 2-1).

At the core of the command-and-control model was a negotiated budget, usually a set of financial numbers, which the company needed to reach by the end of a period, usually a fiscal year. The problem was that setting annual budgets (often reinforced by fixed financial targets and incentives or a fixed performance contract) and then placing everyone under pressure to meet

FIGURE 2-1

The traditional planning and budgeting model

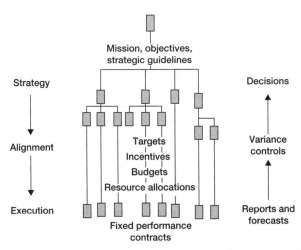

them was a recipe, not for exceptional performance (unless the market was conveniently heading north at the same time), but for a mad scramble at the end of every period as managers throughout the organization found ways (by fair means or foul) to meet them.

Despite today's uncertain environment and their efforts to break free from this top-down, rigid model in which top management makes the best decisions, middle managers control performance, and frontline managers follow the plan, most organizations remain prisoners of this so-called command-and-control management model. While this model has been subject to much criticism over recent years (it focuses on the hierarchy rather than the customer, stifles sharing and innovation, and requires high costs to support the bureaucracy), we must remember that, like mass production, it served industrial economy companies and their customers extremely well. Most managers have grown up and feel comfortable with it and find it hard to imagine a viable alternative.

Enlightened leaders no longer accept this view. They believe that discontinuous change is now the norm. They see planning as a continuous, inclusive process, driven by events (such as the launch of a new product or a competitive threat) and emerging knowledge, and not constrained by the financial reporting cycle. They see the organization in a new light. Instead of the traditional pyramid with the CEO at the apex, they turn the organization on its side, facing the customer (see figure 2-2). Accountabilities flow from left to right.

While the executive team sets the high-level goals and strategic direction based on an annual review, its primary role is to challenge and support frontline (value center) teams that sit in the value zone between the company and the customer. In these organizations, strategic planning relies on fast, relevant, actionable information and responsible people who know what the company expects of them and what to do in any given situation. Most operate with quarterly business reviews using rolling forecasts to test and agree on their action plans. The organization operates as a team rather like an orchestra, with the conductor providing strategic direction, harmonizing and coordinating activities, and setting and upholding values and standards.

Value centers (or business units) act as self-managed teams accountable for continuously improving their performance against peers and best practices. The strategy focus is on learning, adaptation, and renewal rather than on annual planning, budgeting, and fixed targets. Trend reporting, rolling forecasts, and "gap analysis" (i.e., the gap between where you are and the best-practice benchmark) enable managers to ask the right questions and make the right decisions. And the organization collaborates to a much greater extent with external partners. This is facilitated not so much by

FIGURE 2-2

The adaptive planning model

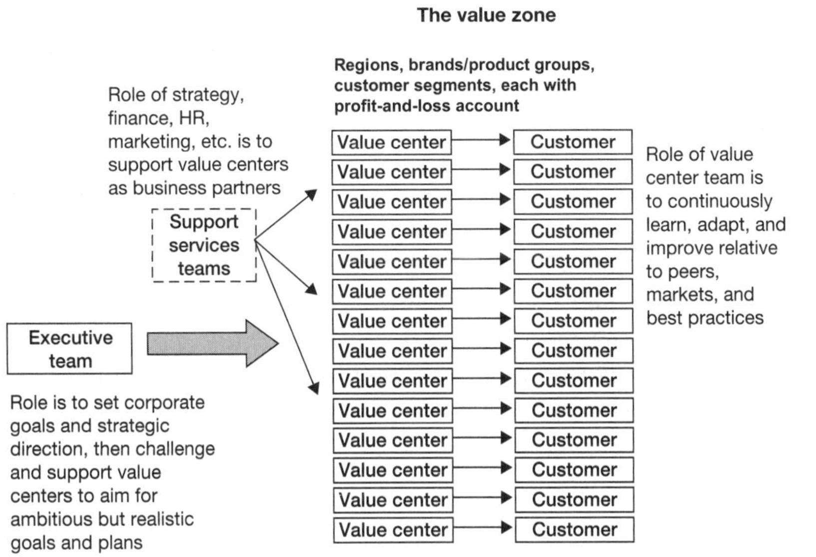

The value zone

Regions, brands/product groups,
customer segments, each with
profit-and-loss account

Role of strategy,
finance, HR,
marketing, etc. is to
support value centers
as business partners

Support
services
teams

Executive
team

Role is to set corporate
goals and strategic
direction, then challenge
and support value
centers to aim for
ambitious but realistic
goals and plans

Value center	→	Customer
Value center	→	Customer
Value center	→	Customer
Value center	→	Customer
Value center	→	Customer
Value center	→	Customer
Value center	→	Customer
Value center	→	Customer
Value center	→	Customer
Value center	→	Customer
Value center	→	Customer
Value center	→	Customer
Value center	→	Customer
Value center	→	Customer

Role of value
center team is
to continuously
learn, adapt, and
improve relative
to peers,
markets, and
best practices

implementing expensive systems but by building relationships and removing barriers such as annual fixed targets and incentives that encourage hoarding rather than sharing.

Many organizations either have moved or are moving to the new model, including Swedish bank Svenska Handelsbanken, Southwest Airlines, Norwegian oil company Statoil, American Express, Malaysian telecommunications company Telekom Malaysia, and Danish medical products company Coloplast.

As the HCL Technologies experience illustrates, the strategic planning process is evolving as technology enables more people to participate. And because many strategic initiatives now involve the Web and digital technology, it makes sense that more (younger) people have a voice.

What is the performance potential of this practice?

- **To set goals and direction.** The primary aim is to agree and communicate to everyone a clear set of goals and directions that define which products, markets, and territories the organization will operate in over the next five years or so.
- **To grow and endure.** The aim of every business should be to grow and endure over the long term. An effective strategy that is regularly renewed helps to achieve this aim.

Opening up the planning process at HCL Technologies

The Indian IT company, HCL Technologies, has gone much further than most in opening up the planning process. Hundreds of people, including members of the team, peers, and senior executives, can now read a strategic plan. CEO Vineet Nayar was influenced by watching his kids using new communications technologies such as Facebook and YouTube. He realized that they were used to sharing just about everything with their family and friends and wondered why communication in a large organization should be different. So he opened up the planning process. Three hundred to four hundred people can review the plans.

He recalled three interesting lessons: One, because your subordinates are going to see the plan, you cannot lie. Two, because your peers are going to see it, you are going to put your best work into it. Third, people learn not from the boss but from reviewing somebody else's presentation.[a]

[a] Adam Bryant, "He's Not Bill Gates, or Fred Astaire," *New York Times*, February 14, 2010, http://www.nytimes.com/2010/02/14/business/14cornerweb.html?_r=1&pagewanted=print.

- **To enable the organization to respond rapidly to change.** Though still retaining a formal annual process that addresses the big questions, planning is becoming more continuous, thus enabling managers to respond rapidly to emerging threats and opportunities.
- **To stimulate imaginative or breakthrough thinking.** The aim is to beat the competition by producing a constant stream of new products, processes, and business models.

What actions do you need to take to maximize the potential of this practice?

ACTIONS TO AVOID

- ✖ **Avoid making strategy a destination.** Many CEOs complain about lack of visibility and poor response times when the unexpected event happens. None of this is surprising when you consider that many leaders are fixated on meeting a predetermined target and constantly realign strategy, structure, and systems to cope with unanticipated change. This not only drains managers' energy and upsets morale but also increases complexity and cost. It's a high price to pay for being too strategy focused. Marching the organization to the drumbeat of a fixed strategy without the flexibility to respond to emerging threats and opportunities can be a recipe for disaster. Make strategy a direction rather than a destination.

✖ **Avoid being too rigid and inflexible.** In a fast-changing and highly uncertain world, organizations need to be flexible. They need to review strategy as and when required rather than tied to accounting cycles, such as fiscal years. Markets and customers do not abide by your accounting cycles, so get in tune with their needs and stop being introspective.

✖ **Be careful using balanced scorecards.** Many organizations use balanced scorecards to formulate their strategy and align metrics and actions. Though scorecards can add huge value to the process, they can also, if poorly implemented, make the organization even more rigid and inflexible. Many lead to a plethora of annual targets that bind managers to an annual performance contract, and this contract is often tied to incentive compensation. (See chapter 4 on the balanced scorecard.)

✖ **Stop spending months on the budgeting process.** In many organizations, the strategic planning and budgeting processes form one protracted planning process that can take many months to complete. But more detail does not lead to more accuracy or more control. So cut the budgeting process to a few weeks and focus on the key variables—revenue streams, high-impact costs, and fixed or working capital requirements. Better still, move from detailed annual budgets to rolling forecasts. (See chapter 33 on rolling forecasts.)

✖ **Avoid making strategy an exclusive, top-down process.** Too many organizations continue to separate strategy from execution. The best ideas are more likely to come from junior employees than board-level executives, so devolving strategy to teams close to the customer makes sense.

✖ **Stop spending too much time on long-range planning.** Many influential people now think that long-range planning is futile. Author James Brian Quinn captured the seductive beliefs about planning that exist in most organizations today when he said that, "a good deal of corporate planning is like a rain dance; it has no effect on the weather that follows, but those who engage in it think it does. Moreover, it seems to me that much of the advice and instruction related to corporate planning is directed at improving the dancing, not the weather."[3] Former Southwest chairman Herb Kelleher takes a similar view: "Over the years," he said, "we developed not only a different strategy but also a different strategic planning process. Basically, we just don't do it. In an industry where a two-week plan is likely to become obsolete, to spend days debating whether we're to serve Trenton, New Jersey [five years from now], is a meaningless exercise."[4]

ACTIONS TO TAKE

- ✓ **Clearly articulate your strategy.** Can you summarize your company's strategy in thirty-five words or less? Would your colleagues express it the same way?
- ✓ **Strike the right balance between stability and flexibility.** While strategy should not be too rigid, no organization can keep changing its course or its core competences. So it needs to have a sensible balance between high-level direction (two to five years out) and short-term tactical change.
- ✓ **Keep the annual review to the big questions.** The board should set long-term directional goals and strategic aims that it reviews annually. During this review, the board should address the big questions. Have the needs of

Clearly articulating your strategy is crucial

According to Harvard professors David Collis and Michael Rukstad, very few executives can honestly say yes when asked if they can summarize their company's strategy and how their colleagues would articulate the strategy. Those that can do this effectively, they note, often turn out to be industry stars. They spell out what's required.

First, start with a definition of the *objective*, or the goal that the strategy is designed to achieve. Since most firms compete in a more or less unbounded landscape, it is also crucial to define the *scope*, or domain, of the business. Perhaps most important, companies need to have a clear sense of *advantage*—that is, the means by which the business will achieve its stated objective. Defining the objective, scope, and advantage requires trade-offs. If a firm pursues growth or size, profitability will take a backseat. If it chooses to serve institutional clients, it might ignore retail customers. If it derives its competitive advantage from scale economies, it will not be able to accommodate idiosyncratic customer needs. Before developing your strategy and crafting your statement, you'll want to carefully evaluate the industry landscape. This includes segmenting customers and identifying unique ways of delivering value to the ones the firm targets. It also calls for an analysis of competitors' current strategies and a prediction of how they might change. The key is to find the sweet spot where the firm's capabilities and customers' needs align in a way that competitors cannot match.[a]

[a] David J. Collis and Michael G. Rukstad, "Can You Say What Your Strategy Is?" *Harvard Business Review*, April 2008, 82–90.

our customers changed? Are our products and services still appropriate? Is our value proposition still valid? Do our chosen value drivers and key performance indicators (KPIs) still reflect the way that value is driven in the business? Do our core competences still support the value proposition? Most businesses need to address these questions only every three to five years, but in fast-changing markets, they may need to address them much more frequently.

✓ **Implement a quarterly business review (QBR).** Organizations subject to continuous change might set regular (monthly or quarterly) strategic reviews or make a review dependent on some significant event. Such events can be positive (e.g., introducing new products or a new business model) or negative (e.g., reacting to competitive threats). The point is that these reviews are not time dependent and thus can occur when needed. QBRs typically start by looking at the latest performance information and then reviewing whether business as usual will take the company to where it needs to be. If not, then the team should think about which new initiatives are appropriate and act on them.

✓ **Fund the best action plans, not negotiated budgets.** In a rolling review process (divorced from annual budgets and resource allocations), the aim is to fund the best current opportunities. This opens the window for new ideas and leads to a more adaptive organization.

✓ **Devolve planning and decision making to frontline teams.** While high-level goals and strategies are set at the board level, most strategic thinking and action planning takes place in teams closer to the front line. At General Electric, group executives demand that their business unit managers give one-page answers to five strategic questions: (1) What does your global competition look like over the next several years?; (2) What have your competitors done in the last three years to upset those global dynamics?; (3) What have you done to them in the last three years to affect those dynamics?; (4) How might your competitors attack you in the future?; (5) What are your plans to leapfrog the competition? What they don't require is a detailed business plan with fifty pages of numbers and charts.[5]

✓ **Encourage creative thinking.** If leaders really want to stimulate creative thinking, they need to eradicate the fear of failure and create a "no blame" culture. This means not only abandoning annual fixed targets that lead to incremental thinking but also allowing managers to make mistakes. Author Charles Handy uses an aviation metaphor to explain the point: "In aviation, the trainer allows the pilot to get it wrong provided that the mistake will not crash the plane. It is the only way the trainee will learn to fly alone."[6]

Consider using discovery-driven planning

Discovery-driven planning reverses the sequence of some steps in the standard approvals process. Its logic is simple. As Clayton Christensen, Stephen Kaufman, and Willy Shih explain:

> If the project teams all know how good the numbers need to look in order to win funding, why go through the charade of making and revising assumptions in order to fabricate an acceptable set of numbers? Why not just put the minimally acceptable revenue, income, and cash flow statement as the standard first page of the gate documents? The second page can then raise the critical issues: "Okay. So we all know this is how good the numbers need to look. What set of assumptions must prove true in order for these numbers to materialize?" The project team creates from that analysis an assumptions checklist—a list of things that need to prove true for the project to succeed. The items on the checklist are rank-ordered, with the deal killers and the assumptions that can be tested with little expense toward the top. If a critical assumption proves not to be valid, the project team must revise its strategy until the assumptions upon which it is built are all plausible. If no set of plausible assumptions will support the case for success, the project is killed.[a]

[a] Clayton M. Christensen, Stephen P. Kaufman, and Willy C. Shih, "Innovation Killers: How Financial Tools Destroy Your Capacity to Do New Things," *Harvard Business Review*, January 2008, 98–105.

✓ **Give everyone a strategic voice.** Often the best ideas for strategic renewal reside within the heads of younger managers who, in most organizations, do not participate in the strategy process. Leaders need to find a way to get them involved. HCL Technologies' idea of opening up the planning process to peer review is one approach.

✓ **Communicate strategy effectively.** All the weeks of thinking and preparation will be of no avail unless everyone understands the company's strategic direction and medium-term goals. So effective communication is essential. There are many ways to communicate, including town hall meetings, Web sites, bulletin boards, scorecards, and newsletters. The process also needs to have continuous feedback so that strategy is updated when necessary.

✓ **Use scenario planning to respond rapidly to unpredictable events.**
Managers can play the "what if?" game many times over as they look at
the various ways that the future might unfold and the implications of
different outcomes. While Southwest leaders think long-range planning
is a waste of time, they believe in scenario planning. The company's executive planning committee meets periodically to create future scenarios
for the airline. For example, if it is considering a new city to fly to, it will
look at what the competition might do, how many more planes it will
need, where it will get them from, and so forth. "Future scenario generation," as Southwest calls it, enables it to prepare in a way that provides
direction yet allows it to maneuver on many fronts.[7]

✓ **Provide coaching, information, and tools.** Teams that have previously
been "doers" rather than "thinkers" can take some time to embrace the
new planning process. They need coaching and support from more experienced colleagues, and they need tools, models, and information to help
them. Some leading organizations use the balanced scorecard to fill this
void. The balanced scorecard is organized around four perspectives—
financial, customer, process, and learning and growth. It enables teams to
link their measures and actions with their strategy through a strategy
map (see chapter 4 on the balanced scorecard).

Conclusions

Strategy formulation is the foundation of any management model. Unless
managers can formulate and describe their strategy clearly and communicate
it throughout the firm, they have little prospect of implementing it successfully. Leaders need to free managers from the shackles of bureaucratic
strategy-formulation processes and harness the intellectual capital inherent in
their people. But doing this without dismantling the rigid annual planning
and budgeting process and replacing it with a more devolved and adaptive
model is hard.

FURTHER READING

Campbell, Andrew, and Marcus Alexander. "What's Wrong with Strategy?"*Harvard
Business Review*, November–December 1997, 42–51.

Collis, David J., and Michael G. Rukstad. "Can You Say What Your Strategy Is?" *Harvard
Business Review*, April 2008, 82–90.

Drucker, Peter F. *Managing in a Time of Great Change*. Boston, MA: Plume, 1998.

Eisenhardt, Kathleen M. "Has Strategy Changed?" *Sloan Management Review*, Winter 2002,
88–91.

Goold, Michael, Andrew Campbell, and Marcus Alexander. *Corporate-Level Strategy:
Creating Value in the Multibusiness Company*. New York: John Wiley & Sons, 1994.

Hamel, Gary. *The Future of Management*. Boston: Harvard Business School Press, 2007.

Hamel, Gary. *Leading the Revolution*. Boston: Harvard Business School Press, 2000.

Hamel, Gary, and C. K. Prahalad. *Competing for the Future.* Boston: Harvard Business School Press, 1994.

Hope, Jeremy. *Reinventing the CFO: How Financial Managers Can Transform Their Roles and Add Greater Value.* Boston: Harvard Business School Press, 2006.

Hope, Jeremy, Peter Bunce, and Franz Röösli. *The Leader's Dilemma: How to Build an Empowered and Adaptive Organization Without Losing Control.* San Francisco, CA: John Wiley & Sons, 2011.

Hope, Jeremy, and Robin Fraser. *Beyond Budgeting: How Managers Can Break Free from the Annual Performance Trap.* Boston: Harvard Business School Press, 2003.

Kaplan, Robert S., and David P. Norton. *The Strategy-Focused Organization: How Balanced Scorecard Companies Thrive in the New Business Environment.* Boston: Harvard Business School Press, 2001.

Mankins, Michael C. "Stop Wasting Valuable Time." *Harvard Business Review,* September 2004, 58–65.

Mintzberg, Henry. *The Rise and Fall of Strategic Planning: Reconceiving Roles for Planning, Plans, Planners.* New York: Free Press, 1994.

Morlidge, Steve, and Steve Player. *Future Ready: How to Master Business Forecasting.* Chichester, UK: Wiley, 2010.

Ohmae, Kenichi. *The Mind of the Strategist: The Art of Japanese Business.* New York: McGraw-Hill, 1996.

Porter, Michael E. *Competitive Strategy: Techniques for Analyzing Industries and Competitors.* New York: Free Press, 1980.

Porter, Michael E. "What Is Strategy?" *Harvard Business Review,* November–December 1996, 61–78.

3

STRETCH GOALS

What is this practice and how effective is it?

Stretch goals are invariably based on negotiating short-term fixed targets and have recently become more pervasive in both the private and the public sectors as senior executives look to make managers more accountable for delivering improved results. But do stretch goals deliver the expected results? In some cases, the answer is yes, but the collateral damage is often too great to bear as managers resort to a range of unethical practices to meet the numbers. We examine the evidence and suggest ways that leaders can drive step changes—a set of rapid improvements in performance where measured improvements rapidly increase, creating an improvement graph similar to ascending stairs—in performance without the damaging effects of fixed targets.

Alternative names and related topics: stretch targets; aspirational goals; goal setting

While most organizations set ambitious corporate-level goals, such as "to be number one or two in the industry," the annual target-setting process tends to fixate on an agreed-on number. First, executive teams give their investors a target. Fifteen percent earnings-per-share growth used to be the benchmark, though this has been adjusted downward in recent years. Then this commitment cascades down the organization so that each division, business unit, product team, and back-office function has a share of the target. When aggregated, all the shares add up to the corporate number (or perhaps a higher number if the top executives want to have some cushion between their internal targets and the numbers they have committed to Wall Street).

This process is usually the front end of the annual budgeting round and can take many months and multiple iterations before it is finally accepted.

Game playing is rife. Whereas business teams aim for a modest increase over the previous year, senior executives demand that they stretch their targets to meet the big number. The result is usually a compromise. Annual targets are seductive, as they give managers a number to reach that defines not only their target but also their bonus and possibly their promotion prospects. So much is riding on how this figure is settled and how individual managers and their teams perform against it.

If key assumptions prove to be invalid and outside the control of the local team, executive management may account for these uncontrollable variances, and, in most cases, the bonus will be unaffected. Indeed, in many cases, the target itself will be adjusted to take account of these changes in assumptions. In recent years, targets have been changed four or five times as oil prices, property values, customer demand, and exchange rates gyrate from one extreme to another. Ironically these discussions take the form of granting managers relief from unanticipated headwinds. Rarely do they ever cover unexpected favorable conditions that made reaching the targets much easier.

But there has always been a flip side to target setting. While accountability might appear to be clear, the behaviors it can drive cast a long shadow over any value it produces. For example, because managers know they will be evaluated against the target, they are resistant to any stretch. The likely result is an incremental target based on a few percentage points change from the previous year. Another problem is that annual fixed targets focus people on meeting the numbers rather than on adapting to emerging threats and opportunities, possibly leading to catastrophic failure. Also, fixed targets rely on the fear of failure to force people to pursue the accepted target at almost any cost. Thus, the targets stifle innovation and can lead to unethical behavior.

Traditional target setting assumes a dim view of human motivation. Indeed, many senior executives believe that only by negotiating a stretch financial target with a manager will they be able to maximize profits. But the same executives wouldn't trust that manager to set such a target. In other words, senior executives think that by agreeing on a fixed target and controlling performance against it, they have control of the results. This is one of the great illusions of command-and-control management. Jack Welch spotted this many years ago when he said, "Making a budget is an exercise in minimalization. You're always trying to get the lowest out of people, because everyone is negotiating to get the lowest number."[1]

If you think that targets damage behavior only occasionally, then consider what damage they can do to business results and customer relationships. Think of a purchasing manager with a target of reducing cost who orders in bulk or pays suppliers late but feels no accountability for the poor quality of the products he bought, the costs of high inventories, or the

Setting aspirational goals at an Asian telecom company

Many leaders are abandoning the annual target-setting process and encouraging their teams to set their own goals, above and beyond what the traditional negotiating process would have produced. These goals are aspirational and directional. They usually describe where a company wants to be in three or five years relative to its peers. The teams can determine a range of goals. For example, an Asian telecommunications company has set these three-year aspirational goals:

1. To become the number-one telecom in the Asia-Pacific region, based on earnings before interest, taxes, depreciation, and amortization (EBITDA) and return on invested capital (ROIC).
2. To be in the top 10 percent of its peers, based on customer satisfaction and loyalty.
3. To be number one in terms of customer fulfillment (e.g., fastest broadband).
4. To be in the top-three employers, based on attracting and keeping the best talent.
5. To be in the top three corporations, based on an index of corporate social responsibility (awarded annually in a size adjusted national competition).[a]

[a] Presented at the Beyond Budgeting Round Table European Meeting (BBRT 45), Copenhagen, Denmark, March 23, 2010.

deteriorating relationships with suppliers. Think of a pension salesperson who sells products that give her the highest commissions but who is not accountable for providing her client with funds that best fit that client's needs. And think of a mortgage broker who ignores risk controls and sells mortgages to people who can't afford them to achieve his maximum bonus. In all these cases, the manager or salesperson has met his or her obligations—to meet the target—but has left the customer dissatisfied and the company worse off.

Setting aspirational and directional goals can inspire and motivate teams. The process recognizes that everything is connected, and achieving any one goal depends on making good progress toward all the others. Each team defines its key success factors and sets medium-term goals based on them. But these goals are relative rather than fixed. In other words, the company measures the teams on the results relative to others, not against a fixed number. This is crucial to the stretching process.

Identifying comparable relative measures can be a problem at the corporate level but can usually be found (albeit with a time lag). Typical sources include industry trade associations, customer data, industry analysts, or competitive cost structure analysis. But peer comparisons inside the organization are much more straightforward. Business units, branches, plants, brands, service teams, and any business segment where there is more than one team can be compared with each other. In these cases, relative performance information is readily accessible.

Once the teams agree on the relative performance goals, there is little need for negotiation. They continuously evaluate performance based on progress toward the goals. Most teams set their sights on consistently being in the top quartile or decile of their peer group. The context for success should be the team's view of best-in-class performance within its peer group and how long it will take to become number one. Managers are willing to accept or propose these stretch goals because they are used for direction setting and evaluation of progress. Their teams' performance will subsequently be measured and rewarded using a range of relative indicators, such as peer-group performance, internal and external benchmarks, and market movements. Baseline goals set a lower level of expectations.

What is the performance potential of this practice?

- **To improve profit potential.** The aim is to raise profits beyond "last year plus 3 percent" and get teams to maximize their performance potential.
- **To build greater team commitment to improvement.** Goals expressed in the right way can be inspiring and lead to greater commitment to success.
- **To encourage innovation.** Most CEOs complain that their organizations are insufficiently innovative. Stretch goals raise the performance bar above business as usual and thus put the pressure on teams to find innovative ways to achieve them.

What actions do you need to take to maximize the potential of this practice?

ACTIONS TO AVOID

- ✖ **Stop turning targets into fixed-performance contracts.** If you continue to engage in an annual, negotiated, or top-down target-setting process, it is highly unlikely that any real stretch will emerge. Managers will play it safe and negotiate incremental targets.

✖ **Stop being a slave to analysts (and managing earnings).** If senior executives are unwilling to stop providing analysts with specific growth or profit targets, breaking free from fixed targets inside the business is difficult.

✖ **Stop cascading targets down the business.** If targets are imposed or negotiated, the best political operators win and the best business builders lose.

✖ **Avoid specific goals.** In an unpredictable world, goals are best set as ranges rather than single-point targets.

✖ **Stop basing performance evaluation and rewards on fixed targets.** Again, if targets are fixed and linked to performance evaluation and rewards, managers will play the negotiating game and opt for lowball targets.

✖ **Stop creating a climate of fear.** If the message of the prevailing culture is to meet the numbers or else, the fear of failure generated will militate against stretch targets.

✖ **Stop denying teams any involvement or ownership.** If top managers impose or even negotiate targets, there is unlikely to be much ownership or commitment. Few people become committed to someone else's target or plan.

ACTIONS TO TAKE

✓ **Frame group success in terms of peer-to-peer comparisons ("be the best").** Persuade investment analysts and regulators that while the company may still give profit estimates, these will not be fixed commitments. Persuade them to see success in terms of peer-to-peer comparisons (above average, top quartile, top decile, or number one). Agree on a list of peers (company to company) against whom performance will be compared.

✓ **Ensure that the executive team sets aspirational, medium-term goals and directions.** Consider using the balanced scorecard to develop corporate strategy maps to help teams set strategic priorities that inform local plans, but don't use scorecards as top-down performance contracts. Many of Toyota's goals are purposely vague, allowing employees to channel their energies in different directions and forcing specialists from different functions to collaborate across the rigid silos in which they usually work. For example, Katsuaki Watanabe, vice chairman of Toyota, has said that his goal is to build a car that makes the air cleaner, prevents accidents, makes people healthier and happier when they drive it, and gets you from coast to coast on one tank of gas. Zenji Yasuda, a former Toyota senior managing director, points out the wisdom of painting with broad strokes: "The vague nature of this goal confers freedom to researchers to open new avenues of exploration; procurement to look for new and unknown suppliers who possess needed technology; and sales to consider the next steps needed to sell such products."[2] These goals provide a context, but not a contract, for improvement and send a message to all teams that helps them set their own goals.

✓ **Support continuous, relative improvement ("be the best") as the primary definition of success at every level.** Frame goals in terms of relative improvement. For example, a goal might be to move from third-quartile to first-quartile performance within three years. Avoid specific financial numbers. Choose ratios and ranges. Once external or peer-based benchmarks are selected, there is little need for negotiation. Teams continuously evaluate performance based on the progress made against the benchmarks. Most teams set their sights on consistently being in the top quartile of their peer group. Typical goals include a return-on-equity and cost-to-income ratio. The idea is for teams to make step changes and thus be prepared to think the unthinkable. Another, similar approach is to base goals not on specific benchmarks but on continuously improving relative performance against the competition. By definition, managers can only estimate these goals; they cannot know them in advance. The goals can be internal (e.g., branch to branch), or external (e.g., business to business).

✓ **Ensure that the executive team supports, but doesn't control, the goal-setting process.** The team's role is to challenge ambition, encourage innovation, and engage in a dialogue about risks, rewards, and resource requirements.

✓ **Enable teams at every level to set their own goals.** The traditional goal-negotiation process is a great inhibitor of ambition. Starting from the previous period's results invariably leads to incremental change rather than stretch goals. Once goal setting is divorced from performance evaluation and rewards, new behavior is quickly evident. Teams start to set more ambitious goals, knowing that they will not form a contract against which they must deliver. In other words, the fear of failure has been removed.

✓ **Use benchmarking to encourage teams to raise their game.** Senior executives can reasonably ask, "If another team can do this, then why can't you? But use benchmarks only to challenge and stretch rather than to judge and blame. (See chapter 8 on benchmarking.)

✓ **Use ranges rather than single-point goals.** Many business leaders demand single-point targets and forecasts, but these can lead to short-term gap-filling decisions and undermine long-term strategy. They also lead to minimal targets and suboptimal performance. Some firms have overcome these problems by moving to ranges and scenarios in which managers set expectations across a range of outcomes and, of course, always

---

Stretch at General Electric

In 1999, Jack Welch commented on his experiences at GE: "Stretch is a concept that would have produced smirks in the GE of three or four years ago, because it essentially means using dreams to set targets—with no real idea how to get there . . . If they don't have the team operating effectively, you give them another chance. If they fail again, you hand the reins to another person. But you don't punish for not meeting big targets. If ten is the target and you're only at two, we'll have a party when you go to four. When you reach six we'll celebrate again. We don't waste time and money budgeting 4.12 to 5.13 to 6.17."[a]

[a] Robert Slater, *Jack Welch and the GE Way* (New York: McGraw-Hill, 1999), 170.

---

aim for the best options. At each performance review, managers submit new action plans and the best ones are funded. The aim is always to maximize the performance potential of the team. This removes the target ceiling and much of the dysfunctional behavior that is often a feature of poor goal setting and forecasting.

✓ **Enable teams to reset goals as required.** In a relative measurement system, specific or even range goals are just aspirations, and these change as and when the performance of industry leaders changes. No one is committed to a fixed number, and there is no realignment of budgets. At Handelsbanken, branch managers can change their goals when they wish. They do not need to communicate them to a higher authority. There is no contract or commitment. The only contract is to do their best to improve their performance, and the test is how well they have done compared with peers and market competition.

✓ **Focus performance reviews on trajectories and gaps.** While leaders challenge managers to stretch their performance, they know that it is not the goals that are important but the trajectory of results. Gaps are based on the difference between your current performance and the relative goal you have set (top quartile, decile, or number one, etc).

✓ **Use league tables with care.** League tables serve as a simple way to compare groups of like branches, geographic regions, divisions, or companies. While regularly published in industries such as investment banking or advertising, they are also used within many other companies and across multiple industries. The tables are constructed by ranking members of the group across a key performance trait. In terms of use, companies should just publish the results without comment. Peer pressure works best when it is understated; every team should know which team it needs to compare itself to.

✓ **Balance internal competition and cooperation.** Ensure that there is no competition for customers (e.g., local versus national sales teams).

Conclusions

Einstein once said that doing the same thing over and over again expecting a different result is the definition of insanity. That just about sums up the addiction to target setting in both the public and the private sectors. Targets are seductively simple, but they apply linear logic to a complex, unpredictable world. If leaders really want to grow the top line and respond rapidly to emerging events, they must stop tinkering with targets and focus their attention on devising fair ways to evaluate and recognize performance.

FURTHER READING

Hope, Jeremy. *Reinventing the CFO: How Financial Managers Can Transform Their Roles and Add Greater Value*. Boston: Harvard Business School Press, 2006.

Hope, Jeremy, Peter Bunce, and Franz Röösli. *The Leader's Dilemma: How to Build an Empowered and Adaptive Organization Without Losing Control*. San Francisco, CA: John Wiley & Sons, 2011.

Hope, Jeremy, and Robin Fraser. *Beyond Budgeting: How Managers Can Break Free from the Annual Performance Trap*. Boston: Harvard Business School Press, 2003.

Ordóñez, Lisa D., Maurice E. Schweitzer, Adam D. Galinsky, and Max H. Bazerman. "Goals Gone Wild: The Systematic Side Effects of Over-Prescribing Goal Setting." Working paper 09-083, Harvard Business School, Boston, 2009, www.exed.hbs.edu/assets/goal-setting.pdf.

4

BALANCED SCORECARD

What is this practice and how effective is it?

The balanced scorecard is a framework for linking strategic goals to measures and action plans. Strategy maps link critical processes enabling managers to focus on key areas of measurement and improvement. But despite a multiplicity of best-practice cases and hundreds of consulting firms selling solutions, the failure rate remains high. One reason is that too many scorecards become nothing more than annual contracts—similar to budgets with additional bells and whistles—that are glued too tightly together and that stifle ambition and flexibility. We look at how some organizations are using scorecards to empower and engage their people in setting ambitious goals and aligning measures and actions with them.

Alternative names and related topics: strategy-focused organization; strategy mapping; cause-and-effect analysis

Robert Kaplan and David Norton developed the balanced scorecard (BSC) in the early 1990s as a response to performance management systems that were focused on budgets rather than strategies. While the BSC started life as a better measurement system, over the course of the 1990s a number of firms—or more accurately, business units within firms—began to use the BSC as a framework for formulating and executing their strategy. The BSC offered a new opportunity to align measures, goals, and actions with a clearly defined strategy. It is one of modern management's great success stories.

The BSC is based on four perspectives (financial, customer, process, and learning or growth). It tells the strategy story through cause-and-effect relationships and communicates it through key strategic themes, measures, and targets based on growth and productivity improvement, usually known as a

The five common traits of the balanced scorecard

After analyzing hundreds of balanced scorecard implementations, Kaplan and Norton recognized that five common traits emerged that set the BSC within the context of an organizational change program rather than a metrics program. They listed these in their second book, *The Strategy-Focused Organization*.[a]

1. Mobilize change through executive leadership. The BSC should present a vision for change supported by executive leaders.

2. Translate strategy into operational terms. By better utilizing existing tangible and intangible assets within a clear strategic framework that can be described and communicated throughout the business, managers can translate strategy into operational terms.

3. Align the organization to its strategy. Any number of individual business unit strategies across large and complex organizations can be integrated by breaking out of the functional barriers and creating strategic themes that transcend traditional boundaries.

4. Make strategy everyone's job. By bringing strategy into the everyday working lives of thousands of employees, leaders can raise strategic awareness across the whole organization and reinforce the right behavior by setting appropriate reward and recognition systems.

5. Make strategy a continual process. By taking it out of the realms of an annual process and into the everyday decision-making actions of operating managers, leaders can turn strategy from an annual event into a continual process.

[a] Robert S. Kaplan and David P. Norton, *The Strategy-Focused Organization: How Balanced Scorecard Companies Thrive in the New Business Environment* (Boston: Harvard Business School Press, 2000).

strategy map. Figure 4-1 shows a simple strategy map for a low-cost airline. To increase profitability—the financial perspective—it needs to both operate with the minimum number of planes and increase its volume of customers. To win more customers, it must ensure that flights are on time and that it offers low prices—the customer perspective. To operate with low prices, it must turn planes around quickly at the gates—the process perspective. To turn planes around quickly, it must train ground crews and align their performance evaluations with this objective—the learning perspective. Zooming in on the customer perspective shows how objectives, measures, goals, and initiatives are

FIGURE 4-1

A simple strategy map for a low-cost airline

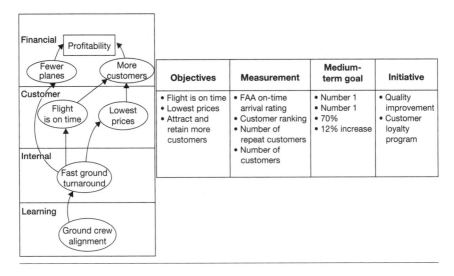

Objectives	Measurement	Medium-term goal	Initiative
• Flight is on time • Lowest prices • Attract and retain more customers	• FAA on-time arrival rating • Customer ranking • Number of repeat customers • Number of customers	• Number 1 • Number 1 • 70% • 12% increase	• Quality improvement • Customer loyalty program

derived and aligned. Notice that goals are derived from objectives and measures, and that actions follow goals.

The Norwegian oil company, Statoil, is a powerful advocate of the BSC. Calling it "Ambition to Action," Statoil uses it to drive performance improvement across the whole organization. There are over eight hundred Ambition-to-Action scorecards in the company. But there are differences between the standard approach and how Statoil uses the BSC. First, the BSC is just one of four walls governing performance management and decision making. The others are the company's values, decision thresholds, and management judgment. Second, they do not cascade down through line-of-sight alignment. This means that upper level goals are not pushed down to lower levels as is often seen in command-and-control environments. Instead, each team sets its own goals, metrics, and actions—though there is a robust dialogue with senior managers—using higher-level BSCs, including the corporate scorecard, to translate higher-level goals and plans into local ones. In other words, the BSC is not imposed from the top down; it is not even mandatory. And third, there is no annual budget. Getting rid of the budget eliminates forces that can drive performance and decisions in other directions and collides with the BSC. The corporate scorecard is the only item the board approves each year. According to project leader Bjarte Bogsnes, when the budget was eliminated, it was like "turbocharging" the scorecard.

While many organizations such as Statoil have gained major benefits from the BSC, there are many others that have been disappointed. The trouble is that in many cases they use the BSC to reinforce the command-and-control management model. But for leaders who want to build more devolved and adaptive organizations, it can be a dangerous practice. Too many scorecards become annual fixed-performance contracts similar to budgets but with some nonfinancial goals and measures attached. The trouble is that while the scorecard process drives the company in the direction of medium-term strategic goals supported by cross-functional initiatives, the budgeting process drives the company in the direction of short-term financial goals supported by individual departmental initiatives.

The IT industry is particularly culpable in this regard. Its software systems tend to assume that users will set targets against which their performance will be monitored. Incentives are then attached to these targets. In one company we visited, there were twenty-two targets, with an incentive element attached to each one. If the BSC appears to be just another budget with annual negotiations of targets and resources, then it is not surprising that local managers will fail to embrace its real strengths. In such a situation, the message will be a familiar command-and-control one, thus undermining any notion of empowerment and trust. BSC simply appears as just another top-down control tool.

Another problem is when a company asks the BSC to do too much. It is not an effective resource management framework, nor is it designed to coordinate plans and actions across the organization. Gluing multiple scorecards together to form a coordinated plan reverts to the problems of rigid planning and budgeting associated with the old system. That's why Statoil steered clear of these actions.

The primary problem is that too many leaders use the BSC to paper over the cracks of a crumbling hierarchy rather than use the power of the BSC to devolve strategy and decision making to frontline teams. In other words, the BSC can be used as a force for either empowerment or control, but the vast majority—wittingly or unwittingly—become tools of top-down control. They can easily lock managers into rigid strategies and annual contracts unless the feedback and learning loops are fully engaged; they rarely are. They can lead to additional complexity and reporting unless other mechanisms, such as budgets, are neutralized; they rarely are. And they can be time consuming and expensive to implement.

As at Statoil, scorecards are at their best when not aggregated but only loosely connected with others, thus enabling teams to think through and describe their improvement strategies and align goals and actions with them. But the implementation devil is in the details. If your organization is already

---

The balanced scorecard can also be an inhibitor of innovation

In an article entitled, "The Tyranny of the Balanced Scorecard in the Innovation Economy," Sven Voelpel, Marius Leibold, Robert Eckhoff, and Thomas Davenport noted, "As heavy hiking boots are a blessing when trying to climb a mountain, and a curse for the 100 meters sprint, the BSC in the innovation economy exerts a tyrannical impact and influence on the firm and its shareholders."[a] They go on to say not only that strategy is too hard-wired but also that the external innovation connectivity of an organization is hampered by the BSC, which is mostly an internal document. This is a critical limitation on its ability to account for the external environment and systemic linkages. In other words, the BSC is a management and measurement tool that is primarily concerned with "driving performance" and "translating strategy into action" efficiently *within* an organization. It widely ignores the needs of an interlinked and highly networked economy in which companies co-evolve and where competition partly gives way to cooperation.[b]

[a] Sven C. Voelpel, Marius Leibold, Robert A. Eckhoff, and Thomas H. Davenport, "The Tyranny of the Balanced Scorecard in the Innovation Economy," *Journal of Intellectual Capital* 7, no. 1 (2006): 43–60.

[b] Voelpel, Leibold, Eckhoff, and Davenport, "The Tyranny of the Balanced Scorecard in the Innovation Economy," 51.

---

well managed, with a clear strategy, well-designed processes, and managers who have the freedom and capability to formulate goals and plans and make effective decisions, then the benefits from implementing the BSC will be limited. But if your company is not well endowed with these management strengths—and most organizations aren't—then the balanced scorecard could be the answer to your problems.

What is the performance potential of this practice?

- **To place strategy at the core of management.** While many organizations spend a lot of time formulating their strategy, that strategy quickly gets derailed as the annual budget takes over. The BSC is an attempt to redress this imbalance.
- **To align measures, actions, and rewards with strategy.** Most performance measures are derived from the financial information system, but most

managers know that the key success drivers are nonfinancial. The BSC provides a framework for placing these nonfinancial measures where they should be—in front of managers every day.

- **To find and act on the key value drivers.** Every organization has a small number of key value drivers (20 percent of drivers create 80 percent of value), but few managers know what they are. Through well-crafted strategy maps, managers can identify their key drivers and take action to maximize their impact.

What actions do you need to take to maximize the potential of this practice?

ACTIONS TO AVOID

- ✖ **Avoid key performance indicator (KPI) scorecards.** Remember that the scorecard is about management, not measurement. Just looking at the four perspectives and then directing teams to find the best KPIs to focus on is not the right way forward. Measurement comes after agreeing on a clear business purpose and strategy; measures should be derived from them. Actions follow measures. Norton advises users *not* to start with an emphasis on metrics: "Start with your strategy and use metrics to make it understandable and measurable, that is, to communicate it to those expected to make it happen and to manage it."[1]

- ✖ **Don't cascade scorecards down or aggregate scorecards up the organization.** The board should not use the corporate scorecard or its power and authority to direct and dictate lower-level goals and plans. Otherwise, teams will gravitate toward incremental improvements and stifle innovation. Nor is it desirable to aggregate scorecards upward, especially if the business is anything less than simple and homogenous. Each business unit team should be encouraged to create its own scorecard that is informed by corporate goals and scorecards but not dictated by them.

- ✖ **Stop using the scorecard as another tool of command and control.** Managers should use the scorecards with "soft" rather than "hard" hands. In other words, they should use them as a framework for helping local teams formulate and communicate their strategies rather than preprogram what they do. If line managers see the BSC as just another reporting tool that will further complicate their working lives, then they will do their utmost to undermine it. The real strength of the scorecard is to involve the whole team in formulating and executing goals and plans and thus building ownership and commitment to achieving them. Enlightened managers see the BSC as a framework for adaptive management rather than annual planning and control.

Don't rely on strategy maps before they can be tested

Managers are too often mesmerized by the cause-and-effect relationships they see on strategy maps. They believe that if you can connect the dots between actions (causes) and results (effects), then you have cracked the strategy problem. While strategy maps help managers see the links between the different perspectives of the scorecard and the key processes that drive those links, cause-and-effect linkages are more difficult to fully understand than many managers recognize. The time lags between cause and effect, for example, can be longer than anticipated.

According to author and consultant Mark Graham Brown, "many executives have become disillusioned with strategy maps which often fail to produce process metrics that can be linked to important outcomes. What these executives have discovered is that most strategy maps are not based on research and data collection, but on prevailing opinions, logic, and wishful thinking. While process measures are showing green, outcomes remain in the red zone. The underlying problem boils down to one significant truth: Strategy maps are often a systematic documentation of a long string of assumptions and hypotheses that are rarely tested. Because the diagrams look so convincing, no one thinks to question their validity."[a] Companies like Sears and Hilton Hotels have accumulated data on hundreds of their properties (stores and hotels) and now are well positioned to test their strategic hypotheses on an ongoing basis.[b] Until that level of detail is available, managers should use strategy maps as a compass rather than a road map.

[a] Mark Graham Brown, *Beyond the Balanced Scorecard* (New York: Productivity Press, 2007), 186.
[b] "Ask the Source," *CIO Magazine*, September 19, 2002, www2.cio.com/ask/source/2002/session27.html.

✖ **Stop basing the scorecard process on annual targets and measures.** Too many firms treat the scorecard like an annual planning and target-setting process. To maintain its relevance, the scorecard needs to be more flexible and subject to continuous feedback and learning. The team-based scorecards must be loose and flexible rather than hierarchical glue that binds them together and makes change difficult. Leaders need to dismantle the process of setting annual targets and monitor variances against them. If the scorecard becomes another fixed-performance contract with target-actual-variance reports, all ideas about focusing managers on strategic goals will be lost. The same gaming that goes on around financial targets will apply to scorecard targets, which leads managers to agree only to targets they can meet safely and means only incremental change.

✖ **Remember that strategy is more about innovation and initiative than incremental improvement.** The whole scorecard process can be overwhelming, causing you to forget about the need to encourage innovation and initiative. This encouragement cannot be programmed into an annual exercise or confined to strategy retreats. Given the right climate, innovative strategies and initiatives can occur at any time and should not be stymied by rigid scorecards or budgets.

✖ **Avoid a collision with the budget.** Budgets and scorecards come from different cultural worlds. Yet most implementations fail to understand this fundamental difference. Budgets determine how people think and act. They contain powerful behavioral antibodies. Unless proposed changes to any core management process sit comfortably with budgeting, they are likely to be either neutralized by its immune system or rejected altogether. Introducing one will require changes in the other.

✖ **Stop forcing cross-company coordination.** Strategic alignment usually means forcing disparate units to integrate their BSC plans and actions, so the organization falls back into the trap of rigid planning and coordination. If senior managers try to glue every scorecard together, then the organization will itself be too tightly glued and thus incapable of responding to change. Coordination should happen continuously between teams within the context of supplier-customer relationships.

✖ **Avoid using too many measures.** Many efforts at implementing the BSC founder on the rocks of performance measurement. Too many scorecards are full of irrelevant measures that fail to provide useful information about what is happening now and where the business is heading. Few measures lead to learning and improvement or change behavior. A practical guide is to have three to five measures for each perspective with a ratio of nonfinancial to financial measures of 5 to 1. An effective measure should help managers understand and improve performance and, to this extent, should be an integral part of the work they do. Few measures pass this test.

✖ **Follow the order of strategy or purpose-measurement-goal-action.** Too many scorecards fail to get this order right. They wrongly rush into short-term targets and actions and then look at how they should measure the outcome. Each element of strategy should have a clear goal, and every process should have a clear purpose. It is clear if it can be measured. Only then can managers know whether the purpose is met and thus if further action is required.

✖ **Don't rush into using personal scorecards.** Many organizations mistakenly take the alignment of strategy, goals, measures, and actions down to the level of individual employees and include them as part of the annual appraisal process. This can destroy flexibility, sharing, and teamwork if individuals are driven by simplistic targets underpinned by assumptions that rapidly lose focus as circumstances change.

✖ **Don't rush into linking incentives to scorecard goals and measures.** Many leaders believe that unless they link incentives to scorecard goals, managers will not take the scorecard seriously. While this might be true to some degree, there are real dangers in this approach. If leaders choose the wrong goals and measures, for example, managers could waste lots of time and energy pursuing the wrong objectives. Moreover, they might need to change the objectives depending on the actions of competitors and customers. Another danger is that if the data is not robust (e.g., if customer satisfaction surveys jump around for no apparent reason), managers whose bonuses are based on the results will lose faith in the BSC and begin to undermine it. Using scorecard measures with hindsight to support judgmental criteria about management performance is a better approach. Measures on their own never tell the whole story.

✖ **Don't assume a verifiable link between nonfinancial indicators and financial results.** Despite many attempts to achieve this holy grail, the links are tenuous at best, partly because the time lags are difficult to gauge; by then, many other factors will influence financial outcomes. However, the intuitive reasoning is compelling, provided that key processes keep improving (i.e., quality and speed improve and costs are reduced).

ACTIONS TO TAKE

✓ **Use corporate scorecards to set directional goals.** Corporate scorecards should represent a high-level view of what success for the organization will look like two to five years out. That is the role of the board. This scorecard provides a framework for all operating teams as well as functions and departments to formulate their own scorecards including their goals, measures, and action plans. At Statoil, the BSC objectives and goals are all that the board approves each year.

✓ **Translate rather than cascade goals, metrics, and actions.** Cascading scorecard targets, metrics, and actions down the organization risks creating inflexible contracts. It is better to enable and encourage each team to look at the scorecards of the level above and the scorecards of their peers so that they can align their goals, metrics, and actions accordingly. Statoil takes this approach.

✓ **Use the scorecard to empower teams.** Scorecards can be an effective tool to transfer the scope and authority for goal setting and planning to front-line teams. Building strategic capability within hundreds of teams across a midsize to large organization is a major benefit of using the scorecard, as long as it is used for empowerment rather than control.

✓ **Use the scorecard to define a team's success.** Scorecards are best used to enable each team to formulate, articulate, and execute its strategy. They can help each team think about why it exists and what it needs to do to maximize the value it contributes.

✓ **Use the scorecard to set ambitious goals.** The scorecard should be used as a framework for setting ambitious goals underpinned by well-thought-out plans to achieve them. This process can be pressure tested by involving the whole team as well as senior executives and peers.

✓ **Use the scorecard to find key value drivers.** The scorecard is an excellent tool for identifying key processes and value drivers that have the greatest impact on customer and, ultimately, shareholder value. If you look back at figure 4-1, the key value driver in a low-cost airline is likely to be "fast ground turnaround" as this enables or inhibits both revenue growth and operational improvement, both of which drive profitability. But without drawing a strategy map, this might not be so obvious.

✓ **Use the scorecard to find the best KPIs.** A well-designed scorecard should tell a team a great deal about what KPIs to use to monitor and control performance. Most teams don't need more than three to five KPIs for each scorecard perspective, but can extend this when KPIs are turned into analytics. (See chapter 32 for more on KPIs and chapter 34 for more on analytics.)

✓ **Use the scorecard to derive action plans.** Firms waste huge amounts of resources each year on projects that have little to do with strategy. The scorecard can help overcome these problems by providing a clear framework for aligning action plans with strategic goals. But be wary of funding cuts that can affect these plans. While strategic initiatives usually last for two to five years, budgets are invariably annual.

✓ **Add perspectives if it makes sense.** Many organizations have moved away from the standard four perspectives. Statoil, for example, has added "health and safety," which is a key performance perspective in the oil industry. In high-level meetings, Statoil executives discuss health and safety first, and finance last.

✓ **Ensure that data is accessible, clean, and accurate.** Too many BSCs fail because of lack of data integrity. Lost or duplicate documents and wrong postings, journals, and allocations can play havoc with the credibility of reports. Choosing measures that are hard to track and that require huge amounts of effort to report on also undermine the BSC's credibility. This problem can become a nightmare if incentives are attached to those measures. Data needs to be accessible in a timely way; users need to see it as credible. Employees will be unforgiving if they believe that they have done better than the figures show.

✓ **Engage everyone in the scorecard process.** Making strategy everyone's job depends on leaders involving frontline people in strategy and empowering them to make key decisions. But letting go is difficult for many leaders who spent years to reach the top of the organization. Leading organizations post progress reports—on graphs and charts—on the intranet and on office walls, so people become attached to the BSC. This drives continuous improvement.

Conclusions

The BSC has been around for fifteen years or so and has established itself as a key management tool. But too many organizations get the implementation badly wrong and waste huge amounts of time and money. They should ask themselves if the BSC is the right tool to solve their problems. Often these problems have to do with poor organization design and complex, dysfunctional systems that need rethinking from first principles. In other words, the BSC can make complex systems even more complex and thus have the opposite effect from the one intended.

How the scorecard is interpreted is of paramount importance. As a tool of empowerment, the impact can be a force for good. But as another tool of command and control, the impact will invariably be negative, with people seeing more work and few benefits.

The BSC represents a significant investment and should not be contemplated without careful appraisal and planning. The prevailing culture is critical. The BSC works best within an organization that has set its course to become more devolved and adaptive (i.e., when it is used as a tool for devolved management rather than top-down control). That is its conceptual strength and its practical weakness.

FURTHER READING

Brown, Mark Graham. *Beyond the Balanced Scorecard.* New York: Productivity Press, 2007.

Hope, Jeremy. *Reinventing the CFO: How Financial Managers Can Transform Their Roles and Add Greater Value.* Boston: Harvard Business School Press, 2006.

Hope, Jeremy, Peter Bunce, and Franz Röösli. *The Leader's Dilemma: How to Build an Empowered and Adaptive Organization Without Losing Control.* San Francisco, CA: John Wiley & Sons, 2011.

Hope, Jeremy, and Robin Fraser. *Beyond Budgeting: How Managers Can Break Free from the Annual Performance Trap.* Boston: Harvard Business School Press, 2003.

Kaplan, Robert S., and David P. Norton. *Alignment: How to Apply the Balanced Scorecard to Corporate Strategy*. Boston: Harvard Business School Press, 2006.

Kaplan, Robert S., and David P. Norton. *The Balanced Scorecard: Translating Strategy into Action*. Boston: Harvard Business School Press, 1996.

Kaplan, Robert S., and David P. Norton. *Execution Premium: Linking Strategy to Operations for Competitive Advantage*. Boston: Harvard Business School Press, 2008.

Kaplan, Robert S., and David P. Norton. "Having Trouble with Your Strategy? Then Map It." *Harvard Business Review*, September–October 2000, 167–176.

Kaplan, Robert S., and David P. Norton. "Measuring the Strategic Readiness of Intangible Assets." *Harvard Business Review*, February 2004, 52–63.

Kaplan, Robert S., and David P. Norton. *The Strategy-Focused Organization: How Balanced Scorecard Companies Thrive in the New Business Environment*. Boston: Harvard Business School Press, 2000.

Kaplan, Robert S., and David P. Norton. *Strategy Maps: Converting Intangible Assets into Tangible Outcomes*. Boston: Harvard Business School Press, 2004.

Kaplan, Robert S., and David P. Norton. "Using the Balanced Scorecard as a Strategic Management System." *Harvard Business Review*, January–February 1996, 75–85.

Niven, Paul. *Balanced Scorecard Step-by-Step: Maximizing Performance and Maintaining Results*. Hoboken, NJ: John Wiley & Sons, 2002.

5

DYNAMIC RESOURCE MANAGEMENT

What is this practice and how effective is it?

Dynamic resource management enables organizations to allocate resources to the best current opportunities. But few organizations operate this way. Most allocate capital during the budget round and allow business leaders to initiate many projects that have dubious merit in terms of adding value. We will examine how better organization design and information systems can help leaders to improve their capital management and support those business segments that warrant more capital and curtail or terminate those that don't.

Alternative names and related topics: risk management; decision analysis; investment decision analysis; corporate portfolio management; investment optimization

Most organizations allocate capital in the annual budget, though they may not allocate much of that capital to specific projects. In other words, a percentage of allocated capital is subject to further approval procedures. In this way, the internal bank is only open for four to six weeks a year—when budget allocations are agreed on—which, in a fast-changing world, is a major impediment to any organization that needs to respond rapidly to threats and opportunities.

Strategy expert Gary Hamel is highly critical of this process. He notes that funding for innovative ideas must survive the upward march through corporate hierarchy.[1] Hamel's scathing attack on the resource-allocation processes of large organizations rings true. They are too often based on company politics rather than strategic common sense. Thus, new ideas are stifled in favor of pouring good money after bad into loss-making projects.

Why is the quality of decision making so poor?

In a recent McKinsey survey of 2,207 executives, only 28 percent said that the quality of strategic decisions in their companies was generally good, 60 percent thought that bad decisions were about as frequent as good ones, and the remaining 12 percent thought that good decisions were altogether infrequent.[a]

The obvious question is why? McKinsey researchers used regression analysis to calculate how much of the variance in decision outcomes was explained by the quality of the process and how much by the quantity and detail of the analysis. The answer: process mattered more than analysis—by a factor of six. This finding does not mean that analysis is unimportant, as a closer look at the data reveals: almost no decisions in the sample made through a very strong process were backed by very poor analysis. Why? Because one of the things an unbiased decision-making process will do is ferret out poor analysis. The reverse is not true; superb analysis is useless unless the decision process gives it a fair hearing.

To get a sense of the value at stake, McKinsey also assessed the return on investment (ROI) of decisions characterized by a superior process. The analysis revealed that raising a company's game from the bottom to the top quartile on the decision-making process improved its ROI by 6.9 percentage points. The ROI advantage for top-quartile versus bottom-quartile analytics was 5.3 percentage points, further underscoring the tight relationship between process and analysis. Good process, in short, isn't just good hygiene; it's good business.[b]

[a] See "Flaws in Strategic Decision Making: McKinsey Global Survey Results," mckinseyquarterly.com, January 2009.

[b] Dan Lovallo and Olivier Sibony, "The Case for Behavioral Strategy," *McKinsey Quarterly*, February 2010, 34–35.

Another problem is that most organizations don't track investments effectively. One report concluded that as many as 75 percent of IT organizations had little oversight over their project portfolios and employed unrepeatable, chaotic planning processes.[2] The reality is that many organizations spend billions on the wrong businesses, products, and projects. The amount of waste is huge.

How much to invest in one business or another, how much to invest in new products or new ventures, and how to evaluate performance across the strategic portfolio are issues that go to the core of effective corporate strategy. These are truly strategic choices that once made are *difficult or costly to reverse.*

The trouble is that only a few people, often with their own political agendas, make these types of decisions, and their batting averages are generally poor. While operating through only a handful of large divisions has long been an effective way to prepare managers for the top jobs and to limit the number of direct reports the CEO has to manage, the divisions make it difficult for managers to see clearly where value is actually created or destroyed. The division and functional heads usually decide whether and where to place investment funds and how to make key trade-offs between innovative—but long-term—growth opportunities and short-term demands to meet the numbers. The evidence suggests a bias toward meeting short-term demands. One McKinsey study concluded that only 59 percent of financial executives would pursue a *positive* net present value if it meant missing quarterly earnings targets. Even worse, 78 percent said they would sacrifice value—in some cases, a lot of value—in order to smooth earnings.[3]

The outcome is a host of missed opportunities and a managerial blind spot where high-performing units mask the performance of poor-performing ones. The problem is that senior executives are often unaware that the decisions have been made. The outcome is that there is little transparency in decision making or value creation.

One way that leaders can overcome the traditional resource-allocation system is to see the organization through the lens of a resource portfolio made up of many small self-managed teams (see figure 5-1). The primary change is to create hundreds of value centers around product lines and market niches. By making teams accountable for creating value and justifying their capital usage, firms are more likely to make better resource-allocation decisions and cut huge amounts of waste.

In one example, a large health-care company analyzed one of its divisions by the type of disease to be treated, rather than by the classic functional structure of research, development, sales, and production. This meant adding up all the products the division used to treat each disease, the specialized sales forces serving specialist professionals around the globe, and the development teams working on new medical devices.

In another example, a European bank identified more than fifty value centers where it had once had nine divisions. Each center was built around related products, segments, or geographical boundaries. Examples included consumer finance, asset management for institutional clients such as pension funds, or wealth management for wealthy individuals.[4] The bank's aim was to give value-center teams' profit-and-loss responsibility, as if each was a stand-alone business. Senior executives benefited by having more detail and understanding of

FIGURE 5-1

A portfolio management view of resources

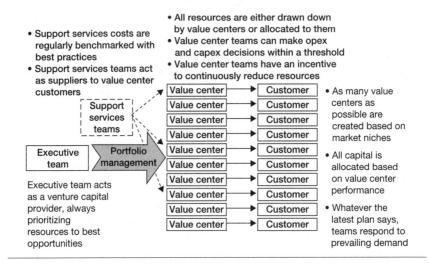

- Support services costs are regularly benchmarked with best practices
- Support services teams act as suppliers to value center customers

- All resources are either drawn down by value centers or allocated to them
- Value center teams can make opex and capex decisions within a threshold
- Value center teams have an incentive to continuously reduce resources

Support services teams

Executive team

Portfolio management

Executive team acts as a venture capital provider, always prioritizing resources to best opportunities

Value center	→	Customer
Value center	→	Customer
Value center	→	Customer
Value center	→	Customer
Value center	→	Customer
Value center	→	Customer
Value center	→	Customer
Value center	→	Customer
Value center	→	Customer
Value center	→	Customer

- As many value centers as possible are created based on market niches
- All capital is allocated based on value center performance
- Whatever the latest plan says, teams respond to prevailing demand

where the bank was creating and destroying value—detail that was previously hidden in budgets and other performance reports. The platform also provided more value-based strategic discussions and improved both accountability and transparency throughout the organization. For example, if there had been any cross-subsidies, they would have become clear. The result was better portfolio management and more control of strategic resources. In effect, leaders saw the investment portfolio through the lens of value centers and operated more like a venture capital company than a central banker. They expected divisional leaders to constantly experiment and spawn new value centers.

While managing so many value centers might appear to increase the CEO's workload, the reverse is often the case. Focusing more on each value center actually increases transparency because both senior executives and value-center managers find it easier to identify and monitor a few KPIs that drive performance improvement, as well as to make more straightforward decisions. In essence, the CEO can use value centers to eliminate several management layers. Instead of aggregating plans and results into complex divisions and then spending time understanding their performance, the CEO is able to make a larger number of more rapid, more insightful, and more value-based decisions at the value-center level.

To support this more dynamic organization, leaders need to replace the annual budget resource-allocation process. Instead, they need to provide resources when required and justified so that resources can follow the best current ideas. Rolling planning reviews, supported by rolling forecasts, offer a better management platform for overseeing this more dynamic resource management process.

American Express didn't know how much of its discretionary spending was on worthwhile projects. Nor did it know if it was optimizing risk across its portfolio. It tracked its investment initiatives on thousands of spreadsheets, but no one could collate the whole picture. By moving from annual budgets to rolling forecasts and from making investment decisions twice a year to 24/7, the company was able to not only speed up the concept-to-launch cycle from months to days but also better manage its portfolio so that it wasted less capital and better managed risk.

American Express also moved more resource decisions to frontline teams (below agreed-on thresholds), with the board or an appointed subcommittee in control of the strategic project portfolio and the prioritization of resources. The investment committee is constantly looking at rolling forecasts and releasing funds on the basis of capacity plans and strategic initiatives. This process tells it what funds are available, how many funds are already committed, and what is left to release into the system. This approach has cut costs dramatically, as capacity is not fixed months or years in advance or based on unrealistic assumptions.[5]

To facilitate these changes, a company needs to realign the management information system around horizontal data flows that cope with sometimes hundreds of profit-and-loss accounts. The data flows should also be able to show peer comparisons, KPIs, economic profit, trends, and forecasts.

What is the performance potential of this practice?

- **To ensure that resources follow the best current opportunities.** In most organizations, the best political operators, rather than the most innovative teams, acquire and spend resources. The aim is to change this approach and provide resources to entrepreneurial teams as and when justified.
- **To improve the alignment between investments and strategy.** Managers reduce waste by ensuring that they derive all investments from a clearly thought-out strategy. Some use the balanced scorecard to provide a robust framework for supporting this process.
- **To reduce waste in both operating costs and capital expenditure.** Most operating managers see budgets as a "license to spend." But when managers use resources only as required, they are less likely to overspend. Moreover, with no budget to act as a floor for costs, managers can seek permanent reductions in their continuous quest for higher levels of efficiency and profitability. The elimination of budget provisions on their own could save most large companies huge amounts.

- **To enable faster response.** Companies can make small-ticket decisions instantly and large decisions every month or so. Thus, new ideas can be fast-tracked to implementation and impact in days and weeks rather than months and years.

What actions do you need to take to maximize the potential of this practice?

ACTIONS TO AVOID

✖ **Avoid the annual allocation process.** Most organizations allocate resources during the annual budgeting process, which forces all teams to prepare and submit most of their project proposals during the annual budget round—a window of only a few weeks. If you managed a bank that opened its doors for only a few weeks each year, how successful would it be? The resource-allocation bank needs to be open 24/7, and funds available to support the best current ideas. The aim should be to shorten the time from project concept to launch from months and years to days and weeks.

✖ **Avoid the central committee decision-making process.** One of the primary purposes of traditional budgeting is to control resources across all operating units and cost centers. Thus, the head office is often seen as the central banker, either constraining or unleashing expansionary proposals.

Gary Hamel on resource allocations

Strategy expert Gary Hamel summarized these problems when he said that resource allocation was the last bastion of Soviet-style central planning and can be found in *Fortune* 500 companies. Hamel explains: "Big companies are not markets, they're hierarchies. The guys at the top decide where the money goes. Unconventional ideas are forced to make a tortuous climb up the corporate pyramid. If an idea manages to survive the gauntlet of skeptical vice-presidents, some distant CEO or chairman finally decides whether or not to invest. You want something new, something out of bounds, something that challenges the status quo? Good luck. It's no wonder so many Silicon Valley entrepreneurs are corporate exiles. After all, the Valley is nothing more than a refugee camp for frustrated entrepreneurs who couldn't get a hearing elsewhere."[a]

[a] Gary Hamel, "Bringing Silicon Valley Inside," *Harvard Business Review*, September–October 1999, 76.

Central bankers are notoriously risk averse, seeing the business more as a portfolio of assets than a portfolio of business opportunities. Resources flow to existing products and businesses rather than to new ideas, they support vested interests rather than new opportunities, and they flow to departmental budgets rather than strategic initiatives.

✖ **Beware of overconfidence.** A December 2009 survey of 463 readers of www.mckinseyquarterly.com underscored the degree to which senior executives sometimes exhibit greater confidence than those further down in the organization. In response to the question, "Does management admit mistakes and kill unsuccessful initiatives in a timely manner?" 80 percent of C-level executives said yes. In contrast, only 49 percent of non–C-level executives agreed with the same statement.[6] At HCL Technologies, CEO Vineet Nayar has opened up key strategic decisions (normally made by the board) to the whole organization. He posed such questions as, "How do we cut costs through the forthcoming recession?" or "What strategic options should we invest in?" and invites employees to come forward with ideas. This "wisdom of crowds" idea is catching on.

ACTIONS TO TAKE

✓ **Create as many entrepreneurial value centers as possible.** Leaders need to pay constant attention to the value-center portfolio by adding new ventures and terminating underperforming units. Value-center teams are responsible for formulating and executing strategy and delivering value or profit. They invariably have their own value streams and profit-and-loss accounts. The teams are typically created around lines of business, brands or product groups, regions or countries, and plants or branches. They start at the lowest level possible (e.g., a small branch of a bank) but can be grouped into numbers of units (e.g., a country or region). The aim is to treat each value center as a stand-alone business. Managers focus on maximizing value as measured by some variant of profit (such as return on sales, return on capital, or economic profit). The aim is that the team sees the value center as its own business and it has maximum freedom to grow and improve it. The teams offer managers a more detailed, more tangible way of gauging business value and economic activity and allow CEOs to spend more time on in-depth strategy discussions.

✓ **Act as a venture capital company rather than a central banker.** Leaders need to view the organization as a portfolio of businesses and investments that seeks to balance risk and reward. In this view, new businesses and investments are consistently encouraged, and poorly performing ones are terminated. The risk that any new venture will fail is quite high—say, six or seven out of ten. But venture capital companies look for the ones that pay off. In other words, they look for a huge upside of, say, 100 to 1 or even 1,000 to 1. Hamel makes an important point here regarding new investments within large organizations:

> Risk is the product of investment multiplied by the probability of failure. A $100,000 experiment with an 80 percent chance of failing is substantially less risky than a $100 million investment with a 1 percent chance of failure . . . Assuming no residual value for either project in the event of failure, the expected downside for the "risky" venture is $80,000 ($100,000 × 80%) and $1 million ($100 million × 1%) for the "sure thing." Yet which would be quicker to win funding in your company? Most companies fail to grasp this simple arithmetic. If they did, they'd be doing fewer big mergers, for example, and would instead be spawning dozens upon dozens of radical low-cost, low-risk experiments.[7]

Hamel's style is designed to make executives uncomfortable, and rightly so. We have seen billions of dollars poured down the drain in the name of shareholder value creation, based on forecasting models with pages of numbers that prove what the project sponsors want to hear but without stressing the risks.

✓ **Prioritize investments according to strategic impact and value creation.** Enlightened leaders focus on two criteria for proposals: *impact*—whether global, regional, or local—and *value*—whether strategic or nonstrategic. (1) Global, strategic proposals are likely to benefit many business units and thus should be decided on and funded by corporate. A new corporate branding exercise or the implementation of an enterprisewide computer system are examples. (2) Global, nonstrategic proposals also affect a number of business units, so again a corporate decision is appropriate. A new office building is an example. (3) Local, strategic proposals usually lie within a particular business unit. Because the proposal is strategic, corporate will want to know about it and ensure that it complies with the definition of a worthwhile strategic investment. (4) Local, nonstrategic proposals usually involve relatively small sums and need to be decided on quickly. Teams should look at the options and decide.

✓ **Prepare the investment case thoroughly.** Major investment decisions are often made quickly without adequate due diligence. This particularly applies to acquisitions where huge risks are taken based on fluffy estimates of synergy-type cost savings and additional market penetration. Huge investment case packs are prepared full of numbers and charts that justify the bottom-line estimates. But there is often a political motive behind the proposal, rather than a compelling and rational strategic case.

Thorough analysis and decision making at Toyota

If decisions involve tens or hundreds of millions of dollars, they should be based on the most thorough investigation possible. Alex Warren, former senior vice president of Toyota Motor Manufacturing in Kentucky, made this observation: "If you've got a project that is supposed to be fully implemented in a year, it seems to me that the typical American company will spend about three months on planning, then they'll begin to implement. But they'll encounter all sorts of problems after implementation, and they'll spend the rest of the year correcting them. However, given the same year-long project, Toyota will spend nine to ten months planning, then implement in a small way—such as with pilot production—and be fully implemented at the end of the year, with virtually no remaining problems."[a]

When Toyota purchased some land for a test track in Arizona, the U.S. lawyer acting for it was amazed at how thorough Toyota was. He commented after the deal, "Toyota stands out as the preeminent analyst of strategy and tactics. Nothing is assumed. Everything is verified. The goal is getting it right."[b]

[a] Jeffrey K. Liker, *The Toyota Way: 14 Management Principles from the World's Greatest Manufacturer* (New York: McGraw-Hill, 2004), 237.

[b] Liker, *The Toyota Way*, 238.

That most acquisitions fail to create wealth for the acquiring company's shareholders is no surprise.[8]

✓ **Keep investment proposals simple.** Most companies write long proposals and memos to justify their case. This is not a learning process, but tells people why you have made a proposal that should be accepted. In contrast, Toyota has communication down to a fine art. It presents all the information needed to make a complex decision on one 11-inch-by-17-inch piece of paper. It is called an A3 report and typically has seven boxes: current situation, proposal, benefits, plan, implementation, controls, and time line.

✓ **Design a standard investment approval process that is common across the organization and can be monitored centrally.** Leading organizations use balanced and weighted approvals criteria including, for example, strategic impact, risk assessment, net present value, cost, time frame, and sustainability impact. They prioritize projects according to strategic impact and value creation and prepare investment proposals thoroughly but implement them quickly. They reckon to spend around 80 percent of their time on preparation and 20 percent on execution, but execute flawlessly the first time.

✓ **Organize and manage meetings to encourage the right debate.** First, make sure the right people are involved. Ensure diversity of backgrounds, roles, risk-aversion profiles, and interests; cultivate critics within the top team; invite contributions based on expertise, not rank; invite experts to attend briefly and present a point of view; keep attendance to a minimum, preferably with a team that has experience making decisions together. Second, create the right atmosphere. Ask others to speak up, starting with the most junior person; show you can change your mind based on their input; strive to create a "peerlike" atmosphere, and encourage admissions of individual experiences and interests that create possible biases. Third, manage the debate. Make sure everyone knows the purpose of the meeting and the criteria to use to make the decision; take the pulse of the room: ask participants to write down their initial positions or their lists of pros and cons. Fourth, follow up. Commit yourself to the decision; connect individually with initial dissenters and make sure implementation plans address their concerns to the extent possible. Finally, conduct a postmortem on the decision once you know the outcome. Periodically step back and review decision processes to improve meeting preparation and mechanics, using an outside observer to diagnose possible sources of bias.[9]

✓ **Identify the biases most likely to affect critical decisions.** McKinsey researchers believe that the open discussion of the biases that may undermine decision making is invaluable. You can stimulate it both by conducting postmortems of past decisions and by observing current decision processes. Are we at risk, in this meeting, of being too action oriented? Do I see someone who thinks he recognizes a pattern but whose choice of analogies seems misleading to me? Are we seeing biases combine to create dysfunctional patterns that, when repeated, can become cultural traits? For example, is the combination of social and status quo biases creating a culture of consensus-based inertia? This discussion will help surface the biases to which the decision process under review is particularly prone.[10]

✓ **Use pre-mortem techniques.** Psychologist Gary Klein reckons that the pre-mortem technique is a sneaky way to get people to do contrarian, devil's advocate thinking without encountering resistance. If a project goes poorly, a lessons-learned session will look at what went wrong and why the project failed—like a medical postmortem. Klein asks:

> Why don't we do that up front? Before a project starts, we should say, "We're looking in a crystal ball, and this project has failed; it's

a fiasco. Now, everybody, take two minutes and write down all the reasons why you think the project failed." The logic is that instead of showing people that you are smart because you can come up with a good plan, you show you're smart by thinking of insightful reasons why this project might go south. If you make it part of your corporate culture, then you create an interesting competition: "I want to come up with some possible problem that other people haven't even thought of." The whole dynamic changes from trying to avoid anything that might disrupt harmony to trying to surface potential problems.

Encourage managers to be open and honest about risk and uncertainty

"A 'confident' presentation that conceals uncertainties is not a demonstration of a desirable social skill. It is a lie deserving a reprimand," notes risk management expert Matthew Leitch. Most business cases and high-level project plans address risk in some way. But it is often included in a subsection of the proposal marked "project risk." The problem, as Leitch points out, is that it's too little, too late: "By the time we write that part of the document we are already committed to our ideas and approach. We've probably defended it verbally in more than one meeting. We identify the approval of the proposal with our personal success."[a]

His advice is that leaders should promote risk management techniques where uncertainty is identified early, before people are personally committed. Risk thinking needs to be part of the way ideas develop, not just part of how they are evaluated. Some techniques are harder to fudge than others, according to Leitch. He gives some examples: "a risk analysis tool that already has the unpopular risks written down so that nobody has to volunteer them; a risk planning tool that already has a framework of responses, and your task is to tailor it, with justifications; risk ratings supported by objective risk factors, not pure subjectivity; and an unyielding requirement to state the source of all data, even if it is just to name the person whose opinion it is."

[a] Matthew Leitch, "Open and Honest About Risk and Uncertainty," July 7, 2004, www.internalcontrolsdesign.co.uk/honest/index.html.

Behavioral economist Daniel Kahneman agrees: "The beauty of the pre-mortem is that it is very easy to do. My guess is that, in general, doing a pre-mortem on a plan that is about to be adopted won't cause it to be abandoned. But it will probably be tweaked in ways that everybody will recognize as beneficial. So the pre-mortem is a low-cost, high-payoff kind of thing."[11]

✓ **Derive investment options from regular strategy reviews.** The vested interests of local teams whose primary aim is to maximize their own resources instead of their business unit rivals drive many initiatives. As a result, many investments have little or nothing to do with the firm's strategy. With often hundreds of initiatives in play at any one time within large organizations, this huge problem represents a significant waste of resources. Leading organizations ensure that all investments pass the strategy test. The balanced scorecard is a particularly useful framework for applying this test and ensuring that all investments are worthwhile.

✓ **Fund initiatives, not budgets.** Some organizations have moved from approving budgets for marketing and capital projects to approving individual initiatives. In other words, frontline teams do not have these budgets. They must bid and compete with other teams for these scarce resources.

✓ **Enable fast access to resources.** If value centers are expected to use their intuition and judgment to make fast decisions, they must have quick access to resources, especially to new operating capacity, including people and technology. But it is rather pointless to go through an extended decision-making process only to find that essential resources are unavailable. Leading organizations calibrate initiatives with available resources. At a large French company, each business team must produce around twenty to twenty-five strategic actions that will support its chosen key value drivers and be implemented over the next few years. Each team must show the impact of each action plan on an impact matrix, which explains how processes contribute to the achievement of each strategic action. These processes are rated as high, medium, or low in terms of how they affect the underlying processes. When completed, the matrix gives a complete picture of the resources demanded and whether or not demands are realistic. This exercise leads to the prioritization of actions and avoids potential bottlenecks, such as overloading key people or IT resources.

✓ **Approve and release noncore funds close to the point of need.** Before spending money, many managers ask, "How much is left in the budget?" rather than inquiring about the necessity and urgency to spend money for a compelling business need. This lack of focus leads to waste rather than value creation. In leading organizations, managers focus on the question, "What is the compelling business case for spending money?" The problem is that the annual budget negotiation sets a floor below which they will not challenge costs. The floor is usually the actual costs for the previous year. Few managers worth their salt will agree to reduce their resources without a fight. They will justify every expense line item and make every excuse for why their business will suffer if resources are cut. Some organizations now use rolling forecasts to support their ongoing resource management decisions. This process of reevaluation and prioritization is continuous. The capital commitments made in the aggregate project portfolio are compared with rolling forecasts of capital available and then evaluated against those projects in the pipeline. This comparison leads to a more informed decision-making process and one in which projects are always being examined to ensure they remain strategic and are meeting their performance milestones.

✓ **Look for alternative investment uses and exit options.** Leading organizations also minimize risk by making decisions as late as possible, but then executing them quickly. They build as much flexibility into long-term decisions as possible. What they don't do is agree to outline capital budgets that give managers license to spend. They see investments as opportunities that, provided they fit with their strategies, can be taken when they become available or when new ideas bubble up the organization.

✓ **Learn from past experience.** Economist Daniel Kahneman believes organizations need mechanisms to review how both individual and group decisions are made. In particular, he observes that most organizations don't learn from their own mistakes; most organizations don't even track their decisions from decision point to final outcome. "They're not investing the smallest amount in trying to actually figure out what they've done wrong. And that's not an accident: They don't want to know," says Kahneman.[12] The best organizations learn from their mistakes and keep improving their batting average.

Conclusions

Senior executives need to stop wasting huge amounts of capital. But to do this effectively, they need to see the organization through the eyes of a venture capital provider and enable and encourage as many new ventures as possible. If they can redeploy 50 percent of the systematically wasted capital into growing businesses or even keep it in the bank, the impact on growth, profitability, and cash flow will be huge.

FURTHER READING

Hamel, Gary. "Bringing Silicon Valley Inside." *Harvard Business Review*, September–October 1999, 70–84.

Hamel, Gary. *Leading the Revolution.* Boston: Harvard Business School Press, 2000.

Hope, Jeremy. *Reinventing the CFO: How Financial Managers Can Transform Their Roles and Add Greater Value.* Boston: Harvard Business School Press, 2006.

Hope, Jeremy, Peter Bunce, and Franz Röösli. *The Leader's Dilemma: How to Build an Empowered and Adaptive Organization Without Losing Control.* San Francisco, CA: John Wiley & Sons, 2011.

Hope, Jeremy, and Robin Fraser. *Beyond Budgeting: How Managers Can Break Free from the Annual Performance Trap.* Boston: Harvard Business School Press, 2003.

Leitch, Matthew. *Intelligent Internal Control and Risk Management.* Burlington, VT: Gower, 2008.

Lovallo, Dan, and Olivier Sibony. "The Case for Behavioral Strategy." *McKinsey Quarterly*, February 2010, 30–43.

Schrage, Michael. "Daniel Kahneman: The Thought Leader Interview." *Strategy + Business*, Winter 2003, 121–126.

6

ENTERPRISE RISK MANAGEMENT

What is this practice and how effective is it?

Enterprise risk management has recently risen in prominence as organizations have lost much respect and credibility following a wave of corporate governance scandals. One consequence is that many leaders have realized that the risk to their reputations is the greatest risk of all. The reaction of governments predictably has been to tighten regulations and extend punishments for serious miscreants. But do these actions get to the root of the problem? Many of these problems are endemic to the performance management systems and accepted practices, such as aggressive targets and incentives, that are in place in most organizations. We will explore these issues and suggest ways that leaders can deal with them.

Alternative names and related topics: risk analysis; risk mapping; risk planning; corporate governance, risk and compliance (GRC)

Enterprise risk management has emerged out of the dour back-office disciplines of internal control, insurance, and governance. Its elevation to the star chamber of management resulted from a number of corporate disasters over the past ten years, from Enron and WorldCom to Lehman Brothers, UBS, and AIG.

Between 1992 and 2002, government-appointed committees in the United Kingdom and the United States established the principle that senior management is responsible for the maintenance of an effective internal control system. In the United States, the Committee of Sponsoring Organizations of the Treadway Commission (COSO), a group of professional associations of U.S. accountants and financial executives, issued guidelines for internal controls.

It redefined internal control broadly to cover not just controls relating to financial accounting, the typical focus of auditors, but also regulatory compliance matters and operations more generally.

As leaders grapple with one unpredictable event after another, they are reminded that business threats can come from anywhere at any time. These include not only terrorist acts or financial disasters, but also strategic risks such as the emergence of a new competitor, a new technology, or a failure to predict marketplace shifts. But many of the major threats are rarely measured or monitored. To manage such risks, most leaders have realized that they need a more comprehensive system of risk management. These efforts have variously been called "strategic controls" or, more recently, enterprise risk management (ERM). This effort involves mapping all of a company's risks in a uniform way and applying a cross-functional approach to managing them.

The realization of risk has led some companies to seek a closer integration between risk management and strategic planning. It's a shift that some have made explicitly. For example, Duke Energy, a North Carolina–based firm with operations in power generation and natural gas and electricity trading, has put strategic planning in its ERM operation. "It's our responsibility to determine where the capabilities we have at Duke Energy can achieve the best risk-adjusted returns for our investors," says Richard Osborne, the company's chief risk officer and former CFO. Other companies, including Akzo Nobel and Aventis, have linked planning and risk management in less formal ways, but with the same goal: using risk management to drive value creation.

Some organizations have used ERM to prepare a matrix that grades all their operational risks according to severity and frequency on a chart (see figure 6-1). They sort risks into those that are wholly transferred (insured), those that are partially transferred, and those that have not been transferred (the company carries the risk). By showing the board the whole portfolio of risks the company is exposed to, risk managers can explain how the company has dealt with them.

Risk managers divide risks into subgroups, such as market risk (strategies, markets, products, and customers); operational risk (business processes and IT systems); financial risk (investors and capital structure); and reputational risk (exposure to bad press and other disasters that can damage reputation). The idea is to calculate the expected probability of each risk in terms of frequency and severity using a mixture of experience, intuition, and research. Using risk-mapping software, they plot risks on a matrix. They sort the risks by shapes to indicate how each has been addressed. For example, a triangle in figure 6-1 indicates that a risk has had little or no transfer; a square

FIGURE 6-1

Using a management matrix to communicate risk

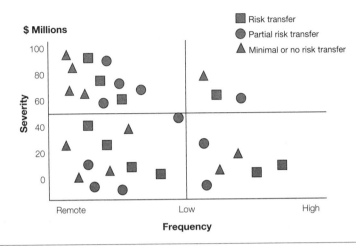

indicates that a risk has been transferred; and a circle shows a partial risk transfer.

ERM represents a shift from managing risks in functional silos to managing them in a consistent fashion across the organization to give senior management a better view of risks and enable a portfolio approach. The more unified a risk management process is across the company, the more satisfied the board will be. Likewise, the more closely risk management is tied to the strategic planning process, the more effective leaders believe it to be.[1]

James Lam, the founder of eRisk and formerly the chief risk officer of Fidelity Investments, argues that one of the key ingredients of successful risk management is having the right reporting. In his view, the ideal monthly risk report to senior management has only two pages and describes three items:

- **Gross losses.** This item helps management understand the operational, credit, and market losses the company has suffered, and shows the trends relative to revenues.
- **Risk incidents.** This item identifies recent risk incidents that may or may not have resulted in loss, but are worth knowing about.
- **Management assessment.** This is a manager's self-assessment: What keeps me awake at night? What should I be concerned about?[2]

Peter Thompson, vice president of finance at PepsiCo, explains how his company's new program has focused on four issues:

- **Define or prioritize risks.** To help prioritize the company's many risks, PepsiCo has created three categories: (1) risks that could break the company, (2) risks that could damage the company, and (3) "noise"— relatively minor risks that don't warrant senior management time. Thompson emphasizes the need to ensure that short-term pressures don't cause the neglect of major long-term risks. "Perception shapes your risk focus, but that perception can be distorted, especially by quarterly earnings pressure," says Thompson.
- **Establish risk tolerance.** This involves determining the level of risk senior management is willing to tolerate for the corporation as a whole and within business units individually.
- **Risk identification.** The main change in corporate behavior is in this area, which has been to alter the focus of internal audit. This has shifted from financial audits to include more operational audits.
- **Risk management or mitigation.** This area focuses on three activities. First, improvement in crisis management, which involves an improved understanding of all the company's business processes. Second, the finance function has worked to make its own processes more risk focused, which include increasing the number and frequency of informal risk reviews. Finally, an effort to update financial policies concentrates on developing a new approach to managing investments.[3]

Some finance executives believe risk management can create competitive advantage in several ways. First, a company that can manage its industry's key risks better than its peers can is in a stronger position to make or sustain a superior profit over time. Second, an ERM system helps CEOs and CFOs to evaluate project risks more thoroughly. And third, integrating risk management and planning can help to identify projects that reduce the company's overall risk and thereby improve its performance.

What is the performance potential of this practice?

- **To enable innovation and growth.** Effective risk management enables managers at all levels to take higher risk or higher reward options.
- **To improve decision making.** Evaluating risk is a key part of every decision. The more effectively a company manages risk, the better its decisions will be.
- **To reduce volatility.** Effective risk management should reduce the roller-coaster effects of decisions that lead to extremes of success and failure.

The dangers noted in *The Risk Management of Everything*

According to Michael Power, author of *The Risk Management of Everything*, there is a danger at the core of risk management, "namely, that the experts who are being made increasingly accountable for what they do are now becoming more preoccupied with managing their own risks. Specifically, secondary risks to their reputation are becoming as significant as the primary risks for which experts have knowledge and training. This trend is resulting in a dangerous flight from judgment and a culture of defensiveness that create their own risks for organizations in preparing for, and responding to, a future they cannot know."[a]

Power believes that internal control systems are also highly problematic. He notes:

> Not only is it difficult to define their effectiveness, which is in principle unknowable, but, more crucially, a growing obsession with internal control (a mutation of the earlier audit explosion) may itself be a source of risk. First, internal control systems are organizational projections of controllability which may be misplaced; such systems are only as good as the imaginations of those who designed them. Second, internal control systems are essentially inward looking and may embody mistaken assumptions of what the public really wants reassurance about. Risk management and certifications of the effectiveness of internal control systems may do little to enhance public trust in senior management of organizations. While practitioners are well aware of the limitations of these systems, "better" control systems continue to be regarded as politically acceptable solutions to crisis, even where it is well known that such systems would not have prevented the crisis in question.[b]

Power believes that "to a large extent internal control blueprints are fantasy policy documents that project comforting images of controlling the uncontrollable . . . Furthermore, reliance on internal control may increase risk if it results in underinvestment in risk intelligence elsewhere."[c]

[a] Michael Power, *The Risk Management of Everything: Rethinking the Politics of Uncertainty* (London: Demos, 2004), 14.

[b] Ibid., 5.

[c] Ibid.

- **To protect your reputation.** Risk management should help leaders to avoid the disaster scenario whereby they place the whole organization at risk of failure.

What actions do you need to take to maximize the potential of this practice?

ACTIONS TO AVOID

✖ **Be wary of the myths surrounding risk management.** The lessons from both quality management and regulatory compliance tell us that at the core of risk management is a nagging contradiction. As Michael Power explains, "On the one hand, there is a functional and political need to maintain myths of control and manageability, because this is what various interested constituencies and stakeholders seem to demand. Risks must be made auditable and governable. On the other hand, there is a consistent stream of failures, scandals and disasters which challenge and threaten organizations, suggesting a world which is out of control and where failure may be endemic, and in which the organizational interdependencies are so intricate that no single locus of control has a grasp of them."[4] Power is right. Leaders who believe they have an effective risk management system, like BP thought, could be in for a shock, as many risks remain unpredictable. In some cases, spending more time and energy working out how to react effectively might be better.

✖ **Be wary of sophisticated risk models.** While organizations need to comply with legal requirements, leaders should be skeptical about the value of risk models, compliance rules, risk indicators, and enterprisewide risk management systems. Almost every failed bank had invested huge sums in these systems, but few anticipated what happened from 2007 to 2009. Power gives a vignette as an example of how risky risk management processes can be and illustrates why relying on rules and procedures can give a false sense of security. For example, an auditor discovered major fraud when he noticed that a paper purchase invoice had no creases and had never been folded. Audit procedures include methods for vouching for the arithmetical accuracy of such documents, for agreeing on the numbers to the accounts, and for agreeing on the independent nature of the invoice. But no process would allow someone to see what this auditor saw—that if an invoice had not been folded, it probably had not arrived by mail. And why was this significant? Inquiries later revealed that the company had fraudulently constructed the invoice to create a fictitious transaction. An auditor concerned solely with official processes would not have seen the purchase invoice in this all-encompassing way.[5]

✖ **Be wary of "risk appetite" controls.** Many organizations try to set out formal risk-appetite controls, whether they are for the organization as a whole or for specific risks. But according to risk expert Matthew Leitch, they have been oversold.[6] Specifying boundaries or limits for risk is almost impossible, except in specific areas.

✖ **Be wary of relying on risk registers.** Don't just make a list of risks and make notes against them to record supplementary information. Risks are not so easily divisible. The temptation is to subdivide risks to fit within acceptable risk thresholds.

✖ **Be wary of risk metrics.** Some organizations have devised hundreds of risk metrics that they regularly report on to senior executives. BP had hundreds of metrics on everything from lost time to accidents to maintenance problems on its oil rigs, but it didn't alert anyone to the potential disaster looming in the Gulf of Mexico. In other words, it had many controls, but they did not add up to effective control.

✖ **Be wary of a culture of resisting bad news.** If senior managers hear only what managers want them to hear, then you might be creating a disaster waiting to happen. Recognize people positively for sharing bad news immediately.

✖ **Don't rely on whistle-blowers.** The landmark Sarbanes-Oxley Act of 2002 mandated that audit committees of publicly traded firms must give whistle-blowers a way to anonymously disclose possible financial fraud without fear of prosecution. But researchers have uncovered disturbing unintended consequences of the regulation that may be rendering it ineffective. Namely, audit committee members appear to be less likely to take action on anonymous tips than on non-anonymous complaints, and in some cases, they are motivated to ignore anonymous whistle-blowers because if their claims prove to be true, it could indicate that the committee failed to oversee the company's activities satisfactorily. This result mirrors a National Bureau of Economic Research study that found the instances of fraud detected by whistle-blowing actually fell from 21 percent to 16 percent after Sarbanes-Oxley set up the anonymous channels.[7]

ACTIONS TO TAKE

✓ **Engage the board in risk management.** While the board cannot know the details of every decision being made and the risks involved, it can agree on and communicate a clear policy about how it views risk. Defining "risk appetite," "risk tolerance," or simply setting the tone at the top are all expressions that attempt to define how the board views risk. And given the potential disasters that lurk around the corner, any self-respecting board should escalate risk monitoring to a key function of the board rather than delegate it to a subsidiary function. But many boards pay lip service to risk management. Lehman Brothers had a strong risk management function, yet its risk committee (a subcommittee of the board) met only twice per year. Further, while the makeup of the board was quite impressive, the experience of board members in managing businesses such as Lehman's was thin.[8] Author Michael Schrage recommends that boards create an explicit risk manifesto that describes and governs how directors will define and oversee ERM.[9]

✓ **Set up a small team of talented executives to look at a range of risk scenarios.** The board should appoint small teams of talented managers to imagine future scenarios and the probabilities of occurrence to initiate an intelligent discussion of risk. The board should also talk with shareholders to better understand their views about risk and learn from experiences elsewhere.[10]

✓ **Prepare a risk matrix.** While you cannot identify all risks, it makes sense to present them in ways that show the board a complete picture of risk exposure and what decisions have been made to cover or not cover each one.

✓ **Ensure that leaders take an ethical stance.** Unethical actions never pay. Take the earnings restatements for which the CFO is responsible. A recent study shows that CFOs at firms that were forced to restate earnings were more likely to get fired because of their aggressive financial reporting than CFOs at firms that did not restate earnings. The results also show that CFOs terminated in the post–Sarbanes-Oxley era had a harder time finding new jobs than they did before the legislation was enacted, suggesting that it has succeeded in holding CFOs more accountable for their actions.[11]

✓ **Make risk management a core competence.** Organizations face risks whenever they make decisions in pursuit of their objectives. But these risks are exacerbated when companies are growing and there are higher levels of optimism. The way that board members manage risks is a vital element of effective corporate governance. While they need effective audit functions, they depend more on the discipline and vigilance of teams as well as the dialogue and challenge of leaders that take place prior to making key decisions.

✓ **Focus on four levers of control.** Robert Simons argues that modern firms need four types of controls: belief systems, boundary systems, diagnostic controls, and interactive control systems.[12] These controls provide a framework for decision making at every level. They enable consistent and coherent decisions to be made at all levels at all times. *Belief systems* are designed to ensure that the behavioral context within which managers

Understand the risks embedded in management systems

When compelled to reassess their compliance and risk management systems, most firms found they were inadequate. Harvard professor Robert Simons points out that firms are particularly exposed to three types of risk: *growth* (pressures for performance, rate of expansion, and inexperience of employees); *culture* (rewards for risk taking, resistance to bad news, and level of internal competition); and *information management* (transaction complexity and velocity, gaps in diagnostic measures, and degree of decentralized decision making).[a] Some of the most toxic risks are embedded in management systems. Top of the league are aggressive targets and incentives. Any risk manager worth his or her salt should look at these risk drivers first. But they are likely to run into some of the most powerful forces in the organization, including the board itself, which gain most from incentive packages. This is one reason most of the failed banks ignored these problems—the CEO was the major beneficiary!

[a] Robert Simons, "How Risky Is Your Company?" *Harvard Business Review*, May/June 1999, 85–94.

work is rooted in the firm's core values. *Boundary systems* specify and clarify the rules of the game. These include codes of conduct, minimum standards, and ethical behavior. *Diagnostic control systems* describe planning and strategic management systems. These systems are designed to monitor the progress of the firm as it proceeds toward its goals. *Interactive control systems* describe a different approach, one that relies even more on trust and continuous communication. They attempt to understand *why* performance is good or bad and thus promote a real learning process.

✓ **Design and use a standardized risk-adjusted decision process.** Most organizations use tried and tested capital approval processes with a number of gates through which each project must pass as it works its way toward approval and execution. The gates usually involve a business case, financial investment, and projected return; whether the project has sufficient strategic impact; and whether the risk associated with the project's outcomes is acceptable. However, the location of the risk assessment within the process is critical. More often than not, risk is included in a subsection of the proposal marked "project risk." The problem is that by this stage the project team is emotionally and politically committed to the proposal and aims to "sell" the risk assessment to the higher authority. Thus, any hope of an unbiased risk-evaluation process has evaporated.

Conclusions

Despite all the money spent on risk management over recent years, the ultimate shield against excessive risk taking and poor decision making is cultural. It involves setting the highest performance and ethical standards and abandoning the worst aspects of the fixed-performance contract. It also means looking at the whole picture and not just focusing on a few problems that need to be fixed. Trust, transparency, and accountability are the key words.

FURTHER READING

Leitch, Matthew. *Intelligent Internal Control and Risk Management.* Burlington, VT: Gower, 2008.

Leitch, Matthew. "Open and Honest About Risk and Uncertainty," July 7, 2004, www .internalcontrolsdesign.co.uk/honest/index.html.

Power, Michael. *The Risk Management of Everything: Rethinking the Politics of Uncertainty.* London, UK: Demos, 2004, http://www.demos.co.uk/files/riskmanagementofeverything .pdf?1240939425.

Schrage, Michael. "Daniel Kahneman: The Thought Leader Interview." *Strategy + Business,* Winter 2003, 121–126.

Simons, Robert. "How Risky Is Your Company." *Harvard Business Review,* May-June 1999, 85–94.

7

KNOWLEDGE MANAGEMENT

What is this practice and how effective is it?

Knowledge management is about making the most effective use of the intellectual capital of a business. It involves *wiring together* the brains of appropriate people so that sharing, reasoning, and collaboration become almost instinctive and a part of everyday work.[1] But there are many barriers to sharing knowledge in the hierarchical organization, where annual budgets and boundary walls often present insurmountable obstacles. We will look at how organizations are breaking down barriers and building a more collaborative culture.

Alternative names and related topics: intellectual capital management; learning organizations; communities of practice

It is rather ironic that as the digital age closes in around us, organizations are depending more on *people* than ever before. Even today's most powerful computers can't match the intelligence of a worm. Their increasing ability to capture, process, and distribute highly structured information is a wonder of the age, but businesses still require the intelligence and experience of human beings to turn that information into useful knowledge and good decisions. As Peter Drucker once noted, "knowing how a typewriter works does not make you a writer. Now that knowledge is taking the place of capital as the driving force in organizations worldwide, it is all too easy to confuse data with knowledge and information technology with information."[2]

In his book *Gaining Competitive Advantage Through Knowledge Management*, Dr. Cyril Brookes described knowledge management as "making the most effective use of the intellectual capital of a business. It involves *wiring together* the brains of appropriate people so that sharing, reasoning and collaboration become almost instinctive and a part of everyday work."[3] Quality guru W. Edwards Deming said that "experience alone, without theory, teaches management nothing about what to do to improve quality and competitive position, nor how to do it."[4] In other words, a very experienced person can have little knowledge.

The new language of the knowledge-based company can be somewhat confusing. Terms such as "intellectual assets" or "intangible capital" are frequently used interchangeably. There are two basic distinctions: The first is *knowledge and learning*, which concerns how organizations and individuals acquire, disseminate, and deploy knowledge, and how cultural and technological forces can help or impede this process. The second defines the *collective body of "intangible" assets*, which can be listed, measured, and, with difficulty, valued.

Unlike information, knowledge itself is a fuzzy concept concerned with human cognition and awareness. Knowing a fact is little different from knowing a skill, but knowing how someone, perhaps a customer or competitor, might react to a piece of information requires human intuition and judgment. This combination of context, memory, and cognitive process separates human knowledge from any other form, such as knowledge-based systems. Moreover, there are two types of knowledge: *explicit knowledge* (skills and facts that

---

Four levels of knowledge

James Brian Quinn, Philip Anderson, and Sydney Finkelstein suggest that we need to recognize four *levels* of knowledge: (1) "cognitive knowledge (or know-what)" derives from basic training and certification; (2) "advanced skills (know-how)" translates book learning into effective execution; (3) "systems understanding (know-why)" builds on the first two and leads to highly trained intuition—for example, the insight of a seasoned research director who knows which projects to support; and (4) "self-motivated creativity (care-why)," which drives creative groups to outperform groups with greater physical or financial resources. They suggest that the first three levels can also exist in the organization's systems, databases, or operating technologies, but the fourth can derive only from its culture. Yet most enterprises focus virtually all their training attention on developing basic skills and little or none on systems or creative skills.[a]

[a] James Brian Quinn, Philip Anderson, and Sydney Finkelstein, "Managing Professional Intellect: Making the Most of the Best," *Harvard Business Review*, March–April, 1996, 72.

people can write down and teach to others), and *tacit knowledge* (skills, judgment, and intuition that people have but can't easily describe).

In the 1980s, Lew Platt, then CEO of Hewlett-Packard, said, "If only HP knew what HP knows, we would be three-times more productive."[5] Many large organizations have accumulated a huge amount of knowledge, but it resides in the heads of its people and is therefore inaccessible to those who need it. Knowledge management seeks to use the organization's collective knowledge more productively and thereby improve competitive advantage. Advanced technology has doubtless dealt organizations a new deck of cards with which to leverage people's knowledge to a much higher plateau. Whether it be improving competencies and processes, facilitating more devolved decision making, improving customer support, winning important orders, or reducing mistakes and missed opportunities, the application of knowledge is playing an ever-increasing role in organizational success.

How firms manage knowledge falls into two schools of thought. On the one hand, we have the *information school*, which believes that knowledge comprises objects that can be identified within information systems. It believes in a sort of trickle-down theory of knowledge sharing and learning. In other words, if a company pours enough information in at the top level (i.e., into its knowledge-based systems), enough sharing and learning will eventually pervade the lower organizational levels. On the other hand, we have the *behavioral school* that sees knowledge management as a dynamic process within which skills and know-how are constantly changing. The information school, which has its roots in computing, artificial intelligence, systems management, and reengineering, sees excellent knowledge-based *systems* as the ultimate answer—in first understanding human *behavior* and then winning the hearts and minds of key people. Its roots are in sociology, anthropology, psychology, and organizational behavior.

John Seely Brown and Estee Solomon Gray note: "Organizations are webs of participation. Change the patterns of participation, and you change the organization . . . At the heart of participation is the mind and spirit of the knowledge worker. Put simply, you cannot compel enthusiasm and commitment from knowledge workers. Only workers who choose to opt in—who voluntarily make a commitment to their colleagues—can create a winning company."[6]

Knowledge-based competitive advantage can occur in many ways. For example, hotels can create personal profiles of guests and ensure that they look after their special needs across the global network. Credit-card companies can monitor spending patterns and detect potential fraud or misuse. Maintenance engineers and medical practitioners can solve problems using special knowledge-based diagnostic systems. The knowledge-based organization

---

Learning is about work, work is about learning

Communities of practice are social groups built around informed participation. Consider the experiences of engineers at Fuji Xerox in Hong Kong. None of the approximately two hundred service engineers working throughout the territory has office space. They move freely around their "patch"—a group of about two hundred customers to whom they are responsible for servicing certain machines. The engineers receive calls from the Fuji Xerox call-center during the day and, when they meet next morning, together decide when and how they will respond. As they deal with different customers, they build up a pattern of customer profiles and preferences. The more they meet, the more they share their individual knowledge of customers and the quirks of the machines they are responsible for fixing. The managing director, Ramagopal Rao, explained that, "the engineers have a level of trust in each other because they are targeted, assessed, measured, and evaluated as a group . . . That fosters an enormous amount of interaction, and it makes them share what they know." The advantages are that there are fewer overheads (no submanagers, assistant managers, managers, group heads, and so on); there is no hierarchy to slow down the transmission of decisions and decision making; and engineers naturally work together for the greater good of the work group and, ultimately, the entire organization.[a]

[a] Karen Winton, "Knowledge Management: An Unnatural Act?" *CFO Asia*, October 2002, www.cfo.com/article.cfm/3006922.

---

is also able to monitor the performance of its key processes. For example, it can track how much value-adding work its business units, teams, and employees are performing; which services particular customers value (and how much extra they will be prepared to pay); why customers defect; and which suppliers provide the best quality. In other words, when knowledge is applied to business processes, it is the why, where, when, and how questions that are answered—not merely the final accounting result.

Perhaps the greatest barrier to effective knowledge management is the annual fixed target that focuses managers on their own performance. That those organizations operating without fixed targets and individual incentives (i.e., fixed performance contracts) share knowledge and collaborate more effectively than those that don't is no coincidence. Egon Zehnder International (EZI) is a classic example. EZI is the third-largest executive search firm in the world. Since its foundation in Zurich in 1964, the firm has been a model of equality, collegiality, noncompetitive internal sharing, and nonhierarchical organizational structures. It selects employees whose interests dovetail with those of the firm and develops people to foster deep collaboration. It charges clients fixed fees and pays no bonuses based on revenues earned. And it evaluates potential partners for their effectiveness at collaboration. In the executive search industry, the average turnover rate among partners is 30 percent. EZI's attrition rate is dramatically lower, averaging only 2 to 5 percent annually.[7]

Even command-and-control leaders are being converted. John Chambers, CEO of Cisco Systems, is one. "If you'd have told me I was going to blog three or four years ago, I'd have said, 'Take it to the bank. That's not going to happen,'" said Chambers. "But blogging is the way I communicate with our

---

The impact of social networking

Knowledge sharing has been given a huge boost in recent years with the rise of social networking sites such as Facebook. Younger managers now joining the workforce are used to sharing knowledge about their personal lives, and they are bringing their expectations into the workplace. At HCL Technologies, leaders support the growth of "employee first councils" that help employees connect with team members who share similar interests and passions. With a Web-based platform, the new initiative rapidly spawned a host of communities around cultural, recreational, and job-related issues. Each council elects its own leader, and today, more than twenty-five hundred employees serve in that role. The CEO's team also launched thirty-two issue-specific councils focused on key business and technology issues, such as cloud computing. These loosely structured teams quickly demonstrated their value and have become a critical source of new ideas and strategic insights. When one of the councils reaches a consensus on a particular recommendation, it transfers it to a dedicated group that pushes the idea toward execution. Three years after launching this concept, 20 percent of HCLT's revenue is coming from initiatives launched in these communities of interest.[a]

[a] www.blogs.wsj.com/management/.../hcl-extreme-management-makeover.

employees—almost all video. Our utilization of discussion forums is not up 160 percent over the last year, it's up 1,600 [percent]. Taking YouTube capabilities and bring them internal—we call it CiscoVision—is up 3,100 [percent], with 54,000 employees out of 66,000 using it in the last year. Using Webex capability, where you collaborate both internal and external through firewalls, utilization is up 3,900 percent."[8]

Although there is much talk of the benefits of managing knowledge, few companies have yet been able to tie tangible results to these programs. Indeed, many remain skeptical. Do organizations need expensive systems and incentives to encourage their people to share knowledge? Perhaps breaking down the boundary walls that surround business units and departments would be a more effective and cheaper approach? The likely reason knowledge isn't shared is the self-interested behavior the budgeting, target-setting, and incentive systems encourage. These are the real barriers that need to be removed.

What is the performance potential of this practice?

- **To provide a more systematic approach to measuring and managing intellectual capital.** In the vast majority of firms, the subject of intellectual capital is not on the agenda. Though managers may know of the term, they have no means of measuring or managing it. Knowledge management is to intellectual capital what financial management is to financial capital. It provides a framework that enables managers to link intellectual capital to financial results. The balanced scorecard is one such framework.

- **To encourage managers to share valuable knowledge across the organization (avoiding reinventing the wheel).** In the traditional hierarchical organization, managers are primarily concerned with their own functions and departments and will tend to hoard knowledge rather than share it. Their aim is to meet their targets and budgets and gain as many resources from corporate as possible in their pursuit of growth opportunities. In a more cohesive organization within which managers connect and combine to satisfy internal and external customers, knowledge sharing becomes a more natural process.

- **To build and retain organizational memory so that valuable knowledge is not lost when people leave.** In some firms, employees feel that their best interests are served by keeping their knowledge to themselves rather than sharing it with others. This is also to their personal advantage when they leave the firm. By providing easy ways to record knowledge and good practice, firms can build a memory bank that future generations of managers can access.

What actions do you need to take to maximize the potential of this practice?

ACTIONS TO AVOID

✖ **Question the belief that information input equals knowledge output.** Building knowledge-based systems, no matter how ingenious, does not mean that people will use them, or that if they do use them, that the benefits will justify the costs. Information overload is a serious problem as designers have encouraged more communication via mobile devices and service providers have thrust more information on users. Users are realizing that information "just in case" is both wasteful and time-consuming, causing a decline rather than an improvement in performance. What they need is information "just in time," and this has caused designers to rethink their systems. The new approach is to enable users to design their own information screens with direct links to those sources they find valuable. Thus, they are separated from the barrage of largely irrelevant information that was previously aimed at them, even though their interest level was minimal.

✖ **Don't force knowledge sharing.** Research on software firms, including more than eighty interviews with corporate executives, general managers, and frontline employees, suggested that the most successful collaborations between multiple business units within firms occur not when they are mandated by management, but when self-interested managers spot opportunities to collaborate and share resources with one another. One reason is that managers at individual business units understand their immediate needs better than corporate executives who take a higher-level view; another is that business unit managers will pursue joint projects only when they believe those projects will benefit their own department. The key finding was that effective collaborations bubble up from small events within individual units—for example, when one engineer finds out that an engineer at another business unit is trying to solve a similar problem—and are polished and expanded by self-interested business unit managers at that level who realize they can extend the value from the collaboration.[9]

✖ **Question how new ideas are adopted.** According to MIT professor Edgar Schein, organizational learning is a three-step process. First, an idea is articulated by academics; then it is picked up by members of the consulting community, who sell the program to their corporate clients; and finally the program is implemented within the firm. But this is where its success or failure depends crucially on its acceptability to the communities of practice. If, for example, members of the operator culture recognize the need for real change in operations, they will attempt to learn from the consultant's prescription, but as they will likely find it incomplete or ineffective, a learning consortium emerges. The community of practice now takes over the problem, gives its stamp of approval, and the task is completed. Managers have great problems trying to understand and build any meaningful systems around this process of learning.[10] Indeed, sharing knowledge outside the community is extremely hard to enforce. One of the reasons many laudable initiatives fail is likely because they hit these invisible barriers. Take, for example, a new reporting system or a new quality program. Either the finance or the quality people are unlikely to share the same community of practice as divisional managers or frontline operators. Salespeople or engineers, for example, instead of seeing such initiatives as improvements to operating capability, may well see another "flavor of the month" initiative, with more work for no extra reward (in their eyes, any benefits will accrue to someone else). The battle is not with the design of new ideas and initiatives, but with cross-cultural commitment.

✖ **Avoid budget boundaries and barriers.** Perhaps the main reason most knowledge-sharing initiatives fail is because managers are driven by the economics of self-interest. They agree on targets and are rewarded for meeting them. This encourages the hoarding, rather than sharing, of knowledge, as the enemy is more often seen as competing internal business units instead of the external competition. Jack Welch called the sharing of knowledge and best practices "boundaryless behavior." "The sweetest fruit of boundaryless behavior," he noted, "has been the demise of 'Not-Invented-Here' and its utter disappearance from our company."[11] Such behavior "elevates ideas based on their merit, not on the rank of the person who came up with them."[12]

ACTIONS TO TAKE

✓ **Relate knowledge management to business purpose.** Too many organizations mistakenly treat knowledge management as an end in itself. If the evangelists fail to connect with real business issues, then the project will drift and fade away. The aim should be to use knowledge management to help managers better deal with problems and opportunities. Responding more rapidly to business proposals, sharing best practices, and reducing cycle times are all ways to use knowledge management systems to add value.

✓ **Consider using peer pressure to kick-start the program.** Don't expect users to be enthusiastic about knowledge-based systems. Even within consultancy firms packed with powerful knowledge workers, managers have had great difficulty getting wide use of knowledge-sharing networks. Some have had more success applying peer pressure and veiled threats, including the impact of nonconformance on pay and promotion. The exercise of peer pressure and the recognition and rewards attached to the individual contribution for the good of the team (and subject to peer reviews) are crucial factors in the adoption of knowledge-based systems.

✓ **Facilitate online communities and conversations.** Author Alan Webber makes an interesting observation when he notes that it is through *conversation* that knowledge workers define the organization. Conversations, not rank or title or the trappings of power, determine who is literally and figuratively in the loop and who is not. At McKinsey, the art of conversation has been wired into its business operations and has transformed the business into a truly interactive knowledge organization. McKinsey's former director of knowledge management, Brook Manville, supervised a network dedicated to providing "a marketplace of readily accessible ideas." On-call consultants are also available on a rotational basis (rather like doctors) to host conversations with or between staff members who are looking for ideas.[13] Companies are now using Facebook and other social networking sites to link their people together, a potentially much lower-cost solution than investing in major IT systems.

✓ **Harness the power of communities of practice.** Communities of practice are small sub-groups of people who have mutual respect, share some common values, and generally get the important work done. Manville defined a community of practice as "a group of people who are informally bound to one another by exposure to a common class of problem."[14] Communities of practice are usually small groups, no more than fifty, who've worked together for a period of time. They are not necessarily a team, a task force, or any other authorized group. They are peers in the execution of "real work." What holds them together is a common sense of purpose and a real need for each person to know what the others know. Communities of practice can be found in every part of an organization, and most people belong to more than one. Until new ideas are safely embedded within these groups, it is safe to assume that real learning has not yet taken place. This is why classroom teaching is rarely as effective as learning "on the job." In other words, the age-old systems of apprenticeship and mentoring remain the most effective methods of learning.

✓ **Start small and grow incrementally.** Knowledge management projects are notoriously difficult to justify on an ROI basis, making it hard to gain approval for major investments. Knowledge management expert Hubert Saint-Onge believes that 50 percent of all ROIs are bogus. Rather than

> ## Invest in helping people use, rather than search for, knowledge
>
> "Knowledge management" in organizations has become synonymous with "knowledge searching." Web crawlers and other data-mining programs swarm over terabytes of documents and e-mails looking for clues that can help connect information seekers with sources. Clever icons adorning desktops promise to instantly deliver users to the right expert. Organizations deploy network analysis tools to identify their key knowledge brokers—people who provide directions and access to knowledge repositories. Is this effort (and spending) worthwhile? Maybe not, say researchers Al Jacobson and Laurence Prusak. They suggest that, valuable as these efforts have been to date, future payoffs will depend less on enhancing systems that track down information than on devising strategies to help employees use what they've found. They discovered that employees spent, on average, less than 17 percent of their time searching and scheduling, and more than 80 percent eliciting, interpreting, and applying. The results are consistent across organizations and for workers of all ages, positions, and lengths of tenure. This surprising finding suggests two things: First, IT investments in search technologies appear to be working, and additional investments of the same kind are likely to yield only marginal benefits. Second, and more important, managers should focus on understanding why some employees are more adept than others at gathering knowledge and customizing it for their own use.[a]
>
> [a] Al Jacobson and Laurence Prusak, "The Cost of Knowledge," *Harvard Business Review*, November 2006, 34.

cook up a hard-dollar ROI that you may not be able to deliver on, it's far better to underpromise and overdeliver. And it's generally easier to justify a smaller project that way because there's less at stake.[15] So instead of treating knowledge management like an all-encompassing enterprise resource planning (ERP) system, it's better to start with a few small initiatives, build trust and confidence, and grow the system over a longer period of time. Even a small failure won't necessarily derail the project. A lot of early knowledge management efforts failed because they added cumbersome steps to the jobs of already overworked employees. So when things got busy, workers just didn't bother with the extra steps.

By starting small and focusing on one job at a time, you can build knowledge management into a job function in a way that actually helps employees do their jobs better, faster, or more easily. Professor Thomas Davenport calls this "baked-in" knowledge management. "You need to embed knowledge into the structure of the job that knowledge workers already pursue so it can't be avoided. Doing so makes it much easier to measure the impact and justify it economically," Davenport explains.[16]

✓ **Don't give up on ROI.** According to consultant Don Cohen's research, some firms do successfully measure return on their knowledge management investments, but only for certain kinds of work. For instance, oil companies have shown that sharing technical knowledge among drilling teams reduces problems and speeds the process, saving tens of millions of dollars a year in the cost of establishing new wells. Xerox's Eureka database for communicating copier-repair tips among technicians cuts costs by about 10 percent. Xerox arrived at that figure by conducting a controlled experiment to compare the efficiency of groups that did or did not use the database. In instances like these, the key to measurability is focusing on activities that are too complex to be captured in a standard set of instructions but are repeated, with variations, again and again. With things like strategy consulting or basic research, though, it's often impossible to connect knowledge supplied with dollars earned or saved so directly. Leaders of the knowledge-based organizations that have the most vibrant knowledge management programs approach the measurement problem by accepting soft indicators that knowledge management is earning its keep rather than demanding hard numbers that may be misleading. They realize that a telling anecdote is a better measure than a precise but irrelevant number. Knowing what you're striving for with your knowledge management makes it much easier to determine whether you're getting value for the money spent—even if the ROI never shows up on a balance sheet.[17]

Conclusions

Knowledge management is not just another competitive weapon to extract from the consultant's toolbox. It is a long-term program involving cultural change that goes to the heart of business transformation. The research into organizational learning is lighting the way. And the advent of Web 2.0, with its social networking, wikis, and blogs is opening up the huge potential of knowledge sharing.

FURTHER READING

Collison, Chris, and Geoff Parcell. *Learning to Fly: Practical Lessons from One of the World's Leading Knowledge Companies*. Milford, CT: Capstone Publishing, 2001.

Cross, Rob, and Lloyd Baird. "Technology Is Not Enough: Improving Performance by Building Organizational Memory." *Sloan Management Review*, Spring 2000, 68–78.

Davenport, Thomas H., and Laurence Prusak. *Working Knowledge: How Organizations Manage What They Know.* Boston: Harvard Business School Press, 1998.

Firestone, Joseph M., and Mark W. McElroy. *Key Issues in the New Knowledge Management.* Burlington, MA: Butterworth-Heinemann, 2003.

Groff, Todd R., and Thomas P. Jones. *Introduction to Knowledge Management: KM in Business.* Burlington, MA : Butterworth-Heinemann, 2003.

Hansen, Morten T., Nitin Nohria, and Thomas Tierney. "What's Your Strategy for Managing Knowledge?" *Harvard Business Review*, March–April 1999, 106–119.

Harvard Business Review on Knowledge Management. Boston: Harvard Business School Press, 1998.

Hope, Jeremy, and Tony Hope. *Competing in the Third Wave: The Ten Key Management Issues of the Information Age.* Boston: Harvard Business School Press, 1997.

Malone, Thomas W., Kevin Crowston, and George A. Herman, eds. *Organizing Business Knowledge: The MIT Process Handbook.* Cambridge, MA: MIT Press, 2003.

Quinn, James Brian. *Intelligent Enterprise.* New York: Free Press, 1992.

Senge, Peter M. *The Fifth Discipline: The Art and Practice of the Learning Organization.* New York: Currency/Doubleday, 1994.

Stewart, Thomas A. *Intellectual Capital: The New Wealth of Organizations.* New York: Currency/Doubleday, 1997.

Wenger, Etienne, Richard McDermott, and William M. Snyder. *Cultivating Communities of Practice: A Guide to Managing Knowledge.* Boston: Harvard Business School Press, 2002.

Zack, Michael H. "Developing a Knowledge Strategy." *California Management Review*, Spring 1999, 125.

8

BENCHMARKING

What is this practice and how effective is it?

Benchmarking enables firms to compare their performance with best-in-class results elsewhere. It entails analyzing in detail the performance of companies deemed to be best in class at performing certain processes and activities. Moreover, these companies need not necessarily be in the same industry as the analyzing company. The focus is on the ability to perform selected activities well, such as billing, distribution, and customer service. But comparing apples with apples can be difficult, and benchmarking can lead to a culture of blame and thus the wrong management behavior. We will look at how to use benchmarking in a positive way to stretch performance.

Alternative names and related topics: best practices analysis; process improvement; continuous improvement

In the past, most firms were content doing better than last year. But first the Japanese and then the growth of world-class practices made firms realize that to compete effectively, they must strive to be as good as their toughest competitors. This realization led to the growth of benchmarking in the late 1980s and 1990s. Lawrence Bossidy, CEO of Honeywell, once said that benchmarking "is not industrial tourism. It is looking at specific practices, getting the benefit of expertise, bringing it back, and having no inhibitions about adopting it and letting people know where it came from."[1]

A benchmark is a standard of performance. As a financial management improvement strategy, benchmarking helps organizations identify standards of performance in other organizations and to import them successfully to their own. It allows them to discover where they stand in relation to others. By identifying, understanding, and comparing the best practices and processes of others with its own, an organization can target problem areas and develop solutions to achieve the best levels of performance. A public-sector organization can borrow the best practices of the private sector, and vice versa.

When examining and comparing the best practices of others, an organization will often perform what is called a gap analysis, a way to identify the performance or operational differences between your process and that of your benchmarking partners, and to understand why the differences exist. One way to identify these gaps is through a technique called activity modeling, a useful method for understanding how a business process really works by first describing how things are ("as is" modeling), and then how you want them to be ("to be" modeling).

There are a number of different ways to approach benchmarking. The most common benchmarking exercises are those done between companies within the same field or sector. The now-famous International Motor Vehicle Program (IMVP), coordinated at MIT from 1985 to 1990, involved auto manufacturers in Europe, the United States, and Japan, and had the specific goal of explaining why Japanese companies performed better than their U.S. and European counterparts. Interindustry benchmarking became popular in the early 1990s, with consortia of companies from sometimes widely differing sectors getting together to study each other's management practices to see if they could learn generic lessons.

Internal benchmarking between divisions or business units within a single company or large group of companies is common. Some benchmarking is done as a cooperative exercise, with companies exchanging knowledge (more or less) openly; in other cases, a neutral moderator such as the American Productivity & Quality Center (APQC), a consulting firm or business school team helps protect confidentiality and ensure that no trade secrets are divulged.

While benchmarking is still in its infancy in many firms, its use is invariably limited to quality or process improvement. To be successful, organizations should have a clear idea of their own critical success factors (e.g., reduction in cycle time or excellent customer service), and knowledge of their own processes before they start to benchmark. Benchmarking need not necessarily be among companies in the same industry. The focus is on the ability to perform selected activities well, such as billing, distribution, and customer service.

The term "benchmarking" can also simply mean "peer comparisons," without any underlying knowledge sharing. Thus, one branch of a bank or one hotel in a chain might compare its performance with other branches and hotels, which is often a better measure of performance than achieving a negotiated target. Jack Welch was a great believer in this process. He once commented that most managers "think incrementally primarily because they think internally. Changing the culture—opening it up to the quantum change—

means constantly asking not how fast am I going, how well am I doing versus how well I did a year or two before, but rather, how fast and how well am I doing versus the world outside. Are we moving faster, are we doing better against that external standard?"[2]

Welch promoted benchmarking at GE for many years. He attributed much of the company's sustained success to breaking the barriers of internal thinking and benchmarking with other leading-edge companies. The result of this process was to prove to frontline managers that big performance leaps were possible and thus to build the confidence essential to their achievement. Welch described what GE learned from its benchmarking partners: "Wal-Mart taught us the direct customer feedback technique we call Quick Market Intelligence. We learned New Product Introduction methods from Toshiba, Chrysler, and Hewlett-Packard, and advanced manufacturing techniques from American Standard, Toyota, and Yokogawa. Allied Signal, Ford, and Xerox shared their insights into launching a quality initiative. Motorola, which created a dramatically successful, quality-focused culture over a period of a decade, has been more than generous in sharing its experiences with us."[3]

Benchmarking at Hilton Hotels

"Hilton Hotels uses internal benchmarking to establish targets for its individual properties. Each year, it expects each property to close the gap between its current performance and that of one of Hilton's top-tier (or 'green zone') hotels. This is how it works: let's assume that a low-performing hotel has a current score of 50 on a particular metric such as customer satisfaction, whereas the best performance score for a comparable property is 90—that's a difference of 40. Hilton would set a target for this property to close the gap by, say, 25 percent each year. So the target for next year would be 60, and the following year (assuming the best-practice score doesn't move), 67.5, and so on. This approach acknowledges that step changes in performance take time. The Hilton approach to target setting also recognizes that improvement becomes more incremental as properties approach performance 'perfection.' "[a]

[a] Robert S. Kaplan, "Target Setting," *Balanced Scorecard Report*, May–June 2006, http://www.nationalcollege.lmmattersonline.com/courses/hmm10/goal_setting/resources/B0605C.pdf.

Learning from the successes—and indeed the failures—of others is an important way of gathering knowledge. That said, benchmarking does have its drawbacks. Author of *Reinventing Management*, Julian Birkinshaw, reckons that the form of benchmarking that many companies practice is tyranny. "If you keep track of how you are doing using narrow indicators of performance against your immediate competitors, and if your competitors do the same, you will end up running round in circles. Your management practices will converge, and your customers will no longer be able to tell you apart. Benchmarking is useful for companies that are a long way behind the curve, but if you are doing well it is a dangerously self referential exercise," notes Birkinshaw.[4]

Human resources expert Jeffrey Pfeffer thinks that "the problem with benchmarking lies in the way it is usually practiced: it is far too 'casual.' The logic behind what works at top performers, why it works, and what will work elsewhere is barely unraveled, resulting in mindless imitation . . . As a wise executive once said, 'We have been benchmarking the wrong things. Instead of benchmarking what others *do*, we ought to copy how they *think*.'"[5]

One common problem concerns the quality of the information that companies in benchmarking exercises provide to their peers. Everyone in a benchmarking group wants to get something, but few want to give much away. They may withhold information because they perceive it to be commercially sensitive. In extreme cases, companies have fed false or misleading information.

What is the performance potential of this practice?

- **To encourage managers to set stretch goals (if they can do it, why can't we?).** If managers accept that similar organizations or teams have achieved much higher-level results, then they are much more likely to set their sights on more ambitious goals.
- **To encourage innovation and breakthrough thinking.** Many organizations are too introverted, never learning from how other organizations work. The best organizations are constantly on the lookout for breakthrough ideas wherever they can find them. Formal benchmarking or just sharing knowledge with others are ways to do this.
- **To encourage managers to examine present processes by checking fundamental assumptions that often lead to self-improvement.** Most business processes are less efficient (take too long, cost too much) than they should be. Without looking at external best practices, it is hard to see how they can be improved. Benchmarking provides new opportunities to rethink how processes are designed and executed.

What actions do you need to take to maximize the potential of this practice?

ACTIONS TO AVOID

✖ **Don't act before looking first at self-improvement.** The best organizations continuously examine their work flows to see how they can improve them. But they don't start by bringing in consultants. Too often, people in white coats who are remote from the actual work lead benchmarking. The best organizations' first step is to ask their own people on the front line. It is cheaper and far more effective to involve your own people in self-improvement. They know the problems and probably have some brilliant ideas for solving them if only invited. Consider what happened at one Hewlett-Packard factory many years ago when four out of every one thousand soldered connections were defective. Not bad for those days, but when the engineering consultants were called in, they cut the defect rate in half by modifying the process. Then HP turned to its own workers. They practically rebuilt the operation—and slashed defects a thousandfold, to under two per million.[6]

✖ **Look outside before looking in the mirror.** Rick Roth, chief research officer with the Hackett Group, warns corporate executives against doing what his firm's precise and timely analyses practically beg them to do. "Don't take the benchmark and see how it applies to your company," he emphasizes. "Focus on what you're trying to change first then identify which type of benchmarking will help get you there."[7]

✖ **Question whether you can attribute the success of the target benchmark organization to the practice or process to be benchmarked.** The drivers of success are often cultural, rather than mechanistic. Teamwork, openness, self-questioning, cooperation, and creativity are just some of the ways to describe successful organizations. But these factors don't easily lend themselves to benchmarking.

✖ **Be wary of parachuting techniques into your organization that may make matters worse.** Another problem is that learning one technique and parachuting it into your organization may not be the right way forward. Remember that all processes and systems are interconnected, so changing one is likely to have an impact on another. Performing one process faster may cause more problems if it creates bottlenecks further down the line. Look at the wider system implications and ensure that you effect a coherent change. Copying a best practice rarely works in practice, as no two operations are exactly the same. The best approach is to understand the ideas behind the best practice you're observing and then adapt those ideas to fit your own processes and culture.

Beware of superstitious learning

As Jeffrey Pfeffer and Robert I. Sutton point out, "If you can't explain the underlying theory, you are likely engaging in superstitious learning, and you may be copying something irrelevant or even damaging—or only copying part (perhaps the worse part) of the practice." They give the example of the "rank and yank" employee appraisal system at GE. Many companies that imitate this system, note Pfeffer and Sutton, and "take only the A, B and C rankings and miss the crucial subtlety that an A player is someone who helps colleagues do their jobs effectively, rather than engaging in dysfunctional internal competition."[a]

[a] Jeffrey Pfeffer and Robert I. Sutton, "Evidence-Based Management," *Harvard Business Review*, January 2006, 63–74.

✖ **Avoid using benchmarking as a big stick.** Benchmarking in the wrong, command-and-control hands can easily be seen as a big stick with which to beat managers into submitting to impossible targets and then judging and blaming them if they don't perform. Many managers react suspiciously to achievements elsewhere and invariably claim that "we're different" and can't be compared with them. Benchmarking should be a tool for learning and improvement that challenges and engages process owners. In other words, they must see benchmarking as something that they do for their self-improvement rather than something that is imposed on them.

ACTIONS TO TAKE

✓ **Study the whole system rather than one technique.** Learning one technique and adopting it without considering its impact on other processes may not be the right approach. Look at the wider system implications, and ensure that a coherent change is effected.

✓ **Compare apples with apples.** No team will take benchmarking seriously unless it is convinced that the comparisons are fair. What one person means by accounts payable can be very different from what another person means. Benchmarking consultants spend much of their time and energy nailing down these definitions. Only then will one team notice how many full-time employees they have compared.

✓ **Provide open and honest information.** While companies must obviously protect commercial sensitivity, benchmarkers need to be as open as

Data quality matters

Experts identify two potential problems with the information companies use in benchmarking projects: fuzzy metrics and dirty data. Rick Roth of the Hackett Group insists that database size matters much less than how well the measures are defined: "When I say accounts payable, which activities in accounts payable does that mean? Does that only refer to accounts payable under the CFO? Or does that mean all accounts payable activities? Does that include technology costs? Does it include the cost to support accounts payable processes? Those and many other similar clarifications are critical to the kind of strong definition that enables apples-to-apples comparisons." The data that benchmarking firms receive from clients usually needs thorough cleaning, Roth says. "Did people answer in the way that you asked the question?" he asks. "Are they giving you actual data, budgeted data or forecasted data? If they're giving you cost, is it fully loaded cost or direct cost? Does the direct cost include an allocation of overhead? Does it include their travel costs? Does it include their travel plans? Have they included incentive stock options?"[a] The lesson is that the benchmarking organization needs to understand the customer's business or industry. That's particularly the case for competitive benchmark studies.

[a] Eric Krell, "Why Benchmarking Doesn't Always Lead to Best Practices," *Business Finance*, October 2003, www.businessfinancemag.com/magazine/archives/article.html?articleID=14008.

possible with their peers. In benchmarking, as in life, you don't get something for nothing, and it is important to share your best practices in order to learn from others. One problem, of course, is that the information that may be most valuable in terms of benchmarking is often that which is most sensitive; giving away one's own secrets of best practice may hand an advantage to the competition. This problem bedevils every benchmarking exercise to some extent, but you can overcome by having a neutral mediator who can provide and receive information anonymously, protecting confidentiality to a certain degree.

✓ **Focus on internal as well as external benchmarking.** When most people think of benchmarking, they assume it applies to industry best practices. But you can gain much from internal peer comparisons. In large organizations, there are likely to be multiple offices, branches, plants, IT teams, customer service teams, and so forth. The performance of each team will vary significantly from the average. One major advantage is that you can do internal comparisons regularly and quickly because data is readily available. Handelsbanken uses peer comparisons (branch versus branch; region versus region; and bank versus bank) to drive continuous improvement throughout the organization.

✓ **Set realistic time horizons for improvement.** Benchmarking can be useful when it gives ambitious improvement targets some credibility in the sense that another organization has achieved them. But most such targets need a reasonable time to reach (usually two to three years). This is a major problem if a company measures and rewards performance in the context of fiscal year-ends, the typical case within a complex target-setting environment.

✓ **Adapt rather than copy.** Copying a best practice rarely works in practice, as no two operations are exactly the same. The best approach is to understand the ideas behind the best practice and then adapt those ideas to fit your own processes and culture.

Conclusions

Benchmarking is the practice of being humble enough to admit that others are better at something than you and wise enough to learn how to match or even surpass them. If well implemented, it can lead to stretch goals and step changes in performance. Though most benchmarking takes place at a detailed process level, there is significant scope for sharing knowledge within firms and across industries to gain some idea of what good practice is. Leading organizations are always looking out for business improvement ideas. But parachuting a best practice into the organization is not always the best approach. Taking the ideas and adapting them to fit a company's individual circumstances offer a better chance of success.

FURTHER READING

American Productivity & Quality Center, www.apqc.org.

Boxwell, Robert J., Jr. *Benchmarking for Competitive Advantage.* New York: McGraw-Hill, 1994.

Camp, Robert C. *Business Process Benchmarking: Finding and Implementing Best Practices.* Milwaukee, WI: American Society for Quality, 1995.

Coers, Mardi, Chris Gardner, Lisa Higgins, and Cynthia Raybourn. *Benchmarking: A Guide for Your Journey to Best-Practice Processes.* Houston, TX: American Productivity & Quality Center, 2001.

Czarnecki, Mark T. *Managing by Measuring: How to Improve Your Organization's Performance Through Effective Benchmarking.* New York: AMACOM, 1999.

Harrington, H. James. *The Complete Benchmarking Implementation Guide: Total Benchmarking Management.* New York: McGraw-Hill, 1996.

Iacobucci, Dawn, and Christie Nordhielm. "Creative Benchmarking." *Harvard Business Review,* November–December 2000, 24–25.

McNair, C. J., and Kathleen Leibfried. *Benchmarking.* New York: HarperBusiness, 1992.

Reider, Rob. *Benchmarking Strategies: A Tool for Profit Improvement.* New York: John Wiley & Sons, 1999.

Spendolini, Michael J. *The Benchmarking Book*, 2nd ed. New York: AMACOM, 2003.

Stauffer, David. "Is Your Benchmarking Doing the Right Work?" *Harvard Management Update*, September 2003, 1–4.

9

SUSTAINABILITY

What is this practice and how effective is it?

Sustainability is not a passing fad. Nor is it a public relations exercise. It offers a host of new opportunities to reduce waste, cut costs, and develop new and exciting products and services. But it means rethinking some deeply ingrained management practices, such as the way firms set financial targets and budgets that collide with many principles of sustainability. We will look at these issues and try to bridge the gap between what's good for the firm and what's good for the environment.

Alternative names and related topics: triple bottom line; sustainable development; living asset stewardship

While most quality improvement programs are aimed at being "good enough" or "meeting industry standards," rather than achieving "perfection" or "zero waste," the ultimate aim of sustainability programs is "zero adverse impact." To accomplish this, some organizations are using a life-cycle assessment (LCA) technique that tracks the environmental impact of their products and services along a continuous path from initial product design through production, resource use, supply chain effects, packaging, shipping, retailing, purchase, and ultimate disposal. Their goal is to replicate the dynamics of natural systems, so that waste from a product or process becomes food for another, or is sequestered within a closed-loop system until it can be rendered back into food.[1]

The idea of corporate sustainability—that increased profits through more innovation and lower costs (through less waste) can and should go hand in hand with social and environmental responsibility—has been around for a long time. A recent *BusinessWeek* article reports on a 2010 study by author Andrew Savitz and notes that sustainability has reached a tipping point with the most significant finding that "despite the economic downturn and a flurry of global challenges, corporate commitment to environmental, social, and governance issues remains strong: 93 percent of CEOs see sustainability as critical to their company's success. This signals a fundamental shift in mindsets since this survey was last conducted in 2007. Then, sustainability was starting to reshape the rules of global business. Now, it has become a strategic priority for CEOs around the world."[2]

According to McKinsey's Sheila Bonini and Hans-Werner Kaas, managing sustainability begins and ends with the accountability of senior executives. In a recent study, less than 13 percent of Russell 1000 companies reported having an executive-level committee responsible for sustainability efforts, and less than 6 percent had a C-level executive on the hook for making progress in this area.[3] Lacking this kind of accountability, companies struggle to integrate sustainability into their core planning effectively and to make the right decisions about allocating resources to get the job done. Moreover, when senior executives don't visibly wave the flag for sustainability, the organization—probably rightly—infers that this is not a strategic priority.[4]

Joseph Bragdon, Director of the Sustainability Institute, believes that the real cost issue most corporations face today is not overspending on so-called "nonessentials," but a kind of "underspending." When companies systematically mistreat people and nature in their pursuit of short-term profit, they destroy the means of their existence, and undermine the trust and credibility they need to cultivate long-term profit. If they do this long and carelessly enough, eventually their businesses become vulnerable and collapse from within. That is why the average life expectancy is only forty to fifty years—far shorter than the perpetual life for which it was designed.[5]

One business group, the World Business Council for Sustainable Development, lists hundreds of international members. According to the council's Web site, these companies share the belief that "the pursuit of sustainable development is good for business and business is good for sustainable development." In all, some five hundred organizations publish sustainability reports according to Global Reporting Initiative (GRI) guidelines. Some countries, such as France, South Africa, and the Netherlands, now mandate environmental or social sustainability reporting as a condition of being listed on their stock exchanges.[6]

The GRI focuses on the "triple bottom line" of economic, environmental, and social impacts of corporate performance. *Economic impacts* (the GRI acknowledges indirect economic impacts, but it has not identified a generic set of performance indicators) includes customers, suppliers, employees, providers of capital, and the public sector. *Environmental impacts* include materials, energy, water, biodiversity, emissions, effluents and waste, suppliers, products and services, compliance, and transport. And *social impacts* include

Focusing on social issues can be a challenging and disruptive process

Transforming a profit-driven company into one that values social issues can be a challenging and disruptive process, but companies such as the Starbucks Corporation and Timberland Company have managed the transformation successfully. Authors James Austin and Ezequiel Reficco looked at these companies for lessons on how firms can better create a culture of corporate social responsibility. The first step, they conclude, is for management to champion the value of social and environmental projects, and to make this approach part of the company's core purpose. A second crucial step is to provide incentives and rewards for employees who generate social value. At Timberland, for example, employees can earn up to forty hours of paid time off for volunteering in their communities. Collaborating with socially conscious organizations is also essential. Starbucks entered into a partnership with Conservation International, a nonprofit organization focused on protecting the earth's biodiversity, to promote environmentally sustainable coffee production among Mexican farmers. Through this partnership, Starbucks was able to increase its capacity to work with small farmers. Companies that wish to promote social responsibility do not see social issues as separate from or secondary to the bottom line. Instead, they find innovative ways to create both societal and business value.[a]

[a] James Austin and Ezequiel Reficco, "Corporate Social Entrepreneurship," working paper 09-101, Harvard Business School, April 2009.

labor practices, health and safety, training and education, diversity and opportunity, human rights, strategy and management, bribery and corruption, and competition and pricing.[7]

But we should not be fooled by such guidelines and reports. Many of today's fallen corporate angels, according to Bragdon—among them AT&T, Ford, and Xerox—tried to adopt the outward appearance of sustainable organizations but failed because their managements were too bureaucratically isolated, too fond of their own ideas, too dismissive of frontline employees, and too focused on quantitative objectives. Although the leaders of all three companies have made extraordinary efforts to be diverse, employee friendly, and environmentally responsible, their workplace cultures utterly undermine these efforts. Employees instinctively know when market share and profit count more than ethics and citizenship. They have a hard time getting inspired and energized when managers talk down to them, withhold vital information, and treat them as potential costs.[8] The litmus test of any serious sustainability crusader is whether it has truly integrated sustainability into its culture and into its performance management systems. Those organizations that will do almost anything to meet this quarter's numbers are unlikely to qualify. That excludes many on the GRI list.

Finnish paper company Stora Enso, with more than $16 billion in annual sales, is a sustainability crusader with impeccable credentials. As the world's oldest company and largest paper company, it continues to build relational equity by caring for the environment—the biodiversity of its timberland, the well-being of its employees, and the health of its host communities. Stora's tolerance for open dialogue and new ideas continues unabated. To promote the broadest possible outreach, the company transparently reports its financial, social, and environmental objectives, and its progress in attaining the triple bottom line. Then it welcomes stakeholder feedback. It also regularly polls employees about their job satisfaction and ideas for improvement.[9] Within its industry, Stora is the sustainability leader and by far the most financially secure.[10]

General Electric has finally come off the sustainability fence

According to GE's CEO Jeff Immelt:

> Once we had done our homework, we launched "ecomagination" with 17 products we could point to. As always, we were metrics driven. We said that our $10 billion of revenue from products tapping renewable energy sources like the sun and wind had to go to $20 billion in five years. The $750 million we were spending on R&D for clean technologies had to go to a billion and a half. Our own greenhouse gas emissions had to come down by 1% by 2012 . . . There were plenty of guys on our energy team who hated this in the beginning because half of their customers were saying *they* hated it. Never mind that half of the customers loved it. We just kept talking. "Here's where we're going. Here's why we think it's good for both of us. And it's going to come someday anyhow, so let's get ahead of it."[a]

[a] Thomas A. Stewart, "Growth as a Process, An Interview with Jeff Immelt," *Harvard Business Review*, June 2006, 60–70.

The important rule to remember is: *everything is connected to everything else.* Cause and effect may not be immediate. The period between toxic releases into the workplace and employees' health claims may be a matter of years. The lag between reckless burning of carbon-based fuels and our recognition of global warming was decades long. *But in the end, everything gets counted.* Companies can and should build such knowledge into their metrics systems. Those that do are far better prepared for stability and success in the long run than those that don't.[11]

What is the performance potential of this practice?

- **To reduce waste.** The aim is to cut waste both within the organization and in the wider ecosystem.
- **To build new products and services.** The sustainability movement is spawning a whole new range of products and services that firms can develop and market. Governments around the world are also supporting these products with marketing and grants.
- **To become a better corporate citizen.** There is evidence to suggest that a large group of investors takes note of a company's commitment to sustainability.

What actions do you need to take to maximize the potential of this practice?

ACTIONS TO AVOID

- ✖ **Stop paying lip service and take sustainability seriously.** Too many organizations treat sustainability as a public relations exercise, as they produce glossy reports to push their "green" credentials. "There are companies using [sustainability reporting] more for a PR exercise, and others that mean what they say," says Eric Israel, managing director in the forensic practice at KPMG LLP in New York."[12]
- ✖ **Challenge economies-of-scale thinking.** Professor H. Thomas Johnson believes that there are now ample technologies available to support efficient small-scale operation of almost every commercial activity. Some examples include the continuous-casting, minimill technology that transformed steelmaking in the last thirty years, small-scale refineries and chemical plants for almost all current petroleum and chemical processing, and Japanese paper-products plants that efficiently produce on a much smaller scale than American papermakers, for example, might think possible.[13]
- ✖ **Be wary of short-term budgets and targets.** The ideas of sustainability don't sit comfortably with typical corporate financial budgets and targets. Sure, managers might set budgets and targets for sustainability, such

as the reduction in carbon emissions, but when profits are under pressure, where do managers look to make savings? It is easy to believe that the sustainability budget would be one of the first to cut.

ACTIONS TO TAKE

✓ **Examine the evidence.** Rather than fighting a rearguard action against a sustainability movement that is here to stay, leaders should apply their analytic rigor to testing and strengthening their own sustainability programs. They should examine the evidence. They should look at such companies as Toyota, Nokia, 3M, Stora Enso, and a host of others and measure how their sustainability programs have lowered costs—in some cases, dramatically—and contributed to consistent improvements in shareholders' wealth.

✓ **Embrace lean (or systems) thinking.** Sustainability and lean thinking make for natural bedfellows. Both are about eliminating waste. Lean is a philosophy that rejects mass production (with all the waste it produces) and aims to make only exactly what customers need with no waste at all. If every organization embraced lean thinking, many of the world's problems would be solved in a few years. But lean thinking is diametrically opposed to traditional management and will take many more years before it becomes the management standard.

✓ **Measure what's important.** Measuring and reporting return on investment is the key to engaging with influential people both inside and outside the company. At Dow Chemical, executives are overseeing development of a second set of ten-year goals for companywide sustainability (to 2015, building on a first set of goals originally developed in 1994). Both plans not only address key sustainability challenges but are also driving the creation of significant financial value. For instance, Dow invested $1 billion from 1994 to 2005 to reduce its energy consumption and improve its water and energy productivity, reaping $4.3 billion in cost savings. Savings continued to accrue from these efforts, amounting to over $8.6 billion by the end of 2008.[14]

✓ **Start measuring the triple bottom line.** Use current guidelines to start measuring the economic, environmental, and social impacts of corporate performance. Danish company Novo Nordisk's accounting system tracks every effluent and waste stream from every plant in its system, as well as those of its suppliers and shippers. From this data, Novo can calculate its total systemic impact on global warming, ozone depletion, acidification, and eutrophication. Novo then publishes the data collected by its eco-accounting system on its Web site and in annual sustainability reports. Novo uses these reports to enrich discourse on its processes and their impacts—both inside the firm and at "stakeholder forums." The knowledge it gains from these feedback sessions is then invested back into improving its processes.[15] Its internal accounting practices include a series of eco-productivity indexes that measure its efficiency in using energy, water, raw materials, and packaging.[16]

Conclusions

Today's best-run companies—and smartest investors—see sustainability for what it truly is: a strategic business driver that will separate the winners from the losers in the next few decades. Waste-reduction and new business opportunities are everywhere you look. Perhaps the easiest way to communicate the impact so far is to say that only 2 percent of the studies show that managers who dedicate corporate resources to social performance—taking actions that consider the interests of society—impose a direct cost to shareholders. Companies can do good *and* do well, even if they don't do well *by* doing good.[17]

FURTHER READING

Bragdon, Joseph H. *Profit for Life*. Cambridge, MA: Society for Organizational Learning, 2006.

Eccles, Robert G., and Michael P. Krzus. *One Report*. Hoboken, NJ: John Wiley & Sons, 2010.

Johnson, H. Thomas. "Confronting the Tyranny of Management by Numbers." *Reflections: The SoL Journal on Knowledge, Learning and Change* 5, no. 4 (2004): 1–11.

Senge, Peter M., and Goran Carstedt. "Innovating Our Way to the Next Industrial Revolution." *MIT Sloan Management Review* 42, no. 2 (2001): 24–38.

Part II

Shareholder and Customer Value

10

INTANGIBLE ASSETS

What is this practice and how effective is it?

Intangible assets or capital represent not only patents and copyrights—which are often shown on the balance sheet—but also other assets, including leading brands, loyal customers, and key capabilities such as new product generation—which are not. Their value is usually understood to be the difference between a company's market capitalization and its net tangible assets. Despite the ebbs and flows of share prices over the past twenty-five years, the value of intangibles has grown significantly, particularly in people businesses such as software, advertising, and financial services. Intangibles are increasingly seen as the key drivers of future success. We will examine how managers can identify these assets and maximize their impact.

Alternative names and related topics: intellectual capital; human capital; market-to-book ratio

With all the regulatory scrutiny and media attention that public companies get today, you would think there is little that isn't known about them. But what's available in the public domain may only scratch the surface of what comprises an organization's true value. Underneath all of the hard numbers about buildings, plants, and inventories lies a subterranean mountain of soft data about such intangible assets as R&D expertise, leading brands, excellent processes, talented people, IT networks, innovation capabilities, and loyal customers that traditional accounting measures don't capture.

Intangible assets underpin up to 80 percent to 90 percent of many share values. Some, such as patents, copyrights, trademarks, and goodwill arising after acquisitions, may already be included in the balance sheet. But their true worth—the difference between market and book values—remains hidden inside the *invisible balance sheet*. Whether they realize it or not, investors are making huge bets on these assets each day without any idea of their underlying worth. Are these bets justified or are they mere acts of faith? What do investors know about these assets—their existing and future returns—and how well they are managed and protected? Neither internal managers nor external investors or regulators seem to know what to do about them. The truth is that published accounts and their associated performance measures were developed for a *tangible world* in which assets can be counted and audited. But for a predominantly *intangible world*, we must find new measures of performance and value.

Until 2001 in the United States, the acquiring firm was required under generally accepted accounting principles (GAAP) to amortize goodwill in subsequent years as an expense. Then, in a halfhearted and barely perceptible nod to the importance of intangible assets, the Financial Accounting Standards Board (FASB) stopped requiring companies to amortize goodwill as a lump sum. Some intangibles with a definite useful lifespan, such as a patent, may still be amortized. Those with an indefinite useful life, such as a trade secret, can't be amortized but are subject to an impairment test. That means that companies must record losses, such as a decline in brand value after a product recall. Other intangibles—for example, the value of an acquired workforce—are explicitly not included. This 2001 improvement in M&A accounting rules ignores the much larger issue: how to account for intangible assets that are created organically by and within an organization, not those that are acquired.[1]

Two years later, in 2003, the Securities and Exchange Commission (SEC) established new guidance for Management Discussion and Analysis (MD&A) statements. MD&A statements address the disclosure of nonfinancial performance measures that are material to a company's financial health. The SEC didn't use the word specifically, but some of these measures include intangibles, such as patents, technical licensing arrangements, and customer-vendor relations. Companies are now allowed to detail the number of patents in their portfolios, along with generally accepted industry performance measures, such as the number of citations by other patent applications or the cash flow from royalties. But they are barred from discussion of valuation or depreciation of those assets. The practical result, as in the case of the Google Network, is that investors are left to infer value from how the assets are disclosed.[2]

When asked why companies do not account for their intangible assets, accounting professor Baruch Lev answered that, "intangible assets, such as new discoveries like drugs, software programs, brands or unique organizational design and processes that provide a competitive advantage, are by and large not traded in organized markets, and the property rights over these assets are often not fully secured by the company. The risk of these assets—for example the risk involved in developing a new drug or software program—is generally higher than that of physical assets. Therefore, under current GAAP, these expenditures cannot be capitalized."[3]

The implications of Lev's observations are clear. Maximizing the value of intangible assets has a far greater impact on shareholder value than maximizing financial assets. Though experts have different views about how to define intangible assets, we will settle on four primary components: structural capital, human capital, innovation capital, and market capital (see figure 10-1).

- **Structural capital** includes excellent processes supported by equally excellent IT networks and databases. And when you consider that most business problems are concerned with processes rather than people (according to W. Edwards Deming), then you can see why structural capital is so important. Attention to structural capital has enabled many companies to uncover significant cost savings.

- **Human capital** includes all individual capabilities—the knowledge, skill, and experience of the company's employees. Such companies as Whole Foods, Handelsbanken, Southwest Airlines, and W.L. Gore have all found a strong relationship between the capabilities of their people (who work in self-managed teams), low staff turnover, high customer loyalty, and sustained competitive success. They all recruit and develop people who can operate within a high-responsibility environment. This is their real competitive advantage.

FIGURE 10-1

Component parts of intangible capital

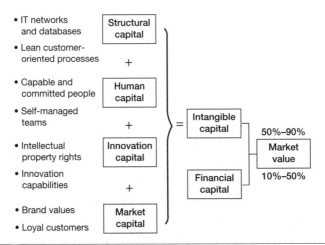

- **Innovation capital** refers to the renewal capability and the results of innovation in the form of protected commercial rights, intellectual property, and talents used to create and rapidly bring to market new products and services.[4] Management systems such as aggressive targets and misaligned incentives that focus on short-term results rather than long-term value creation facilitate or destroy innovation capital.
- **Market capital** is equivalent to the value that any potential purchaser would have to pay for the brand and customer portfolio. Several studies have tried to value brands. The most comprehensive of these is Interbrand Group's study, "Best Global Brands 2010," which concluded that, on average, brands account for more than one-third of shareholder value (in some cases, they can account for more than 70 percent of value).[5] Building the value of *market capital* depends on knowing how to satisfy customers' exact needs and, just as importantly, how to do this profitably.

While Lev is downbeat about the prospects of valuation anytime soon, he is more optimistic about providing lots of useful information about intangibles. "Take human capital," notes Lev. "I'm not asking you to value it outright, but I would like to know what your retention rates and investments in employee training are, particularly compared to other companies. I don't expect companies to provide extensive information about the future, because I don't think they know. But some things they definitely know, like investment in training. I don't think revealing that would have any damaging effect. To the contrary, it could ultimately benefit the company for outsiders to know what investment is being made in employees. This ensures investors that the company understands the enormous value of human capital and is investing wisely in its own future."[6]

Despite Lev's views about measurement, measurement research has been accelerating in three key areas: human capital, market capital, and brand values. Let's start with human capital. According to McKinsey partner Lowell Bryan, it's time to recognize that financial performance increasingly comes from returns on talent, not on capital. To boost the potential for wealth creation, strategically minded executives must embrace a radical idea: changing financial performance metrics to focus on returns on talent rather than returns on capital alone. This shift in perspective would have far-reaching implications—for measuring performance, for evaluating executives, even for the way analysts measure corporate value. Only if executives begin to look at performance in this new way will they change internal measurements of performance and thus motivate managers to make better economic decisions, particularly about spending on intangibles.

Bryan notes that from 1995 to 2005, the top thirty of the very largest companies in the world (ranked by market capitalization) have seen their median

Valuing intangibles in aggregate

While Baruch Lev acknowledges the difficulties of valuing individual intangibles, he does have a formula for valuing intangibles in aggregate that can enable business leaders and investors to estimate whether the market has over- or undervalued them: "It starts with the assumption that an enterprise's performance, as reflected by its operating earnings, is generated by its physical and financial assets, enabled by intangibles. Since most tangible and financial assets are commodities, it is unlikely that by themselves they can contribute to above-average earnings performance. So the value of intangible capital is derived by subtracting from earnings the average contribution of physical and financial assets in the company's industry. What remains is a figure that indicates the contribution of intangible assets to the company's performance and provides the basis for the valuation of intangible capital."[a]

[a] Baruch Lev, "Sharpening the Intangibles Edge," *Harvard Business Review*, June 2004, 109–116.

market capitalization grow at a 17 percent compound average growth rate, yet their compound return on invested capital (ROIC) only grew 3 percent. Over the same period the average number of employees grew at a compound rate of 8 percent, while the profit per employee rose at a compound growth rate of 9 percent. The change in human talent (which as an intangible assets is not reflected on the balance sheet) provides a better explanation of results than the financial metrics.

Concentrating on this formula—as opposed to returns on capital—offers several advantages. For one, unlike ROIC, profit per employee is a good proxy for earnings on intangibles, partly because the number of people a company employs is easy to obtain. Capital, perhaps surprisingly, is subject to the vagaries of accounting definitions and such corporate finance decisions as debt-to-equity ratios, dividend policies, and liquidity preferences. As any executive will testify, talent—not capital—is usually the scarcer resource.[7]

Let's turn to market capital. In a groundbreaking 2006 study, University of Michigan business professor Claes Fornell and colleagues showed the relationship between customer satisfaction and financial success by creating a hedge portfolio in which stocks are bought long and sold short in response to changes in the American Customer Satisfaction Index (ACSI). Developed by the University of Michigan's National Quality Research Center, the ACSI is an indicator of economic success that reflects levels of customer satisfaction with goods and services purchased from about two hundred companies in more than forty industries; it's based on interviews with more than sixty-five thousand U.S. consumers each year.

How are these results possible, given efficient-market theory, which says you can't consistently outperform the market? According to Fornell, the results are possible because today's stock valuation methods fail to incorporate the kind of information that forms the basis for making stock trades in the ACSI portfolio. If they did, the ACSI portfolio would closely track the S&P 500. Customers' attitudes improve or deteriorate as people notice consistent quality differences. Changes in companies' customer satisfaction scores don't happen overnight; they have to work their way through complex value chains that ultimately affect quarterly profits and stock prices. (This accounts for the modest performance difference between the ACSI portfolio and the S&P 500 in the study's early years.) As the ACSI companies have attained higher levels of customer satisfaction and the laggards have been sold short, the fund's performance has significantly improved. A decrease in Home Depot's ACSI score, for instance, led the fund to sell the do-it-yourself retailer's stock short—and that was consistent with the company's poor financial performance and downgrades by stock analysts, even before the current housing downturn added to the company's woes.

The implications of the ACSI study will differ from one company or industry to another. In businesses with long purchasing cycles, like life insurance and durable goods, changes in customer satisfaction will take awhile to make a difference in a company's sales, ability to increase prices, and so on. (After all, how often do you need to replace your dishwasher?) In many service-intensive industries, however, if a company's customer satisfaction increases, customers will be quick to adjust their behavior and tell other people, whose own purchase behavior is also likely to change quickly.

Now that this market inefficiency has been exposed, business leaders—especially CFOs—have a responsibility to seriously question decision-making criteria that result in stronger short-term earnings but could weaken customer attitudes and relationships. The stakes are high. Leaders who do not actively work to increase customer satisfaction will be responsible for damaging their companies' future earnings and shareholder value.[8]

Brand valuation also moved forward. The brand-valuation technique developed by British company Interbrand Group is based on an earnings multiple that is determined by brand *strength*. The brand-strength analysis involves a scoring system based on seven key criteria shown together with their maximum scores.

Despite these examples, there is little interest in valuing intangibles, except within the Nordic countries and in Japan. There has been little interest in the

United States or United Kingdom. One explanation for this attitude is that executives don't believe the risk of disclosure is worth the benefit. They worry about giving away proprietary information. Shareholder liability is another problem. Because lawyers representing shareholders can work on contingency and have been known to troll for companies to sue, public firms will often disclose only what they absolutely must. Most experts on intangibles agree that liability issues are stopping even companies that would like to disclose their intangible assets from doing so.[9]

What is the performance potential of this practice?

- **To drive wealth creation.** Intangible capital is often the primary driver of wealth creation, so identifying its component parts is an important step.
- **To prioritize improvement initiatives.** Identifying your intangible assets and evaluating your strengths and weaknesses enable you to prioritize your improvement initiatives.
- **To value a business.** If intangible assets represent the majority share of your market value, you should make every attempt to measure them and improve their worth.

What actions do you need to take to maximize the potential of this practice?

ACTIONS TO AVOID

✖ **Stop trying to formulate and justify the balance sheet values of intangibles.** Intangible assets have long been treated as a soft currency not to be taken too seriously, but all this is changing as managers recognize how critical they are in the battle for competitive advantage, especially now that innovation, speed, quality, and customization have become its defining factors. So focus on identifying and improving their value *and* productivity.

✖ **Don't rely on the accounting profession to value intangibles.** The international accounting standards committees and the auditing profession have always been skeptical about intangible assets. You can understand it from their point of view. How can we audit and verify values that have not been subjected to the test of market worth (i.e., there is no transaction to audit)? This position is unlikely to change any time soon.

ACTIONS TO TAKE

✓ **Identify your key intangibles.** Do an audit of your intangible assets. Make a rough and ready evaluation of which are strategic and significant. The balanced scorecard can help teams focus on the key processes, IT capabilities, people competences, and so forth required to turn soft intangibles into hard numbers. Also assess how effective you are at managing and improving them. This should point you in the right direction toward the actions you need to take. It will also indicate where you are weak and where you have serious gaps.

✓ **Educate managers.** Most managers understand financial budgets and what they need to do to achieve them. But they are less aware—and most are probably totally ignorant—about what are intangible assets and what they can do to increase their value. Finance managers have an important role to play in educating managers of the importance of these assets and lead a discussion about what can be done to raise their value.

✓ **Build the value of intangibles.** Lev gives the example of Walmart's now-famous system in which its suppliers have direct access to its inventory. "When you buy something there, the bar code is read, [and that purchase information] goes directly to Procter & Gamble, which is in charge of maintaining the inventory. Wal-Mart got rid of inventory maintenance completely. And it has a market value which is substantially larger than its book value, yet it doesn't have any patents or trademarks. So where is this value added coming from? What is this huge asset that is there in addition to the stores and the inventory? It's these new types of intangibles, this new way of doing things and [the sustaining of] that advantage," says Lev.[10]

✓ **Focus on key value drivers.** Knowledge of intellectual capital enables managers to better see their key value drivers. What drives brand growth? What drives customer loyalty? What drives process excellence? Finding the key drivers focuses everyone on what's really important in the business.

✓ **Measure intangibles where possible.** While progress is patchy, there are a number of proxies to use to monitor the value of intangibles within the organization. Profit per employee is a good example. Leaders should make the number of employees a key factor in strategic thinking. And they should keep a clear eye on ROIC, but more as a way of ensuring that the company earns more than the cost of that capital than as an aspiration in its own right. With these metrics, the company can set its goals for the return on intangibles (that is, profit per employee) and growth (the number of employees), as well as its return on capital, which is largely a sanity check. Together, these three metrics squarely highlight—and drive—market capitalizations.[11]

Conclusions

In a dynamic business world, businesses need to be fast on their feet and create the future, rather than be a slave to it. They need to harness all the intangible capital of their people. They need to free frontline teams from the shackles of suffocating bureaucracy and enable them to share ideas, collaborate with each other, and feed knowledge back to product designers and other key people in the organization. Organizations that identify, prioritize, and improve the value of their intangible assets are usually remarkably successful at pursuing organic growth.

FURTHER READING

Caruso, Denise. "The Real Value of Intangibles." *Strategy + Business*, Autumn 2008, 27–32.

Edvinnson, Leif, and Michael S. Malone. *Intellectual Capital.* New York: HarperBusiness, 1997.

Hope, Jeremy, and Tony Hope. *Competing in the Third Wave: The Ten Key Management Issues of the Information Age.* Boston: Harvard Business School Press, 1997.

Lev, Baruch. "Sharpening the Intangibles Edge." *Harvard Business Review*, June 2004, 109–116.

11

ECONOMIC VALUE ADDED

What is this practice and how effective is it?

Economic value-added (EVA) models, if well implemented, will encourage managers to act like owners and consider their decisions in the context of whether they will increase shareholders' wealth. Accounting profits have proved time and again to be a poor indicator of future success. Remember Enron, WorldCom, and Tyco? EVA goes a long way toward meeting some of the criticisms of published accounting information. But for some managers, its concepts are challenging and difficult to translate into operational decisions. We will look at how to use EVA to improve decision making.

Alternative names and related topics: value-based management; shareholder value analysis; discounted cash flow

Most investors use variants of return on capital employed to measure company performance. But this ratio—usually defined as profits after tax as a percentage of the total share capital of the business—is easily manipulated. Take the profit figure. One of the easiest ways to make quick improvements to profits is to reduce expenditures on discretionary and intangible investments. For example, when sluggish sales or increasing costs make profit targets hard to achieve, managers might try to prop up short-term earnings by cutting expenditures on R&D, promotion, distribution, human resources, and customer service—all of which can be vital to a company's long-term performance. The immediate effect of such reductions is to boost reported profitability, but at the risk of sacrificing the company's competitive position.

Traditional methods of calculating accounting profits and capital employed fail to take account of many of the values and measures that give investors clues about the performance of intangible assets, even though, as we noted earlier, these assets now dominate the value of many companies. Economic value added (EVA) is an attempt to make accounting numbers more relevant by turning accounting profits into rough measures of "free cash flow" that many people believe more closely correlates with shareholder value (EVA adjustments add back many noncash expenses, such as goodwill). EVA is, however, not exactly a new idea. It has its roots in residual value accounting that was popular for a time in the 1960s and 1970s.

EVA is different from accounting profit in that it deducts the full cost of capital, thus providing shareholders with a measure that shows the real underlying increase in their wealth. It is defined as the (adjusted) after-tax profit for the period less the (weighted average) cost of capital. Thus, if a company has after-tax profits of $20 million, shareholders' funds of $100 million (with a cost of capital of 12 percent), and borrowing of $50 million (with a net of tax interest cost of 4 percent), its EVA would be $6 million (profit of $20 million less equity cost of $12 million and debt cost of $2 million). Advocates believe that EVA is an estimate of true "economic" profit, or the amount by which earnings exceed or fall short of the required minimum rate of return that shareholders and lenders could get by investing in other securities of comparable risk.

EVA has the advantage of being conceptually rational since it starts with familiar operating profits and simply deducts a charge for the capital invested in the company as a whole, in a business unit, or even in a single brand or plant. By assessing a charge for using capital, EVA makes managers more aware of managing assets as well as income, and helps them properly assess the trade-offs between the two. This broader, more complete view of the economics of a business can make dramatic differences. By relating income streams to the full costs of producing them, managers can see the true value of product lines and business segments.

EVA aficionados like to display the results in a "waterfall" chart that lines up the value streams across the portfolio from the most valuable, in economic value terms, on the left to the most destructive on the right, weighted to show how much of the company's resources are tied up in each. Surprises often result. Indeed, this was the case at one U.K. retailer. Most managers believed that the company's prescription drug business was where the real profits were made, only to discover that, once they applied EVA, nothing could be further from the truth. It was its Cinderella operation—the retail stores—that proved to be the outright winner. As a result, the company reduced its investment in the drug business—finally exiting it altogether—and boosted the retail operation by investing heavily in cosmetics, toiletries, and over-the-counter medicines.

EVA at Diageo

Managers at global alcoholic beverage company Diageo started to look at the economic value of Scotch whisky. Analyzing the real cost of holding long-term inventory proved to be an illuminating exercise. The costs of maturing Scotch whisky, sherry, and port tied up capital in such a way that, in one particular case, the process sometimes destroyed value, even though Scotch at premium prices tends to generate good returns. By contrast, an EVA analysis highlighted drinks such as vodka and liqueurs that the company could sell within weeks of distillation as the real value creators. As a consequence, managers switched funds from the lower value-added brands to the higher ones and diverted their advertising expenditure accordingly. Following this study, the firm decided to extend the discipline of economic profit throughout the organization, while finding an executive compensation scheme that was consistent with EVA. According to Diageo's former CEO, John McGrath, EVA can go right down to the production line. As he explained: "EVA might seem like common sense, but the idea is to turn complex concepts into practical advice on a personal basis. For instance, reducing levels of breakdown, improving productivity, lowering costs, and increasing value."[a]

[a] This case is an annotated version from "Tracking Down Value," by John McGrath, Chief Executive, Diageo PLC, which appeared in *FT Mastering Management Review*, December 1998, and reproduced on the Stern Stewart Web site at www.sternstewart.com/action/diageo.php.

Some senior executive teams believe that EVA is the elusive link between the real performance of a business and its market value. This has spurred such companies as General Electric, Coca-Cola, Anheuser Busch, Quaker Oats, Eli Lilly, Monsanto, Diageo, and Cadbury to align their *internal* measures with EVA, in some cases, down to divisional levels.

But there are potential problems with EVA. For example, it can encourage managers to focus too aggressively on shareholder value and overlook other stakeholders' needs such as those of employees, customers, suppliers, and the environment. Its decision model can also encourage managers to rely too much on financial forecasts and net present value calculations when, for the most part, they are imprecise. And it can lead to the rejection of many strategies and improvement projects, when a more judgmental approach might have suggested they were sensible options.

A full implementation of EVA requires huge amounts of information that are not generally available from within a normal accounting system. Thus, consultants need to spend months translating vertical accounting results into horizontal economic results. The costs for a large organization can be millions of dollars.

However, many leaders believe this is money well spent. For the first time, they can break down the business into a number of value centers such as business units, divisions, and product groups, and understand which add and which destroy value. In a typical large firm, many business segments add little or no value, but the firm needs EVA analysis to find out which they are. EVA's real power is that it makes managers think and act as if they were owners of the business. Shareholders, of course, have alternative choices for how they invest their money, and this opportunity cost also influences the discount rate to use.

In practice, EVA can be tough to implement especially at lower management levels. AT&T, for example, phased out its use of EVA and returned to accounting measures such as earnings per share. According to one article, between 40 percent and 50 percent of all companies trying value-based metrics abandon them between the third and fifth year of implementation.[1]

There is little doubt that by setting improvement goals that must cover the cost of capital (however defined) as opposed to, for example, beating last year's results, managerial thinking and performance are more clearly aligned with that of shareholders' interests (and common sense). But like most measurement systems, if employed too rigidly—especially if also linked to rewards—EVA measures can lead to behavior that damages long-term success. That's why experienced users measure and reward performance over rolling periods of around three years.

What is the performance potential of this practice?

- **To encourage managers to act like owners and consider their decisions in the context of whether they will increase shareholders' wealth.** EVA forces managers to look at strategic options and improvement decisions on the basis of which alternatives will maximize shareholder value. Thus, meeting income targets is insufficient. Managers must see results after the costs of funds used have been deducted. Managers must always have one eye on the balance sheet and operate with the minimum of resources.
- **To enable managers to see which business segments and product lines add value and which don't.** Traditional accounting systems focus on income and costs generated by pieces of the hierarchy such as departments, functions, divisions, and subsidiaries. They cannot see the value created (after charging all below-the-line costs including capital) of product lines, customer segments, and distribution channels, as these

EVA Momentum

In 2009, Bennett Stewart, of Stern Stewart, the leading advocate for EVA, wrote an article in which he claimed that "EVA Momentum" is the one measure that explains the whole story of an organization's performance. According to Stewart, it represents the change in a firm's economic profit in a given period divided by its sales in the *prior* period. For example, if a company increases its economic profit by $10 million on last year's sales base of $1 billion, then its EVA Momentum is 1 percent. Put another way, it is the *size-adjusted* change in economic profit, and it qualifies as the missing link in business management. For all other ratios, notes Stewart, performance benchmarks are ambiguous and hard to define. How high should profit margins be, for instance? What improvement in days-on-hand is a reasonable target? The answers are ultimately somewhat arbitrary and highly debatable. But by virtue of deducting the cost of capital, EVA Momentum incorporates an objective hurdle rate that is set in global capital markets.

Stewart claims that EVA Momentum is eminently suited to serve as the corporate objective function—the single ratio that every business should aim to maximize over time. So long as a company is mature enough to consider earnings per share, EBITDA, or return on capital as relevant financial metrics, the management team is likely to be far better off using EVA Momentum in place of such traditional metrics to summarize and grade its performance, set financial goals, anchor a scorecard of metrics to value, diagnose competitive strengths and weaknesses, formulate strategies, and even to meter discretionary pay awards.[a]

[a] Bennett Stewart, "EVA Momentum: The One Metric That Tells the Whole Story," *Journal of Applied Corporate Finance* 21, no. 2 (Spring 2009): 74–86.

value streams flow horizontally across the business. After a full implementation of EVA, managers will be able to see economic profits horizontally across the business. They will be able to determine which products and business segments add value and thus where to place their investment dollars.

- **To focus managers on the balance sheet as well as the income statement.** In the traditional model, all the focus is on the income statement. Few plans and budgets have targets linked to the balance sheet. Thus, many assets are underutilized and, in some cases, are totally redundant, yet they remain hidden in the balance sheet. EVA managers are suddenly aware of the resources they use to generate income and thus are more focused on ensuring that assets are deployed to their maximum extent and redundant assets are eliminated. The impact on cash flow can, of course, be extremely positive.

- **To provide a reward mechanism that compensates managers for increasing shareholder value.** Most managers are rewarded for meeting financial targets and budgets. The link between this and increasing shareholder value is tenuous at best. One of the strengths of EVA is that it can be used to reward managers for increasing shareholders' wealth. However, any incentive scheme needs to take account of short-term actions; thus, many companies spread rewards over a number of years to ensure that decision outcomes are sustainable.

What actions do you need to take to maximize the potential of this practice?

ACTIONS TO AVOID

- ✖ **Don't use the traditional hierarchy to determine key economic segments.** Knowing the *net* contribution, after the costs of capital, of each segment of the business is a powerful insight into where managers should focus their strategy and resources. But this insight critically depends on managers redrawing the organization map so that income streams from product lines and business segments can be related to the resources they consume. Redrawing the map serves two purposes: first, it builds executive consensus around shareholder value, and second, the outcome produces business units with enough financial integrity that executive teams can take full responsibility for economic profit. However, the time and cost involved in this type of analysis can be prohibitive. Some organizations have spent tens of millions of dollars. Perhaps business leaders would be better off reducing the complexity of their organizations and making it easier to relate the capital used to the income streams generated.

- ✖ **Be wary of driving the wrong behavior.** Many managers see an easy way to make the EVA number look better, and that is to cut the asset base. If this means running down excess capacity or selling off redundant assets, then that's a logical outcome. But too often it can mean failing to invest in growth capacity—there is usually a time lag between investment and increasing cash flows—and being too aggressive with working capital. Paying suppliers late improves the EVA result but upsets suppliers who may well decide to deal with customers that play fair with them.

✖ **Be wary of tying rewards to EVA results.** Many advocates, including Bennett Stewart, strongly believe in linking incentives to EVA. But, in some cases, once the early and easy gains have been made, managers can become addicted to bonus payments and will sometimes take any action necessary to achieve them, even if this means destroying long-term value. Stewart recommends that rewards should be earned over a period of time, say, a rolling three-year period, rather than based on short-term results. According to McGrath, "employee incentives must be tied to the shareholder value program. It is the incentive that changes behavior, and changing behavior is what changes companies. This has certainly been the case within Diageo."[2]

✖ **Be wary of a fluctuating capital base.** The value of many assets can fluctuate according to a number of uncontrollable factors such as currency movements, changes in commodity prices, and share values themselves. This is why EVA tables tend to ignore financial services and some utility companies. Nor are these problems confined to commodity businesses such as oil companies. Many so-called trading companies now include a substantial element of financial services and commodity dealing. GE, Ford, and Tesco are all examples.

✖ **Don't try to implement EVA intuitively.** Implementing EVA intuitively rarely works. According to McGrath, "a company has to go through the hard work of understanding how it works, introducing the detailed processes and imposing the disciplines. It has to win people over."[3] Some EVA consultants reckon it can take up to five years before the full benefits are felt.

ACTIONS TO TAKE

✓ **Use EVA instead of financial targets on scorecards.** Focusing goals on EVA rather than earnings-based budgets provides a better context for success and is likely to encourage more cash-generating actions.

✓ **Devolve EVA-based decisions to frontline teams.** If you use EVA as a tool for top-down control, don't expect too much enthusiasm within frontline teams. Better results come from involving local teams and empowering them to look at their assets from an economic perspective. For example, managers at long-time EVA adherent Briggs & Stratton, used to measure performance at their larger unionized plant. Eventually however, the company's managers decided EVA was not the right system for that facility and began to employ productivity as their preferred measure. Why? Because the majority of the factory's workers had no effect on decisions that related to capital expenditures. Meanwhile, most of the workers at the company's nonunion foundry believed they could have an effect on capital spending decisions. Briggs & Stratton realized that it could train those workers to understand just how that process occurs. In 2001, Briggs & Stratton president John Shiely told *CFO Magazine*, "The algebra is different [in such a small plant.]" At Briggs & Stratton, managers have since solidified EVA's drivers at the foundry such as molding efficiency, uptime, scrap rework, and attendance. According to Shiely, identifying those drivers that employees can recognize as measuring their performance "is the big issue as you push [EVA] down in the organization."[4]

✓ **Keep the application of EVA concepts simple.** According to consultant Mark Graham Brown, EVA fell out of favor when companies got tired of paying the consultants. He believes that the biggest problem with EVA is that no one understood it. Any metric that is so complicated that you need consultants to compute it is not likely to stay on the corporate dashboard of KPIs. (A corporate dashboard is a way of displaying the organization's key performance indicators on a single display, similar to the dashboard of an automobile.) "I have not seen or heard of any company tracking EVA in at least 5 years," notes Brown.[5] Many organizations customize EVA to produce a model they are comfortable with, which often involves a trade-off between accuracy and simplicity. The U.K. manufacturer, Tomkins, uses a version of EVA it calls "bonusable profit" to measure business unit performance and reward managers for success. Bonusable profit is business unit operating profit after deducting a notional tax charge and deducting a capital charge on the total investment in that business, including goodwill. Managers receive a percentage of bonusable profit as a very substantial part of their remuneration. Former CFO Ken Lever commented, "We have adapted the [EVA] concepts to suit us and not worried too much about the academic purity. To us, it is whether it is directionally correct and encourages the right behavior that really matters. The difference is that our managers can understand it, whereas EVA itself can be a difficult and complicated concept to understand because it requires all sorts of adjustments, such as the capitalization of training, R&D, etc. We didn't want to do all that."[6]

✓ **Spend time educating employees.** All employees need to understand why the organization has adopted the EVA model and how it will affect their work. They also need to know the proxies they can use as value drivers and KPIs that support the EVA model. This education program is particularly crucial if rewards are to be linked to EVA performance. Employees should also be aware that there is a danger that the intense focus on shareholder value will crowd out other considerations in the decision-making process. Not every decision can be reduced to value-based criteria. In many cases, economic results are subject to long-term forecasts based on weak assumptions.

✓ **Accurately measure the cost of capital.** Calculating the cost of capital for EVA purposes can be a tortuous and very imprecise science. According to research across a range of well-regarded U.S. companies, there is significant variation in the way they derive the numbers, particularly regarding the cost of equity capital. The researchers caution that, at best, the cost of capital is an uncertain estimate.[7]

Conclusions

The management literature is replete with examples of poor accounting measures. While the reported balance sheet is lacking information on its most important intangible assets, the profit-and-loss account gives precious little indication of real managerial performance. Neither EVA nor other measures that use published accounting data fully redress the problem. While EVA can be complicated and expensive to implement, there are many satisfied users who swear by it. Despite the many pitfalls, if done well, the results might be worth the effort.

FURTHER READING

Copeland, Tom, Tim Koller, and Jack Murrin. *Valuation: Measuring and Managing the Value of Companies,* 2nd ed. New York: John Wiley, 1995.

Ehrbar, A. *EVA: The Real Key to Creating Wealth.* New York: John Wiley, 1998.

Grant, James L. *Foundations of Economic Value Added,* 2nd ed. Hoboken, NJ: John Wiley, 2002.

Hope, Jeremy. *Reinventing the CFO: How Financial Managers Can Transform Their Roles and Add Greater Value.* Boston: Harvard Business School Press, 2006.

Hope, Jeremy, and Robin Fraser. *Beyond Budgeting: How Managers Can Break Free from the Annual Performance Trap.* Boston: Harvard Business School Press, 2003.

Hope, Jeremy, and Tony Hope. *Competing in the Third Wave: The Ten Key Management Issues of the Information Age.* Boston: Harvard Business School Press, 1997.

Knight, James A. *Value Based Management: Developing a Systematic Approach to Creating Shareholder Value.* New York: McGraw-Hill, 1997.

Luehrman, Timothy A. " What's It Worth?: A General Manager's Guide to Valuation." *Harvard Business Review,* May–June 1997, 132–142.

Martin, John D., and J. William Petty. *Value Based Management: The Corporate Response to the Shareholder Revolution.* Boston: Harvard Business School Press, 2000.

Rappaport, Alfred. *Creating Shareholder Value: A Guide for Managers and Investors.* New York: Free Press, 1997.

Stern, Joel M., and John S. Shiely, with Irwin Ross. *The EVA Challenge: Implementing Value-Added Change in an Organization.* New York: John Wiley & Sons, 2001.

Stewart, G. Bennett, III. *The Quest for Value.* New York: Stern Stewart, 1993.

12

KEY VALUE DRIVERS

What is this practice and how effective is it?

Key value drivers are the processes and practices that have the greatest impact on shareholder value. Valuation theory tells us that the market value of the firm is the sum of the present value of its future free cash flows. But what drives these cash flows? There are a small number of key value drivers, but few organizations understand what they are or how to maximize their impact. We will look more deeply at the value-driver model and suggest ways of identifying key value drivers and how managers can best use their power.

Alternative names and related topics: performance drivers; driver analysis; shareholder value analysis

A key value driver (KVD) is any variable that drives value for shareholders. But few firms can identify their KVDs and thus use them for forecasting and improvement. Identifying your KVDs can take a deep understanding of the business and much trial and error. Often, value drivers are combinations of variables. Alfred Rappaport, the founding father of value-based management, believes that most businesses can focus on just three to five indicators and capture an important part of their long-term value-creation potential.[1]

As most finance students know, the value of a firm is based on the present value of its future cash flows. In fact, there are two distinct components: (1) present value of free cash flows from existing assets and (2) present value of free cash flows from growth opportunities (see figure 12-1). For a high-growth firm, a significant part of its value can lie in the second variable (cash flows from growth opportunities), and this is likely to depend on its ability to innovate in every part of its business.

As figure 12-2 shows, KVDs can be useful at three levels: the generic level where cash profits ("cash in") and invested capital ("cash out") are combined

FIGURE 12-1

The value of a firm

$$\text{Value of firm} = \begin{array}{c} \text{Present value of free} \\ \text{cash flows from} \\ \text{existing assets} \end{array} + \begin{array}{c} \text{Present value of free} \\ \text{cash flows from} \\ \text{growth opportunities} \end{array}$$

FIGURE 12-2

Levels of value drivers

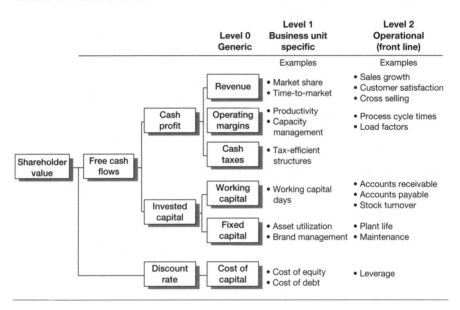

to compute free cash flows for the firm as a whole. At the business unit level, variables such as sales growth and customer mix are particularly relevant. And at the operational level, KVDs are defined as precisely as possible and tied to specific decisions and metrics that frontline managers can control. The balance sheet must also be included. Some experts believe that 100 percent of value created comes from no more than 50 percent of the capital employed.[2]

The value-based management (VBM) approach attempts to create streams of value relating to products, brands, channels, and customer segments (also known as value centers) that can be associated with their costs and the resources they use. Once they have identified the value stream and its associated assets, managers can use VBM models to evaluate its net present value. By placing values on these business components and then aggregating them, the VBM methodology can derive the total value of a business. This is not as easy

The four rules of value creation

1. Companies create value by generating future cash flows at rates of return greater than the cost of capital. The combination of revenue growth and return on invested capital (ROIC) drives value creation.
2. Value is created when companies generate higher cash flows, not by rearranging investors' claims on those cash flows.
3. A company's share price is driven by changes in investor expectations, not just the company's actual performance (the greater the expectation built into the share price, the harder it is to keep up).
4. The value of a business depends on who is managing it and what strategy he or she pursues.

Source: Tim Koller, Richard Dobbs, and Bill Huyett, *Value: The Four Cornerstones of Corporate Finance* (Hoboken, NJ: John Wiley & Sons, 2011), 4–6.

as it appears because accounting systems run vertically up and down the hierarchy, whereas economic value runs horizontally along product and customer-based value streams.

VBM expert Peter Kontes reckons that redrawing the organization map is the key. "Most organizational boundaries are political," notes Kontes. "The new map should be economic, defining units that can be managed for value largely independently of other units—for example because they have few shared costs."[3] Redrawing the map serves two purposes: first, it builds executive consensus around shareholder value, and second, the outcome produces business units with enough financial integrity that executive teams can take full shareholder value responsibility.

Most managers have an intuitive or implicit understanding of what drives actual and potential performance. American Express, for example, has three KVDs that leaders monitor: average card-member spending, card attrition rates, and average assets per financial client.[4] In creating the framework for a new forecasting system, business units had to identify KVDs based on company-specific algorithms. The key question was: how would $1 in billings or one additional card member affect the bottom line? Previously, staff had given a lot of attention to the impact of salaries and benefits on net profits. Managers had believed that all they needed to know was the cost of adding or eliminating an employee. However, they found that these numbers had only a 5 percent effect on the net figures. What they needed to identify were the volume drivers, those that influence 80 percent of the numbers. This turned out to be only fifteen lines on the profit-and-loss statement. "If we identified our drivers correctly, we would accurately gauge the P&L," explained project leader Jamie Croake.

The team found that billings were what really drove American Express's businesses—how much card members spent at restaurants, on airline tickets, and for major purchases. Two specific drivers behind this volume were the number of American Express cards and the average spending per card. Knowing those two items allowed them to calculate the billings numbers. These numbers, in turn, affected quite a few other items on the profit-and-loss statement, such as membership rewards, level of delayed billings, amount of interest income, measure of risk for bad debts, and so forth. The trick was to create the algorithms that accurately forecast the billings.[5]

To see how a value-based model works, consider the list of value drivers for a distributor shown in figure 12-3. In this example, value is derived from a combination of gross margin, warehouse costs, and delivery costs. Gross margin is determined by gross margin per transaction and the number of transactions. Warehouse costs are a function of the number of retail stores per warehouse and the cost per warehouse. And delivery costs are determined by the number of trips per transaction, the cost per trip, and the number of transactions. Analysis of these variables might, for example, show that the

FIGURE 12-3

Value drivers for a distributor

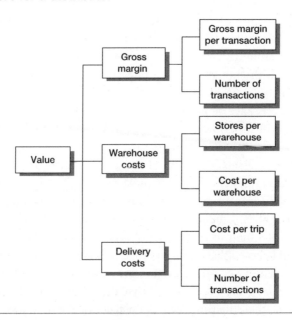

number of stores per warehouse significantly affected the cost per transaction: the more stores that could be served by a single warehouse, the lower the warehouse costs relative to revenues.

The scale economies can be substantial enough to support a strategy of growth through urban concentration, rather than a shotgun approach of scattering new stores over a wide area. The number of stores per warehouse thus becomes a key value driver. Further analysis might reveal that the number of delivery trips per transaction was very high. Whenever there were errors in an order or goods proved defective, multiple deliveries had to be made to a single customer. In one example, a retailer found that it was making an average of 1.5 trips per transaction, compared with a theoretical minimum of 1.0. Management believed this was high for the industry and thought it should be reduced to 1.2. Attaining this performance would increase value by 10 percent. So trips per transaction became an operating value driver as the company began to monitor its monthly performance.[6]

Other examples of KVDs include:

- The speed and quality of completing a loan in a bank, as this directly affects capacity and customer satisfaction.
- The turnaround time of a plane for an airline, as this directly affects asset utilization and costs. For example, Southwest Airlines reckoned early in its life that cutting ground time to ten minutes would reduce operating expenses by 25 percent (it needed far fewer expensive planes). Even with the growth of carry-on luggage and increasingly congested airports, the average turnaround time is still only twenty-five minutes, about half the industry average.
- The speed of finalizing an insurance claim, as this directly affects costs and customer satisfaction.
- Sales per square foot for a retailer, as this directly affects revenue and margins.
- Zero defects for a car manufacturer, as this directly affects customer satisfaction and loyalty.
- Customer satisfaction in a bank or car rental company, as this builds loyalty and leads to cross-selling and higher profits.

Cycle times are often key drivers in many businesses. Take Progressive Insurance, which focused on speeding up the process of settling claims, an idea that sounds counter intuitive to many finance managers. The idea was to unload payments as quickly as possible by getting its claims adjusters out of the office and at the scene of the problem. The logic behind such a radical notion was that happier customers and more productive claims reps would more than make up for the lost interest income. At Progressive, that radical notion is spelled IRV, "immediate response vehicles," a fleet of cars loaded with enough communications gear—laptops, printers, and cellphones—to allow adjusters to settle claims right at the scene of an accident. Not only did the program help improve customer retention by 20 percent, it also helped Progressive to cut labor costs. Progressive's mobile adjusters can handle nearly twice the workload they could before the changes.[7]

Identifying KVDs can be difficult because an organization has to think about its processes in a different way. Also, existing reporting systems are often not equipped to supply the necessary information. Approaches based on available information and purely financial measures rarely succeed. What is needed instead is a creative process involving much trial and error. Nor can value drivers be considered in isolation from each other. Taken alone, a price increase might boost value but not if it results in substantial loss of market share. In seeking to understand the interrelationships among value drivers, scenario planning is a valuable tool for assessing the impact of different sets of mutually consistent assumptions on the value of a company or its business units. Typical scenarios include what might happen if there were a price war or if additional capacity came online in another country. Thinking about such issues helps management avoid getting caught off guard and brings to life the relationship between strategy and value.

What is the performance potential of this practice?

- **To educate and focus everyone on KVDs.** Value drivers are often not intuitive, so managers need to spend time educating their people.
- **To drive innovation.** Identifying KVDs leads to a focus on innovative ways to maximize their impact.
- **To maximize shareholders' wealth.** Ultimately, the impact of identifying KVDs and maximizing their impact is to increase the value of the organization.

What actions do you need to take to maximize the potential of this practice?

ACTIONS TO AVOID

✖ **Stop basing key decisions and improvement initiatives on earnings rather than free cash flows.** Alfred Rappaport notes that "companies that fail to embrace this first principle of shareholder value will almost certainly be unable to follow the rest. Unfortunately, that rules out most corporations, because virtually all public companies play the earnings expectations game. What's so bad about focusing on earnings? First, the accountant's bottom line approximates neither a company's value nor its change in value over the reporting period. Second, organizations compromise value when they invest at rates below the cost of capital (overinvestment) or forgo investment in value-creating opportunities (underinvestment) in an attempt to boost short-term earnings. Third, the practice of reporting rosy earnings via value-destroying operating decisions or by stretching permissible accounting to the limit eventually catches up with companies. Those that can no longer meet investor expectations end up destroying a substantial portion, if not all, of their market value. WorldCom, Enron, and Nortel Networks are notable examples."[8]

ACTIONS TO TAKE

✓ **Teach managers the importance of free cash flow.** Free cash flow is "operating cash flow" (net profit after tax adjusted for noncash items such as depreciation and goodwill) minus capital expenditures. In other words, free cash flow represents the cash that a company is able to generate after laying out the money required to maintain or expand the company's asset base. Free cash flow allows a company to pursue opportunities that enhance shareholder value. Without cash, it's tough to pursue new opportunities, make acquisitions, pay dividends, or reduce debt. A company's cash flow statement is so vitally important, it's ironic the statement is least scrutinized by analysts who are obsessed with earnings per share. Enron never provided a balance sheet in a timely fashion, and only one analyst complained. Enron gave even *less* vocal analysis to the cash flow statement. Cash flow statements are also harder to fudge than income statements. The income statement is typically clouded by interest earned or paid, fluctuations in tax rates, one-time events, and numerous distorting but as yet legal accounting maneuvers. By contrast, while the cash flow statement isn't foolproof, it still gives investors a *much* clearer view of a company's cash-generating (and keeping) capabilities. And that's what's important.

✓ **Make strategic decisions that maximize expected value, even at the expense of lowering near-term earnings.** Companies that manage earnings are almost bound to break Rappaport's second cardinal principle (the first was "stop basing key decisions and improvement initiatives on earnings rather than free cash flows"). Indeed, most companies evaluate and compare strategic decisions in terms of the estimated impact on reported earnings, when they should be measuring against the expected incremental value of future cash flows instead. Expected value is the weighted average value for a range of plausible scenarios. (To calculate it, multiply the value added for each scenario by the probability that that scenario will materialize, then sum up the results.) A sound strategic analysis by a company's operating units should produce informed responses to three questions: First, how do alternative strategies affect

Some organizations use analytics to identify key drivers

A number of years ago, restaurant chain Ruby Tuesday discovered through its business intelligence (BI) analysis that in one restaurant, "customers were waiting longer than normal for tables and for their orders once they were seated. It was a recipe for customer dissatisfaction and, of course, poor sales. Was the restaurant not adequately staffed? Was the problem with the kitchen staff, a server, an assistant manager, a general manager—or with something beyond the company's control, like the location? Managers then assessed the time it took for a table to change hands from one patron to the next, using the BI system to calculate the time between when a waiter opened a check on the point of sale to the time the customer paid the tab. CIO Nick Ibrahim says the average time it takes a restaurant to turn over a table from one customer to the next is forty-five minutes. So if the company sees that it takes fifty-five to sixty minutes to close a check at a particular restaurant, people aren't getting their food as fast as they should. (The problem is rarely a matter of diners lingering over their meals, especially if it's taking the waiters at every table fifty-five minutes to close the check.) Management concluded, based on this information and by visiting the restaurant, that the long wait times were a result of increased demand. The area had been through an economic boom, and the restaurant was running at full capacity. The company made changes to the layout of the kitchen, the placement of food, and the location of cooks, so that everyone had easy access to the food and equipment they needed to produce dishes faster, to move more customers through the restaurant, and ultimately to increase sales. The changes increased the rate at which tables were turned by 10 percent, which in turn decreased wait times for customers.[a]

[a] Meredith Levinson, "The Brain Behind the Big, Bad Burger and Other Tales of Business Intelligence," *CIO Magazine*, March 15, 2005, www.cio.com/archive/031505/intelligence .html.

value? Second, which strategy is most likely to create the greatest value? Third, for the selected strategy, how sensitive is the value of the most likely scenario to potential shifts in competitive dynamics and assumptions about technology life cycles, the regulatory environment, and other relevant variables?[9]

✓ **Educate managers in value driver analysis.** The more managers who understand KVDs and their potential impact on the business, the better the company is placed to drive performance improvement. This role is key for finance.

✓ **Identify and eliminate key drivers that *destroy* value.** Many drivers add cost but no value, and need to be exposed and eliminated. For example, in one organization, managers thought that sales growth was a KVD, but when they tested it within the valuation model, they found that increasing sales actually *reduced value*. The company was not earning its cost of capital, so as sales increased, profits increased, but not enough to cover the cost of capital on the additional asset investments. Thus, for every dollar increase in sales, the firm's value was lowered. Only if margins increased above a particular threshold would value have increased.

Conclusions

Managing earnings is an obsession with many CEOs who are continuously under the spotlight of the investment community. They constantly tamper with the business by raising or cutting discretionary expenditures, such as R&D, marketing, and improvement initiatives, to meet investors' expectations. The fixation with meeting budgets and managing earnings makes it difficult to focus on KVDs. Maximizing free cash flows is the name of the game.

FURTHER READING

Martin, John D., and J. William Petty. *Value Based Management: The Corporate Response to the Shareholder Revolution*. Boston: Harvard Business School Press, 2000.

Rappaport, Alfred. "Ten Ways to Create Shareholder Value." *Harvard Business Review*, September 2006, 66–77.

13

REVENUE GROWTH ANALYSIS

What is this practice and how effective is it?

Revenue growth analysis enables managers to understand where their past growth has come from and thus places them in a better position to make the right growth-based decisions. While many organizations have been adept at cutting costs, few are equally good at growing revenues. As sales and marketing people focus on negotiating sales targets based on a range of products and services, there is less understanding of where revenue comes from. Is it existing customers, new customers, adjacent markets, new markets, and so forth? We will examine how to do this analysis and how to use it to improve revenue growth.

Alternative names and related topics: revenue driver analysis; sources of revenue statement; double-digit growth analysis

When asked how the income statement and balance sheet for a company driven by organic growth look different from the financials for a company that grows mainly through productivity and acquisition, GE's CEO Jeff Immelt replied, "Higher revenue, of course—and in our case, more of it global, because the market's more global."[1] He went on to say that, "every initiative needs a metric. To find the right one, we studied about 30 companies. We looked at the percentage of sales attributable to products introduced in the past three years and maybe 15 other things like that . . . We finally came up with organic revenue growth as the only output function that goes straight into the ledger. We believe that we can grow faster than world GDP . . . It's good to have aspirational goals in a company like GE."[2] Immelt made another key point: "If we can create a sales and marketing function that's as good as finance at GE, I'll change this company."[3]

As Immelt is aware, it is impossible to know if your innovation strategies—or any other for that matter—are working if you haven't a clue what's happening to your sales growth. Over the past few decades, many firms have produced acceptable levels of revenue growth based on expanding products and have been paying little attention to the top line, with the result that the growth in revenues has far exceeded the growth in earnings. Many executive teams have forgotten how to grow profitably, but this doesn't stop them from pursuing growth strategies *unprofitably*. There are many ways to achieve unprofitable growth, including engaging in price wars, overpaying for acquisitions, and buying customers.

The reality is that most firms simply monitor sales against agreed-on targets and budgets. But because sales analysis is usually done by product line, geographic market, or internal business segment, there is no way of knowing if you are growing faster, slower, or in line with the market; whether you are losing too many customers; or whether you are successfully entering new areas of business or new markets. In other words, while most firms analyze costs to three decimal points, they have no useful information on sales growth. "You should know how much revenue is coming just for showing up," says Adrian Slywotsky, vice president at Mercer Management Consulting and coauthor of *How to Grow When Markets Don't*.[4] He explains that companies that don't understand their revenue growth is coming only from market expansion can be lulled into complacency. And once their market matures and growth slows, they're left unprepared. This missing data provides vital clues about the health of the business, including sales growth and gross margins. In an IBM survey, better information about customer management was at the top of the CFO wish list.[5]

Author Michael Treacy believes that the revenue growth plan needs to be built around five possible sources of revenue (see "Using a More Analytical Approach"). The question he asks is, "What are we going to do to drive improved performance in each of these five areas?" The basic method of compiling a sources-of-revenue-statement (SRS) is fairly straightforward; most of the information needed is readily available. But the effort does require two estimates: an accurate measure of how fast the market is growing, and customer churn rates. To produce a SRS, five steps are required in addition to establishing total revenues for comparable periods.[6]

1. Determine revenue from the core business by establishing the revenue gain or loss from entry to or exit from adjacent markets and the revenue gain from new lines of business, and subtracting this from total revenue. (In table 13-1, 185.4 − 4.6 − 7.5 = 173.3.)

Using a more analytical approach

An increasing number of companies are taking a more analytical approach and beginning to learn more about revenue growth. With the right discipline and analysis, they believe that growing revenues can be as straightforward as cutting costs. Michael Treacy, author of *Double-Digit Growth*, has developed a "sources-of-revenue statement" (SRS) that is helping firms come to grips with these problems. According to Treacy, there are five possible ways to grow:[a]

1. Continuing sales to established customers (known as base retention). Reducing customer churn will increase your growth rate.
2. Sales won from the competition (share gain). The second way to grow is the first thing people think about, and it's the hardest to achieve: to grow market share. To do so, not only do you have to win, but somebody else has to lose, and most people, most companies, and most competitors don't enjoy that experience.
3. New sales from expanding markets. The third way to grow is actually the easiest: market positioning. Simply move into markets that are growing, and let your boats float along with everybody else's.
4. Movement into adjacent markets where core capabilities can be leveraged. The majority of these efforts fail, usually because the analysis of whether the company really had an immediate practical advantage was done poorly.
5. Entirely new lines of business unrelated to the core. The fifth source of revenue, the one that Treacy advises the majority of firms to forget about (although you see a small number of firms succeed this way), is simply to grow in new and unrelated marketplaces and businesses.

[a] From Joseph McCafferty, "Testing the Top Line," *CFO Magazine*, October 2004; and Michael Treacy, *Double-Digit Growth: How Great Companies Achieve It—No Matter What* (New York: Penguin 2003).

2. Determine growth attributable to market positioning by estimating the market growth rate for the current period and multiplying this by the prior period's core revenue (in table 13-1, 10-0).
3. Determine the revenue not attributable to market growth by subtracting the amount determined in step two from that determined in step one (173.4 − 10.0 = 163.4).

4. To calculate base retention revenue, estimate the customer churn rate, multiply it by the prior period's core revenue, and deduct this from the prior period's core revenue (172.6 − 28.5 = 144.1).

5. To determine revenue from market-share gain, subtract retention revenue, growth attributable to market positioning, and growth from new lines of business and from adjacent markets from core revenue (163.3 − 144.1 = 19.2).

Using the SRS model to look more deeply into the performance of business units can be a powerful tool for understanding growth. The example in table 13-1, according to Treacy and Jim Sims, suggests that "this company appears to be losing customers in a slow-growing (5.8%) market. But that is an oversimplification that masks different challenges for each of its divisions. Division 3 for instance is failing to take advantage of a fast-growing (18.7%) market whereas Division 1 is growing faster than its market by holding on to much of its customer base and making successful forays into adjacent markets."[7]

Treacy and Sims believe that the extra work involved in producing these estimates is worth it. When companies look at the amount of revenue coming from each source, and the changes in each, they can spot opportunities or weaknesses and allocate resources more effectively. "It really becomes powerful when you get down to the business-unit level," they say.

Discounts are a potential black hole in the calculation of revenue growth. Jeff Immelt was amazed when he discovered how much discretion GE salespeople had in pricing. "Not long ago," he noted, "a guy here named Dave McCalpin did an analysis of our pricing in appliances and found out that about $5 billion of it is discretionary. Given all the decisions that sales reps can make on their own, that's how much is in play. It was the most astounding number I'd ever heard—and that's just in appliances. Extrapolating across our businesses, there may be $50 billion that few people are tracking or accountable for. We would never allow something like that on the cost side. When it comes to the prices we pay, we study them, we map them, we work them. But with the prices we charge, we're too sloppy."[8]

A recent study within the software industry—though few respondents had any hard historical data—guesstimated that negotiated discounts equaled 25 percent of booked revenue, on average, and often exceeded 50 percent. If figures this large were to appear on a P&L statement, they would be subject to detailed analysis and executive-level control.[9]

One of the more obvious ways that profit drains away comes from the different ways that the same customer can obtain discounts that are never brought together in one place inside the accounting system. Table 13-2 shows an invoice that starts with a dealer list price of $100. It then shows how extra

TABLE 13-1

SRS statements

	Total company		Division 1		Division 2		Division 3		Division 4	
	$million	Percent	$million	Percent	$million	Percent	$million	Percent	$million	Percent
Prior year revenue (A)	172.6		41.3		52.1		62.4		16.8	
Revenue lost to churn (B)	(28.5)	−16.5	(0.8)	−1.9	(6.3)	−12.1	(18.0)	−28.8	(3.4)	−20.2
Base retention revenue (C)	144.1	83.5	40.5	98.1	45.8	87.9	44.4	71.2	13.4	79.8
Gross share gain (D)	19.2	11.1	2.4	5.8	10.9	20.9	2.7	4.3	3.2	19.0
Market positioning revenue (E)	10.0	5.8	4.3	10.4	(6.3)	−12.1	11.7	18.7	0.3	1.8
Adjacent market revenue (F)	7.5	4.3	1.5	3.6	0.0	0.0	6.0	9.6	0.0	0.0
New line of business (G)	4.6	2.7	0.0	0.0	0.0	0.0	0.0	0.0	0.0	0.0
Current year revenue (H)	185.4	107.4	48.7	117.9	50.4	96.7	64.8	103.8	16.9	100.6

Note: $H = C + D + E + F + G$
$C = A - B$

Using an SRS at Alcoa

Alcoa is one organization that has taken Michael Treacy's ideas seriously and is reaping the rewards. "The idea is to bring the same systematic analysis to growing revenue that we have brought to cost cutting," says Franklin Feder, vice president of analysis and planning at Alcoa Inc. Alcoa is deploying Treacy's model within all of its thirty business units. The move is the latest in a program started in 2001 to focus on profitable organic growth. "We have always been obsessed with cutting costs," says Feder. "Now we are trying to bring that same discipline to growing revenue." Its new revenue discipline starts with a look at year-over-year growth in the five categories for each business unit. While estimates of market growth and churn rates are readily available for some units, the figures for others require a combination of internal and outside research. Feder says that the statements are generated by a team made up of marketing and finance personnel working at the business-unit level, and that some unit managers now use the information on a quarterly basis.

However, Alcoa's approach doesn't end there, as the company is applying its SRS not only to revenue but also to margins. "It's not enough to simply grow revenue organically—we want to grow where we are most profitable," says Feder. To do that, the company leverages the work it has done in activity-based costing, which enables it to allocate costs and revenues to different market and customer types. Although Alcoa's program is still in its infancy, Feder says the company already has a better idea of its true sources of growth, and business managers can make better decisions about where to allocate resources. The company hasn't yet decided to tie the model to compensation, which would be the logical next step.[a]

[a] Joseph McCafferty, "Testing the Top Line," *CFO Magazine*, October 2004.

discounts gradually decrease the value of the invoice until it settles down at $75—a massive 25 percent reduction that may be invisible to everyone.

Some of these discounts are agreed on with salespeople, some with marketing, and some with the accounts receivable team. But the point is that they are often posted to separate general ledger accounts and never appear in a customer profitability statement. If you have also given a reduced price to clear some older products or for any other reason, it is easy to see how any sale can slip quickly into the red zone. Of course, some of the discounts depend on

TABLE 13-2

Car dealer's invoice

Dealer list price		$100.00
Order size discount	1.50	
Competitive discount	1.00	
Invoice price		**$97.50**
Payment terms discount	5.00	
Annual volume bonus	6.00	
Cooperative advertising	3.50	
Special promotions	8.00	
Net price		**$75.00**

volume, which reminds us of the old saying, "We might lose money on this transaction, but we'll make it up on volume."

At Nucor Steel, the price that you see is the price that you get. Former CEO Ken Iverson explains his philosophy on pricing:

> Nucor publishes its prices, like everyone else in the steel industry. But *un*like most everyone else, the prices we publish for our steel products are the prices we charge. To everyone. No special discounts. No exceptions. Why is this important? Over the years, we've heard from dozens of customers who've told us that discounting had a negative effect on their business. For example, the manager of a service center (a steel distributorship) in Iowa told me that he got burned when he bought a large order of steel from a big producer, paying a sum close to the published price. A week later, the same steel maker sold a large order of the same product—at a very steep discount—to a steel broker who competed with the service center ... By not offering discounts, Nucor treats all customers equally. We give them a level playing field. And we make dealing with us about as simple as a business transaction can be.[10]

While analyzing revenue growth involves a few estimates, it seems worth the effort. Knowing where your sales growth is coming from (or not) is an important step in knowing how to stimulate new growth. It also enables managers to think more constructively about the key growth issues instead of wasting their time negotiating budgets.

What is the performance potential of this practice?

- **To drive sales growth.** Knowing your history of sales growth places you in a better position to focus on how to increase it.
- **To diversify the portfolio.** Looking at a wider set of growth options enables managers to consider how to diversify their offerings and attack other markets.
- **To align rewards with real growth.** Aligning sales incentives with organic growth is a key part of driving growth in the business.

What actions do you need to take to maximize the potential of this practice?

ACTIONS TO AVOID

- ✖ **Stop compensating salespeople for market growth and start compensating them for growing market share.** Treacy and Sims envision a time when companies spend as much time analyzing revenue as they do costs, and when revenue accounting focuses on more than when revenue is recognized. "It's not going to happen overnight. After all, cost accounting has a 100-year head start," they say. "It's convenient to blame the market when things don't go well," they add, "but it's not fair. Revenue growth is controllable."[11]

- ✖ **Be wary of deep discounts, and understand how much they are costing you.** Authors Jim Geisman and John Maruskin suggest that leaders ask themselves these questions: "Are discount dollars being invested in the customer segments and product categories that provide the greatest strategic value to the company? Do discount levels associated with a particular customer segment or product category vary widely, beyond what can be attributed to differences in deal size? Are discounts fairly consistent over time, or do they rise sharply at the end of the quarter? Is excessive discounting a widespread, relatively uniform problem in the company?"[12] Perhaps the best approach is to follow the Nucor Steel's philosophy and stick to the published price list. While some deals might be lost, the upside of keeping a level playing field as well as providing excellent services will probably outweigh any downside.

ACTIONS TO TAKE

- ✓ **Start looking at the business through a growth portfolio lens.** Most management teams don't know their growth history, so measure performance for the past five years in each of the growth perspectives and set stretch goals for each one.[13]

✓ **Use your knowledge to build plans that focus on key areas of growth.** Teams should take the right actions to achieve their growth goals by researching the market opportunities and evaluating what it takes to stretch their performance.

✓ **Spread the risk.** Rather than putting all your eggs in one growth-scenario basket, such as a few large initiatives, it makes sense to try a number of different ideas, thus spreading the risk.

✓ **Expand growth capabilities.** Management capacity rather than market demand is often the primary constraint on growth. You may need to build operating capacity before you can achieve all your growth ambitions.

✓ **Prepare an SRS.** Treacy's methodology is well thought-out but tricky to prepare in practice. Nevertheless, it will provide valuable insights into which divisions and products are providing growth and which aren't. It will also provide a platform for managers to think about their future growth strategies.

✓ **Make growth through innovation your top priority.** Tell key managers that they are accountable for growth. It must be one of their top priorities. Trying to innovate without knowing where you are today is not the best place to start the growth journey. Knowing your current sales growth performance is the key step in applying your creative ideas to the growth process.

✓ **Think about how to grow within existing customers and products.** According to Slywotsky, "a few smart companies have figured out how to create new growth with the same product and the same customer. Instead of investing in an improved product or finding new customers, they address the issues and hassles that surround their product. We call this 'demand innovation.' For example, a few years ago, GM introduced OnStar, a vehicle communications service that now brings GM around $1 billion annually in high-margin subscription revenue. Instead of introducing a car that served a different customer, GM created a platform for new growth that surrounded its existing products and served an unmet need of its established customers. There are many other examples. Installation, maintenance, financing, training, or outsourcing can all serve unmet needs of your established customer and create a platform for new growth."[14]

Conclusions

Most of the ideas in this section come from Treacy's book, *Double-Digit Growth*, that just about encapsulates what the aim of every customer-facing team should be aiming for every year. Treacy offers this thought: "the economy, though important, is but a small factor in the growth potential of any company. Competition, though fierce, can be outfought and outflanked. Customers, though demanding, want to grow with value-creating suppliers."[15] Treacy's ideas are compelling and deserve your attention.

FURTHER READING

Slywotzky, Adrian, Richard Wise, and Karl Weber. *How to Grow When Markets Don't: Discovering the New Drivers of Growth*. New York: Warner Books, 2003.

Treacy, Michael. *Double-Digit Growth: How Great Companies Achieve It—No Matter What*. New York: Penguin, 2003.

Treacy, Michael, and Jim Sims. "Take Command of Your Growth." *Harvard Business Review*, April 2004, 127–133.

14

CUSTOMER VALUE PROPOSITION

What is this practice and how effective is it?

Customer value propositions help leaders decide which strategic position to take. There are three classic value propositions: product leadership, operational excellence, and customer intimacy. Companies need to focus on one of these and ensure that their processes and metrics underpin them. But few firms do this well, leading to strategic confusion and poorly aligned processes. We will look at how the best organizations have clearly defined value propositions and how they use them to beat the competition.

Alternative names and related topics: market strategy; customer value analysis; market segmentation

Michael Porter's work focused on two basic strategic positions: low cost and differentiation. Both were based on *product or service economics*. However, in recent years, the economic focus has moved toward the customer, thus recognizing a new strategic position—customer intimacy—a strategic position that focuses on *customer economics*.[1] One way to think of these three strategic positions is in terms of the *customer value proposition*. The three classic value propositions are *product leadership* (best product), *operational excellence* (lowest-cost product), and *customer intimacy* (best customer solution). Every strategic position looks for ways of bonding with the customer, thus making it costly or difficult for the customer to switch to other products, services, or suppliers. Determining your core value proposition is not easy. Most senior managers like to think their company is good at every one of them. However, while this might be true, the theory goes that you need to be *exceptionally* good at one of them, and it is this one that distinguishes you from the competition.

How do you define customer value?

Michael Treacy and Fred Wiersema define customer value as "the sum of benefits received minus the costs incurred by the customer in acquiring a product or service. Benefits build value to the extent that the product or service improves the customer's performance or experience. Costs include both the money spent on the purchase and maintenance as well as the time spent on delays, errors and effort. Both tangible and intangible costs reduce value." They also note that price, product quality, product features, service convenience, service reliability, expert advice, and support services can either create or destroy value for the customer. The value added or destroyed depends on how much the value exceeds or falls short of customer expectations.[a]

[a] Michael Treacy and Fred Wiersema, *The Discipline of Market Leaders* (London: HarperCollins Publishers, 1995), 19–20.

Table 14-1 shows the three classic customer value propositions and how companies need to excel at particular components of customer value (price, quality, time, functionality, service, customization, and image). But this does not mean they can relax in other areas. They must at least meet industry standards.

Product leadership companies compete primarily on *innovation and speed.* Thus, their main objective is to produce innovative products and services and bring them to market faster than the competition. Customers expect the latest, state-of-the-art products and feel-good brands. The business model is based on conceiving attractive new products and services and commercializing them as rapidly as possible. The shorter the cycle, the less time is available for profitable sales and, thus, the fewer funds for further development. The only way to win is to be first to market and so get the maximum length of time to reap the returns on investment. All later entrants inevitably must compete on price. Product leaders achieve a number of benefits. For example, they have the opportunity to set industry standards. Their key operating processes include R&D, commercializing products and services, marketing, and brand management. Their typical key performance indicators (KPIs) include top-line growth, market share by brand, time to market, percentage of sales from new products introduced in last three years, talent recruitment, and number of patents filed. Exemplars include innovation-driven companies such as 3M, Apple, and Samsung and feel-good brand companies such as Versace and Goldman Sachs.

TABLE 14-1

Three classic customer value propositions

Components of value proposition	Product leadership	Operational excellence	Customer intimacy
Price	Meet industry standard	**Combination of price, quality, and ease of purchase**	Meet industry standard
Quality	Meet industry standard		Meet industry standard
Time	**State-of-the-art products and services**	Meet industry standard	Meet industry standard
Functionality		Meet industry standard	Meet industry standard
Service	Meet industry standard	Meet industry standard	**Customized products and personal service**
Customization	Meet industry standard	Meet industry standard	
Image	**Feel-good brand**	**Smart shopper**	**Trusted partner**

Operational excellence companies compete on the basis of *low cost and high quality*. Thus, their primary objective is to have lean processes and make products right the first time. Customers look to buy products and services on the basis of good value, high quality, and ease of purchase. They demand high quality, but they are not prepared to pay premium prices or go out of their way to make a purchase. These companies have high fixed costs; they need to make large volumes essential to achieving low unit costs. To achieve this, they must develop competence platforms that include effective management of the supply chain and high levels of efficiency in managing inventories and logistics, but above all, suppliers must ensure that their operating processes are fast, efficient, and lean. Most exponents of operational excellence have one primary objective in mind: *keep operations simple*. Key operating processes include supply chain management, production, distribution, and service. KPIs include working capital turnover, product market share, quality, productivity, process cycle times, customer satisfaction, and product profitability. Exemplars include Walmart, Tesco, McDonald's, UPS, and Toyota.

Customer intimacy companies compete on the basis of *customer service and relationships*. Their objective is to acquire the right customers, keep them forever, and provide as many related products and services to them as possible. Customers are interested in getting exactly what they want, even if they have to pay a higher price or wait a bit longer to get it. Such customers buy from suppliers that they can identify with their own special needs. Thus, Handelsbanken provides customized pension policies, and Southwest Airlines caters to people who want to fly from point to point at convenient times and at low prices. Customers see these companies as being responsive to their needs, and they repay this responsiveness with loyalty. Key processes include customer knowledge management, solutions development, and service and support. KPIs include market share by customer, customer retention, customer complaints, employee satisfaction, new customer acquisitions or defections, customer profitability, and profit per employee. Exemplars include Whole Foods, Handelsbanken, and Southwest Airlines.

Although the three operating models bear similarities, each one is constructed to meet the needs of its (different) target customers. Porter notes that cost is generated by performing *activities* (steps within the value chain) and that cost advantage arises from performing particular activities more efficiently than competitors. Performance of activities, then, constitutes the basic ingredients of competitive advantage.[2] The particular value proposition dictates which activities should be undertaken, and the operating model should be designed to ensure that they are performed effectively.

Well-thought-out value propositions can last for a number of years, sometimes for decades. But a fast-changing economy carries many new traps for the unsuspecting high flier. Which killer business model is just around the corner in your industry? Strong core competencies and improving operating models are the best protection, but managers cannot afford to lower their guard.

What is the performance potential of this practice?

- **To clearly articulate and communicate how your business will compete.** This means that each part of the organization knows what part it has to play in achieving its strategic goals.
- **To align processes, measures, actions, and rewards with strategy.** The core value proposition enables the organization to align its processes, measures, actions, and rewards with its strategy and thus ensure that every team is on the same page at the same time.

What actions do you need to take to maximize the potential of this practice?

ACTIONS TO AVOID

✖ **Don't assume that everyone knows or agrees on what your value proposition is.** Our experience is that when executive teams sit around a table to discuss and agree on their core value proposition, they rarely agree. This confusion will be reflected in conflicting strategies and operating processes. So, gather together and hammer out an agreement and then align key processes with the chosen proposition.

✖ **Don't assume that the same value proposition applies to every business.** In a multibusiness organization, different value propositions can apply to different businesses.

ACTIONS TO TAKE

✓ **Define your core value proposition.** Seeing the business through the eyes of the customer helps to position the company's products and services and thus focus on how to create and deliver exceptional customer value. Examine the specific dimensions of value that you must excel at and agree on action plans that will enable you to compete successfully on your chosen dimensions. While the firm must meet industry standards in other elements of value delivery, the chosen value proposition is the one where competencies and performance must be exceptional and thus enable you to distinguish yourself from the competition. You must engage the senior executive team in this dialogue. Most teams fail to agree on their core value proposition, resulting in confusion further down the hierarchy.

✓ **Align operating processes.** Just agreeing on your value proposition is insufficient. The whole company must be aligned with it. This includes operating processes, measures, and rewards.

✓ **Meet threshold standards in the other dimensions of value.** Remember that your chosen value proposition means you have to be world class or much better than your competitors (regularly number one or two in your peer group), but that you cannot relax in the other dimensions of value. You must at least maintain the average of your peers.

✓ **Dominate your market by improving value year after year.** Once you have chosen your core value proposition, you need to go on to dominate your market. This means relentless continuous improvement at your chosen competencies and processes. You need to continuously benchmark against your peers to ensure that you maintain your leadership position.

✓ **Evolve the model continually.** Every market leader is a target for imitation and is vulnerable to imaginative competitors willing to challenge the existing rules of the industry. Competencies and operating models must be constantly improved, even if this means denying easy short-term profits. How many companies would introduce new products long before existing profitable products have reached their "sell by" date? Apple, Samsung, and Canon do this regularly. They compete with themselves to stay alive. Too many companies spend the valuable time of their best people supporting yesterday's products and starving tomorrow's opportunities of essential resources.

Conclusions

Despite the appeal of the core value proposition, leaders need to be aware that strategy is not formulated in a vacuum, nor is it the result of some clever computer model that simulates all possible outcomes. It is rooted in experience and assumptions, usually forged in the first flush of sustained managerial success and then laid down in procedures, systems, and working practices. But at some future point, these accepted practices become out of kilter with the external environment. The story is familiar. Companies such as GM, IBM, and Sears developed a finely tuned synthesis between their competencies and their customers—a strong and watertight synthesis that survived for two or three generations (including a depression and a world war)—only to see it ruptured when fundamental assumptions about managerial philosophies, lines of authority, and measures and rewards were suddenly found wanting, as new competitors and emerging technologies changed the rules. Not only do competencies turn to rigidities, but the whole philosophy of business is unhinged as new realities place their very survival at risk. Fortunately, these particular organizations were strong enough to survive the shock and withstand the painful period of reconstruction, a process that can take a whole generation, with no guarantee of final success. Alas, business history is littered with the bones of those that never made it.

FURTHER READING

Hope, Jeremy, and Tony Hope. *Competing in the Third Wave: The Ten Key Management Issues of the Information Age.* Boston: Harvard Business School Press, 1997.

Porter, Michael E. "What Is Strategy?" *Harvard Business Review,* November–December 1996, 61–78.

Reichheld, Frederick F., with Thomas Teal. *The Loyalty Effect: The Hidden Force Behind Growth, Profits, and Lasting Value.* Boston: Harvard Business School Press, 1996.

Reichheld, Frederick F. *Loyalty Rules! How Leaders Build Lasting Relationships in the Digital Age.* Boston: Harvard Business School Press, 2001.

Treacy, Michael, and Fred Wiersema. *The Discipline of Market Leaders.* London: HarperCollins Publishers, 1995.

15

CUSTOMER RELATIONSHIP MANAGEMENT

What is this practice and how effective is it?

Customer relationship management (CRM) models aim to more clearly identify what companies need to do not just to satisfy customers but also to build their loyalty and profitability. A whole software industry has risen from nowhere to grab a slice of this market. But it has failed to understand a crucial point. Companies need to make customers want to do business with them instead of trying to sell them products and services they don't want to buy. That's why the vast majority of CRM systems never recover the costs they absorb. We will look at how you can use CRM systems to support strategy rather than just act as a more sophisticated sales tool.

Alternative names and related topics: customer segmentation; customer value proposition; customer service

When presented with the choice of which customer value proposition is "core to the company" (product leadership, operational excellence, or customer intimacy), in our experience, most leaders choose customer intimacy or customer relationship management. They all like to believe that they are excellent at building customer relationships, that this is *the* primary goal of the firm. This belief has led to an explosion in CRM systems over the past fifteen years. Banks, utilities, telecoms, major retailers, and government agencies have all made huge investments in these systems and, in many cases, built call or service centers around them, often located in low-cost countries.

But for most buyers of these systems, the appeal is being able to standardize the sales or service process and improve their ability to make contact with many more customers, more often, and at the lowest cost. Building relationships is of course the aim, but when it comes to implementation and operation of these systems, it slips down the pecking order. In 1960, Theodore Levitt, in his brilliant article, "Marketing Myopia," noted how important relationships truly are. He believed that an organization must learn to think of itself not as producing goods and services but as buying customers, as doing the things that will *make people want to do business with it.*[1] Most organizations fifty years later still fail to understand this point. They continue to try to persuade the customer to buy what the company decides to make and sell. Likewise, most applications of CRM systems fail to heed his words. They are more refined versions of "make and sell."

This tells us that few managers understand what CRM as strategy really means. According to authors Michael Treacy and Fred Wiersema, companies that adopt such a strategy build bonds with customers similar to those between good neighbors. They don't deliver what the market wants but what a specific customer wants. They make it their business to know the people they sell to and the products and services they need. Their value proposition is: "We take care of you and all your needs" or "We get you the best total solution." Their greatest asset becomes the loyalty of their customers.[2]

Many leaders also recognize that they cannot succeed without the total commitment of their workforce. In other words, the bonds between supplier and customer are, more often than not, bonds between *employees* and customers. In companies that are truly customer oriented, management has designed or redesigned the business to support a number of key processes, including solution development and specialist advice and support.

Despite these important points about "CRM as strategy," most managers see CRM as an *IT system* that enables a better sales and/or support process. It was the potential to codify and improve the sales process and track customer behavior that led to the explosion in the sales of CRM software packages in the late 1990s. CRM systems are usually the province of the marketing or sales department that designs them to gather huge amounts of information about customer behavior and then direct their frontline people to promote one product or another, according to previous buying patterns or lifestyle profiles.

The trouble with most CRM systems is that they treat customers as data, not as real people. Call centers, for example, are notorious for employing low-skilled employees (with high staff turnover rates) who make customers feel undervalued or even badly let down by their supplier.

The success rate of CRM systems has been patchy to say the least. Several surveys note that around half fail to provide an adequate return on investment.[3]

This is a huge failure, given that large organizations can spend tens of millions of dollars implementing them. One reason for this level of dissatisfaction is that managers think they are buying a CRM solution from an IT vendor, but they haven't carefully defined their business case. Few organizations have identified the fundamental problem—a misalignment between inside-out planning and sales processes and outside-in CRM strategies.

"Too many companies forget there's a 'C' in 'CRM,'" says Tom Connellan, consultant and best-selling author of *Inside the Magic Kingdom*, which describes how Disney creates great customer experiences. He also tells a story about one of his clients, a major Midwestern insurance firm, that decided it would respond to all customer applications within twenty-four hours, instead of the usual seventy-two hours. But its field agents balked, saying it would take them at least forty-eight hours to pull together the supporting information for each applicant. Connellan suggested the company run the idea by twenty or thirty of its most loyal customers and gauge their response. "Their response was, 'So what?'" Connellan says. "The difference between twenty-four and forty-eight hours mattered not one whit." He says that "involving top customers in what the CRM system should deliver can help companies define their CRM goals and strengthen their customer relationships."[4]

A true CRM model involves a commitment to a strategy supported by well-designed processes, improvement goals, measures, and actions that support that strategy. It rejects the plan-make-and-sell model that remains at the core of most performance management systems. But few organizations are prepared to abandon this "company first" planning process, which remains the difference between value-adding CRM systems and those that just provide better customer information.

What is the performance potential of this practice?

- **To build long-term customer relationships.** In many organizations, the sales force has targets to reach and thus sees customers as sales objects—a means of reaching those targets. This leads to a culture of special deals as the quarter- and year-ends loom. CRM is a strategy for building loyal and profitable customers (i.e., those that return again and again to repurchase).
- **To provide frontline teams with a full picture of the customer relationship so that an intelligent dialogue can take place.** Well-designed CRM systems enable frontline people to see a snapshot of all recent interactions, which puts them in a position to have an intelligent, personalized dialogue.
- **To increase profitable sales.** In most organizations, sales growth comes from marketing and product promotions. Good customer relationships are a bonus. CRM companies believe that focusing on customer loyalty is the best way to grow profitable sales. Loyal customers incur

---

The flawed logic in CRM systems

Consultant Mark Graham Brown believes that the flawed logic in CRM programs is that it presumes you can engineer a relationship with a customer with as much precision as you can design the products and services you sell. This is simply not the case. "Selling is 40 percent science and 60 percent art," says Brown. "Yet many CRM programs focus on following the same series of behaviors with each customer. The most successful salespeople are those who can tailor their approach to each individual customer, which means getting to know them and doing more listening than talking. Using an engineering approach to sales tends to work well only with products that pretty much sell themselves, like fast food or cars."[a]

[a] Mark Graham Brown, *Beyond the Balanced Scorecard* (New York: Productivity Press, 2007), 65.

---

no setting-up costs, nor do they require much marketing. In fact, they are the best form of marketing available. Satisfied customers tell others about their experiences.

What actions do you need to take to maximize the potential of this practice?

ACTIONS TO AVOID

- ✖ **Avoid buying a technology solution.** CRM is more about strategy than technology. While technology can be a powerful enabler, it is just that–an enabling tool. Leaders would be better advised to spend time educating their people on the merits of CRM and explaining the firm's strategy and how it is aligning its core processes to support that strategy. The moment that technology becomes the primary focus, the game is lost, which is why, in so many cases, CRM achieves the opposite of what its sponsors want. It destroys customer loyalty.

- ✖ **Stop using CRM as just a better sales tool.** Many CRM systems are designed to step a salesperson through the stages and actions of the sales cycle. "If only we could capture and 'standardize' the sales process, we could improve our results dramatically," think senior executives. But life is never so simple. The best salespeople don't follow rigid steps. They use their knowledge, guile, and personality as much as they extol the virtues of their company's products. Forcing them into rigid standards will probably stifle their effectiveness.

✖ **Be wary of the impact of sales incentives on customer relationships.** Anyone who has had a visit from an overly aggressive pensions salesperson knows the problem. These people are on commission to sell specific products and set out to prove why you should buy what they recommend and will use any data at their disposal to prove their point. Setting aggressive sales targets and providing incentives for salespeople to meet them is the antithesis of CRM (meeting customers' needs). But it takes much courage to change this business model, perhaps the litmus test of a true transformation to a CRM philosophy.

✖ **Avoid making too many unsolicited calls.** What is the hidden cost of cold calling? Certainly, you are creating zero goodwill and probably a negative relationship value. Perhaps the really difficult question is: do customers really want managing? Our suspicion is that most want to be aware of the choices they have available when they want to buy something, but they don't want their privacy invaded by unsolicited mail and phone calls. The problem underlying this approach is that the company is not thinking or caring about the customer at all. The philosophy of CRM should be about sensing and responding to customer needs. For example, Dell does huge amounts of marketing through advertising and direct mail. It then makes it easy for customers to engage with the company when the customer is ready to do so. Most call or service centers fail the test of excellent customer service.

ACTIONS TO TAKE

✓ **Align CRM with a clear customer strategy.** What is your customer value proposition? Is it product leadership, operational excellence, or customer intimacy? Can you get consensus? (Boards rarely agree.) What does this tell you about your customers' needs and your CRM strategy? And what does it tell you about your operating processes and how they support your core value proposition? Too many CRM systems are implemented without addressing these important questions. How can you design a system without knowing your strategic priorities?

✓ **Redesign sales and support processes from the customer's perspective.** Many CRM systems can make problems worse by focusing on recording, scanning, queuing, batching, counting, routing, and archiving data—each process is prone to errors and rework—instead of rethinking the system from the customer's perspective. The belief is that there is real value from such a rigorous tracking system and that everyone can see the status of each part of the customer transaction. Managers should make every effort to ensure that only clean data enters the system and monitor the performance of the whole process, not just its component tasks to avoid many problems later.

✓ **Clarify who owns the customer.** It is not atypical in large companies to find that all customers are up for grabs; that is, any business unit has the right to fight for a customer's business. Even more common is dual responsibility for large customers where both the global accounts team and the local sales team are trying to maximize sales to the same customer and both are rewarded for doing so. While this approach might inject a strong competitive element into the sales process, it neither fosters good customer relationships nor helps internal coordination. At Handelsbanken, customers are attached to their nearest branch and are owned by the branch, whatever their size. Some large customers find this difficult at first–they want to talk to someone at head office–and not all accept it, but those that do usually build a strong local relationship that invariably leads to long-term profitability.

✓ **Devolve the responsibility for customer relationships to frontline people.** Frontline teams need to be empowered to spend time understanding customer needs and working out how best to respond to them. And given that each customer is attached to a team, the accounting system should be able to post all income and cost transactions to that customer's account, thus building an ongoing picture of customer profitability. This enables frontline staff to make educated business-case decisions concerning particular orders. Enlightened organizations encourage a "can do" and "no blame" culture and empower frontline teams to serve and satisfy customers' needs.

✓ **Segment customers according to need.** Knowing customers' exact needs and then responding to them is the primary goal of CRM. But such a goal is not often included on the agenda of most sales planning meetings. Most companies construct and monitor sales plans by segmenting customers according to product group, size, lifestyle, or some other grouping that reflects ways of selling products or services through segments and channels. This doesn't help when salespeople focus on achieving fixed targets based on revenue, product volume, or gross margin. It is even worse when multiple teams compete for the business of the same customer. In the call-center context, it involves tracking how many calls agents make and how long they spend on them. The problem is that customers don't care about internal targets, incentives, and measures. That is why the annual process of setting them is out of kilter with CRM. The process makes people think in terms of separate activities rather than a seamless system and seduces leaders into believing that coordination and cohesion can be centrally planned and controlled.

✓ **Provide customer contact people with a complete picture of the customer relationship.** Few CRM systems enable frontline staff to see the whole customer picture. According to one study, the average agent needs to access five to ten different legacy systems, which means customers must wait thirty to forty seconds while the agent tracks down relevant data.[5] Well-implemented CRM systems enable staff to make key customer connections (e.g., between customer needs, existing and future products, and customer problems).

✓ **Provide channels to feed customer knowledge back to product designers and customer support managers.** Too few organizations systematically receive feedback from customers on their products and services. And even fewer use this feedback to provide their designers with ideas for improvement. The CRM channel is an ideal medium for recording these ideas, and, without going through a regimented questionnaire, sales and support staff should be encouraged to have this kind of dialogue and record the results.

✓ **Ensure that frontline agents can solve customer problems at the first point of contact.** Walk into almost any call center and the first thing you'll see is a huge electronic billboard flashing statistics such as caller wait time, call-abandonment rate, and average call duration. The message is one of efficiency rather than service. But customers whose needs aren't met won't put up with shoddy service. "If you're not providing a very good service level, customers will call through again, and you'll end up with more call volume because you did not resolve the query the first time," says Michele M. Crocker, vice president of distributor services for Herbalife, a weight-loss, nutrition, and personal care products company. Surprisingly, good service doesn't always mean longer talk times. When Judy Nelson, first vice president of Merrill Lynch Global Private Client Services, instructed the seven hundred–plus agents at the two call centers she manages to focus on solving clients' problems instead of worrying about call duration, customer satisfaction increased, on average, 5 percent to 6 percent. And the average length of calls actually declined approximately 5 percent. "The directive to spend as much time as we need to solve the client's issues made me feel great coming to work for Merrill Lynch because I knew they really cared about the client," says veteran agent Paul Keller.[6]

✓ **Measure end-to-end customer outcomes.** Consider a water utility with a manual of standards that defines excellent performance. Service staff must respond to problems within two working days. There are targets for the time it takes to phone customers, send a surveyor if there's a structural problem, send a plumber to fix the problem, and for performing each activity according to detailed specifications. But the experience of the customer is not on the measurement radar screen. A customer with a leaking drain can suffer interminable delays waiting for this system to take its course while the water meter is ticking and the house is damaged. But measuring each activity allows the company to claim that its standards of service are excellent. Measures should focus on flow (the end-to-end customer delivery cycle), rather than how much of any activity has been completed. The result is that everyone focuses on improving the work by applying their own and other people's knowledge.

✓ **Make service a way of life, not just a business technique.** This imperative is borrowed from Southwest Airlines. CRM should be a *support* system, not the whole process. Great service is personal and therefore, in a large organization, it must be part of the culture. Former Southwest president and COO Colleen Barrett is clear that the company will support just about any employee initiative that improves the satisfaction of customers: "We will never jump on employees for leaning too far toward the customer, but we come down on them hard for not using common sense."[7] She has also said, "We are not an airline with great customer service. We are great customer service organization that happens to be in the airline business."[8] The best salespeople are often those who build *long-term relationships* with customers. They are there when customers return. At Toyota Japan, it is said that the only way to lose your salesperson is to leave the country. How can people in service centers form long-term relationships? People don't have relationships with organizations. They have them with real people.

Conclusions

Few leaders have gotten the message: great service leads to *lower costs*. CRM systems should enable great service and not be used solely as a customer contact database on steroids! CRM is a philosophy rather than a process or IT system. It is also a tough challenge.

FURTHER READING

Cooper, Kenneth Carlton. *The Relational Enterprise: Moving Beyond CRM to Maximize All Your Business Relationships.* New York: AMACOM, 2002.

Day, George S. "Which Way Should You Grow?" *Harvard Business Review*, July–August 2004, 24–26.

Day, George. "Why Some Companies Succeed at CRM (and Many Fail)." Knowledge@ Wharton, January 2003.

Dyche, Jill. *The CRM Handbook: A Business Guide to Customer Relationship Management.* Boston: Addison-Wesley Publishing Company, 2001.

Hope, Jeremy, and Tony Hope. *Competing in the Third Wave: The Ten Key Management Issues of the Information Age.* Boston: Harvard Business School Press, 1997.

Reichheld, Frederick F. *The Loyalty Effect: The Hidden Force Behind Growth, Profits, and Lasting Value.* Boston: Harvard Business School Press, 1996.

Reichheld, Frederick F. *Loyalty Rules! How Leaders Build Lasting Relationships in the Digital Age.* Boston: Harvard Business School Press, 2001.

Rigby, Darrell K., and Dianne Ledingham. "CRM Done Right." *Harvard Business Review,* November 2004, 118–129.

Rigby, Darrell, Frederick F. Reichheld, and Phil Schefter. "Avoid the Four Perils of CRM." *Harvard Business Review,* February 2002, 101–109.

Seddon, John. *Freedom from Command & Control–A Better Way to Make the Work Work.* Buckingham, England: Vanguard Education Limited, 2003.

Shaw, Robert. *Improving Marketing Effectiveness.* London: Economist Book, 1998.

Treacy, Michael, and Fred Wiersema. *The Discipline of Market Leaders.* Reading, MA: Addison-Wesley, 1996.

16

STRATEGIC AND PROFITABLE CUSTOMERS

What is this practice and how effective is it?

Strategic and profitable customers are the ones that every organization wants, but accounting systems are hopeless at telling managers which they are–and there aren't usually many of them. Managers need to systematically evaluate their customers and decide which ones deserve the "satisfaction" dollars and which don't. But few organizations do this well. We will suggest some simple techniques that can add huge amounts of value.

Alternative names and related topics: customer profitability analysis; customer segmentation analysis; strategic customers

Despite the huge sums they spend on CRM systems and other tools, few companies have a clue about which customers to keep, which have untapped potential, which are strategic, which are unprofitable, and which they should abandon. They aim most marketing programs at replacing the 20 percent of customers they expect to lose each year, without any consideration of whether resources would be better spent on keeping customers than attracting the replacements. Authors Frederick Reichheld and W. Earl Sasser Jr., have noted that a 50 percent cut in defections will more than double the average company's growth rate.[1]

According to Robert Kaplan, in virtually every customer profitability study ever done, around 15 to 20 percent of customers generate 100 percent or more of profits. In one insurance company, for example, the most profitable 40 percent of customers generated 130 percent of annual profits; the middle 55 percent of customers broke even, and the least profitable 5 percent of customers incurred losses equal to 30 percent of annual profits.[2]

John Whitney suggests a rough-and-ready evaluation guide for customer evaluation.[3] Just imagine sitting down with a small team of marketing, sales, customer service and support, order processing, credit control, and accounting people. Now imagine you have a list of customers (or groups of similar customers) on the table. The team then goes through the list asking questions about which customers are strategic and significant and which are profitable.

The team starts with questions about strategy. Do customers fit neatly with our core competencies, and thus are we in a better position to serve them than our competitors? If they do not fit the strategy of a particular business unit, can they be switched to others in the group that better meet their needs? This review might also reveal deeper problems. What if we discover that few, if any, customers are aligned with our competencies? Does one customer influence others? Dealing with one customer in a particular area or technology platform can be the gateway to many others–whether a community, territory, a group of companies, or perhaps an economic web. Many other strategic relationship questions spring to mind. Is the customer likely to grow? Can we learn from the customer? Can we follow a particular customer into a new market opportunity? Does the customer have special technology or excellent systems from which we can benefit? Unless you ask these types of questions, customers' underlying importance will remain unrecognized and their potential unexplored. How important is the customer in terms of the percentage of total revenue and gross profit?

Size is also significant. For example, does the customer figure in the top 20 percent? But size is not always correlated with profitability. The warning signs are usually there, if you look close enough. For example, do large revenue-generating customers place onerous demands on sales, production, and management time? Do they place thousands of small one-off orders or demand special promotions and extra stocking arrangements, all of which might offset the benefits of volume purchases? In other words, large customers should be the largest contributors to profits and are not easy to replace. With these customers, it is important to spend time investigating possible improvements in the terms of trading. For example, can you combine multiple small orders in some way to reduce costs or perhaps establish computer links to speed operations and reduce handling costs? Moreover, size may not relate just to the current level of business, but can also signify huge untapped potential. Are we the customer's number-one supplier, or are we low on the list? Acquiring this knowledge provides some guidance as to how you might structure future deals with this customer.

Determining which customers are profitable is not subject to precise analysis. In fact, there is a strong case for also using judgment–supported by financial evidence–to evaluate which customers are profitable. Answering questions such as whether they demand extra free services, special promotions, and discounts; whether customers pay on time; whether they require unusual capital costs such as high stock levels or extended credit; whether their orders are well prepared and right the first time; whether their billing is straightforward or complex; whether they require extra costs for distribution such as small deliveries to multiple sites; and whether in general they are difficult to deal with and demand lots of management time can go a long way toward understanding whether customers are profitable (see table 16-1).

There are real advantages in this type of structured analysis. The marketing manager can directly link her spending with closely targeted customers, the sales manager can educate his sales force in the business case of the specific customer transaction, the accountant can provide meaningful reports on the profitability of worthwhile customers, and the support manager can make intelligent choices about who to support with free services and who to charge.

Since the introduction of time-driven activity-based costing (ABC), customer profitability analysis has become easier to use. Time-driven ABC enables managers to look at the cost of one hour of a team's time–such as a

TABLE 16-1

Customer profitability evaluation guide

Annual revenues from customer or customer group	$xx			
Less: Direct costs (e.g., discounts, rebates, etc.)	($x)			
Less: Cost of goods sold	($x)			
Direct profit from customer (or customer group)	$xx			
Slow pay	High	Medium	Low	N/A
Unusual fixed capital costs	High	Medium	Low	N/A
Complexity of order entry	High	Medium	Low	N/A
Billing complexity	High	Medium	Low	N/A
Distribution complexity	High	Medium	Low	N/A
Customer service complexity	High	Medium	Low	N/A
Senior management time required	High	Medium	Low	N/A
Other costs	High	Medium	Low	N/A

customer service team–and charge any time used to a particular customer. However, there are problems. Why did the team spend that time? Who caused the problem? And if it was caused by something the company didn't do right the first time, why should the customer suffer the cost?

Some organizations also measure the *lifetime profitability* of a customer. Customers can buy once and be worth very little, or they can buy consistently over a lifetime and be worth a fortune. The impact of retention levels on profitability and thus on customer value can be huge. Tom Peters provides the following anecdote to illustrate the long-term effects of customer profitability: "Grocer Stew Leonard got me started on this," says Peters. He then quotes Leonard: "'When I see a frown on a customer's face, I see $50,000 about to walk out the door.' His good customers buy about $100 worth of groceries a week [this quote is from 1987!]. Over ten years, that adds up to roughly $50,000 . . . Average lifetime auto purchases will total about $150,000, not including repair work. Given the remarkably low dealer loyalty of car buyers these days, might it not make a difference if dealers and their employees focused on this big number?"[4]

The impact of retention levels on profitability and thus on customer value is immense. Research has shown that customer profits rise with the length of the trading relationship. The factors are: (1) the *cost of acquiring a customer*, (2) the *base (or gross) profit* from the goods or services provided to the customer, (3) the profit from *increased purchases* arising from the additional spending of satisfied customers, (4) the *reduced operating costs* of serving loyal customers, (5) the profit from transactions with new customers who have been *referred by loyal customers*, and (6) the profit from the *price premium* charged to loyal customers who are less sensitive to price.

How a company acquires customers can also make a difference to profitability. In one study involving three hundred new customers of a bank, 71 percent of respondents felt that the bank had induced them to join, leaving 29 percent who joined of their own free will. A year later, those who had been induced by the bank were half as profitable as those who had joined willingly (and these were 80 percent less likely to defect).[5]

One approach to the question of whether customers (individuals or groups) are worthwhile is to use a customer decision matrix that looks at customers from both strategy, significance, and profitability perspectives (see figure 16-1). This approach, while not rooted in numerical accuracy, has the benefit of being reasonably fast and directs the attention of managers to the right questions. Instead of discussions about market share, market-based promotions, discounts, and other special offers, questions are now being asked about the central issues of strategy and profitability. Each decision point can then address further questions of resource allocation. What action shall we

FIGURE 16-1

Which customers are worthwhile?

Strategic?	Significant?	Profitable?	Customer type	Percent sales	Percent profits	
Yes	Yes	Yes	A	20%	+150%	These are the customers you need to keep at all costs. Pour resources into them.
Yes	Yes	No	B	20%	-20%	Work on the profitability problem through a mix of pricing, service, delivery, etc.
Yes	No	Yes	C	10%	+20%	Consider other channels to reduce costs. If business is low but potential is high, work hard to increase.
Yes	No	No	D	5%	-5%	Being strategic is not enough. Try other ways to improve scale and profits. Otherwise, exit leaving a way back in.
No	Yes	Yes	E	10%	+10%	If customer does not fit your value proposition, don't provide any special attention. If the customer demands special offers, then exit.
No	Yes	No	F	20%	-40%	This is the real test. Size is not enough. Exit fast before your profits are drained even further.
No	No	Yes	G	5%	+5%	Your long-term profits lie with strategic and significant customers. Spin off to a distributor.
No	No	No	H	10%	-20%	These are easy. Just say goodbye.

take based on this analysis? For example, which channels should we expand and contract? Which customer groups are profitable and how can we increase profits in targeted areas? In the search for new customers, the marketing department can benefit from understanding better which potential customers are likely to be worthwhile and which are likely to be a waste of time.

Understanding which customers are strategic and profitable goes to the core of Handelsbanken's strategy. Excellent people providing high-quality services do not want to be wasted on customers that abuse the system or those that demand high discounts and absorb too much management time. The bank uses a crude form of ABC to derive customer and branch profitability. Each year, it produces a set of standard process costs that it applies to various types of customer transactions, such as opening and closing accounts, arranging loans and mortgages, and so forth. Each month, a reconciliation takes place between the notional and actual results.

What is the performance potential of this practice?

- **To determine which customers are worthwhile.** Many customers lose money for the company, but accounting systems can't tell who they are.
- **To help with pricing policy.** Customer segments that are marginally profitable or actually losing money should be candidates for price increases.
- **To know which customers (and segments) to target.** Customer profitability analysis can provide useful data on which customer segments to grow and which to run down.

What actions do you need to take to maximize the potential of this practice?

ACTIONS TO AVOID

✖ **Stop segmenting customers by territory, lifestyle, age, and so on.** Start segmenting customers according to whether they are strategic, significant, or profitable. This will also help you to segment them according to what sort of relationship they require (e.g., strategic support or transaction only).

✖ **Don't rely on gross profits from the accounting system to inform you about customer profitability.** Because accounting systems gather, record, and report costs and profits by function and department, determining exactly which customers are profitable is an effort fraught with problems. The best that most accounting systems can achieve is some measure of gross profitability, but as a general rule, many costs classified as fixed actually vary with customer demands. In fact, some studies show that up to 60 percent of sales value is taken up in customer-driven costs.[6]

✖ **Don't assume that unprofitable customers are bad customers.** If you discover that a high percentage of your customers is unprofitable, this does not mean you should abandon them. The key step is to arrange a meeting and discuss options for reducing transaction costs or other opportunities for improving profitability. Only when you have tried all ideas, should you abandon a strategic but unprofitable customer.

✖ **Don't just focus on recent customer profitability.** The lifetime profit potential of a customer is what's important. But equally be wary of salespeople claiming that all customers are strategic and they will all be profitable tomorrow.

✖ **Stop compensating salespeople for reaching revenue or gross profit targets.** If salespeople are compensated for achieving revenue quotas or gross profit targets, then it stands to reason that they will have no interest in the *net* profitability of customers. They will likely focus on short-term sales opportunities rather than keeping customers for the long term.

ACTIONS TO TAKE

✓ **Set up a customer review team.** Gather together a cross-functional team that has direct contact with customers and challenge it to segment customers and then evaluate whether they are strategic, significant, or profitable. Prepare action plans for each group and for each large customer.

✓ **Look at each customer segment as an opportunity rather than a problem.** The gaming or casino industry is rife with conventional wisdom—spend money on facilities, attract the high-rollers, offer free accommodation, and so on–but when Gary Loveman arrived at Harrah's as CEO, he decided to do some rigorous research. One discovery was that spending money on employee selection and retention, including giving people realistic job previews, enhancing training, and bolstering the quality of frontline supervision, reduced staff turnover and produced more committed employees. Harrah's was able to reduce staff turnover by almost 50 percent as a result. Loveman had reasoned, using academic research on service effectiveness, that more experienced, committed, and better managed employees would improve customer service, which in turn would bolster guest satisfaction and, ultimately, their willingness to return. This attention to employees, plus Harrah's investment in data warehousing and analytics that permitted the company to track and analyze guest behavior, had a far bigger payoff than throwing money at facilities.[7]

✓ **After understanding their true nature, fire bad customers.** "A textbook case of firing bad customers can be found in Larry Selden's book, *Angel Customers and Demon Customers.* Selden explains how companies like Best Buy realized that many of their costs were being generated by relatively few, badly behaved customers. For instance, people who chronically buy and return items generate massive costs in terms of back-office and inventory activity. So Best Buy can now track and discourage this sort of behavior. Clothing retailers have adopted this approach as well. Internet bank ING Direct regularly fires needy customers who make too much use of its telephone service or back-office capabilities. And American Express actually offers a select group of customers a $300 gift card to pay off their balances and shred their cards."[8]

✓ **Monitor lifetime profitability.** Customers can be profitable one year but unprofitable the next, depending on product order mix and other factors. It is important to monitor lifetime profitability and be alert to changes in the profitability curve.

✓ **Monitor discounts.** Discounts can be a hidden cost that can turn what appears to be a profitable customer into an unprofitable one. Too many customers take liberties with discounts, so you should monitor them carefully.

✓ **Focus the majority of "satisfaction" dollars on strategic and profitable customers.** It sounds obvious, but your most important customers should receive the bulk of your satisfaction dollars. In other words, you should build close relationships and be alert to any signs of dissatisfaction. When these signs appear, you must deal with them immediately.

✓ **Look at the "long tail" of marginal and unprofitable customers.** You need to agree on a strategy for how to tackle large individual customers (for example, by taking costs out of the relationship) and groups of smaller customers (for example, by making them Web-only customers or handing them to distributors).

Conclusions

Marketing people need the help of accountants, and accountants must learn how to help marketing people. What use are customers, even the very loyal ones, if they are unprofitable and of marginal strategic value? Accountants can help marketers understand which customers to keep (what level of resources to commit) and give them an idea how much they are adding to or subtracting from the value of customer capital. But you should take care in assessing profitability. Many customers create extra work and unwarranted costs, such as undue demands on management time, credit problems, extra staff training due to high staff turnover, and so on. Many of these costs (e.g., the use of technical people to help with demonstrations or other types of support) are not easy to identify within accounting systems. However, many customers are hassle free. Customer profitability analysis over the right period clarifies the economics of the customer relationship.

FURTHER READING

Hope, Jeremy, and Tony Hope. *Competing in the Third Wave: The Ten Key Management Issues of the Information Age.* Boston: Harvard Business School Press, 1997.

Hope, Tony, and Jeremy Hope. *Transforming the Bottom Line: Managing Performance with the Real Numbers.* Boston: Harvard Business School Press, 1996.

Reichheld, Frederick F. *The Loyalty Effect: The Hidden Force Behind Growth, Profits, and Lasting Value.* Boston: Harvard Business School Press, 1996.

Reichheld, Frederick F. *Loyalty Rules! How Leaders Build Lasting Relationships in the Digital Age.* Boston: Harvard Business School Press, 2001.

Shaw, Robert. *Improving Marketing Effectiveness.* London: Economist Book, 1998.

Treacy, Michael, and Fred Wiersema. *The Discipline of Market Leaders.* Reading, MA: Addison-Wesley, 1995.

Whitney, John O. "Strategic Renewal for Business Units."*Harvard Business Review,* July–August 1996, 84–98.

17

LOYALTY MANAGEMENT

What is this practice and how effective is it?

Loyalty management is the process of managing and measuring customer loyalty and ultimately improving the long-term performance of the business. But loyalty is often confused with satisfaction. Recent research on measuring loyalty offers companies new opportunities to turn loyalty management into a winning formula. But few companies have heard the message or reaped the benefits. We will learn from recent research how firms can focus on loyalty as a key strategic theme.

Alternative names and related topics: service-profit chain; customer aggravation index; customer retention; customer surveys; net promoter score

In the industrial age, owning production and distribution capacity was the primary source of strategic control. Now that control is in knowing how to satisfy customer needs. Loyal customers–those that repurchase again and again–are the ones that every company wants. Their impact on the bottom line can be huge. This comment, by *Fortune* Magazine writer Rahul Jacob, captures the loyalty impact:

> Increase it, and a beneficial flywheel effect kicks in. Powered by repeat sales and referrals, revenue and market share grow. Costs fall because you don't exert excess energy foraging to replace defectors. Loyal customers expect a good price, but they crave value most of all. Rather than becoming an enemy, price then becomes a tool to filter out buyers who'll bolt for a penny. These steady customers are also easier to serve; they understand your modus operandi and make fewer demands on employee time. But when they ask, do come running. The payback? A Bain & Co study

---

The flaws in customer satisfaction surveys

Until 1991, Xerox's goal was to achieve 100 percent of scores in the four or five category (i.e., it was looking at satisfaction scores in isolation). Its subsequent analysis of repurchase behavior (specifically, the repurchase of Xerox products in the ensuing eighteen months) showed that a totally satisfied customer, who had awarded a score of five, was six times more likely to repurchase than was a merely satisfied customer, who had awarded a score of four. The Xerox experience had profound implications. Simply satisfying customers who have choices is not nearly enough to ensure loyalty. What is needed is total satisfaction (a five on a one-to-five scale, and a nine or ten on a one-to-ten scale).[a]

If companies rely exclusively on satisfaction surveys to give them clues to profits, they run a real risk, because to a large extent the surveys may be asking the wrong question. The real question is not whether customers are satisfied with the product or existing level of service. Rather, it is whether the value they receive will keep them loyal. In other words, satisfaction indexes report (necessarily) what customers *say*; profitability comes from what customers *do*. If customers fail to return to repurchase products or reuse services, they are giving the company the thumbs-down signal. They are acting in a way that says the value they receive isn't up to the mark. But in survey after survey, report after report, between 60 percent and 80 percent of all lost customers say they are either satisfied (scale of four) or even very satisfied (scale of five) prior to defection.[b]

[a] James L. Heskett, Thomas O. Jones, Gary W. Loveman, W. Earl Sasser Jr., and Leonard A. Schlesinger, "Putting the Service-Profit Chain to Work," *Harvard Business Review*, March–April 1994, 164–174.

[b] Frederick F. Reichheld, "Learning from Customer Deflections," *Harvard Business Review*, March–April 1996, 56–69.

---

estimates that a decrease in the customer defection rate by 5 percent can boost profits by 25 percent to 95 percent."[1]

Despite the huge sums spent each year on customer satisfaction surveys and audits, knowing how to measure and thus improve loyalty has been, until recently, an inexact science. Customer satisfaction surveys don't even come close. The problem is that customers can be satisfied, but their repurchase levels can be miserably low. The link between satisfaction and repurchase or loyalty can be tenuous and sometimes downright misleading.

According to Frederick Reichheld, loyal relationships are affairs of the analytical and emotional sides of your brain. He explains:

> The analytical side of a customer is interested in the best value, features, quality, price–functionality, in other words. Those are the things you can get pretty well from today's survey. On the other hand, what surveys do terribly is the emotional connection in a relationship–the feeling that a company knows you, values you, listens to you, and shares your values. When you do those surveys, it usually screams out that you know nothing about that customer or their purchase history, and you're giving them a mixed message on whether you listen to them. Although you're asking them to take time to fill out the survey, they never hear back from you about what you're going to do in response to the results. So in and of itself, the survey almost destroys half of the relationship you're trying to build.[2]

Satisfaction surveys in isolation can be an insidious trap and a potentially lethal tool as far as predicting profitability is concerned. Satisfaction in itself is a temporary feeling and very difficult to measure in a meaningful way, which is precisely why companies use such simple–and simplistic–rankings. Nor do retention rates capture the essence of loyalty, though most companies measure and base rewards on them. Though they do correlate with profitability, they fail as predictors of growth. That's because they track defections–the degree to which a bucket is emptying rather than filling up. They are also poor indicators of loyalty in situations where customers are held hostage by high switching costs or other barriers, or where customers naturally outgrow a product because of their age, increased income, or other factors.[3]

Reichheld's research has profound implications for marketers and sales managers. Keeping surveys simple and feeding back fast results is something the marketing industry is not used to. But frontline managers need such results to respond rapidly to customer feedback and improve their performance. Also tying these results to employee recognition and rewards can change management behavior in a positive way.

However, consultant and author Mark Graham Brown is not impressed by Reichheld's net promoter score measure. He prefers a "customer aggravation index," whereby focus groups highlight the particular problems that upset them and then weight the most important factors. For example, late flights are bad, but canceled flights are even worse. Once the list is prepared, a company can monitor and measure it. Finnish paper company Stora Enso reckons that this measure has a high correlation with customer loyalty.[4]

One recent, common approach to customer loyalty has been the loyalty program, often including loyalty cards. But they are rarely fully costed and even more rarely justified. Frequent flyer programs, for example, are

New measures of loyalty

Frederick Reichheld has researched customer loyalty for over two decades. Even he was astounded when one company, Enterprise Rent-A-Car, suggested to him a new way to measure loyalty that actually correlated with growth and profitability. And when he applied these ideas to a whole range of industries, he found a consistent correlation. The first insight was that only one or two questions were needed—bad news for the marketing industry. In fact, most companies need to ask only one question: "How likely is it that you would recommend 'company X' to a friend or colleague?"[a]

But the real breakthrough was in measurement. Using a survey scale from one to ten, Reichheld discovered that the difference between "promoters" (those that scored a nine or ten) and "detractors" (those that scored between zero and six), known as the *"net promoter"* score, had a statistically valid correlation with growth and profitability. No airline, for example, has found a way to increase growth without improving its net-promoter score.

Enterprise Rent-A-Car pays new staff 50 percent more than the competition, yet has the lowest prices in the industry. The secret is the measurement of loyalty and then tying results to recognition and rewards. The company discovered that customers who gave the highest rating to their rental experience were three times more likely to rent again than those who scored the next grade. Though the measurement system cost $4 million to implement, the company reckons the investment is one of the best it's ever made. Tying results to rewards was a key step. Now branch managers are not eligible for promotion unless their performance matches or exceeds the average score.[b]

[a] Frederick F. Reichheld, "The One Number You Need to Grow," *Harvard Business Review*, December 2003, 47–54.

[b] Ibid.

estimated to cost airlines between 3 percent to 6 percent of revenues. Most schemes are "defensive," designed to protect their existing customers, rather than "offensive," designed to attract new customers. All companies are trying to attract the most profitable customers, but these are often the least loyal or the most polygamous in that they utilize multiple programs. In other words, your most profitable customers are also likely to be your competitors' most profitable customers as well. Extensive research shows that only 10 percent of consumers who buy products such as coffee, breakfast cereals, newspapers, aviation fuel, toothpaste, gasoline, television programs, airline tickets, and ethical drugs are 100 percent loyal to a particular brand over a one-year period.[5] The trouble is that so many companies are now locked into loyalty programs that they are on a treadmill of high-cost promotions that have lost their strategic purpose.

Researchers also found that in consumer markets, the most effective way to increase profits is not to pour more resources into trying to get existing customers to buy more, but to get more customers by gaining more distribution outlets. All a customer loyalty program is likely to do is cost more money to provide extra benefits to some customers (most do not care about them). They don't have much impact on brand value.[6]

Other researchers are not so impressed. Michael Treacy, author of *Double-Digit Growth*, notes that the best way to fix base-retention problems is to focus on customer loyalty as a kind of Holy Grail. "Like knights-errant on an endless quest, managers ride on for years, tilting with competitors, enduring endless rejection, in their pursuit of individuals and organizations that will remain faithful," notes Treacy. "These people, the theory goes, have a natural tendency to be loyal; once they are in the fold, they can be kept there by giving them superior value."[7] But Treacy believes the theory is wrong. The quest for loyal customers is largely wasted effort. And the notion that current customers will remain simply because of bolt-on improvements in a company's value proposition is naive.

Treacy goes on to say that if there were ever any customers who would never abandon you for a competitor's product, they are nowhere to be found today. Sentimental loyalty doesn't exist. He also notes that companies that have committed themselves to complicated schemes for customer loyalty management don't have much to show for it. He cites two companies—Lexus and American Airlines—that have invested heavily in loyalty programs without much effect.[8]

Focusing on customer loyalty, as opposed to satisfaction, represents a fundamental rethinking of customer management. And given the huge amounts spent on satisfaction surveys and loyalty programs, managers really need to reconsider whether these are value for the money. The loyalty bonds are often, rather inconveniently, between employees and customers, and more attention should be paid to attracting and developing the right people and keeping them for a longer period of time.

What is the performance potential of this practice?

- To build lasting relationships with the right customers—those that are strategic and profitable—and capture a larger share of their business.

Many customers lose money and only buy from you when their main supplier has a problem. You need to find out who they are and build relationships with those customers you really want to keep.

- **To generate sales growth by increasing the number of referrals from customers and employees.** Customer referrals are the cheapest and most powerful way to attract new customers. And they tend to be the "right" ones.
- **To attract and retain employees whose skills, knowledge, and relationships are essential to superior performance.** Satisfied customers improve employee satisfaction levels in a mutually reinforcing way. This feeds into the employee contact network and attracts their colleagues.
- **To improve long-term financial performance from loyal customers.** Effective loyalty management can be correlated with long-term sustainable growth in profitability.

What actions do you need to take to maximize the potential of this practice?

ACTIONS TO AVOID

- ✖ **Don't leave loyalty management to the marketing department.** Marketing people both inside and outside the organization have a vested interest in the spurious science of customer surveys and the complex algorithms they use to produce results that rarely help managers to make good decisions.
- ✖ **Stop allowing annual targets to undermine loyalty management.** Many firms budget huge sums for acquiring new customers to replace those they expect to lose every year. And even more reward their salespeople for acquiring new customers or meeting financial targets based on sales growth or gross profitability. These incentives can undermine all the good work done elsewhere on loyalty management. Loyalty leaders such as Enterprise Rent-A-Car tie rewards to net promoter scores and compare these scores across the business.
- ✖ **Stop basing sales compensation only on financial targets.** If salespeople are rewarded only for sales and gross profits, they will have no interest in satisfying customers profitably. So start rewarding salespeople for customer satisfaction and loyalty as well as sales and profits.
- ✖ **Be skeptical about loyalty programs.** If you are locked into a loyalty program or thinking of launching one, then design the program to support the product or your company's value proposition. Forget free gifts and other freebies; they are just froth—nice to have but with no lasting effect. (One positive effect might be to get other distributors to stock your products.) Design the program to maximize the buyer's desire to make another purchase. Airlines are good at this: the more you fly with them,

the more benefits you get on the rewards escalator. Fully cost the program; a number of costs are obvious–such as marketing, database management, cost of cards, communication costs, and so on–but many costs aren't (how much management time is taken up? what is the opportunity cost of the whole investment?). Would you be better putting your money into everyday low prices? Companies striving to generate customer loyalty should avoid five common mistakes: Don't create a new commodity, which can result in price wars and other tit-for-tat competitive moves. Don't cater to the disloyal by making rewards easy for just anyone to reap. Don't reward purchasing volume over profitability. Don't give away the store. Finally, don't promise what you can't deliver.[9]

✖ **Question customer satisfaction surveys.** Scrap the traditional customer satisfaction survey with its long list of questions that focus on every aspect of a customer's thinking and behavior. Surveys should be short, easy to complete, and frequent.

ACTIONS TO TAKE

✓ **Ask the right customer satisfaction questions.** Reichheld found only a few questions to be relevant. By far the most important was, "How likely is it that you would recommend 'company X' to a friend or colleague?" In circumstances where this question wasn't relevant (e.g., where suppliers are chosen strategically at a high level, as in the software industry), then a second question is useful, though more abstract than the first: "Does the product or service set the standard of excellence in its industry or deserve your loyalty?"[10]

✓ **Focus on the net promoter score and compare units across the organization.** Reichheld's research focuses on the net promoter score (the difference between the percentage who score a nine or ten and those who score between a zero and six). Monitoring this figure, he believes, will tell leaders a great deal about current and future financial performance and should be one of *the* key performance indicators in the business. It can also be used to drive continuous improvement within frontline units across the organization. These units can be compared against each other to encourage units to strive to be the best and use the motivational power of peer pressure as a spur to improvement.

✓ **Use a scale of one to ten.** The scale is important. Most surveys use one to five, from "very dissatisfied" to "very satisfied." But Reichheld believes that more granularity is necessary to derive the "promoters" (a score of nine or ten) and "detractors" (a score of zero to six).

✓ **Consider using a customer aggravation index.** Mark Graham Brown believes that a customer aggravation index is a better option than a net promoter score. According to Brown, the key is that the data is not gathered via a survey. Instead, focus groups rate and rank the severity of the aggravations to identify the factors that aggravate a customer. Once you have the data, you count the number of times each aggravating event occurs and multiply the frequency by the severity weight.[11]

✓ **Demand fast results–in days, not weeks.** For survey results to be action-able, they need to be taken and translated into useful information within days rather than weeks or months. Only then will managers have the opportunity to contact recent defectors and understand why they have made a decision to buy elsewhere and whether they can change the defectors' minds.

✓ **Analyze defections.** To glean incisive information from defectors is not easy. Unless obtained by someone with knowledge of the business, such information is likely to be useless. Experienced managers–not those who managed the account–who can analyze the causes of dissatisfaction and rec-ommend remedial action should conduct the interviews with defectors.

✓ **Tie recognition and rewards to net promoter scores.** Customer-facing teams (e.g., sales, service, and support) should have an element of their rewards based on the net promoter score. When they implemented this practice at Enterprise Rent-A-Car, performance saw marked improve-ment. Keep your rewards at the team level.

✓ **Devise ways to turn customers from detractors into promoters.** Armed with fast feedback on promoters and detractors (and defections analysis), managers are in a strong position to take action. Is there a pattern emerg-ing that explains what's happening and what needs to be done? Are com-petitors' actions having an impact? Is the company not performing other services well enough (e.g., customer service or training)? Answers to these questions can help managers take the right remedial action.

✓ **Design customer service and support around small teams.** One of Reichheld's rules of loyalty has to do with reducing business complex-ity to promote speed and flexibility for customer transactions. He notes: "There are a lot of ways to keep things simple, but maybe more important than any other is the size of the teams that your company is organized into. Enterprise Rent-A-Car has only eight people per branch. The competition, many of whom are bankrupt, have four times that team size."[12]

✓ **Recognize that customers relate to people, not corporations.** If you have high staff turnover in the customer contact parts of your business, then you will likely struggle to keep your customers loyal. Finding and keeping the right people is the other side of the customer loyalty coin and one of the keys to building loyal customers.

✓ **Align CRM systems with loyalty management.** Managers need to switch the emphasis of their CRM systems from monitoring customer behavior and selling products to managing loyalty. Taking every opportunity to ask the key satisfaction question and recording it on the customer's CRM file would go a long way to providing a monitoring system that would alert managers to any danger signs.

Conclusions

Loyalty management is a compelling idea that we should take seriously. But to get the most out of it, we need to heed the lessons of Reichheld's research. He reminds us that it's crucial to distinguish between measuring customer satisfaction and loyalty, especially when it comes to conducting customer surveys. "The difference between the two is, loyalty links up to growth and cash flow; satisfaction doesn't," he said. "If you go to all the people who are promoters and ask them the satisfaction question, they give higher scores than they do on the question that asks if they would recommend your company to a friend. So satisfaction is a lower threshold of success. It tends to focus on a transaction, a one-time moment of truth, whereas loyalty gets at the relationship issue," says Reichheld.[13]

FURTHER READING

Brown, Mark Graham. *Beyond the Balanced Scorecard.* New York: Productivity Press, 2007.

CIO Insight Editors. "Expert Voices: C.K. Prahalad & Venkat Ramaswamy on CRM." *CIO Insight,* December 2003, 32–37.

Dinsdale, J. Scott, and Dr. Jim Taylor. "The Value of Loyalty." *Optimize,* April 2003, 32–42.

Dowling, Grahame. "Customer Relationship Management: In B2C Markets, Often Less Is More." *California Management Review,* Spring 2002, 87–104.

Hope, Jeremy, and Tony Hope. *Competing in the Third Wave: The Ten Key Management Issues of the Information Age.* Boston: Harvard Business School Press, 1997.

Reichheld, Frederick F. *The Loyalty Effect: The Hidden Force Behind Growth, Profits, and Lasting Value.* Boston: Harvard Business School Press, 1995.

Reichheld, Frederick F. *Loyalty Rules: How Today's Leaders Build Lasting Relationships.* Boston: Harvard Business School Press, 2003.

Reichheld, Frederick F. "The One Number You Need to Grow." *Harvard Business Review,* December 2003, 46–54.

Reinartz, Werner, and V. Kumar. "The Mismanagement of Customer Loyalty." *Harvard Business Review,* July 2002, 4–12.

Thompson, Harvey. *Who Stole My Customer? Winning Strategies for Creating and Sustaining Customer Loyalty.* Upper Saddle River, NJ: Financial Times Prentice Hall, 2004.

Part III

Lean Cost Management

18

TOTAL QUALITY MANAGEMENT

What is this practice and how effective is it?

Total quality management (and ISO 9000 and its subsequent series of numbers) promises better quality products and more-satisfied customers. Most governments and large, global organizations now demand that their suppliers be "ISO9000 certified" before they will deal with them. However, total quality management has a reputation for being bureaucratic and lacking practical application because it imposes rigid—one size fits all—standards not just on product development but also on a company's management processes. Few people would argue against total quality, but is standard practice the best way to achieve it? We will look at the balance of the argument.

Alternative names and related topics: ISO 9000; quality assurance; Malcolm Baldrige Award

The explosion of the total quality movement in America can be traced back to an NBC TV show in June 1980 entitled *If Japan Can, Why Can't We?* in which quality guru W. Edwards Deming was asked, "Why are we failing to compete with the Japanese?" His one-word answer was, "Quality." A Ford manager was watching and brought Deming and his ideas to his company, resulting in the Team Taurus that eventually led to Ford's best-selling car.

Through the 1980s until his death in 1993, Deming became a management legend and is rightly credited with making Western organizations aware of the quality improvement methods that the Japanese introduced after World War II. However, few organizations have adopted his philosophy as laid down in his famous fourteen principles.[1]

We can trace the quality movement in Britain to assembly problems in the munitions factories during World War II. To solve the problem of faulty bombs, the Ministry of Defense placed inspectors in factories. Suppliers had to document how products were made and then employ inspectors to check the work. Government inspectors would then provide an extra check. This approach enabled companies to claim that their products met specifications and that their output was consistent. U.K. occupational psychologist John Seddon notes: "The inherent logic was quite straightforward and remains appealing—you control how you do the work and hence you make what you say you are going to make. These ideas solved the problem of bombs going off in factories. 'Quality' became associated with 'conformance' rather than 'improvement' and 'quality assurance' implied that 'conformance had been assured' through inspection."[2]

According to Seddon, we are now witnessing a decline in companies' use of ISO 9000 in many of the countries that were first to jump on the bandwagon. For example, in Britain, France, and Germany, ISO 9000 registration is decreasing. But in the "new" economies, ISO 9000 is rampant. In China, growth is phenomenal, and the standard is regarded as essential for world trade. Despite its membership in the EU being years away, Romania considers the ISO 9000 an essential ticket to European trade. Even in Japan, growth of ISO 9000 is strong because of marketplace coercion: "you comply or we won't buy" is the rallying call. As growth has mushroomed around the world, parasitical inspection organizations have exploited their opportunity.[3]

Most quality control programs are well intentioned but frequently reinforce the top-down command-and-control management model. The standard is the only truth and must be followed without question. As many lean experts understand, it is important to see the organization as a system and ensure that products and services flow through the system smoothly and without errors. As Deming said, 95 percent of problems are in the system and are not concerned with people. Quality manuals do not recognize this insight. Deming also said that wherever leaders throw out and replace work standards, quality and productivity goes up substantially and people are happier on the job.[4]

What is the performance potential of this practice?

- **To provide consistent product quality.** Quality was a hit-or-miss affair prior to the implementation of quality control procedures. As some managers put it: "Our quality control systems were based on customer feedback." The software industry gained an unenviable reputation in this regard. Products now go through rigorous quality control procedures so that most problems are rectified before they reach the customer.

- **To provide a robust system that is auditable.** Before ISO 9000, individual organizations that may or may not have had the requisite standards developed quality control systems. Now quality control is subject to detailed international standards that can be audited and verified. This provides suppliers and customers with benchmarks that give them the confidence to engage with a partner.
- **To reduce costs through less rework.** Without process mapping and analysis, most managers can neither see the amount of rework that takes place nor how it is caused. Quality processes identify the causes of rework and thus give managers the opportunities to eradicate them.
- **To improve customer satisfaction.** Without effective quality systems, the customer bears the brunt of quality problems; they are likely to vote with their order pads and defect to the competition. ISO 9000 has applied rigorous quality standards and thus has reduced the likelihood of customers suffering high levels of dissatisfaction.

What actions do you need to take to maximize the potential of this practice?

ACTIONS TO AVOID

- ✖ **Stop focusing on volume and aim for quality.** Most manufacturers aim to maximize volume first and then have inspection and rework departments deal with any quality problems that arise through the production process. The problems associated with this approach are encapsulated in an observation Jim P. Womack, Daniel T. Jones, and Daniel Roos made when they recounted their visit to a German auto plant: "At the end of the assembly line was an enormous rework and rectification area where armies of technicians labored to bring the finished vehicles up to the company's fabled quality standard. We found that one-third of the total effort involved in assembly occurred in this area. In other words, the German plant was expending more effort to fix the problems it had just created than the Japanese plant required to make a nearly perfect car the first time."[5]
- ✖ **Be careful about who is responsible for quality.** Often, both the inspector and the person being inspected are caught up in the psychology of inspection; each is prone to assuming that the other will be responsible. This is a recipe for increasing errors. Inspection of any kind always increases errors. As Deming said, "inspection does not improve quality, nor guarantee quality. Inspection is too late. The quality, good or bad, is already in the product."[6] Quality should be designed into the system rather than inspected for.
- ✖ **Be wary of too much emphasis on compliance and control.** ISO 9000 can be excessively bureaucratic and lead managers to checking boxes rather

Traditional U.K. and U.S. approaches to quality management

Following visits to Japan in the 1970s, U.K. industrialists "began to copy some Japanese practices, for example, quality circles and suggestion schemes," but "they failed to 'see' what was behind these practices—a fundamentally different way of thinking about the design and management of work. Unaware of this crucial distinction, the U.K. Department of Trade and Industry held road shows on the benefits of BS 5750 registration and provided funding to encourage organizations to use consultants to support its implementation.[a] The recommended method of implementation was (and still is) as follows:

1. Look at your current organization to see how it compares with the requirements of the standard.
2. Decide what corrective action is needed to conform to the standard.
3. Prepare a program of work.
4. Define, document, and implement new management systems and procedures.
5. Prepare a quality manual.
6. Hold a preassessment meeting (to help the client establish his suitability for going forward to assessment and thus registration).
7. Pass the assessment test (the inspector determines whether the organization conforms to its documentation).
8. Register.[b]

In the 1990s, the British standard 5750 was adopted as the international standard ISO 9000. Quality assurance, according to the standard, is a *way of managing* that prevents nonconformance and thus assures quality. John Seddon makes the point that this is what makes ISO 9000 different from other standards: it is a *management* standard, not a *product* standard. It goes beyond product standardization: it is standardizing not *what* is made but *how* it is made. But Seddon believes that customers take a total view of an organization—how easy it is to do business with—with respect to all the things of value to them. ISO 9000 requires managers to "*establish and maintain a documented quality system as a means of ensuring that a product conforms to specified requirements.*" Loosely translated this is, "say what you are going to do, then do it."[c]

In the United States, the quality movement was given a boost by the establishment of the Malcolm Baldrige National Quality Award—an annual award that recognizes U.S. organizations in the business, health-care, education, and nonprofit sectors for performance excellence. The program and award were named for Malcolm Baldrige, who served as U.S. Secretary of Commerce during the Reagan administration (Baldrige died in a rodeo accident in 1987 shortly before the U.S. Congress approved the award). The Baldrige Award is the only formal recognition of the performance excellence of both public and private U.S. organizations given by the president of the United States. For its first three years, it was administered by the American Productivity & Quality Center (APQC) and the American Society for Quality. Subsequently, the award's administration passed to the National Institute of Standards and Technology, an agency of the U.S. Department of Commerce.

The Baldrige Award promotes awareness of performance excellence as an increasingly important element in competitiveness and information sharing of successful performance strategies and the benefits derived from using these strategies. To receive an award, an organization must have a role-model organizational management system that ensures continuous improvement in the delivery of products and/or services, demonstrates efficient and effective operations, and provides a way of engaging and responding to customers and other stakeholders. The award is not given for specific products or services. Currently, up to three awards may be given annually across each of the six eligibility categories—manufacturing, service, small business, education, health care, and nonprofit/government; however, a total of seven is the most that have ever been in a single year and that has only happened twice. As of 2010, ninety-one awards have been given to eighty-seven organizations.[d]

[a] John Seddon, "A Brief History of ISO9000—Where Did We Go Wrong?" www.lean-service.com/6.asp.

[b] Ibid.

[c] Ibid.

[d] U.S. National Institute for Standards and Technology Web site on Baldrige Award recipients, http://www.nist.gov/baldrige/baldrige_recipients2010.cfm

than improving systems. Just implementing ISO 9000 to get the certification may be necessary to compete in certain industries, but it is by no means sufficient to embed a culture of quality in the organization. This requires strong leadership and a focus on systems improvement.

✖ **Be wary of the culture of target setting and measurement.** Deming was scathing about targets and measures. "Eliminate targets, slogans, exhortations, posters, for the work force that urge them to increase productivity," he said. "'Your work is your self-portrait. Would you sign it? *No*—not when you give me a defective canvas to work with, paint not suited to the job, brushes worn out, so that I can not call it my work. Posters and slogans like this never helped anyone to do a better job.'"[7] He believed that posters and exhortations were directed at the wrong people. "They arise from management's supposition that the production workers could, by putting their backs into the job, accomplish zero defects, improve quality, improve productivity, and all else that is desirable. The charts and posters take no account of the fact that most of the trouble comes from the system," said Deming.[8] He goes on: "Goals are necessary for you and for me, but numerical goals set for other people, without a road map to reach the goal, have effects opposite to the effects sought."[9]

✖ **Beware of processes that conform to standards but make customer service worse.** Almost all large organizations have certificates of quality standards and are able to say that they have passed every test. But their service remains abysmal. Anyone who has experienced service from utilities, telecoms, and banks knows this. One customer of a U.K. bank had paid her minimum balance on her credit card and gone to Australia for several weeks to visit her daughter. She had been a loyal and trouble-free customer for forty years. But she returned to find the bank hadn't received the payment and received a letter detailing the action it was proposing to take; she was horrified. The gulf between measurement rhetoric and service reality can be huge. Quality standards can be followed to the letter, but the overall customer service can be awful.

✖ **Don't think that completing ISO 9000 certification means that you have finished with quality.** ISO 9000 further reinforces the idea that work is divided into management and worker roles. Seddon believes that it was the fundamental mistake of twentieth-century management, for ISO 9000 continues the tradition that "managers decide" and "workers do." This tradition has led to control—through adherence to procedures, budgets, targets, and standards—all of which cause suboptimization. It is a way of thinking about management that began in mass production systems and has been the starting point for defining the purpose of management.[10]

ACTIONS TO TAKE

✓ **Embed quality in the system rather than use bureaucratic inspections.** There are no separate quality inspection departments at Toyota. It embeds quality in processes and people. At Toyota, there is an open "visual control system" that includes the famous *andon* cord that workers can pull (it's like a clothesline that runs around the plant) to stop the line. Most problems are solved within a minute. According to Teruyuki

Minoura, former president of Toyota North America, "it is essential to halt the line when there's a problem. If the line doesn't stop, useless, defective items will move on to the next stage. If you don't know where the problem occurred, you can't do anything to fix it. That's where the concept of visual control comes from. The tool for this is the *andon* [cord which when pulled turns on an] electric light board [which alerts everyone to where the problem is located]."[11]

✓ **Ensure that people who understand the work design the quality systems.** A U.K. government employee who was frustrated by the damage ISO 9000 had done to his organization sent this e-mail to Seddon:

> Twelve months ago over "two feet" of procedures arrived on my desk with the instructions that they are to be implemented immediately. Implementing those procedures increased our workload by, I would guess, 10 to 15 per cent. This was the start to ISO 9000. We found that everything was beautifully detailed. There were sub-tasks for each procedure, with a person responsible for each. But nobody was actually responsible for ensuring the overall activity was achieved. Innovation was totally stifled, the only way to do it was by the procedure. . . . Many procedures had been written by people who didn't understand the work. In some cases the procedure was absurd in its impracticality. Twelve months later the amendments to the procedures are flying around at a furious rate to try and correct for the fact that people cannot (or, I have to admit in some cases, will not) follow all the procedures. . . . We got ISO 9000. Was it worth it? In my opinion, no.

✓ **Focus on zero defects.** Perhaps the most striking difference between mass production and the system at Toyota lies in their ultimate objectives. Mass producers set a limited goal for themselves—"good enough," which translates into an acceptable number of defects, a maximum acceptable level of inventories, and a narrow range of standardized products. Toyota, on the other hand, sets its sights explicitly on perfection. According to H. Thomas Johnson, it is the balanced, cyclical pattern of continuous flow in the work of every person, not driving people to meet quantitative targets, that explains Toyota's long-term success.[12]

Conclusions

Seddon believes that ISO 9000 is not improving organizations because it is based on bad theory. Underlying it are concepts of specification and control, rather than understanding and improvement, the heart of real quality. Customers will recognize that ISO 9000 has led organizations to focus on procedures rather than service, encumbering the service experience. Managers point to the excessive bureaucracy and work whose only purpose is to meet the requirements of their ISO 9000 assessor.[13]

FURTHER READING

Deming, W. Edwards. *Out of Crisis*. Cambridge, MA: MIT Press, 1982; 26th ed., 1998.

Oakland, John S. *Total Quality Management: The Route to Improving Performance*. Burlington, MA: Butterworth-Heinemann, 1993.

Seddon, John. *Freedom from Command & Control—A Better Way to Make the Work Work*. Buckingham, England: Vanguard Education Limited, 2003.

19

ACTIVITY-BASED COSTING

What is this practice and how effective is it?

Activity-based costing (ABC) models enable managers to understand product and customer *net* profitability by providing better methods of attributing overheads. But few challenge the need for these costs in the first place, many of which are caused by the controlling bureaucracy. More-enlightened managers use ABC to see whether costs should be incurred at all, but its implementation can be complicated and expensive. We will examine these issues and look at the latest incarnation of ABC, which offers far better opportunities for success.

Alternative names and related topics: activity-based management; customer profitability analysis; product-line profitability

Peter Drucker once noted that, "while 90% of the results are being produced by the first 10% of events, 90% of the costs are being increased by the remaining and result-less 90% of events."[1] In other words, economic results are, by and large, directly proportionate to revenue, while costs are directly proportionate to transactions. Consider the implications of this view of costs for a typical company. A handful of customers produce all the profits; a few salespeople produce the bulk of "good" orders; a small number of products, services, and distribution channels produce all the profits; and a small proportion of the work done in the research labs, the factory, and the office actually adds value to customers. Traditional accounting systems make no attempt to connect indirect costs with revenue streams—other than by largely arbitrary methods of allocation—and, thus, managers have little hope of discovering which costs are worthwhile and which are not. When work audits are carried out or where specific research is conducted, the results invariably show that between 20 percent and 50 percent of work is either unnecessary or of poor quality.[2]

An obvious question now arises: how can managers identify those 80 percent to 90 percent of products and customers that absorb all the costs but contribute very little to the success of the business? Or phrased in a slightly different way: which products, customers, and business segments are profitable? To answer this question, accountants clearly need a better understanding of the causes of indirect costs and how they support products and customers. Traditional costing systems, such as standard costing, were primarily concerned with questions of cost control and inventory valuation, rather than cost reduction and business improvement. With the inexorable rise of indirect costs driven by variety and complexity, these methods were providing increasingly distorted results.

By the mid-1980s, U.S. companies John Deere, Hewlett-Packard, and Textronix, and European companies Siemens, Ericsson, and Kanthal were experimenting with different transaction-based approaches to product costing. In 1985, the Consortium for Advanced Manufacturing–International (CAM–i) brought together thought leaders from leading companies, consulting firms, and academics to discuss costing issues in advanced manufacturing environments. Included in this group were Harvard academics Robert Kaplan and Robin Cooper. The discussion of these ideas developed many innovative management accounting ideas. The leading one became what is now known as activity-based costing (ABC). ABC analysis presents a clearer picture of product costs through a better identification of the costs of activities (such as machine setups or purchase orders) consumed by products. Using ABC, managers could more clearly relate many indirect costs to the products and customers that consumed them, giving managers a more accurate picture of product and customer profitability. While this data helped designers better understand the cost implications of their design options and helped managers to improve their product-mix decisions, ABC was initially seen as no more than a better method of cost allocation and of marginal benefit in improving profitability.

Two crucial breakthroughs were required before ABC could fully deliver on its initial promise. These came in a seminal article by Cooper and Kaplan entitled "Profit Priorities from Activity-Based Costing," in which they explained the causes of costs in terms of the production hierarchy and excess capacity.[3] They noted that costs were caused at four different levels: (1) individual unit level (labor, materials, energy); (2) batch level (setups, material movements, inspections); (3) product-line level (engineering specifications, process engineering, engineering change notices), or (4) facility level (building costs, plant maintenance, administration). Similarly, sales costs were caused at the brand, channel, and customer level. Cooper and Kaplan asserted that all costs can be attributed to one of these levels and thus *only by changing the capacity constraints at each level could costs be controlled.* These insights explained how two factories with identical physical outputs might have completely different cost structures. Kaplan and Cooper used the example of a pen factory to illustrate their point. Suppose one factory produced 1 million standard pens of one color, and another produced the same number of pens but in two thousand different colors and varieties. It is hardly surprising that the second factory would have much higher levels of costs to support its product mix and multiple production runs. But these expenses are not incurred at the product-unit level; they are incurred at the batch, product line-sustaining, and facility levels.

Of course, this simple example does not mean that pursuing a policy of product variety is necessarily wrong. Competitive imperatives may demand this approach, but ABC makes it clear to designers and managers that prices should reflect these extra costs; otherwise, these products will be unprofitable. Traditional systems fail to reveal these important differences. Kaplan and Cooper note that high-volume products should be produced in facilities optimized to perform unit-level activities, whereas low-volume, high-variety products should be produced in facilities that are finely tuned for batch and product line-sustaining activities (such as a job shop with skilled versatile employees and general-purpose equipment).[4]

The second theoretical breakthrough was equally important. Whereas traditional systems allocate all costs to products and services, ABC measures the cost of the resources *consumed* by products and services, *not the resources available.* A new equation was now visible: *cost of resources supplied = cost of resources used + cost of unused capacity.* Cooper and Kaplan explain the principle of excess capacity in relation to a purchase-ordering department in which there are ten people (the resource supplied) whose aggregate cost is $25,000 per month and whose process capacity is 1,250 purchase orders per month (the activity performed), giving a cost per order of $20. But if only 1,000 orders are processed, excess capacity is $250 \times \$20$ or $5,000. The manager is now aware of the extent of resource usage and over a period of time can reduce or increase capacity costs. What was seen as a fixed cost under the traditional system can now be seen as a variable cost under ABC.[5]

The ABC view of cost behavior challenged the conventional wisdom that the best approach to reducing product costs was to find cheaper suppliers, buy in greater bulk, install higher-performance machines, build more automated warehouses, spend money on industrial engineering studies to shave a few decimal points off hourly labor costs, and ultimately relocate production to lower labor-cost regions. Instead, ABC suggested to managers that many of their best cost-reduction opportunities were within their own grasp. For example, they should reduce setup times, improve plant layout, reduce the need for inspection, build close relationships with fewer high-quality suppliers, use just-in-time inventory control, integrate buying and payment systems, question product variants that add little extra value to customers, and design products with fewer parts. The challenge to the traditional cost mentality could not have been greater.

ABC burst onto the management accounting scene in the late 1980s following the success of *Relevance Lost–The Rise and Fall of Management Accounting* by H. Thomas Johnson and Robert Kaplan. Shortly after the book was published, Johnson distanced himself from ABC. It is instructive to understand why. "Simply because improved cost information becomes available," he noted, "a company does not change its commitment to mass produce output at high speed, to control costs by encouraging people to manipulate processes, and to persuade customers to buy output the company has produced to cover its costs."[6] In other words, according to Johnson, ABC is a solution to the wrong problem. Enlightened managers know that the right problem (and opportunity) is to look at reducing *total costs* rather than unit costs. The task should be to get rid of overheads, not waste time trying to find better ways of allocating them. Systems thinkers, like Johnson, believe that ABC is trapped in a time warp of mass production and all the cost-allocation problems that it entails.

What is the performance potential of this practice?

- **To provide a better understanding of cost drivers.** Traditional cost management doesn't focus on the causes of costs. ABC enables managers to see these causes and thus places them in a much better position to understand good costs and bad costs.
- **To distinguish between value-adding and nonvalue-adding costs.** Most managers strive to eliminate nonvalue-adding costs but without ABC analysis, it is not easy to identify them. If this analysis is done well, managers are in a good position to eliminate huge swaths of costs.
- **To facilitate product and customer profitability analysis.** In most large organizations, many products and customers are unprofitable after managers apply all the below-the-line costs of supporting them. ABC offers managers the opportunity to back the winners and discard the losers.
- **To understand the full costs of customization.** Customers increasingly expect customized products and services. But what's the cost? Without ABC analysis, it is not easy to find out.

An ABC revival

In the past few years, after sagging interest, Robert Kaplan and Steven Anderson have introduced "time-based" ABC and given ABC new momentum. This method is simpler since it requires, for each group of resources, estimates of only two parameters: how much it costs per time unit to supply resources to the businesses activities (the total overhead expenditure of a department divided by the total number of minutes of employee time available) and how much time it takes to carry out one unit of each kind of activity (as estimated or observed by the manager). "For example, if a customer support department has a cost of $70 per hour, and a particular transaction for a customer takes 24 minutes (0.4 hours), the cost of this transaction for this customer is $28."[a]

This approach, they argue, overcomes a serious technical problem associated with employee surveys: the fact that when asked to estimate time spent on activities, employees invariably report percentages that add up to 100. Under the new system, managers take into account time that is idle or unused. Armed with this data, managers then construct time equations, a new feature that enables the model to reflect the complexity of real-world operations by showing how specific order, customer, and activity characteristics cause processing times to vary.

Kaplan and Anderson conclude by saying that,

Over the past 15 years, ABC has enabled managers to see that not all revenue is good revenue and not all customers are profitable customers. Unfortunately, the difficulties of implementing and maintaining ABC systems have prevented them from being adopted on any significant scale. Time-driven ABC has overcome these difficulties, offering a transparent, scalable methodology that is easy to implement and update. It draws on existing databases to incorporate specific features for particular orders, processes, suppliers, and customers. ABC is no longer a complex, expensive financial-systems implementation; the time-driven ABC innovation provides managers with meaningful cost and profitability information, quickly and inexpensively.[b]

[a] Robert Kaplan, "A Balanced Scorecard Approach to Measure Customer Profitability," HBS Working Knowledge, August 5, 2005, http://hbswk.hbs.edu/item/4938.html.

[b] Robert S. Kaplan and Steven Anderson, "Time-Driven Activity-Based Costing," *Harvard Business Review*, November 2004, 131–138.

What actions do you need to take to maximize the potential of this practice?

ACTIONS TO AVOID

✖ **Avoid putting the accountants in charge.** While integrating ABC into the mainstream accounting system sounds like a job for the accountants, it is different from promoting and implementing ABC concepts. One of the reasons Bob Lutz was so successful at Chrysler was because he kept the ABC project away from the finance people. The point is that accountants are likely to see ABC as an accounting solution to an accounting problem, whereas Lutz and others see it as a real opportunity to provide business managers with information that will help them make better decisions.

✖ **Stop basing ABC calculations on negotiated budgets.** While traditional companies use ABC to challenge the value of direct product-based costs, they do not see it as a tool for challenging all costs. Thus, ABC focuses on the reduction of *existing costs*, while rarely challenging if those costs or the processes of which they form part *should exist at all*. Johnson once said that "the pathway to global competitive excellence is not reached by doing better what should not be done at all."[7] This is exactly the point.

✖ **Don't just see ABC as a project-based system.** There is an inevitable clash of cultures between traditional accounting measures (including budgets) and activity accounting. Whereas traditional measures focus on revenues and costs by function and department, ABC measures focus on customer-oriented processes that cut across the hierarchy. Thus, in only a few companies has ABC become a mainstream management information system. However, because managerial recognition and rewards remain tied to accounting results, ABC systems are often left uncared for and suffer terminal decline. This is tragic because ABC information includes many of the golden nuggets that managers need to make value-based decisions.

✖ **Beware of line managers perceiving ABC as just another control system.** Unless carefully presented, ABC can appear to frontline people as just another accounting system that involves more work and results in the loss of jobs. It can also be too complicated. Users should keep activity analysis at a fairly high level and resist the temptation to treat ABC like a time-and-motion system.

ACTIONS TO TAKE

✓ **Prepare a process or activity map for the ABC process.** Preparing a process map showing activities (pieces of work) is the critical first step in building an ABC model.

✓ **Translate accounting costs–cost centers, and so on–into activity costs.** This involves analyzing how people spend their time–not what departments spend, but how they spend it.

✓ **Use ABC analysis to distinguish between value-adding and nonvalue-adding work.** Activity-based systems rarely attempt to distinguish between value-adding and nonvalue-adding time, and thus any poor-quality work is charged to the user or business unit alongside good-quality work. Many managers believe implicitly that the way to improve competitiveness is to lower unit costs by increasing scale and speed. But doing the *wrong* things better, faster, or on a greater scale does not lead to improved competitiveness.

✓ **Use activity analysis to challenge operating costs.** ABC can provide managers with an alternative view of costs based on the work that people do (i.e., their activities, such as visiting customers) rather than the general ledger view of cost (e.g., the cost of the salaries and benefits). Thus, if managers can see what it costs to deal with mistakes or carry out rework and shed light on any other areas of nonvalue-added work, then they are placed in a much better position to deal with the root causes of the problems.

✓ **Use ABC to provide customer profitability analysis.** Making fast decisions at the front line, especially where customized solutions are involved, means that managers need to know the costs and profitability of the proposed transaction. This is difficult without full customer costing. But the question of customer profitability is surrounded by myths and false premises. Some managers, for example, believe that provided the gross profit from sales (which *can* usually be measured) contributes to fixed overheads, no further analysis of the customer relationship is necessary. Knowing the costs of a customized transaction is becoming increasingly important, as more firms offer tailored solutions but prices rarely take account of such variations. Differences in price (excluding quantity discounts) for the same product and for similar transactions can be as much as 30 percent, but such differences bear little relationship to the costs of serving the customer.[8]

✓ **Consider switching to time-based ABC.** This method is potentially simpler to use and may have a greater chance of long-term success. It provides a meaningful way to measure varying degrees of idle capacity rather than burying it in average activity rates. After the initial set-up it relies on drivers that can be readily tracked by operating personnel. This can also be used in interim cost estimating.

Conclusions

ABC is a significant step forward from standard costing and enables managers to see more clearly the true costs of products and service and thus set more appropriate prices. Time-driven ABC has also made it easier to implement and use. But ABC has failed to challenge the mass-production, command-and-control view of management. Rather than finding better ways to allocate overheads, the focus should be on eliminating them.

FURTHER READING

Cokins, Gary. *Activity-Based Cost Management: An Executive's Guide.* New York: John Wiley & Sons, 2001.

Cooper, Robin, and Robert S. Kaplan. *Cost and Effect: Using Integrated Cost Systems to Drive Profitability and Performance.* Boston: Harvard Business School Press, 1997.

Cooper, Robin, and Robert S. Kaplan. "The Promise–and Peril–of Integrated Cost Systems." *Harvard Business Review,* July–August 1998, 109–119.

Forrest, Edward. *Activity-Based Management: A Comprehensive Implementation Guide.* New York: McGraw-Hill, 1996.

Hicks, Douglas T. *Activity-Based Costing: Making It Work for Small and Mid-Sized Companies,* 2nd ed. New York: John Wiley & Sons, 2002.

Hope, Jeremy, and Tony Hope. *Competing in the Third Wave: The Ten Key Management Issues of the Information Age.* Boston: Harvard Business School Press, 1997.

Hope, Tony, and Jeremy Hope. *Transforming the Bottom Line: Managing Performance with the Real Numbers.* Boston: Harvard Business School Press, 1995.

Johnson, H. Thomas. *Relevance Regained.* New York: Free Press, 1992.

Johnson, H. Thomas, and Anders Bröms. *Profit Beyond Measure.* London: Nicholas Brealey Publishing, 2000.

Kaplan, Robert S., and Steven R. Anderson. "Time-Driven Activity Based Costing (TDABC)." Working paper 04-045, Harvard Business School, Boston, 2003.

Miller, John A. *Implementing Activity-Based Management in Daily Operations.* New York: John Wiley & Sons, 1996.

Player, Steve, and Carol Cobble. *Cornerstones of Decision Making: Profiles of Enterprise ABM.* Greensboro, NC: Oakhill Press, 1999.

Player, Steve, and James W. Gibson Jr. *Activity-Based Costing in Wholesale Distribution: Winning the Profitability Battle.* Washington, DC: Distribution Research & Education Foundation/NAW, 1997.

Player, Steve, and David Keys. *Arthur Andersen's Lessons from the ABM Battlefield,* 2nd ed. New York: John Wiley & Sons, 1999.

Player, Steve, and Roberto Lacerda, *Arthur Andersen's Global Lessons in Activity-Based Management.* New York: John Wiley & Sons, 1999.

Pryor, Tom. *Using Activity Based Management for Continuous Improvement: 2000 Edition.* Arlington, TX: ICMS, 2000.

20

BUSINESS PROCESS REENGINEERING

What is this practice and how effective is it?

Business process reengineering burst onto the scene in the early 1990s with the promise of transforming organization structures from vertical functions into horizontal processes that focus on delivering seamless solutions to customers. The dividend was supposed to be faster processes and lower costs. But evangelists didn't take account of the human reaction, and many projects foundered. Too much emphasis was on "business reengineering"—get rid of jobs—and not enough on "process improvement"—improve the flow of work and, ultimately, product quality and customer service. We will look at the power of process mapping and how reengineering techniques can add real value.

Alternative names and related topics: cycle time reduction; horizontal organizations; process redesign; process management

In the early 1990s, two articles, one in *Sloan Management Review* by Thomas Davenport and another in *Harvard Business Review* by Michael Hammer, reported on the growing wave of process innovation and radical business process change. "Don't Automate, Obliterate" became the clarion call of those who set out to reengineer businesses by shifting management's focus from optimizing specialized functions carried out by individual departments to the cross-functional business processes that deliver value to customers. In 1993, Hammer and James Champy published their blockbuster book *Reengineering the Corporation*, and the business process reengineering (BPR) revolution was born.

Davenport's article rammed home the point—that the way most firms organize their work is guaranteed to create huge amounts of waste. Since then,

"Staple yourself to an order"

In a classic 1992 article entitled "Staple Yourself to an Order," Benson Shapiro, V. Kasturi Rangan, and John Sviokla made this comment:

> The order management cycle offers managers the opportunity to look at their company through a customer's eyes, to see and experience trans-actions the way customers do . . . In the course of the order management cycle (OMC), every time the order is handled, the customer is handled. Every time the order sits unattended, the customer sits unattended. Paradoxically, the best way to be customer-oriented is to go beyond the customer to the order; the moment of truth occurs at every step of the OMC, and every employee in the company who affects the OMC is the equivalent of a front-line worker . . . The best way for managers to learn this lesson is effectively to staple themselves to an order. They can then track an order as it moves through the OMC, always aware that the order is simply a surrogate for the customer . . . Here's what managers don't do: they don't travel horizontally through their own vertical organization. They don't consider the order management cycle as the system that ties together the entire customer experience and that can provide true customer perspective.[a]

[a] Benson P. Shapiro, V. Kasturi Rangan, and John J. Sviolka, "Staple Yourself to an Order," *Harvard Business Review*, July–August 1992, 113–122.

many firms have adopted a process-based management structure in an attempt to align their operations with the needs of the customer. Davenport has defined a process as "a specific ordering of work activities across time and place, with a beginning, an end, and clearly identified inputs and outputs: a structure for action."[1] Cross-functional processes offer managers a clearer view of which work should be done and, when new technology is applied, how such work can be done faster and more effectively. Teams are integral to the process-based structure, and process owners are accountable for continuous performance improvement. Business processes appear at two levels: core processes such as new product development and customer service, and smaller subprocesses that define the activities to be accomplished within the core processes.

The changes in speed, cost, and customer service can be dramatic. James Womack and Daniel Jones, for example, argue that by eliminating unnecessary steps, aligning all steps in an activity in a continuous flow, recombining labor into cross-functional teams dedicated to that activity, and continually striving for improvement, companies can develop, produce, and distribute products with half or less of the human effort, space, tools, time, and overall expense. They can also become vastly more flexible and responsive to customer desires.[2]

The real lesson of process management is to improve the work rather than manage the budget. Viewing costs through the lens of work processes rather than accounting categories provides managers with many new insights into cost-reduction opportunities.

But the macho language of BPR has overshadowed the merits of process design and improvement. In a 1995 article, "The Fad That People Forgot," Davenport deflated the reengineering bubble that by that time had grown into a $50 billion business. Davenport noted, for example, that some firms—especially those that were the principal case studies in *Reengineering the Corporation*—had a "revisionist" view of their reengineering efforts, and none of the companies involved has been able to claim sustained success.[3]

However, Davenport is careful to point out that it is the hype and especially the colorful language of reengineering (e.g., "carry the wounded but shoot the stragglers") that has given these initiatives such a bad name. Remaining a staunch supporter of business process improvement, he notes: "The most profound lesson of business process reengineering was never reengineering, but business processes. Processes are how we work. Any company that ignores its business processes or fails to improve them risks its future. That said, companies can use many different approaches to process improvement without ever embarking on a high-risk reengineering project."[4]

Although BPR ultimately became a dirty word in business, most known for downsizing, it did illuminate the huge potential of process redesign such as reducing handoffs and eliminating disconnects between departments. Where BPR fell down was in its lack of understanding of how people work within processes. In other words, just remapping functions into processes and using IT to join activities together doesn't work on its own. Designers need to understand the interface between process and practice (activities and people). Work is primarily a social activity. Process designers must be aware that they cannot simply design work practices and procedures on flow charts and implement them in the workplace without fully understanding how people actually spend their time. Many process designers see only the authorized or explicit work procedures and fail to see the unauthorized or tacit practices where much of the real work gets done.

In the 1980s, an anthropologist at Xerox's Palo Alto Research Center (PARC) made an interesting observation. Managers were trying to boost the productivity of field service staff, so, instead of simply accepting their descriptions of work activities, the anthropologist actually followed the field staff around. He discovered that reps often made a point of spending time *not with customers, but with one another.* They would gather in common areas, like the parts warehouse or around the coffee machine, and swap stories from the field. Now imagine how a reengineering consultant might view this observation—juicy pickings for increasing time on the job or with the customer. But the consultant would miss the point. The anthropologist saw these *social activities* as an extremely valuable part of the day; the reps were acting as a community of professionals, providing one another with valuable insights into improving their work and learning how to solve customer problems more effectively.[5]

John Seely Brown and Paul Duguid note that many of the celebrated cases of BPR come from a fairly narrow band of operations. Procurement, shipping and receiving, warehousing, fulfillment, and billing are favorites. These generally account for the most impressive results, with inventories transformed into just-in-time delivery, fulfillment, and billing accomplished in days rather than weeks. In these areas of work, they note, processes are relatively well defined. They usually have clearly measurable inputs and outputs. And, as we might expect from a process-oriented view, they emphasize a linear view of how organizations work. To complete a process, something passes from A on to B ending with C—from, for example, receiving to manufacturing to shipping. In such well-defined processes, it is the "longitudinal" links between each stage that appear to matter. Lateral ties among people doing similar tasks—among, for example, the people in shipping—appear at a heavy discount from a process-based perspective. They are generally regarded as nonvalue-adding.[6]

They go on to note that reengineering has had less success in the parts of organizations that are less linear and less clearly defined by process and information. Management, for example, has proved notoriously hard to reengineer. So has research and development. In such areas, life is less linear; inputs and outputs are less well defined; and information is less "targeted." These are, rather, areas where making sense, interpreting, and understanding are both problematic and highly valued—areas where, above all, meaning and knowledge are at a premium.[7]

Hammer, architect of the reengineering movement, was aware of these problems, but he suggested that work issues are secondary to customer issues. "What truly imbues work with meaning," noted Hammer, "is the sense that one's work has a larger purpose, that one's individual activity fits together with the work of others to create a result for a customer, an individual or enterprise that values the result. There is as much community in process as there is in practice. For the individual and the enterprise, fulfillment requires a blend of these two axes."[8]

What is the performance potential of this practice?

- **To reduce costs.** In the typical organizational hierarchy, work is done in well-defined functions and departments. There are multiple handoffs between each team, and, in a manufacturing operation, this leads to buffer stocks to ensure that one process connects with another without disruption. The result is excess cost. In the process-based organization, teams connect and combine to provide a seamless solution to the customer. Only those processes and activities that are necessary and add value to the customer are performed. The result is the elimination of swaths of nonvalue-adding costs.

- **To improve quality.** Despite the implementation of total quality management, quality is inevitably compromised when there are disconnections between processes. Errors and rework are inevitable. Quality is built into well-designed processes and is a key performance indicator for the process team. The result is lower-cost products and higher customer satisfaction.

- **To improve cycle times.** Operating through disconnected functions and departments is invariably slow, as documents and transactions enter queues, then are batched, scanned, and archived at each stage. Speed is of the essence in the process flow system as one team hands over to the next. What's important is that the handover from one workstation to the next goes smoothly.

Be wary of placing too much emphasis on IT

Of course, the design and implementation of IT systems are crucial to an effective reengineering project. But project leaders would be wise to reflect on their use and impact. The emphasis should be on process redesign—the simpler the better—rather than huge sums spent on IT. A joint study conducted by McKinsey, Stanford University, and the University of Augsburg of more than a hundred global electronics companies reminds us that it is managerial ability rather than technology that leads to superior performance. The authors explain why:

> The logic is clear and consistent: delegation reduced delays in getting management approval; dedicated assignments limit distractions; small team size minimizes time spent on coordination; and higher skill levels support the judgment needed for flexibility on schedule and late design changes. Building such capability, however, does not depend on substituting information technology and automation for people. In fact, the successful companies in our sample spend about 25 percent less on

(continued)

information technology and over 50 percent less on automation. Simpler business processes reduce companies' need for IT and automation. The key issue—for both leaders and laggards—is the development of the whole work force through enabling the delegation of responsibility, *not* the size of the investment in information technology.[a]

[a] Arthur P. Cimento and Russell J. Knister, "The High-Productivity Electronics Company," *McKinsey Quarterly*, January 1994), 20–28.

What actions do you need to take to maximize the potential of this practice?

ACTIONS TO AVOID

✖ **Don't sell reengineering based on job reductions.** Because the vast majority of reengineering projects involve job cuts, it is critical to make a compelling business case to both managers and employees for the proposed changes. But changing ingrained attitudes, implementing new information systems, penetrating powerful management cliques, and convincing knowledge workers to share their assets is hard to sell. For example, a statement such as "we are making changes to improve internal processes and customer value" sounds quite different from "we have to make cuts to survive, and this is how we're doing it." Most reengineering programs start on the wrong foot. And because they often follow in the wake of failed restructuring efforts that have left indelible scars on the workforce, employees see them as just another attempt at cost reduction.

✖ **Be wary of redesigning processes that rupture social relationships.** The BPR movement has sold itself on the basis of cost reduction, primarily by cutting jobs. Redesigning linear work flows using the power of information systems is the methodology, but there are serious pitfalls awaiting organizations that blindly follow this path. For example, reengineers can unwittingly slice right through lateral relationships (often called "communities of practice"), thus rupturing some of the main arteries of value-adding work and knowledge sharing. One of the lessons of the BPR movement over the past twenty years is that organizations are not machines that can be reengineered without taking account of the social interactions of people and how they learn from one another.

✖ **Don't alienate employees; involve them.** If employees are involved in the redesign of the processes within which they work, they will be less resistant to change. Imposing process redesign from the top down or from external consultants is almost bound to create employee resistance. Besides, firms such as Toyota have consistently shown that many of the best improvement

But most reengineering programs are carried out in the name of cost reduction; employees see them as yet another top-down management tool that inexorably leads to fewer jobs. The lesson is clear. BPR cannot work without an associated change in culture and reward systems and, to achieve these needs, much more thought, planning, and effort than most project managers have so far demonstrated.

FURTHER READING

Carr, David K., and Henry J. Johansson. *Best Practices in Reengineering: What Works and What Doesn't in the Reengineering Process.* New York: McGraw-Hill, 1995.

Champy, James. *Reengineering Management: The Mandate for New Leadership.* New York: HarperBusiness, 1996.

Davenport, Thomas H. *Process Innovation: Reengineering Work Through Information Technology.* Boston: Harvard Business School Press, 1992.

Frame, J. Davidson. *The New Project Management: Tools for an Age of Rapid Change, Complexity, and Other Business Realities.* San Francisco, CA: Jossey-Bass, 2002.

Grover, Varun, and Manuj K. Malhotra. "Business Process Reengineering: A Tutorial on the Concept, Evolution, Method, Technology and Application." *Journal of Operations Management*, August 1997, 193–213.

Hall, Gene, Jim Rosenthal, and Judy Wade. "How to Make Reengineering Really Work." *Harvard Business Review*, November–December 1993, 119–131.

Hammer, Michael. *Beyond Reengineering: How the Process-Centered Organization Is Changing Our Work and Lives.* New York: HarperCollins, 1997.

Hammer, Michael, and James Champy. *Reengineering the Corporation: A Manifesto for Business Revolution.* New York: HarperCollins, 1993.

Hope, Jeremy, and Tony Hope. *Competing in the Third Wave: The Ten Key Management Issues of the Information Age.* Boston: Harvard Business School Press, 1997.

Keen, Peter G. W. *The Process Edge: Creating Value Where It Counts.* Boston: Harvard Business School Press, 1997.

Sandberg, Kirsten D. "Reengineering Tries a Comeback—This Time for Growth, Not Just Cost Savings." *Harvard Management Update*, November 2001, 3–6.

21

LEAN MANUFACTURING

What is this practice and how effective is it?

Lean manufacturing is nothing less than redesigning organizations around processes, working from the customer backward into the organization, and eliminating waste. Lean challenges traditional command-and-control management in many fundamental ways. For example, teams respond to customer orders rather than follow predetermined plans. And there is less need for top-down control systems and middle managers to connect high-level decisions with frontline actions. But the implementation problems must not be underestimated. One reason the impact of lean has been so marginal is that group finance insists on measuring the performance of individual tasks and departments when it is the whole end-to-end process that matters. We will examine all these issues.

Alternative names and related topics: systems thinking; mass customization; just-in-time

Despite its recent setbacks, Toyota is still acknowledged to be the best manufacturing company in the world. Toyota in Japan succeeded for many years by applying and improving the Toyota Production System (TPS), the legendary system introduced by Taiichi Ohno. This system governed the way Toyota managed its manufacturing plants, but the approach was not properly recorded and was mostly taught by example. The techniques not only helped to build the success of Toyota, but also started the whole lean manufacturing revolution. However, tools and techniques are not the secret weapon for transforming a business. Toyota's success stems from a deeper business philosophy based on its understanding of people and human motivation.

For Teruyuki Minoura, global purchasing director of Toyota, the way TPS develops people is its greatest strength. "Under a 'push' system," he notes,

The Toyota Production System is based on five key ideas

1. **Takt time**, the idea that makes continuous flow possible. It is important never to vary the pace of work. Therefore, as efficiencies are introduced in the factory or design shop, or as the rate of production falls, unneeded workers must be removed from the system in order to maintain the same intensity of work.[a] More experienced plants can run at faster takt times than less experienced ones.

2. **Standardized work** is set and agreed on by teams so that they can see immediately if something "abnormal" occurs. It also enables workers to be flexible. In some plants, workers may move every two hours to a different workstation to avoid boredom.

3. **Jidoka**, which describes the use of machines with humanlike intelligence; they can detect errors and stop themselves.

4. **Just-in-time**, which reflects the belief that waste can and must be avoided in every process. Ohno got this idea from visiting an American supermarket in the 1950s and noticing how shelves were immediately replenished when goods were sold.

5. **Heijunka**, the leveling sequencing of variants in production. Toyota balances the variations by sequencing products so they occur as evenly as possible. Thus, if half of the day's units are vans and half of those have air-conditioning, then work is scheduled so that every fourth unit coming down the line will be an air-conditioned van.[b]

[a] Thomas Johnson and Anders Bröms, *Profit Beyond Measure* (London: Nicholas Brealey Publishing, 2000), 79.

[b] Ibid., 93.

"there is little opportunity for workers to gain wisdom because they just produce according to the instructions they are given. In contrast, a 'pull' system asks the worker to use his or her head to come up with a manufacturing process where he or she alone must decide what needs to be made and how quickly it needs to be made. An environment where people have to think brings with it wisdom, and this wisdom brings with it *kaizen* (continuous improvement)," notes Minoura. "If asked to produce only one unit at a time, to produce according to the flow, a typical line worker is likely to be flummoxed. It's a basic characteristic of human beings that they develop wisdom from being put under pressure."[1]

Perhaps the most striking difference between mass production and TPS lies in their ultimate objectives. Mass producers set a limited goal for themselves—"good enough," which translates into an acceptable number of defects, a maximum acceptable level of inventories, and a narrow range of standardized products. Toyota, on the other hand, set its sights explicitly on perfection. According to H. Thomas Johnson, a balanced, cyclical pattern of continuous flow in to work of every person, not driving people to meet quantitative targets, explains Toyota's long-term success.[2]

But lean isn't just about eliminating waste. It's also about liberating employees from the tyranny of command-and-control management and releasing the energy and creativity of the whole workforce. It is not uncommon for lean organizations to experience a surge in employee satisfaction that invariably leads to a similar effect on customer satisfaction. There is little doubt that people feel more valued if they are able to make a difference to their organization and to the environment. And it makes sound business sense.

So why hasn't lean thinking turned into generally accepted management practice? Perhaps it's because lean is seen as a cost-reduction initiative, and these initiatives have recently slipped down in importance on the management agenda. Many leaders believe they have squeezed their organizations as hard as they dare through relentless benchmarking, reengineering, six sigma, and other improvement projects. Many say that efficiency gains have run their course. The reality, however, is that compared with truly lean organizations, they have barely scratched the surface. The more likely reason is that lean involves moving from the command-and-control hierarchy to managing through horizontal processes and cross-functional teams; this can be a gut-wrenching change. It can appear to threaten some of the most powerful people in the organization, and they are quick to man the hierarchical barricades.

What is the performance potential of this practice?

- **To reduce costs.** With a process rather than a functional view, everyone focuses on improving process performance, especially removing unnecessary work and cost. Over time, these small changes add up to a huge step change in performance.
- **To improve customer satisfaction.** In the "pull" model, organizations build to the customer's order and thus are able to meet a customer's exact (and exacting) needs.
- **To build quality into workplace systems.** Quality is designed into the process rather than "inspected for." Employees have the authority to stop the line to fix quality problems as they occur.

- **To improve decision making.** Managers make small decisions quickly but spend time on major decisions, ensuring that all the variables are checked and verified and then implemented quickly, getting implementation right the first time.

What actions do you need to take to maximize the potential of this practice?

ACTIONS TO AVOID

✖ **Avoid overemphasizing lean tools.** You can make significant improvements in manufacturing performance by creating cells and flow, using takt time, and creating a pull system. But this misses the big opportunity—changing how people work by changing the system. If you look for example at General Motors, where people do a lot of lean interventions, it hasn't fundamentally changed the system; people still set revenue and volume targets, which of course means that they can't create a pull system. "The problem," according to author Jeffrey Liker, "is that many companies mistake lean tools for 'deep thinking.'" Lean thinking based on TPS "involves a far deeper and more pervasive cultural transformation than most companies can begin to imagine."[3] Of Liker's 4Ps (philosophy, process, people/partners, and problem solving), he believes that the vast majority of firms have only tackled "process."

✖ **Abandon targets and use measures to learn and improve.** The whole lean implementation can be undermined by the inappropriate use of targets, measures, and rewards. If these continue to focus on functions, departments, and activities in a way that reinforces the top-down, command-and-control model, then lean is doomed to failure. "Management by a numerical goal is an attempt to manage without knowledge of what to do, and in fact is usually management by fear," said Deming.[4] He also wrote that while we need good results, "management by results is not the way to get good results. It is action on outcome, as if the outcome came from a special cause. It is important to work on the causes of results—i.e., on the system."[5]

✖ **Don't assume that economies of scale always make sense.** All business school students learn about economies of scale, and in the right setting (i.e., avoiding too much duplication), the logic is compelling. But for many processes, the economies of flow (i.e., one-piece flow) have an even greater logic. Creating a smooth flow of work from one team to the next that eliminates unnecessary work and is done right the first time while using the minimum inventory can reduce costs to a greater extent than scale economics *without the side effects* (e.g., poor quality and high inventory). Most Western companies can't understand this. Their business models are based on a plethora of quarterly and annual targets underpinned by aggressive incentive plans. The idea that "lowest cost" comes not from maximizing volume through batch production but from dealing with one order at a time, leveling the flow, and solving quality problems as they arise is an idea most American and European organizations view with suspicion.

✖ **Avoid a conflict with standard costing; eradicate it.** When Western firms tried to copy the techniques of lean production, their accounting and reward systems often went haywire. Initiatives such as just-in-time production and quality programs didn't show up well in variance reports and charts and, in many cases, caused them to disregard the new ideas. Standard cost-efficiency variances, for example, encourage the recovery of all direct labor hours, no matter what the consequences might be for quality or other hidden costs (such as high or unsalable inventories) of the finished output. They encourage long production runs and large batch sizes, whereas just-in-time and total quality emphasize production to demand and high quality. The result is invariably more waste, more indirect labor costs needed to patch up poor quality, higher inventories, and a mad scramble at the end of each accounting period in an effort to hit volume and efficiency targets, all of which leads to *higher costs, lower quality*, and *fewer satisfied customers*. Lean organizations use a combination of target costing and value stream costing to set prices and manage costs. But the emphasis is on *total costs* rather than unit costs.

✖ **Don't treat inventory as an asset to be maximized.** One of the first problems that traditional finance people faced in the lean manufacturing world is the demise of inventory. While it is a huge boost for cash flow, it can cause problems with earnings management. Many firms expand and contract their inventories to meet their targets. In organizations with large inventories, much of the profit is wrapped up in the labor, materials, and overhead carried forward in the closing period's inventory valuation figure. For lean manufacturers, inventory is so low as to be almost immaterial. In fact, you should hardly need to count it; it is likely to amount to only a few days' cost of sales. So treat inventory as a liability to minimize rather than an asset to maximize.

ACTIONS TO TAKE

✓ **Base management decisions on a long-term philosophy.** Lean is not a project to give to a project team, although the planning and evaluation might start that way. Nor is it a series of discrete projects that focus on fixing specific problems. It is a whole management philosophy that all key people must discuss and accept. The second of Deming's fourteen points was "adopt the new philosophy." He believed that higher levels of quality at lower costs are possible if you learn to manage differently. This means learning how to improve systems in the presence of variation (reducing variation in materials, people, processes, and products).

✓ **Use "pull" systems to avoid overproduction.** The removal of waste is a key objective. Ohno defined waste in terms of overproduction, waiting time, transportation, processing, inventory, movement, and making defective products. A key feature of the TPS is the use of customer order information to *pull* material through the plant. At hundreds of workstations along both sides of the line, team members attach and install parts that they pull from line-side conveyance racks that are replenished every hour or so by *kanban* (signboard). The kanban is typically a piece of paper in a rectangular vinyl envelope containing three pieces of information: pick-up; transfer; and production. The kanban carries the information vertically and laterally within Toyota itself and between Toyota and its external partners. It has a number of other functions. For example, it acts as a work order, it prevents defective products by identifying the process making the defectives (defective products are not sent to the next process; the result is 100 percent defect-free goods), and it reveals existing problems and maintains inventory control.[6]

✓ **Level out the workload.** Of course, all manufacturers want to maximize volume. But they need to take into account bottlenecks in the plant and the maintenance of high-quality processes throughout the production cycle. Toyota bases production on takt time. This rhythmic process is rather like the pulse of a heartbeat. It enables products to flow steadily through the plant rather than driving them through at breakneck speed and dealing with problems at the end of the line. It does not allocate resources on the basis of planned production levels, though it does estimate plant capacity according to anticipated demand. If demand rises or falls, then Toyota takes appropriate action; the takt time remains the same, so resources needed—such as people and machines—are automatically adjusted. It minimizes costs by only providing resources to make one vehicle at a time. *Heijunka* is the Japanese word for leveling of production by both volume and product mix. Toyota does not build products according to the actual flow of customer orders, which can swing up and down wildly, but takes the total volume of orders in a given period (in Toyota's case, one day) and levels them out so that the same amount and mix are made each day. The TPS approach from the beginning was to keep batch sizes small and build what the customer (external or internal) wants.

✓ **Stop when there is a quality problem.** Quality inspection is built into the line at Toyota. There is an open "visual control system" that includes the andon cord, which workers can pull to stop the line.

✓ **Establish standardized tasks for continuous improvement.** In most organizations, operational management is highly structured, with layers of supervision. At first sight, Toyota looks similar, but when you take a second look, it is quite different. Paul Adler, an expert in organizational theory, studied Toyota and noticed that jobs were highly repetitive, with short cycle times, often only one minute before repeating.[7] Workers also follow detailed standardized procedures. There are lots of teams, team leaders, and group leaders. In other words, there is an extensive hierarchy. So how does this fit with the type of devolved, organic organization that is the essence of lean? The answer is that with a more trained eye, you can see that it is organic. There is extensive employee involvement and lots of communication, flexibility, high morale, and a strong focus on the customer.

✓ **Use visual controls, so no problems are hidden.** When most of us think about management information and reporting, we think of streams of data flowing through fast computer systems. We think about standard costing and quality control systems and reams of variance reports. But in a Toyota plant, visual information remains important and leads to immediate action. Toyota uses visual control to tell everyone at a glance if they are performing work to critical standards. Such controls might show where items belong, how many belong there, what the standard procedure is for doing something, the status of the work-in-progress, and other information critical to the flow. These controls are not about meeting plans and targets. They are integrated into the work. The visual aspect means that anyone can see if work is deviating from an agreed-on standard and enable immediate corrections to take place. For example, by just observing minimum and maximum levels of inventory compared with the standard enables managers to be highly effective. These controls are kept on *daily* graphs and charts.

✓ **Use only reliable, thoroughly tested technology.** Many leaders fixate on acquiring the latest technology, particularly if it means performing the same process in less time. Thus, they will spend large sums on machines that offer step changes in capacity and lower cost. But, according to the Toyota mind-set, this may not be the best approach. A new machine may be faster and even more reliable, but it may also put the production line out of sync and soak up much of the firm's capital. A better approach may be to go for a more incremental change, that is, acquire similar, though slightly better machines to those already installed that increase capacity only when needed and at a modest cost. Thus, the speed and flow of the line is maintained.

✓ **Grow leaders who live the philosophy.** Lean organizations develop their own leaders. Toyota spends a great deal of time and effort hiring the right people. Author Steven Spear tells a compelling story of how Toyota hired and trained a star American recruit destined for a high-level position at one of Toyota's U.S. plants. Rather than undergo a brief induction and ori-enteering course, the recruit spent months on the job in the United States and then in Japan learning the TPS the long and hard way—by practicing it. This is how Toyota trains any new employee, regardless of rank or function.[8]

✓ **Respect, develop, and challenge your people and teams.** The TPS is built around groups of between twenty to thirty people. This comprises five to eight group leaders, three to five team leaders, and twelve to eighteen team members. Team members perform manual jobs to standards and are responsible for solving problems and improving their work. Team leaders take on a number of jobs traditionally done by white-collar man-agers, such as keeping the line running, producing quality parts, covering absenteeism, training, and meeting production goals. Group leaders per-form a number of functions usually done by support functions in human resources, engineering, and quality. These include manpower and vaca-tion scheduling, production planning, shift coordination, and process trials. There is no such thing as a hands-off leader at Toyota.[9]

✓ **Respect, challenge, and help your suppliers.** The community at Toyota extends beyond the organization's walls. It involves external suppliers and customers. It engages with suppliers to reduce costs throughout the value chain so that they all benefit from the profits that come from selling cars at competitive prices. Instead of treating suppliers like adversaries to beat into submission, lean organizations see them (or at least the key ones) as potential partners in a win-win process of value creation. Toyota does not believe in bullying suppliers. It knows that its best long-term interests are served by developing their capabilities and potential. Toyota helps its key suppliers cut their lead times and costs. However, there is a popular misconception that all frontline suppliers are classified as business partners. The reality is that of the hundreds of first-tier suppliers, only a few are elevated to the rank of partner and share technology, strategy, and information; the rest have specific roles. While Toyota outsources 70 percent of its product parts, it is careful not to include core technologies. This goes back to its belief in self-reliance. If a technology is core to a vehicle, Toyota wants to be the best in the world at developing it. Toyota's suppliers know what is expected of them in, for example, new product development. Once a concept has been approved, there is little latitude for further changes. From that point on—through the prototyping stage—milestones have to be met and target costs and performance levels reached. The whole network of supply is tightly coordinated, as any slippage in targets at one level could have damaging effects elsewhere. There is little sympathy for missed targets.[10]

Make decisions slowly

Toyota emphasizes thorough preparation and consensus decision making. If a decision fails to live up to expectations, then managers will be tolerant, but if the preparation is sloppy, then they will not be tolerant and will likely follow up with a reprimand.

There are five major elements in the Toyota decision-making process:[a] (1) find out what's really going on, (2) understand underlying causes that explain surface appearances—ask "Why?" five times, (3) consider alternative solutions and develop a convincing rationale for the one preferred, (4) build consensus within the team, (5) use simple, efficient methods of communication.

Toyota passionately believes in consensus decision making. Small-ticket decisions are made quickly without any fuss. A small team might agree to do something that it just announces and goes ahead with. For larger decisions, however, there can be many signatures on the proposal sheet. On a new product design, for example, as many as a hundred people examine and sign the "K4" form. Someone from administration who has little to do with development might sign. The idea is to involve people with different perspectives.

Alex Warren, at Toyota's Georgetown, Kentucky, plant, made this observation: "If you've got a project that is supposed to be fully implemented in a year, it seems to me that the typical American company will spend about three months on planning, then they'll begin to implement. But they'll encounter all sorts of problems after implementation, and they'll spend the rest of the year correcting them. However, given the same year-long project, Toyota will spend up to ten months planning, then implement in a small way—such as with pilot production—and be fully implemented at the end of the year, with virtually no remaining problems."[b]

[a] Jeffrey K. Liker, *The Toyota Way* (New York: McGraw-Hill, 2004), 237.
[b] Ibid.

✓ **See for yourself to thoroughly understand the situation.** Lean organizations do not believe in management by remote control. Managers are expected to check and verify the facts before coming to a decision. Local decision making is absolutely critical to Toyota's success. It makes all production decisions within the teams on the front line. *There are no control systems linking high-level decisions with frontline actions.* They are not necessary. The company trusts its workers to make fast, rational decisions as the need arises. Work processes are designed so that people can see problems where they occur, when they occur, and remedy them on the spot, without exceptions and with no catastrophes. Ohno notes that most decisions are made in the plant, for example, when to stop production, what sequence to follow in making parts, or when overtime is necessary to produce the required amount. "These discussions can be made by factory workers themselves without having to consult the production control or engineering departments," he notes.[11]

✓ **Use *kaizen* to embed organizational learning in the culture.** "Standardized work is essential to identifying where things go wrong," Minoura says. "If you're turning out something in a different way from that on the standardized work sheet, or different from the way other people are doing it, that's the definition of a problem. By thinking about what is causing the problem, the problem itself will come into view. When the problem becomes clear this will lead to *kaizen*. If you make it a rule to deal with defects only when they occur, the number of staff you need will drop straight away. Things that are running smoothly should not be subject to any control. If you commit yourself to just finding and fixing problems, you'll be able to carry out effective control on your lines with fewer personnel."[12] Everyone at Toyota is involved in business improvement planning. They have regular meetings to discuss their progress and consider new initiatives. Everyone is expected to contribute, and everyone's ideas are listened to. There are no suggestion boxes anywhere because people are not afraid to talk about new ideas no matter how radical they are. On one of Liker's visits to Toyota's plant in Kentucky, he discovered that over a one-year period, employees had made 80,000 improvement suggestions, and the plant had implemented 99 percent of them.[13]

Conclusions

The impact of lean thinking on most organizations is so compelling that you have to wonder why it has taken so long to grow. The likely answer lies in the deeply ingrained way we manage our organizations. One report identified that the key barriers are companies' attitudes to change, lack of understanding of lean, shortage of the right lean skills (at management, supervisor, and workforce levels), and cultural issues.[14] Another problem is that as project leaders migrate lean thinking from operations up the organization, they come across the functional, hierarchical mind-set that runs counter to the environment required for lean thinking to flourish. Leaders need to be patient. Lean is not a quick fix. Bottom-line results might take some time to materialize. People need time to see what's different and build new competencies. Sometimes, accounting results have to get worse before they get better (though cash flow improves immediately). Some leaders find that hard to accept.

FURTHER READING

Deming, W. Edwards. *The New Economics.* Cambridge, MA: MIT Press, 2000.

Deming, W. Edwards. *Out of Crisis,* 26th ed. Cambridge, MA: MIT Press, 1998.

Hope, Jeremy. *Reinventing the CFO: How Financial Managers Can Transform Their Roles and Add Greater Value.* Boston: Harvard Business School Press, 2006.

Liker, Jeffrey K. *The Toyota Way.* New York: McGraw-Hill, 2004.

Ohno, Taiichi. *The Toyota Production System.* Portland, OR: Productivity Press, 1988.

Seddon, John. *Freedom from Command and Control—A Better Way to Make the Work Work.* Buckingham, England: Vanguard Education Limited, 2003.

Womack J. P., and D. T. Jones. "Lean Consumption." *Harvard Business Review,* March 2005, 58–68.

Womack J. P., and D. T. Jones. *Lean Thinking.* London: Simon and Schuster, 1996.

Womack, J. P., D. T. Jones, and D. Roos. *The Machine That Changed the World.* New York: Rawson Associates, 1990.

22

LEAN SERVICES

What is this practice and how effective is it?

Lean services apply the principles of lean to service organizations ranging from call centers to hospitals. However, unlike manufacturing, where processes can be standardized, service organizations need to absorb much more variety, and therefore standard processes and tasks are less useful. But as we will point out, there is just as much waste in services, and managers need to learn how to identify and eliminate it.

Alternative names and related topics: value analysis; value stream mapping; white collar productivity; just-in-time for the office

Over the past twenty years or so, large services organizations such as retailers, banks, telecoms, professional services firms, and government agencies have all been looking for ways to improve efficiency and reduce costs. They realized that with large IT systems, they could combine many activities and benefit from economies of scale. So they closed branches and offices, consolidated them into larger regional centers, built shared services and call centers, and outsourced many of their routine back-office work. The idea was to separate the front office, which had direct contact with the customer, from the back office, which managed the transactional work. Everything looked rosy on the plans and spreadsheets as the cost savings started to show up. But for most of these organizations, that's not how it worked out in practice.

In many cases, cost savings didn't materialize, so firms brought in lean and six sigma consultants who did some process and "value stream" mapping and broke everything down into standardized tasks.

Lean techniques have helped U.K.-based retailer Tesco grow its share rapidly and become the United Kingdom's market leader in groceries, as well as fuel its global expansion in Eastern Europe and East Asia. Over a twenty-four-hour

---

The six principles of value stream mapping

1. Solve the customer's problem completely by ensuring that all the goods and services work, and work together.
2. Don't waste the customer's time.
3. Provide exactly *what* the customer wants.
4. Provide what's wanted exactly *where* it's wanted.
5. Provide what's wanted where it's wanted exactly *when* it's wanted.
6. Continually aggregate solutions to reduce the customer's time and hassle.

Source: James P. Womack and Daniel T. Jones, "Lean Consumption,"*Harvard Business Review*, March 2005, 58–68.

---

day, by replenishing every store continuously to eliminate the need to hold stock either at the back of the store (like Walmart) or in high-bay storage (like Home Depot), Tesco reorders from key suppliers that produce—in a matter of hours—items that customers have just purchased. What's more, Tesco picks up directly from suppliers' shipping docks at precise times and takes the goods to regional distribution centers where fresh products and fast-moving items are cross-docked onto vehicles delivering to stores. Lean techniques have also allowed the retailer to increase customer satisfaction and loyalty by giving shoppers what they want without wasting their time.[1]

But for many other service organizations, lean has been an empty promise. The problem was that the consultants used the same lean practices they applied in the factory. For example, they set targets for each activity—answer the phone within three rings; handle a call within 420 seconds, and so forth—and measured performance against the target. But deep cost savings still failed to materialize. What many failed to understand was that the problems are different. In service organizations, there are few standards and lots of variety. No two customer requirements, such as sales orders, customer complaints, or mortgage applications, are exactly the same. So how to absorb variety at the highest quality and lowest cost is the greatest challenge.

There was another problem the consultants failed to see. There are two types of demand on any service system. Let's call them "value demands" (what we are here to do) that meet the purpose of a process, such as sales orders or customer service issues, and "failure demands" that are caused by not handling an earlier demand right the first time (repeated demands on the system). Value demands add value; failure demands don't. The trouble is that failure demands can represent a huge proportion of demand activity in any system.

Why does this happen? The likely answer is that most customer service agents are driven by targets and measured on "units of production" (all borrowed from the factory). These targets are based on items such as the number of calls taken, the time to answer, the average time a call takes, abandon rates, and how much work each agent does in a day or week. Now that type of information is useful to plan for the resources needed (number of people, etc.), but as measures of performance, they are counterproductive. If agents can't meet their targets, they start to cheat.

The problem, as lean thinkers understand it, is not the people. *It's the system.* Managers typically change targets and incentives, put people on training courses, and threaten them with their jobs, but in reality, they are working on only 5 percent of the problem. To eradicate the nonvalue calls, lean organizations examine the work flow from the customer's perspective. They find out why the company is not delivering products on time and why it is not calling customers back. They know that if they can get to the root cause of these problems (e.g., by eliminating targets, providing the right training and information, and measuring the customer experience), then they will begin to make real headway. By achieving these relatively simple changes, firms will either create huge amounts of extra capacity or avoid building so many call centers.

The traditional manager has no information about flow. Instead, she will see reams of computer reports about standards, variances, and costs. Consistent with the desire to manage work standards, most managers typically specify procedures for how the work is to be done. Where procedures do not match with customer demands, waste occurs—rework, duplication, lost time, and so on. By contrast, the object of a systems design is to design flow against value— what matters to customers for each type of demand.

Lean services at Fujitsu

Fujitsu Services is one of the largest providers of IT services in Europe, the Middle East, and Africa. After providing technical support for its own products for many years, Fujitsu began to offer services to companies that were outsourcing their customer service and technical support activities. Typically, firms like Fujitsu are paid to respond to user complaints at the lowest cost per complaint handled. This call-center model gives firms no reason to reduce the number of complaints received and, indeed, creates a disincentive: if the call volume falls, so does the revenue. Fujitsu approached the problem with a completely different mind-set. It set out

(continued)

to eliminate the root causes of callers' complaints—and to make a profit doing so.

When Fujitsu took over the help desk contract in 2001 for airline BMI, it immediately analyzed the different types of calls coming in from BMI employees. Then it set to work to understand the problems that gave rise to the calls; to track the time and effort required to fix them; and, most important, to measure the impact on the business of the failures or delays in doing so. Fujitsu found that more than half the calls to help desks were repeat complaints about recurring problems or repair delays. One of the most common reasons for calls—accounting for 26 percent of the total—was malfunctioning printers: Ticketing agents kept finding that they couldn't print boarding passes and baggage tags for passengers at check-in. It was immediately apparent that solving the printer problem was critical to the airline's business. Given tight airport security, the inability to print boarding passes and baggage tags that could be scanned at a number of points could cause flights to miss their take-off slots. Under BMI's previous contractor, the help desk had struggled to get service technicians to respond more quickly so check-in staff wouldn't keep calling with complaints.

Fujitsu's response was to find the most cost-effective way to eliminate the root cause of the printer problem. The answer was to convince BMI senior management to spend money up front to install better printers. As a result, the number of calls about malfunctioning printers was cut by more than 80 percent within eighteen months, which translated into major savings in flight operations far exceeding the cost of the new printers. In addition, Fujitsu improved the technician-response process so that the average time needed to fix printers that still failed fell from ten hours to three. Fujitsu coupled this problem-solving approach with a different business proposition for BMI. Instead of being paid for each call handled, Fujitsu asked to be paid a set fee based on the number of *potential* callers to the BMI system. This allowed Fujitsu to profitably offer BMI a lower bid than its current vendor.

By addressing root causes, Fujitsu reduced total calls to the help desk by 40 percent within eighteen months and improved customer satisfaction. As the company has progressively applied this problem-solving approach to all of its customers, it has moved beyond its original role as a mediator between vendors and frustrated consumers to become an analyst and optimizer of entire IT response systems.[a]

[a] James P. Womack and Daniel T. Jones, "Lean Consumption," *Harvard Business Review*, March 2005, 58–68.

John Seddon believes that the lean approach creates an adaptive organization; as demand changes, people change what they do—something that is impossible to accomplish in a command-and-control design. It puts people back where they belong: managing relationships with customers. Managers' roles change from working in the hierarchy to acting on the system.[2]

What is the performance potential of this practice?

- **To improve the customer experience.** By designing processes from the customer's perspective, firms can eliminate errors and repeat calls, resulting in a much enhanced customer experience.
- **To improve employee satisfaction.** Employees are happier when they can solve customer problems on the first call.
- **To reduce costs.** The potential for cost reduction is huge as work can be completed in half the time, thus requiring fewer people and control systems.

What actions do you need to take to maximize the potential of this practice?

ACTIONS TO AVOID

- ✖ **Avoid separating the front and back offices.** Many organizations have built back-office processing and shared services centers to process the transactional part of the customer service request. The theory is that this increases efficiency, but in practice, costs often rise because the customer fails to provide all the information needed the first time, and so files are opened and closed many times and information (which is copied, batched, stored, and archived) is incomplete and inaccurate. Solving these problems leads to backlogs, overtime, and staff frustration and, ultimately, to higher costs.
- ✖ **Avoid standardization.** There are countless examples of standards in service organizations including standard times for service work queues and standard work measures for employee tasks in the form of targets. While manufacturers use standardization to learn and improve, service organizations need to use actual data (e.g., time taken to execute tasks, volume of tasks done) for learning and improvement. Standard times become arbitrary data, as they do not allow for variation. *The impact of standardization in service organizations is damage to the system's ability to absorb variety and increase costs.*
- ✖ **Eliminate activity targets.** Top-down targets are the nemesis of lean. They focus managers on the boxes on the organization chart and individual activities such as "answer the phone within three rings" rather than on the end-to-end process.

✖ **Stop assuming that people are the problem.** The vast majority of service problems are concerned with the process rather than the people employed to operate within it. Lack of access to fast, accurate, and relevant information is a classic example of why service systems fail.

ACTIONS TO TAKE

✓ **Study the nature and frequency of demand in customer terms.** If you want customers to pull value from the system, you need to know the nature of demands customers place on it. If you don't know this, you risk giving poor service at high cost.[3] Once you know the nature and frequency of demand, you can design processes and train people to meet it. One advantage is that you can focus training on the top-ten problems, and thus cut the training time significantly. Other problems that occur can be dealt with by more experienced people until the new staff builds his or her own knowledge.

✓ **Distinguish between value and failure demand.** Value demands are those you want customers to place on the system. Failure demands are those you don't want. Turning off the causes of failure demand is one of the greatest economic levers available to managers.[4]

✓ **Analyze activity using control charts and the theory of variation.** The theory of variation helps us to understand when there has been a genuine improvement in performance. A stable process, one with no indication of a special cause of variation, is said to be in statistical control, or stable. Its behavior in the near future is predictable. It also has a definable capability (the specifications that it can meet are predictable). Also costs are predictable. Once the process is stable, it can (and should be) improved continuously. Common causes of variation (e.g., poor design, poor working conditions, poor supervision, failure to provide good information) are the responsibility of management, not operators (i.e., they are system problems and common to every worker on the process). According to Deming, without statistical methods, attempts to improve a process are hit or miss, with results that usually make matters worse.[5] The aim in production should be not just to get statistical control, but to shrink variation.[6] In Seddon's experience, using the principles of variation in call centers often leads to more than 100 percent improvement in sales, efficiency, and/or service. Quality improves productivity. It is a better way.[7]

✓ **Rethink measures and incentives.** Forget the twenty to thirty KPIs that relate to activities such as "average speed of answer," "call abandonment rate," "percentage of calls answered within thirty seconds," "average queue time," "average hold time," and "average time to abandon." Instead focus on *people* measures, including satisfaction, absenteeism, and turnover; *process* measures, including failure rates, first-contact resolution, and call handling; and *customer* measures, including service, satisfaction, and complaints.

✓ **Place your best people at the front line.** Instead of batching, sorting, queuing, counting, and dealing with a problem multiple times as the customer provides more information, the best leaders have learned to place highly competent, well-trained people at the first point of customer contact with the scope and authority to deal with and solve the customer problem through to completion. Liverpool Council transformed itself from one of the worst-performing local government councils in the United Kingdom to one of the best. Customer service was key. The myriad delivery departments of the past are gone. There are now just two channels: a call center that accounts for 70 percent of customer contact and a network of one-stop shops providing access to the council's 770 services. The surprise package is the call center. "Liverpool Direct" boasts of being the highest-paying call center in the United Kingdom. It also has the lowest staff turnover at 2 percent. All staff people are experienced council workers (hence, the high costs), but the value they provide can be seen in the number of calls they deal with successfully at the first point of contact. They measure repeat or failure calls, and these are a fraction of the industry average. The whole project is seen as a winner, saving £120 million per year for the council.[8]

Conclusions

One of the greatest services any leader can do for the organization is wage a war against waste. But to do this effectively, he or she needs to blow up the bureaucracy and challenge those resources often protected by some of the most influential people in the firm. Learning and applying the lessons of lean thinking will yield huge benefits, provided that managers have the scope and authority to make the necessary changes. They also need to see these changes as permanent rather than quick fixes; otherwise any benefits will be fleeting.

FURTHER READING

Bowen, D. E., and W. E. Youngdahl. "'Lean' Service: In Defense of a Production-Line Approach." *International Journal of Service Industry Management* 9, no. 3 (1998): 207–225.

Deming, W. Edwards. *The New Economics.* Boston: MIT Press, 2000.

Deming, W. Edwards. *Out of Crisis.* Boston: MIT Press, 1998.

Drew, J., B. McCallum, and S. Roggenhofer. *Journey to Lean: Making Operational Change Stick.* New York: Palgrave MacMillan, 2004.

Johnson, H. T., and A. Bröms. *Profit Beyond Measure.* London: Nicholas Brealey Publishing, 2000.

Liker, Jeffrey. *The Toyota Way.* New York: McGraw Hill, 2004.

Schlesinger, L. A., and J. L. Heskett. "The Service-Driven Service Company." *Harvard Business Review*, September–October 1991, 71–81.

Seddon, J. *Freedom from Command and Control–A Better Way to Make the Work Work.* Buckingham, England: Vanguard Education Limited, 2003.

Seddon, J. "Watch Out for the Toolheads!" www.lean-service.com, 2005.

Womack, J. P., and D. T. Jones. "Lean Consumption." *Harvard Business Review*, March 2005, 58–68.

Womack, James P., and Daniel T. Jones. *Lean Thinking.* London: Simon and Schuster, 1996.

Womack, James P., Daniel T. Jones, and D. Roos. *The Machine That Changed the World.* New York: Rawson Associates, 1990.

23

SIX SIGMA

What is this practice and how effective is it?

Six sigma is an extension of total quality management (it has been described as TQM on steroids). It takes its name from a statistical measure of near perfection which, equated to numerical terms, reaches a goal of 3.4 defects per million units produced. Achieving this level promises lower costs, higher quality, and a more capable workforce. The management focus is on training "green belts," "black belts," and "master black belts," who learn a range of tools that enable them to implement six sigma procedures. But it has a reputation for alienating workers because companies too often impose it from above, with bright young black belts telling seasoned managers how to do their jobs differently. It can also be difficult to implement. We will look at how some large organizations have used six sigma to improve their performance.

Alternative names and related topics: lean manufacturing; total quality management; statistical process control

Six sigma dates back to 1984, when Mikel Harry was an engineer trying to improve the quality of products in the government electronics group of cellphone maker Motorola. He found that the average manufacturing process runs at around what statisticians call three sigma, or 66,800 errors per million. He then set himself a truly audacious goal: to reduce that error rate to six sigma, or a mere 3.4 per million. To make such a giant leap, he felt he couldn't rely on traditional methods. So he invented his own, called DMAIC (define, measure, analyze, improve, and control). Why "sigma"? The word is a statistical term that measures how far a given process deviates from perfection.

Led by a hierarchy of instructors referred to as green belts, black belts, and master black belts, a DMAIC project begins by quantifying the unknown variables around a process. Ford Motor, for instance, learned that the key factor in determining how well its car doors fit—and block out ambient noise and weather—was the location of their center of gravity. Max Allway, head of the Six Sigma Academy's consulting organization, says defining variables clears up a lot of mysteries. As an analogy, he says that stories about dolphins pushing drowning people to shore created a "mythology that dolphins love people." But if you do the sort of hard analysis that DMAIC requires, you find that "research has shown that dolphins don't love people; they simply love to push things. We never heard from the people who were pushed out to sea."[1]

Once all the variables are defined, DMAIC prescribes rigorous statistical techniques for understanding what improvements are crucial to driving down the number of defects. As Allway puts it, "The data take you where you need to go." A typical project—of which there may be dozens or even hundreds under way simultaneously—runs four to six months and saves $150,000 to $500,000 a year, according to the academy.[2]

The six sigma program

The following example of a typical six sigma program comes from Air Academy Associates. It starts with requirements that executives must have a total commitment to the implementation of six sigma and accomplish the following:

1. Establish a six sigma leadership team.
2. Identify key business issues.
3. Assign masters to each key business issue.
4. Assist the masters and leadership team in identifying critical projects that are tied to the key business issues.
5. Assist the masters and leadership team in selecting expert candidates.
6. Allocate time for change agents (experts) to make breakthrough improvements.
7. Set aggressive six sigma goals.
8. Incorporate six sigma performance into the reward system.
9. Direct finance to validate all six sigma returns on investment.
10. Evaluate the corporate culture to determine if intellectual capital is being infused into the company.
11. Continuously evaluate the six sigma implementation and deployment process and make changes if necessary.

Source: "Six Sigma for Manufacturing and Non-Manufacturing Processes'" position paper by Air Academy Associates, http://www.airacad.com/PaperSixSigma.aspx.

General Electric, perhaps the world's greatest exponent of six sigma after following Motorola's lead in adopting these practices, reckons that today's competitive environment leaves no room for error. GE believes that it must delight its customers and relentlessly look for new ways to exceed their expectations. Six sigma quality has become a part of GE's culture. It believes that six sigma is a highly disciplined process that helps it focus on developing and delivering near-perfect products and services. Six sigma has changed the DNA of GE; it is now the way it works, in everything it does and in every product it designs.[3]

But critics see six sigma as "total quality management on steroids," with similar problems. According to U.K. consultant John Seddon, many six sigma programs start with extensive interviews with operating managers. This is not the same as studying the work. In one example he describes, many black belts were trained. Then five consultants interviewed managers for four weeks about their problems and ideas for improvement, but little changed. Notable by its absence was any thinking about the system. Six sigma is top-down project management, rather than knowledge applied to improve the work from a customer perspective. It assumes that the problem is *people rather than systems*.

To Seddon, all of this sounds like the traditional mantra of command and control. In other words, "we know best, and we will train you what to do and reward/punish you if you don't do it right." So how did Motorola and GE claim such dramatic success? While Motorola's fortunes have declined over the past ten years, GE's star has, with a few blips here and there, kept rising. Following its lack of success in previous initiatives, GE was convinced that six sigma was the answer to its prayers. From 1995 to 2000, it invested billions of dollars in six sigma, training tens of thousands of people and initiating thousands of projects. Former CEO Jack Welch gave it power and momentum by telling managers that either they were on board with six sigma or they had no future with the company. Anecdotal success stories are legion, and the company claims that it has benefited to the tune of billions of dollars.[4]

There can be little doubt that such an investment in quality initiatives, however instigated and managed, has been a courageous and well intentioned move, but will it lead to sustainable improvement? In other words, once the pressure is relaxed (and other programs take over), will the company slip back into its old ways? Leaders would likely say no, but without truly embedding quality in processes and people, there is minimal evidence to back this up.

The six sigma movement extols the virtues of tools and training. This invariably involves recruiting bright young, highly paid people who learn the methods and who then go forth and multiply. But what real experience do these people have? How can they possibly sound credible to others who have worked on the line for years? And how do companies then move them into operational jobs when they are so overpaid? Jeffrey Liker, in his book *The*

Toyota Way, expresses his views: "In reality, the training of internal Six Sigma and lean 'experts' serves to reinforce the superficial tool orientation in the vast majority of companies . . . Even Convis [Gary Convis—first president of Toyota America] says it took ten years of living in Toyota for him to understand and he is still learning every day. Yet the companies seeking to benefit from the Toyota Production System and Six Sigma typically train employees for one to two weeks, ask them to do a project, and anoint them as experts."[5]

Toyota inculcates in every new recruit the need to understand and engage in improving their work, as part of everyone's everyday job. People get better with age and experience. It's a deep cultural issue that no amount of policies and procedures can teach. The learning is on the job, through colleagues and mentors. And people stick around long enough to pass on their wisdom. It is a cultural mix of a philosophy, continuous process improvement by people on the job, and committed employees who provide a stream of improvement ideas. While six sigma might kick-start this process, it is not necessarily the long-term answer.

When asked which tool was the most important at GE, Jim Parke, former CFO of GE Capital, replied, "I think the one that has had the most impact on our company is Six Sigma because it has forced everyone to learn a new language. It's a language that says 'good enough' is not acceptable. It teaches everyone to aim higher and demand nothing less than the best. It has also given us a consistently applied approach to problem solving. It's got everyone on the same game-plan; we all now think the same way. It's been through various iterations and continues to evolve, but it's now part of the company's culture. If you take on any project or program, you apply the disciplines of Six Sigma. There's no debate."[6] But GE may be the exception rather than the rule. The six sigma landscape is littered with "part projects" that had some initial success and then faded away. Whether the benefits outweighed the costs is a debatable issue.

What is the performance potential of this practice?

- **To improve the quality of products and processes.** Prior to six sigma, "good enough" or attaining "industry standards" was the aim for many organizational improvement efforts. Six sigma has lifted the improvement benchmark to a much higher level. Indeed, the aim of some companies is for perfection (zero errors).
- **To make cost savings.** Errors and rework cost organizations a fortune. Just reducing them through basic quality control can cut costs, but six sigma is in another league altogether. Achieving six sigma will eliminate the need for expensive rework departments and have a huge impact on costs.

- **To improve the competencies of the workforce.** Many workers are cynical about quality initiatives, as they "check the boxes" rather than truly embrace cultural changes. Beginning a six sigma program is a signal that the management team is serious about improving workers' skills. The individual certifications under six sigma reward workers' extra efforts to become involved, and the green, black, and master black belt certifications enhance worker marketability and earning power. Raising the capability of the workforce in such a way is a powerful approach to long-term business improvement.

What actions do you need to take to maximize the potential of this practice?

ACTIONS TO AVOID

- ✖ **Don't limit six sigma to just manufacturing and logistics.** Daniel Laux, president of the Six Sigma Academy, says it is the methodology's success that has led practitioners to greatly expand how it is used. Initially, six sigma efforts focused on manufacturing and logistics. Laux says they can now apply it to "all industries and all functions." Six sigma can even be used in research and development to find innovative products, notes Laux. This method for minimizing mistakes has become so all encompassing that, according to Laux, some companies view it as "an enterprise wide business strategy."[7] Others disagree. Larry Keeley, head of the design and innovation consulting firm Doblin, is positively caustic about attempts to expand the use of six sigma beyond the original intent. "Consulting firms often need to relearn the truism that once you master a hammer, everything starts to look like a nail," he says. "The recent trend to use Six Sigma statistical process-control metrics for every damn fool thing is just the latest example of the adaptive instincts of modern consulting."[8]

- ✖ **Don't use six sigma initiatives unless you can measure the potential improvement.** "Where you don't do it is where you can't measure the quality of the outcome," says Dave Amos, who oversees six sigma at Ford's design studio, among other areas. Amos says Ford devises "mathematical transfer functions" to translate "critical customer requirements" into engineering language, which works fine for brakes and hood latches. But quantifying the all-important intangibles involved in styling "has been a challenge," he says, "because those [designers] are artists."[9]

- ✖ **Be wary of losing the innovation edge.** A relentless focus on improvement can lead to innovation blind spots. IBM serves as a good example; six sigma, almost a religion there in the early 1990s, was improving product quality across the board. The company won a Malcolm Baldrige National Quality Award at the facility in Rochester that made the AS/400 line of minicomputers. However, the use of six sigma didn't help the company spot a glaring problem: IBM was, in many cases, building the wrong products. While IBM was focused on reducing the defects in its networking equipment, Cisco Systems was innovating and introducing new products known as routers. The same situation occurred with disk drives. While IBM was making incremental improvements to its disk drives, EMC was pioneering a wholly new approach, known as RAID (redundant arrays of inexpensive disks). Cisco and EMC tapped into explosive growth and took the leading position in their markets away from IBM. IBM has never recovered in networking equipment and recently announced plans to essentially leave the hard-disk-drive market.[10]

✖ **Be wary of the destructive impact of black belts.** When the initiative comes to an end, what happens to the smart MBAs whom the firm has hired to implement six sigma? Integrating them into the firm is often difficult because they have not earned their spurs through the normal channels and may lack credibility among their peers.

✖ **Don't underestimate the training overhead.** Implementing six sigma usually involves a huge investment in employee training, as often thousands of people realize the impact of what they are taking on. Raising the capability of the workforce in such a way is a powerful approach to long-term business improvement. Much depends on how the training takes place. If inexperienced black belts impose the new standards on experienced workers, then it is unlikely to lead to the right result.

✖ **Be wary about assuming that financial success will follow.** GE may be the exception. "Despite the extravagant claims," noted management writer and consultant Michael Hammer, "Six Sigma success is not synonymous with business success. Some of its early adopters—Eastman Kodak, Xerox, and Polaroid, among others—have experienced significant business reversals recently. Even Motorola has seen its performance fall and rise and fall again, despite its continuing practice of Six Sigma."[11]

ACTIONS TO TAKE

✓ **Link six sigma projects to business strategy.** Choosing projects that have little impact on performance or a poor linkage with strategy undermines the credibility of six sigma. Sometimes the purpose is gaining black-belt certification for team members rather than achieving anything significant for the business.

✓ **Study the work.** Consultants often focus on tools and metrics and overlook the key step—studying what people do and how to improve the work flow. As with any process study, the first step is to agree on the purpose of the process and then examine the nature and frequency of demand. Once this is done, then you can apply six sigma tools in an intelligent way.

✓ **Ensure that frontline employees are involved.** Six sigma, with its dedicated "belt" infrastructure and standardized DMAIC methodology, is likely a more sophisticated and effective approach than past quality improvement methods. But many initiatives fail when it comes to involving frontline (untrained) employees. If six sigma is imposed on them, they are far more likely to resist the project than if they are invited to play a full part in it.

✓ **Make sure that any credit also goes to the team doing the work.** Nothing is more likely to alienate frontline employees than if the project team gets all the kudos and the frontline workers who make it happen are ignored. This can be particularly damaging if the workforce has gone out of its way to support the initiative. News travels quickly, so don't be surprised if the next project doesn't get the support you expect.

✓ **Be patient.** Patience is another factor in the six sigma equation. "For the first two years, people had to keep telling Jack Welch, 'You're not going to see bottom-line results right away.'"[12] This comment implies that many six sigma initiatives will outlive their initial sponsors. And given that many initiatives are driven by individuals (including many ex-GE leaders), this should ring warning bells for the long-term success of the project. Six sigma is clearly difficult and expensive to implement and is not to be entered into lightly.

Conclusions

Errors and rework cost organizations a fortune. Just reducing them through basic quality control can have an impact, but six sigma multiplies this impact significantly. Achieving six sigma will eliminate the need for expensive rework departments and have a huge impact on costs. But weighed against this is the cost of hiring consultants and their tools and training the workforce. Clearly, leaders need to be aware to ensure that the expected savings are greater than the implementation costs.

FURTHER READING

Biolos, Jim. "Six Sigma Meets the Service Economy." *Harvard Management Update*, November 2002, 1–4.

Breyfogle, Forrest, III. *Implementing Six Sigma: Smarter Solutions Using Statistical Methods*, 2nd ed. New York: John Wiley & Sons, 2003.

Eckes, George. *The Six Sigma Revolution*. New York: John Wiley & Sons, 2001.

George, Michael L. *Lean Six Sigma: Combining Six Sigma Quality with Lean Speed*. New York: McGraw-Hill, 2002.

Hoerl, Roger. "One Perspective on the Future of Six-Sigma." *International Journal of Six Sigma and Competitive Advantage* (IJSSCA) 1, no. 1 (2004): 112–119.

Pande, Peter S., Robert P. Neuman, and Roland R. Cavanagh. *The Six Sigma Way: How GE, Motorola and Other Top Companies Are Honing Their Performance*. New York: McGraw-Hill, 2000.

Pande, Peter S., and Lawrence Holpp. *What Is Six Sigma?* New York: McGraw-Hill, 2002.

Snee, Ronald D., and Roger W. Hoerl. *Leading Six Sigma: A Step-by-Step Guide Based on Experience with GE and Other Six Sigma Companies*. Upper Saddle River, NJ: Financial Times Prentice Hall, 2002.

24

TARGET COSTING

What is this practice and how effective is it?

Japanese lean manufacturers have used target costing for many years to set prices and manage costs. There are many differences between "target" costing and "standard" costing. Whereas standard costing is used to calculate unit costs and value inventory (cost-led pricing), target costing is used to set prices over the lifetime of a product family and then set a target cost that managers must stay within to achieve the return on capital required (price-led costing). We will examine these differences in approach in more depth.

Alternative names and related topics: lean manufacturing; product costing; activity-based costing; profit planning

The basic principle underlying most of the costing systems used today entails an assumption about the behavior of costs. Costs are classified as either *variable* (they vary with volume, for example, with output or revenue), or *fixed* (they don't vary with volume). This simple classification is the root and branch of most costing systems. Accountants construct their budgets on the basis of "recovering" fixed costs, and production managers aim to maximize volume to meet these recovery targets and generate profits once the break-even level has been passed. There is another way of saying this. As more units are produced, more fixed costs are recovered or absorbed by production. Thus, managers often speak in terms of "fixed overhead recovery"—meaning that if more units than expected in the budget are produced, the firm over-recovers its fixed costs and *unit costs fall*, whereas if fewer units are produced, there is an underrecovery of fixed costs and *unit costs rise*. Most volume and many pricing decisions are based on these beliefs. But reality is intruding on the assumptions of this model in ways that challenge its entire plausibility.

By focusing on volume-based methods of allocating costs to products, the changing *mix* of overhead costs has been overlooked, destroying the credibility of accountants' models. Overheads have risen as a proportion of total costs, and direct labor costs have fallen, but questions have been seldom asked about the causes of these changes. Consequently, few have realized that overhead costs are increasingly driven not by volume, but by scope and diversity, caused by a wide variety of customer demands, such as product customization, special packaging, and extended service commitments. The speed and scale of these changes have caught many companies unaware, and they have stretched the plausibility of the traditional methods to the breaking point.

Discussing his own experience, Gary Convis, president of Toyota's Kentucky plant, explained the difference between Ford's and Toyota's approaches to costing. "When I was at Ford, if you didn't run production 100 percent of the shift, you had to explain it to Division. You never shut the line off. We don't run 100 percent of the scheduled time out here. Toyota's strength I think is that the upper management realizes what the andon system is all about . . . They've lived through it and support it. So in all the years I've been with Toyota, I've never really had any criticism over lost production and putting a priority on safety and quality over hitting production targets."[1]

There is little virtue in having an accurate costing system that plots product costs to three decimal places if the actual product costs are much higher than those of competitors. Recognizing this, many Japanese companies have moved from cost-led pricing to price-led costing, also known as target costing. Acknowledged expert Robin Cooper has defined target costing as a structured approach to determining the cost at which a proposed product with specified functionality and quality must be produced in order to generate the desired level of profitability at the product's anticipated selling price.[2] The contrast between the traditional and the target costing approaches is shown in figure 24-1.

The traditional model starts with the product specification, which the design and engineering departments provide. The accountants then apply costs to each component and add the required profit margin to arrive at the projected price. If they judge the market price to be too high, they go back around the same loop until either a different design (with lower costs) is produced, or the product idea is accepted with a lower profit margin or dropped altogether.

The target costing model takes a different view. For example, Toyota starts with a target cost based on the price the market is prepared to accept. Then it tells designers and engineers to meet that cost. It sets target costs for every product component and invites suppliers to tender on the basis of such costs. If suppliers have a problem meeting a particular target cost, Toyota either redefines the product specification within new cost guidelines, or meets with its own suppliers to work out a mutually acceptable way of reducing costs.

FIGURE 24-1

Contrasting traditional and target costing

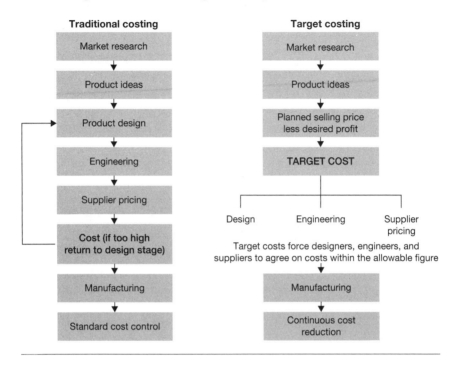

However, what doesn't change is the target cost. All members of the value chain are thus involved in solving cost issues, the incentive being the guarantee of work by the principal manufacturer.

Take the fictitious case of leaders of ABC Widgets, who believe there is a market niche for a widget with certain new features. After researching the market, the marketing department believes that a price of $50 would be appropriate for the new widget. They reckon that the company can sell thirty thousand widgets each year over the next three years at that price, producing annual revenues of $1.5 million. To design, develop, and produce these widgets would require an investment of $2.5 million. The company needs a return on investment (ROI) of 20 percent. The target cost is calculated at $1.5 million revenues less $0.5 million profit ($2.5 million investment × 20 percent return) leaving an allowable cost of $1 million or $33.30 per widget. This $33.30 target cost would be broken into subtargets for the various functions involved in the manufacture, sales, and service of this product. Each team would be accountable for keeping its actual costs within the agreed-on target.

The critical factor in target costing is its focus on reducing product costs at the design and development stage, that is, before the product is committed to

Target costing at Olympus

Olympus Optical in Japan is a global company with 70 percent of the digital SLR camera market. Olympus was a market leader in SLR cameras in the late 1970s, but watched with dismay as competitors introduced high-feature compact cameras that tore into its market share. Although Olympus introduced its own compact range, by the mid-1980s, the company plunged into losses. In 1987, it changed its policy completely to concentrate on the features customers valued and geared its target costs to meet these increasingly volatile expectations. Only when designers and engineers were able to convince managers that market price points could be met, would a camera be committed to production. Only 20 percent of designs were acceptable on the first pass. Those that were not acceptable were subjected to a feature-cost review. In other words, designers and marketers were asked if the "nice to have" features really justified their costs, or whether those features could enhance a product sufficiently to move it up into a higher price bracket.

Olympus applies five cost-management methods to decrease the cost of a product over time. At the conception and design phase, the company uses the target costing method, determining the product's price point and establishing a corresponding cost target. To achieve that target, engineers apply techniques such as reducing the number of parts in the product and eliminating expensive, labor-intensive processes whenever possible. The other four methods come into play during manufacturing. First, Olympus uses product-specific kaizen costing—redesigning the product during early manufacturing runs to replace certain components with cheaper ones and focusing on ways to reduce supplier and labor costs. Second, the company uses general kaizen costing focused on manufacturing, challenging employees to discover ways of meeting cost-reduction goals for production processes. Third, it implements functional group management, in which the production process is separated into autonomous groups whose responsibility is to find ways of increasing output level and revenue. Finally, the product costing method coordinates activities between the other methods and monitors their performance.

Importantly, Olympus does not treat the methods as independent functions but as an integrated system in which the output of one becomes the input of the next. This system reduces the cost of Olympus products during the manufacturing phase by approximately 17 percent annually. These savings accumulate year after year, leading to significant cost reductions over the lifetime of a product.[a]

[a] From Robin Cooper and W. Bruce Chew, "Control Tomorrow's Costs Through Today's Designs," *Harvard Business Review*, January–February 1996, 86–97.

production. Once the target cost has been achieved, low unit costs are not dependent on high-volume production runs. And without the intense pressure created by numerous production changes, companies can develop more stable production processes, operate flexibly, produce only what is demanded, and concentrate on high-quality production. In other words, by managing costs at the design and development stage, they minimize the struggle throughout the production process to keep costs within budget. The focus is on the speed of attaining the target cost, and not on a regular comparison of actual costs with obsolete budgets. The results of this approach are, usually, lower inventories and more satisfied customers.

The target costing approach puts less emphasis on such cost classifications as fixed and variable. Rather, it seeks to minimize *total costs throughout the value chain*. A number of Western car manufacturers such as Mercedes-Benz and Chrysler have now adopted the target costing approach. Mercedes-Benz CEO Helmut Werner has said that "Mercedes now has to produce cars to match market-driven prices, not make the autos its engineers design at whatever the cost."[3] Japanese car manufacturers have built an enviable reputation for bringing new products to market on time and at the right cost. Their methods of target costing and supplier management are at the root of this success. But target costing is not without its problems. A study of Japanese companies suggested that one of the major difficulties is deciding on the tightness of the targets in terms of the effort required to obtain them. Another problem concerns the appropriate level in the cost hierarchy at which targets should be set. The respondents in this study indicated that 41 percent set a target cost for each level, 39 percent at the product level, and 16 percent at the product group level. The product level used varied substantially across industries, reflecting the degree of product variety.[4]

What is the performance potential of this practice?

- **To focus managers on anticipating future cost needs.** By looking at costs over a product's life cycle, managers can anticipate future cost reductions and plan for them from the outset, rather than face a competitive crisis that they are unprepared to meet.
- **To focus management attention on total costs (rather than unit costs).** The standard focus on unit cost concentrates on attribution rather than the causes of those costs, particularly overhead. Target costing focuses managers on managing total costs over a product's life cycle and thus offers a better approach to cost reduction.
- **To involve the supply chain in the cost-reduction process.** Traditional organizations negotiate arrangements with suppliers every year or so. Only in rare cases are suppliers involved in long-term cost planning.

With target costing, key suppliers are part of that planning. And the company shares information with them. By getting suppliers' commitment to a cost-reduction program to meet anticipated price reductions, the main producer can be confident in meeting future cost targets.

What actions do you need to take to maximize the potential of this practice?

ACTIONS TO AVOID

✖ **Don't bully suppliers into accepting impossible targets.** Power over suppliers is important because one of the outputs of a target costing system is the price at which the firm is willing to buy components from its suppliers.[5] However, business partners can often discuss and negotiate targets in the pre-production phase. Toyota submits targets four months after the initial supplier presentation and usually requests small improvements, such as a 4 percent reduction in cost or a 5 percent improvement in performance. But while these performance improvements are forcibly stressed, suppliers understand that there is some element of flexibility. Toyota also sends suppliers a broad specification showing how parts must interact with those of other suppliers. Unlike many Western car manufacturers that increasingly rely on computer-aided design models, Toyota still places a high value on prototyping as a means of finalizing the specification and gaining the commitment of suppliers to meet target costs.[6]

ACTIONS TO TAKE

✓ **Agree on the primary purpose of the target costing approach.** The primary purpose of Nissan's costing is to achieve the target cost by creating downward pressure on suppliers' selling prices and by modifying the functionality of the product. In contrast, Komatsu sets the product's target price and then determines the functionality that can be supported at that price. Olympus determines the distinctive functionality of its products first and then sets target prices.[7]

✓ **Build strategic partnerships with first-tier suppliers.** Toyota and its key suppliers help each other cut lead times and reduce costs. However, there is a popular misconception that Toyota classifies all frontline suppliers as business partners. The reality is that of the one hundred to two hundred first-tier suppliers, it elevates only a dozen or so to the rank of partner and shares technology, strategy, and information. The rest have specific roles.[8]

✓ **Share information.** Target costing depends on extensive knowledge sharing between a manufacturer and its key suppliers. Toyota's suppliers know what is expected of them. They present relevant development ideas thirty-six months prior to production, but once a concept has been approved (twenty-seven months prior to production), there is little latitude for further changes. From that point on—through the prototyping stage—suppliers have to make milestones and reach target costs and performance levels. The whole network of supply is tightly coordinated, because any slippage in targets at one level could have damaging effects elsewhere. Toyota has little sympathy for missed targets.[9]

✓ **Integrate target costing with value engineering.** "Value engineering is an organized effort to analyze the functions of goods and services in order to find ways to achieve those functions in a manner that allows the firm to meet its target costs."[10] This process determines the function of each part of the product and attempts to match the functional cost with the perceived customer value, thus helping to evaluate the target cost. Sometimes, this can involve five or ten reviews, which can take the form of two- or three-day sessions where internal and external advisers meet to thrash out cost-reduction strategies. If they allow a functionality improvement that increases costs, then they must also find savings to offset those additional costs. What doesn't change is the target cost. Such an approach was a culture shock for managers at a new Suzuki plant in Hungary. Deputy Manager for Production Laszlo Pataki commented, "They taught me to concentrate on every detail and ask how to do it cheaper. That was not part of the Hungarian culture. We were never taught value engineering."[11]

✓ **Be prepared for huge amounts of detail and many meetings.** At Nissan, a typical model line has twenty thousand components. However, engineers perform detailed target costing only on two or three representative variations. Each variation contains approximately thirty-five hundred components. and typically 80 percent of the components are common across variations. Therefore, about five thousand components are subjected to detailed target costing. The target costs of the other fifteen hundred components are estimated by comparing them to similar components in the five thousand already subject to target costing.[12]

✓ **Set target prices according to strategic and market perspectives.** Referring to Nissan in the early 1990s, Cooper notes that "the target price was determined by taking into account a number of internal and external factors. The internal factors included the position of the model in the matrix and the strategic and profitability objectives of top management for that model. The external factors included the corporation's image and level of customer loyalty in the model's niche, the expected quality level and functionality of the model compared to the competitive offerings, the model's expected market share, and finally, the expected price of competitive models."[13]

Conclusions

The success of Toyota over recent decades highlights the benefits of target costing. The essence of target costing is its dynamic approach, which drives managers to look for continuous improvement and ways of reducing costs. It has been the secret weapon of Japanese manufacturers through their period of global expansion. Only in recent years have Western companies begun to use its methods. Standard costing and lean manufacturing come from different management philosophies. One is focused on internal costs, while the other is focused on the customer. But the change to target costing is quite difficult and needs careful planning. It also requires real determination to succeed.

FURTHER READING

Cooper, Robin. *When Lean Enterprises Collide: Competing Through Confrontation*. Boston: Harvard Business School Press, 1995.
Liker, Jeffrey K. *The Toyota Way*. New York: McGraw-Hill, 2004.

25

LEAN ACCOUNTING

What is this practice and how effective is it?

Lean accounting is a relatively new term that describes appropriate cost management approaches for lean organizations. It enables operations managers to better understand cost drivers and offers easier ways to understand and manage the costs that contribute to satisfying customers, using "value stream costing." But, as we will illustrate, it means embracing lean manufacturing and overhauling the entire cost accounting system.

Alternative names and related topics: value stream costing; just-in-time management; box reporting

The vast majority of manufacturing companies still use standard costing to control costs and set prices. In standard costing, the cost of producing a particular product is generally defined in terms of variable costs (primarily materials and direct labor) plus an assigned proportion of overheads. As often described, "the standard cost is set at the start of a period according to a number of assumptions, including output, capacity, material usage, labor requirements, machine time, material prices, and overheads. At periodic intervals, this standard cost is compared with the actual cost. The ensuing variances are usually caused by price changes in materials or labor (price variances), or by producing products faster or slower than expected (efficiency variances). Overheads are normally charged to products according to some volume-based allocation method such as labor hours or machine time."[1]

The problem with standard costing, however, is that overheads have grown as a percentage of total costs and thus have made the standard costing model far less accurate. In the 1960s, the typical overhead "burden" rate was around 150 percent of the labor cost; in many firms today, it can be 1,000 percent or even greater. "Although labor represents a smaller and smaller proportion of total costs, it is still the predominant basis of allocating overheads."[2]

To address the problems of standard costing, activity-based costing (ABC) entered the scene in the late 1980s. ABC analysis presented a clearer picture of product costs through a better identification of the costs of activities, such as machine setups or purchase orders, consumed by products. Using ABC, many indirect costs could be more clearly related to the products and customers that consumed them, giving managers a more accurate picture of product and even customer profitability. But as far as product costing was concerned, ABC didn't challenge the mass production approach; it just did a better job of managing it. For those organizations that have moved to lean manufacturing, ABC—at least at the product cost level—becomes less relevant.

Lean manufacturers are less interested in finding better ways to allocate overheads. *Rather, they are looking for ways to eliminate them*, as well as anything else that adds no value to the customer. These inefficiencies typically exist because the system is poorly designed. Standard costing is replaced by value stream costing, which shows how the organization's efforts create value for customers.

Lean accounting is designed to replace traditional measurements of performance with measurements tailored to "lean thinking." Doing so requires companies to fundamentality rework many of their processes so as to incorporate lean principles into their accounting, control, and measurements practices. This transformation allows them to improve their responsiveness toward decision-making, customer valuation, and other assessments, while also cutting waste and inefficiencies. As noted by authors Bruce Baggaley and Brian Maskell, lean accounting provides companies with:

- "A better way to understand costs, product costs, and value stream costs.
- Methods to eliminate large amounts of waste from the accounting, control, and measurement systems.
- Time freed up for finance people to work on lean improvement.
- New ways to make management decisions relating to pricing, profitability, make/buy, product/customer rationalization, and the like.
- A way to focus the business around the value created for customers."[3]

Rather than categorizing costs by department, lean accountants categorize them by value streams. A value stream usually includes a family of similar products and everything done to create value for a customer that can reasonably be associated with that product line or family. "Among the costs in a value stream would be the expenses a company incurs to design, engineer, sell, market, and ship a product as well as costs related to servicing the customer, purchasing materials, and collecting payments on product sales. Value streams cut across functional departments, so one stream can include sales and marketing, production, design, and debt collection costs. Ideally, each employee is assigned to a single value stream rather than split among several, as is traditional with most existing systems . . . While corporate overhead costs are accounted for, they are shown below the line on internal value stream reports, because value stream managers can't control them."[4]

Performance is reported weekly or monthly. The report shows the actual performance trend over a number of weeks compared with a goal based on best-practice standards elsewhere. (See table 25-1 for a typical weekly box report.) The first part of the report shows operational performance; the middle part,

TABLE 25-1

A typical weekly box report

Production weekly Box Report	Week 1	Week 2	Week 3	Week 4	Week 5	Week 6	Goal
Units per person	15.18	15.63	14.70	15.91	15.30	16.99	**20.00**
On-time shipment	82.0%	83.0%	78.0%	79.0%	84.0%	85.0%	**95.0%**
Dock-to-dock days	5.80	5.90	6.00	6.20	6.20	6.00	**5.00**
First time through	65.0%	68.0%	67.0%	70.0%	67.0%	70.0%	**90.0%**
Average product cost	£7.5	£7.3	£7.1	£7.4	£7.6	£7.5	**£6.0**
AR days	65	62	64	68	62	68	**35**
Productive capacity*	26%	25%	26%	25%	24%	24%	50%
Waste	54%	52%	53%	55%	56%	56%	30%
Available capacity	20%	23%	21%	20%	20%	20%	20%
Revenue	**60,000**	**59,000**	**56,000**	**57,500**	**58,250**	**59,500**	**70,000**
Material cost	6,000	5,900	5,600	5,750	5,825	5,950	**5,600**
Conversion cost	33,000	32,450	30,800	31,625	32,038	32,725	**33,600**
Other costs	4,800	4,838	4,368	4,543	4,777	4,939	**5,600**
Value stream GP	**16,200**	**15,812**	**15,232**	**15,582**	**15,610**	**15,886**	**25,200**
RoS	27.0%	26.8%	27.2%	27.1%	26.8%	26.7%	**36.0%**

*% of total capacity used for value-added work (defined as total cycle time × units shipped).

capacity levels and waste; and the third part, financial results. Lean accounting advocates justifiably claim that this type of report offers a clearer picture of performance that nonfinancial specialists can more easily understand and act on.

Costs include materials purchased during the period. Once material inventories are reduced to low levels, additional purchases are simply expensed to the period. Spare parts, tools, and other consumables are purchased as required and also expensed to the period. Labor costs include all those people working within the value stream. Lean manufacturers try not to have shared services groups, but to the extent they do, these costs are shared with each value stream. In some cases, they might be shown as "sustaining costs" and kept outside the main value-stream profit statement. The only allocated cost is the building space and associated overheads. Average product cost is simply the total value stream costs divided by the units produced.

Decision making is also improved. Historically, standard costs are typically used for a range of management decisions including setting prices, evaluating profit margins on product lines and customer orders, measuring factory performance (using efficiency measures, utilization measurement, cost variance, and absorption), encouraging process improvement through analysis of the product costs and the variances, make-or-buy decisions, and inventory valuation. Lean accounting practitioner Bruce Baggaley explains, "When using value stream costing, it is not necessary to know the cost of specific products to make these decisions. A decision relating to make or buy, for example, is addressed with reference to the profitability of the value stream as a whole, not the individual product. Plugging the marginal revenues and costs into the value stream profitability model will quickly reveal the answer."[5]

The Wiremold case

Despite its appeal, there are few examples of lean accounting in practice. One success story was Wiremold, a U.S. maker of racks and duct strips to protect cabling, that started its lean transformation in 1990 when its market value was around $30 million. In 2000, the company was sold to French cable and wiring company Legrand for $770 million. The chief financial officer at the time, Orest Fiume, attributes this success to the implementation of lean manufacturing and lean accounting.[a] A comparison of the changes in the company over this period tells the story (see table 25-2).

According to a blogger and former employee at Wiremold, since the company was acquired by Legrand, it has gone back to its old ways. "Legrand managers did not bother to learn about lean and did not heed Art

[Byrne, the CEO] or Orry Fiume's advice to apply lean management across the corporation. Instead they found reasons not to do Lean—basically, 'we're different'—and Wiremold quickly backslid. In fact, Legrand management seemed to actively dismantle almost everything that Art and his management team and people of Wiremold accomplished. In January of 2006, a standard-cost software system was installed at Wiremold, adding head count to the finance function and thus completing the return to batch-and-queue thinking and management."[b]

TABLE 25-2

Wiremold before and after lean

	1990	2000
Assess value	$30 million	$770 million
Gross profit	38%	51%
Sales per employee	$90,000	$240,000
Throughput time	4–6 weeks	2 hours–2 days
Product development time	2–3 years	3–6 months
Number of suppliers	320	43
Inventory turns	3.4	17.0
Working capital as percent of sales	21.8%	6.7%

[a] Brian Maskell, "Do We Need to Simplify Financial Reporting?" www.maskell.com.
[b] Bob Emiliani, *Better Thinking, Better Results* (Wethersfield, CT: The CLCM, LLC, 2007), 284.

Standard costs are not required for valuing inventory, provided the inventory levels are low and under control. When lean manufacturing is introduced, the level of inventory falls substantially. If the inventory level is low, then its valuation is far less important than when it is high. If, for example, a value stream has three months of inventory, then it is very important to value this inventory in a detailed way using some form of standard costing. However, if the inventory is less than five days, then the importance of the inventory value to the calculation of the company's financial position is probably immaterial.

While value stream costing is used for tracking and accounting for product line costs and making a range of related decisions, it is not used for pricing. Pricing is related to customer value. Thus, there is no direct relationship to product cost. Lean organizations tend to use target costing for setting prices and that allows for total costs over the life cycle of the product.

Lean accounting fills a need for accountants to measure and report performance that fits with lean practice. But lean accounting should be kept in its place as a measurement function. It must not be used to set targets and drive performance from the corporate center; otherwise, the benefits will be short lived.

What is the performance potential of this practice?

- **To support lean manufacturing.** Lean manufacturing is based on the legendary Toyota Production System. However, many attempts to implement lean manufacturing have been blocked by traditional, standard costing systems whose measurement signals actively work against implementation. Lean accounting provides an alternative method of managing costs.
- **To provide managers with more relevant cost accounting information.** Lean accounting presents product costs in ways that production, rather than finance, managers can understand. It eliminates the need for complex cost accounting and inventory valuation systems.
- **To simplify mainstream accounting.** Lean accounting also does away with the need for hundreds of general ledger accounts and cost-center-level analyses. This speeds up the month-end close.

What actions do you need to take to maximize the potential of this practice?

ACTIONS TO AVOID

- ✘ **Don't replace standard costing immediately.** When a company first moves to value stream costing, it usually keeps the standard costing results in place and uses value stream cost reports as supplementary data. But the traditional systems need to be dismantled piece by piece as the underlying operations change. Fortunately, the cost information that managers need to prepare lean financial statements is usually accessible from the traditional accounting system. It's just a matter of reformatting the data. For instance, rather than including labor and overhead expenses in the cost of goods sold, a lean financial statement will show materials, labor, and overhead as separate line items. That way, the company will recognize labor and overhead expenses when it incurs them, rather than having them get wrapped into inventory on the balance sheet.

ACTIONS TO TAKE

✓ **Use value stream costing to manage product costs.** As standard costing is consigned to history, value stream costing takes over the costing role. Instead of focusing on unit costs, value stream costing assumes that all costs—there is no distinction between direct and indirect costs—are debited to a value stream account (i.e., a product line). Overhead costs are related to the value stream as a whole and not to production labor time. The cost of any particular product primarily depends on how quickly it flows through the value stream, particularly the bottleneck operations. Managers are much more interested in the rate of flow through the value stream than with the utilization of resources, people's individual efficiency, or overhead allocations. Many transactions that take time and increase complexity in the traditional system disappear. For example, the costs of material purchases, direct labor earned, and overhead absorbed are recorded in an asset account and tracked until they are sold. Author Brian Maskell, an expert on lean accounting, notes: "Inventory is in the system so long that you have to cycle count it, reconcile it, and provide reserves against it for slow moving and obsolete parts. All of these steps are necessary to ensure inventory is properly valued. In lean, parts move swiftly through the plant and there is just not much inventory on hand . . . Usually, you take a physical and use that to value the inventory. It is simple, straightforward and quick."[6]

✓ **Design and use easy-to-understand reports.** Unlike standard costing reports that are often incomprehensible to the average manager, lean accounting reports follow the logical sequence of the flow of production and sales and are thus easy to understand. They are also produced weekly and enable the production team to respond rapidly to any unusual data.

✓ **Use price-led target costing to set prices and total costs.** Pricing decisions within lean organizations are never made with reference to the cost of the product. The customer value determines the price; customer value has no direct relationship to product cost. Although the logic of target costing is undoubtedly compelling, its methodology is often painstakingly slow and involves many cost-function reviews with designers and suppliers. Conceptually, it is simple to understand, but its methodology can test the patience of the most professional manager.

✓ **Reduce inventories by purchasing only what's needed, when needed.** There is no more need to buy in bulk to gain extra discounts but suffer all the hidden costs of moving, storing, financing, and writing down obsolete stock. The net savings can be huge.

Conclusions

One of the reasons that lean organizations have fewer quality problems and lower costs than traditional firms is that they don't have multiple control systems to connect decisions made at the corporate center with action taken at the front line. They don't have, for example, targets, budgets, standard costing, batch scheduling, or quality control systems—quality is in the line, not inspected for—and all their associated costs. Teams have all the information they need to complete the work. They have plans, forecasts, KPIs, and a stream of business intelligence flowing through their computer systems.

FURTHER READING

Cooper, Robin, and Regine Slagmulder. *Target Costing and Value Engineering*. Montvale, NJ: Productivity Press, 1998.

Hope, Jeremy, and Tony Hope. *Competing in the Third Wave: The Ten Key Management Issues of the Information Age*. Boston: Harvard Business School Press, 1997.

Johnson, H. Thomas, and Anders Bröms. *Profit Beyond Measure*. London: Nicholas Brealey Publishing, 2000.

Liker, Jeffrey K. *The Toyota Way*. New York: McGraw-Hill, 2004.

Maskell, Brian, and Bruce Baggaley. *Practical Lean Accounting*. Montvale, NJ: Productivity Press, 2004.

Solomon, Jerrold. *Who's Counting? A Lean Accounting Business Novel*. Ft. Wayne, IN: WCM Associates, 2003.

Stenzel, Joe. *Lean Accounting*. Hoboken, NJ: Wiley, 2007.

Womack, James P., Daniel T. Jones, and Daniel Roos. *The Machine That Changed the World*. New York: Rawson Associates, 1990.

26

SHARED SERVICES

What is this practice and how effective is it?

Shared services involve the shifting of multiple functions such as finance, information technology, research and development, human resources, and marketing (usually integrated within individual group businesses) to one or more shared services centers. Companies can locate these centers anywhere in the world but are increasingly placing them in low-cost countries such as India. We will examine the pros and cons of shared services and how best to implement them.

Alternative names and related topics: internal markets; outsourcing; offshoring

While decentralization of decision making can lead to significantly lower costs, there are areas of business that will be more efficient and less expensive if they are *centralized*. Many large organizations have moved their back-office functions, such as accounts receivable, accounts payable, and human resources administration, from multiple sites to a small number of shared services centers, saving huge amounts of cost. According to the Hackett Group, leading organizations have reduced routine transaction processing work by 16 percent, reduced their number of systems from 30 per billion dollars of revenue to just 2.8 and cut costs by around 50 percent.[1] Spans of control have also increased from one supervisor covering seven staff in average companies to a range of between one to fifteen to one to twenty in world-class organizations.[2] Another step change in cost reduction comes from locating service centers in low-cost countries such as India.

American Express reduced its forty-six data centers to just two shared centers. Most of its normal accounting, reporting, and transaction processing is now done in Phoenix, Arizona, and Delhi, India. Notes former CFO, Gary Crittenden, "This move was critical to saving a thousand heads and $100 million dollars per annum. Previously a lot of work was being done in individual markets around the world with a few controllers and a few accounting people here and there well away from the corporate head office. That was quite scary. But now it's all housed in a well-controlled environment with high quality standards and practices. We just needed to make sure that the communications were clear between the shared services centers and the markets." According to Crittenden, there are four main advantages: "First, there are considerable cost savings. Secondly, it is easier to make improvements (you can more easily set common standards). Thirdly, it facilitates a more visible career path for back office employees. And fourthly, by having multiple centers it serves as a hedge against the disruption of the back office. These shared services centers have also created more reliable, standardized information for use in the company's business planning efforts."[3]

However, managing the relationship between shared services providers and internal customers can be fraught with difficulty. Some have used service-level agreements to define this relationship, but this is more likely to suggest a legal obligation to support central services units than to simulate a real market with choices and conditions of customer satisfaction. Another problem is how a company defines and charges for internal services. There is nothing worse than operating managers receiving internal service invoices that are unfathomable. They become suspicious and resentful about the head-office burden that their business unit has to carry. The golden rule is to keep the basis of charging as simple as possible. For example, an IT department might provide a menu of services, together with a clear basis for charging out these services. Operating units can then clearly understand the basis of charging and, more importantly, how they can influence the costs they incur. Thus, if they are incurring high charges for a service they don't value, they can use it less or complain and demand that it be improved. This transparency exerts far greater pressure on central costs and makes operating units feel much more like external suppliers with customers to satisfy.

An internal market at Handelsbanken

Handelsbanken uses an internal market to simulate supplier-customer relationships in which the central service "sellers" meet the business unit "buyers." "Buyers check the prices against similar services in the marketplace and ensure that they receive value for money."[a] The central support departments are under constant pressure.

"This annual round of discussions involves real negotiation. A typical comment by a branch manager might be: 'Since we are not increasing our costs, we expect you to do the same.' Where possible, costs are attributed to branches on the basis of actual usage (e.g., by transaction, such as the number of mortgages or loans processed). However, all costs attributed to regions and branches are the *actual costs to the bank*. There is no internal markup or fudging of the numbers.

"In a decentralized performance model [such as Handelsbanken's], the integrity of the numbers is crucial to success."[b] The bank is also careful not to overburden branches with paperwork. Each transaction within the internal market is charged to the branch immediately through a "shadow" accounting system. This means that branch and profit-center managers have a fairly good view on a continuous basis of what is happening. All central and regional costs are roughly cleared to branches each month. So if you add up all the branch income statements, they will give you the total figures for the whole bank, although there are some head-office costs like directors' salaries that are not charged.

Former CFO Lennart Francke is careful to distinguish the internal market from service-level agreements, which he thinks are a sham:

> They talk about service commitments, but in reality they are just contracts driven by central services who have the power to inflict them upon business units. In that sense you probably couldn't apply our system to other centralized organizations because then you don't have the independent buyers that actually are empowered to negotiate transfer prices. The thing to remember is that we have buyers that actually have an income statement that they have to guard and they can act as almost independent buyers. So if a branch doesn't want to buy your product or service they can either buy somewhere else or just discontinue buying your services. It's up to them—they are responsible for their costs and profitability.[c]

By transferring authority to internal customers, the internal market enables Handelsbanken to exert continuous cost pressure on its central services units. Customers are demanding and do not want to be charged with services that they don't need or with excess costs. That explains why Handelsbanken has a very lean head office and has one of the lowest cost structures of any bank in Europe.

[a] Jeremy Hope, *Reinventing the CFO: How Financial Managers Can Transform Their Roles and Add Greater Value* (Boston: Harvard Business School Press, 2006), 132.

[b] Jeremy Hope and Robin Fraser, *Beyond Budgeting: How Managers Can Break Free from the Annual Performance Trap* (Boston: Harvard Business School Press, 2003), 64.

[c] Lennart Francke interview with Jeremy Hope, January 24, 2005.

Many organizations use various forms of transfer pricing when they move products and services from one organizational unit (e.g., a division or business unit) to another. But it is easy to lose clarity and transparency in the performance measurement system through a poorly designed system of transfer pricing. The problem is that accountants are desperately trying to make *financial sense* of business units (spread costs and profits and minimize tax), whereas it is *behavioral sense* that organizations now need. Each company must agree on a set of rules governing the management of and accounting for business units. Teams should know in detail how measures are constructed. They should be clear and transparent so people have confidence in them.

Moving to shared services, however, can destroy rather than add value, especially where there is no service relationship culture. In other words, if the relationship between shared services units and internal customers is too top-down and contract-based, then business units will fail to embrace the changes. Moreover, the pressure to reduce costs that comes from the need to meet "conditions of satisfaction" is missing.

Nor are lean thinkers happy with the idea. They believe that separating the front office and the back office (where the experts work) leads to fragmentation and to deterioration in service quality as well as higher costs. They say focusing on activity targets such as the average time to answer or deal with a call is the wrong approach. What matters is the end-to-end process and how well it is managed. They also believe that the experts should work in the front-office help desk so that any problems can be answered on the first call.

Despite these caveats, grouping *routine* back-office transactional work into shared services centers makes sense for large organizations. But they must be careful how these changes are implemented, as they can easily alienate internal customers. Few central services providers such as finance or human resources have traditionally seen themselves as service providers to internal customers. Unless they are persuaded to change their view, few shared services programs will meet their goals.

What is the performance potential of this practice?

- **To enable often considerable cost savings.** Combining central services into a few cohesive units enables managers to cut out duplicated work and reduce costs.
- **To enable process improvements.** Many firms have large numbers of central services units in different parts of the world, each one with its own way of doing things and each with its own standards that can vary from poor to excellent. Combining central services enables firms to set higher standards across the organization and continuously improve performance.

- **To facilitate a more visible career path for back-office employees.** With many small, central services units, most employees have limited career paths. Frustrated and dissatisfied, they look for more stability elsewhere. By creating larger units, firms can provide a long-term career path for key people as well as meet their personal development needs.

What actions do you need to take to maximize the potential of this practice?

ACTIONS TO AVOID

✖ **Be careful which processes you transfer to shared services centers.** Shared services need to make sense both strategically and economically. Shared services typically work best with transactions that are high volume, similar, and routine. If cost savings are the primary reason, then managers must do their homework. But they must also factor in the disruption costs, which can be substantial. Moving functions from several locations to a central operation will prompt resistance from employees worried about their jobs. Another good reason to create shared services centers is to improve compliance and control. Many companies with existing shared services centers are now extending these facilities to include planning and compliance.

✖ **Be wary of service-level agreements (SLAs) that are too "legalistic."** SLAs that are based on legal negotiated agreements are the wrong approach. They invariably fail to take account of variation, leaving users with assumptions that lead to higher costs than expected—because volumes are lower—or lower levels of quality.

ACTIONS TO TAKE

✓ **Focus on the right processes.** Identify processes that you can consolidate and share without risking service quality. Prime targets include transaction processing, payroll, billing, and human resources administration. But be wary about shared services that involve external customers. The aim here is to ensure that customer problems are satisfied at the first point of contact.

✓ **Select an appropriate operating model.** Companies can outsource operations to full-service providers or establish national, regional, or global shared services centers. The decision depends on corporate objectives, cash flow projections, risk assessments, and potential return on investment.[4]

✓ **Create the right governance structure.** Leading organizations manage their shared services from the group board level; shared services typically report to the CFO, CIO, or COO. This establishes clear lines of accountability. The other focus of governance should be on the customer.

Choose the right charge-back model

Managers need to be extremely careful with transfer pricing, especially if profit markups are involved. There are basically four pricing options: use variable costs only; use full cost (variable cost plus a proportion of overheads); use full cost plus a profit markup; or use full market pricing.

1. **Variable costs** is the lowest-level transfer price and represents only those costs that vary directly with the product or service (e.g., material, labor, and other direct costs of production). They do not include overheads. While simple to use, this method is unlikely to lead to a fair accounting result for the upstream or downstream unit.

2. **Full cost (variable cost plus a proportion of overheads)** is the method preferred by most organizations. It means that each cost center, usually a unit with no external customers, clears its costs over a year and breaks even, in accounting terms. This method has the advantage of being relatively simple and avoids the adverse behavior often associated with the next option (i.e., where a profit figure is included).

3. **Full cost plus a profit markup** is used by some organizations to motivate managers in noncustomer-facing units to give them profit targets. The idea is to simulate market prices and give upstream unit managers incentives to maximize performance. But the opportunities for bad practice and gaming are wide open as managers cut corners or manipulate prices to achieve their numbers.

4. **Full market pricing** is the option used by organizations that also have independent business units sell their products and services to external customers. They are likely to have price lists that can be used for transfer pricing purposes. Thus, they charge the same price to other group businesses as they would to external customers (i.e., the market price model). Most oil companies operate this way.

Source: Jeremy Hope, *Reinventing the CFO: How Financial Managers Can Transform Their Roles and Add Greater Value* (Boston: Harvard Business School Press, 2006), 130–131.

✓ **Focus on internal supplier-customer relationships.** The relationship between central shared services and business units should be similar to an arm's-length supplier-customer relationship, with clear conditions of satisfaction that are measured and monitored.

✓ **Consider using activity-based costing models to determine charges.** By applying activity-based costs to shared service activities and using these as the basis for internal pricing, there is a far greater likelihood of achieving the right price or, if the price is out of line, understanding where to trim costs. Use time-driven ABC (see chapter 19).

✓ **Invest in the right technology.** Most firms find that they spend far more on technology than they originally estimated, up to twice as much in many cases. However, implementing the right systems and especially high-speed and reliable connections across global operations is critical to success. Many of the expected cost savings come from automating routine transactional processes, so the technology platform needs to deliver on these promises.

✓ **Redesign key processes.** Focusing solely on savings in staffing costs doesn't indicate the extent to which a company will save money. In studying this issue several years ago, JPMorgan Chase found that 10 percent to 15 percent of the possible cost savings came from lower labor costs, while 60 percent to 65 percent came from reengineering processes.[5] The message is clear. If you just move the old process from one location to another and reduce the head count to some degree, the payoff will be marginal at best.

✓ **Take your time.** Full rollout can take two or more years. Think through the scope, structure, location, and operating models and whether to involve some outsourcing.

✓ **Measure performance.** Measure customer-oriented performance (cost, quality, and service). Benchmark against comparable services in your industry.

Conclusions

The rise of shared services centers is unstoppable, as communications costs have reduced dramatically over recent years. However, they can easily lead to the wrong behavior and thus an increase in costs rather than the sought-for reduction. The overarching key to success is ensuring that shared services providers see business teams as real customers with needs that require high-quality, low-cost services.

FURTHER READING

Driacoll, Mary. "Moving Up the Maturity Curve of Financial Shared Services." Houston, TX: APQC, January 21, 2011.

Hope, Jeremy. *Reinventing the CFO: How Financial Managers Can Transform Their Roles and Add Greater Value.* Boston: Harvard Business School Press, 2006.

Hope, Jeremy, and Robin Fraser. *Beyond Budgeting: How Managers Can Break Free from the Annual Performance Trap.* Boston: Harvard Business School Press, 2003.

"Success Through Shared Services." Chicago: A.T. Kearney, 2004, http://www.atkearney.com/index.php/Publications/success-through-shared-services.html.

Tham, Irene. "Shared Services: Getting It Right." *The Age,* February 18, 2005.

27

OUTSOURCING AND OFFSHORING

What is this practice and how effective is it?

Outsourcing and offshoring have expanded over recent years as companies hand over individual processes or even whole departments to third-party service providers that have high-levels of expertise in performing certain tasks. But there are many hidden traps, the level of dissatisfaction is high and rising, and some organizations are now reversing the trend. There is much confusion over the merits of outsourcing. We will examine these issues and suggest how organizations can deal with them.

Alternative names and related topics: nearshoring; core competences; strategic alliances; vendor services; partner service models; contract labor

What advice would you give to a member of staff who has a parent suffering from Alzheimer's disease? Most people wouldn't know where to start. That's why a number of companies now provide help-desk facilities that can tap into this kind of expertise and reduce employees' stress. These help-line services are a reminder of what outsourcing should really be about: handing over discrete functions to an outside specialist so that the company and its staff can concentrate on what they do best: adding value for customers. Other examples are catering, cleaning, or, increasingly, IT integration, human resources, customer service, and accounting. And the scale has been increasing. BP has outsourced all its accounting and human resource management. Nike and Hewlett-Packard have outsourced much of their manufacturing.

In the 1970s and 80s, companies focused on process improvement through total quality management. In the 1990s, it was the turn of business process reengineering, which was then followed by six sigma. Yet for many organizations, the anticipated cost reductions have been illusory. That's why increasing numbers of organizations have turned to outsourcing. In some cases, the economic case for outsourcing is overwhelming, particularly if the same job with the same level of competence can be done in India for $10,000 per person compared to a cost of $75,000 in America or Europe. However, for many outsourcing contracts—especially in areas such as IT and human resources—the economics are not so clear, particularly when productivity suffers and service costs start to increase.

According to Thomas Davenport, outsourcing has become easier to manage: "An increasing number of firms offer 'knowledge process outsourcing' in analytical fields including data mining, algorithm development, and quantitative finance."[1] Organizations such as the American Productivity & Quality Center (APQC) are working hard to produce standards for a whole range of processes. These already exist in the field of software development and are starting to have an impact. The Software Engineering Institute has developed a Capability Maturity Model with five levels—initial, repeatable, defined, managed, and optimizing. Firms are evaluated and certified against these

Outsourcing at General Electric

One company that understands outsourcing better than most is General Electric. In the 1990s, it decided to consolidate many of its back-office systems and remove a lot of the manual activities. So it invested in a new operation in India (Genpact), which it rapidly expanded to a total of seventeen thousand people (eleven thousand in financial services). Genpact now manages hundreds of processes—split into centers of excellence—categorized by industry or function. GE units saved an estimated 35 percent to 40 percent on cost alone and another 40 percent when a client relationship reaches three years. By then, the benefits of Genpact's drive for process improvement start to kick in.

This is where CEO Pramod Bhasin thinks the future of outsourcing lies. "Too much of what is happening today is still what one of my customers calls, 'My mess for less.' They're just moving the work, and you're just executing the work. Not enough is being done around process expertise and domain knowledge. Improving the process that's outsourced," he argues, "can deliver savings equivalent to the labor arbitrage benefits."[a]

[a] Abe De Ramos, "The Future of Outsourcing,"*CFO Magazine*, June 15, 2005, www.cfo.com/printable/article.cfm/3860276.

criteria. Many firms in India have now reached the highest levels, and they are winning the lion's share of new business.

Few organizations have managed outsourcing as well as GE. After an onslaught of complaints, computer maker Dell stopped using a technical support center in India to handle calls from its corporate customers—85 percent of its business. Some U.S. customers complained that the Indian technical-support representatives were difficult to communicate with because of thick accents and scripted responses.[2]

In most organizations, while outsourcing often masquerades as strategy, in reality it is usually about cutting costs. Cutting staff, divesting businesses, and getting rid of hundreds of person-years of accumulated skill seem to be a prevailing compulsion among many firms that are seeking to improve profitability by shrinking their size. Taking assets off the balance sheet has its attractions. It can improve return on assets at a stroke, and the reduction in head count can dramatically improve the productivity numbers. Another attraction is the ability to make hard cost-cutting decisions easier by subcontracting them to external parties. This financial engineering angle explains much about why outsourcing is so attractive to Western organizations that are driven by shareholder value.

Outsourcing can also increase business risk. In February 2005, U.S. company ChoicePoint, a major provider of identification- and credential-verification services, sold the personal data of some 145,000 individuals to criminals posing as small firms. In April 2005, several employees at business process outsourcing (BPO) firm MphasiS in Bangalore, India, were caught using client passwords to fraudulently withdraw funds from the New York accounts of Citibank customers. And in June 2005, an employee at BPO firm Infinity e-Systems in New Delhi sold the account numbers and passwords of a thousand bank customers to a reporter from the British tabloid. *The Sun* for $5,000.[3]

There are three types of risk: operational risk (e.g., slippages on time, cost, and quality), strategic risk (e.g., theft of intellectual property such as customer data), and composite risk (e.g., when a company has outsourced a process for so long that it no longer retains any capability to perform it). Managers should fully investigate these risks and weigh the costs and benefits of the outsourcing deal before proceeding.

Smart organizations will outsource if it is strategically compelling (i.e., if it takes advantage of somebody else's capacity to accumulate knowledge faster than it can be done in-house). But they don't outsource on the premise of cost cutting alone. They are also careful when outsourcing problems and risk. The best way to make outsourcing work is to find a service provider (like Genpact) that works continuously to improve processes and thus take problems, waste, and cost out of the system.

McKinsey's 2008 to 2009 survey of the global IT offshoring and outsourcing industry—covering two hundred relationships among companies in Asia, Europe, and North America, including sixty-five of the *Fortune* 200—shows that a number of rising suppliers are changing the long-standing model for contracting offshore services by focusing on the quality of services delivered rather than the usual benchmarks of costs per offshore hire. They are also collaborating with clients in new ways and gaining more control over outsourcing strategies. What's more, the study shows that this new group of IT service providers is developing the broader and deeper pools of talent that global clients increasingly demand and using progressive techniques to manage and retain these workers. Perhaps that's why such companies had the highest rankings for overall client satisfaction and employee retention in the survey, logging high scores across their entire client base and showing a consistent year-on-year improvement. By contrast, clients thought that most of the other established tier-one and tier-two companies were just doing an "average job," and their performance wasn't improving. In another major shift, they can no longer win bids solely by differentiating on price, since almost all suppliers are now cost competitive.[4]

But there is a black cloud looming on the outsourcing horizon. Cloud computing is a potential game changer and is likely to result in major consolidations in the industry, as only mega-players will survive. Cloud technology lets users tap into computing power available via the Internet rather than on a desktop or computer server housed locally. The appeal is scale, flexibility, and efficiency: Thousands of server computers can attack a task more quickly—and cheaply—or handle a patchwork quilt of different technologies that companies use to run their businesses. This approach will let businesses outsource entire tasks such as the tracking of inventory, paying only for the information accessed or used.[5]

According to a *BusinessWeek* article, the outsourcing market is on the verge of experiencing its most massive transformation since the concept arose more than twenty years ago. For outsourcers, cloud computing creates an unprecedented opportunity to reshape how services get delivered. For clients, it opens up a new era characterized by the arrival of new players that are eager to build relationships and showcase their capabilities. That means more choice and a new model that will sustain the price advantage that outsourcing has hitherto provided.[6]

What is the performance potential of this practice?

- **To provide more strategic focus on core competences.** Managers spend huge amounts of time fixing broken processes that can be either "core" or "noncore." In fact, many organizations do not distinguish between those processes that really matter and those that are peripheral. With fewer noncore processes to deal with, managers have more time to spend improving those that are clearly strategic to the business.

- **To reduce costs.** Many organizations suffer from inefficient processes that take too long, deliver poor quality, and cause excess costs. By outsourcing inefficient processes to a service provider that can manage the process more efficiently, there should be a significant cost saving.
- **To reduce compliance problems.** With new regulatory frameworks (e.g., Sarbanes-Oxley), firms are involved in documenting detailed processes and any changes in those processes. This can take time and involve significant work and cost. By outsourcing processes and even whole departments, managers are able to reduce the compliance workload, as they transfer it to the outsourcing contractor.

What actions do you need to take to maximize the potential of this practice?

ACTIONS TO AVOID

- ✘ **Avoid outsourcing on the basis of cost cutting alone.** Relative cost is of course a major consideration in any outsourcing decision, but it should never be the only or principal concern. The outsourcing provider should have real expertise in the chosen activity and be able to improve service quality and reduce costs over time. "Despite the lure of lower costs and the promise of big gains in efficiency and innovation, it may make sense not to outsource at all."[7] Ramesh Venkataraman, McKinsey's technical partner for Asia, advises companies not to send work offshore simply because competitors are doing it. And don't outsource a mess. Ananda Mukerji, CEO of the Bombay call-center operator and researcher, ICICI OneSource Ltd., notes, "If you have a broken process, shifting it overseas won't fix it."[8]
- ✘ **Question why you can't match the outsourcing contractor's costs.** Many companies look at outsourcing with a sense of failure. They say, "Why can't we improve our process efficiencies so we can compete with anyone else in the world?" Employees at Nokia's flagship plant in Salo, Finland, are paid thirty times the wages workers receive in low-cost Asian factories, yet their productivity is so high that Nokia's cost of making and selling the average phone was almost 20 percent less than the average cost for its closest rival. Nucor, in spite of paying the highest wages in the steel industry, has the lowest labor costs per ton of steel produced in the United States.[9]
- ✘ **Don't confuse labor costs with labor rates.** As Jeffrey Pfeffer explains, this confusion can lead to wrong outsourcing decisions. "For the record,"

notes Pfeffer, "labor rates are straight wages divided by time—a Wal-Mart cashier earns $5.15 an hour [Pfeffer was writing this in 1998], a Wall Street attorney $2,000 a day. Labor costs are a calculation of how much a company pays its people and how much they produce. Thus German factory workers may be paid at a rate of $30 an hour and Indonesians $3, but the workers' relative costs will reflect how many widgets are produced in the same period of time."[10] To lower labor costs, managers must pay attention to *both* labor rates and productivity. While this might be obvious, even huge organizations such as Ford and General Motors didn't appear to understand the difference. Another point made by Pfeffer is that, in most industries, labor costs are not a high proportion of total costs, so gaining competitive advantage by cutting them is likely to be minimal. He notes that the cost of direct labor is only 15 percent of the total cost of producing a pair of jeans.[11]

✖ **Be wary of hidden, upstream costs.** "Hidden costs emerged as the biggest complaint among nearly half of the twenty-five major organizations surveyed by Deloitte Consulting, to the extent that they achieved no cost savings at all. More than half absorbed costs that they thought were their supplier's responsibility."[12] Outsourcing contracts are invariably negotiated on the basis of the budgeted costs of the activities or department under consideration, but it is usually difficult to determine whether these budgeted costs cover all the *problem-fixing work* undertaken by a department. In other words, as many activity-based studies have proved, much of the work one department undertakes stems from inefficiencies and problems caused by another department upstream. So, in this situation, who will take on this often unseen workload after the department has been outsourced? The answer is that the remaining staff must work even harder, or the outsourcing contractor will return to negotiate more favorable terms.

✖ **Be wary of contracts based on unit costs per transaction.** Some outsourcing contracts are based on transaction costs, but in many service organizations, there can be large volumes of nonvalue transactions leading to hidden costs. For example, a high percentage of a service center's calls can be failure calls—those that would not occur if something earlier had been done right the first time. However, if these are not recorded separately, with the transaction count included in these calls, the contractor will potentially charge for large volumes of calls that add no value, although the unit cost per call might appear to be falling. The contractor might even demand that you increase IT capacity and provide more resources to cover the apparent increase in activity. This is potentially one of the classic hidden traps of service outsourcing.

✖ **Be wary of the exposure to new risks.** The ethical standards and security procedures within the outsourcing company may not be as good as they claim, thus exposing the company to greater risk. The leaking or illicit sale of confidential information to third parties is a classic example. The consequences and costs can easily outweigh any cost savings of the outsourcing contract.

ACTIONS TO TAKE

✓ **Decide whether to set up your own subsidiary offshore—known as a "captive" operation—or contract with outside specialists.** "The appeal of keeping everything in-house is that you maintain control of proprietary technology and processes. For that reason, Boeing opened its own center in Moscow, where it employs eleven hundred skilled but relatively low-cost aerospace engineers on a range of projects, including the design of titanium parts for the new 787 Dreamliner jet. Likewise, Chicago-based law firm Baker & McKenzie has its own English-speaking team in Manila that drafts documents and does market research. One downside of captive units," warns Gartner Inc., "is that they can wind up costing the head office more than it would to hire large outside outsourcers that spread overhead among numerous customers. For that reason, many companies are aiming for the best of both worlds. Bank of America established its own India subsidiary, yet also teamed up with Infosys Technologies and Tata Consultancy Services to shift 30 percent of its resources offshore. Since 2001, says the bank, offshoring has helped it save $100 million and, more important, improved product quality."[13]

✓ **Choose the managed-service over the staff-augmentation model.** A recent survey shows "that client organizations relying primarily on the managed-service rather than staff-augmentation model reap great advantages: the best and most efficient work, the highest satisfaction levels, and the lowest attrition rates among their suppliers' employees. Managed services may also make it possible for clients and suppliers to improve offshore results more than the traditional approach does. According to an executive at one pharmaceutical company, 'While you do have to invest time up front, managing it on an ongoing basis is much less of a hassle. And you actually get more control when you focus on deliverables and things that matter rather than micromanaging the team remotely which doesn't work and results in a lot of frustration on both sides.'"[14]

✓ **Be clear on what you intend to outsource.** There is as yet no consensus on just what comprises cost accounting or HR benefits management, so there is huge scope for ambiguity and misinformation in negotiating

Build a strategic partnership with the outsourcing provider

Building a good relationship with an outsourcing contractor makes a lot of sense. After all, fractious relationships can only lead to declining service, higher costs, and a potentially awkward termination process that reinstates the work in the company. In fact, half of all strategic partnerships fail, according to a study by MIT's Center for Information Systems Research (CISR). So "when Campbell Soup CIO Doreen Wright was trying to cut costs to fund a multimillion-dollar global investment in SAP, she was surprised to get help from what many might view as an unlikely ally—her outsourcing vendor. Without being asked, IBM reexamined the outsourcing contract and identified several million in services it was providing that could be cut with minimal pain to Campbell. Recognizing the financial hurt that move might cause her partner, Wright took the sting out by working with IBM to identify new outsourcing services (which, by the way, would also further reduce her IT operating budget) and awarded the vendor several other projects in the following months. 'They were very forward-thinking, and there was a tremendous amount of teamwork involved,' says Wright. The result was that Campbell cut its IT costs and was able to go ahead with the SAP project, while IBM actually saw its revenue increase."[a] The success of strategic partnerships depends on mutual benefit. It also depends on both parties working hard at the relationship and dealing with any problems with mutual trust and respect.

[a] Stephanie Overby, "Outsourcing Can Mean Big Deals, Big Savings, Big Problems," *CIO Magazine*, February 1, 2006, www.cio.com/archive/020106/outsourcing.htm.

outsourcing contracts. Therefore, clearly mapping the flow of work that each process covers is essential.

✓ **Measure the existing performance of the processes to be outsourced.** Unless you can measure your own process performance—especially quality, speed, and cost—how can you evaluate the offering from a third party?

✓ **Get your people on board.** Remember that employees and middle managers can make or break a bold outsourcing move. Dutch bank ABN Amro was aware of this risk when it decided in 2004 to boost efficiency and product quality by uniting retail, investment, private banking, and asset management businesses under one technology platform, to be developed offshore. Senior executives feared resistance. "When you first approach outsourcing, it's a religious issue," says Lars Gustavsson, ABN

Amro's London-based group chief information officer. "People either believe in it or they don't." To counter potential opposition, the bank set up a full-time communications department dedicated to explaining the move to middle managers and staff. Senior executives held town hall meetings with employees and involved the unions in managing the shift. And the bank gathered together its twelve chief technology officers into a committee that made decisions by consensus about redeploying the workforce and selecting outsourcing partners.[15]

✓ **Set up a governance structure.** According to Jeff O'Hare, CIO at Cendant, a governance structure should accompany any outsourcing agreement. He recommends that "a governance structure should be included right in the contract, preferably in an exhibit. This way, both parties know what they're signing up for in terms of how the relationship will be monitored and managed from day one. Also, too often service levels are set up based on what metrics the buyer has available rather than on the requirements and expectations of the agreement. This inevitably leads to cross purposes and unmet expectations in everyday execution.[16]

✓ **Rethink internal management roles after outsourcing.** According to David Rhodes, a principal and HR expert at Towers Watson, "Outsourcing creates the ability for HR to transform itself, but unless work gets done to determine what [those individuals] are going to do with the time saved by outsourcing, it tends not to effect any change." In other words, if HR staffers aren't specifically assigned to strategy-setting roles, they often simply seek new administrative tasks after outsourcing takes effect. In fact, says Rhodes, that tendency contributes to the lack of cost savings at many companies. "For a $100 million outsourcing deal, the question is whether you really got rid of that much work or whether it's still deeply embedded in the organization," he says.[17]

✓ **Have a dialogue about process improvement.** Just looking at current performance is not enough. Managers should also ask the outsourcing contractor about how they can make future process improvements and thus make further cost reductions. As we learned in the Genpact example, this can amount to a further cost reduction of 40 percent or more.

Conclusions

One could say that outsourcing has many of the attributes of anorexia nervosa. People with anorexia have a distorted self-image that makes them feel fat even when emaciated; a preoccupation with food, low self-esteem, and emphatic denial of the problem characterize most anorexics. Similarly, executives in companies with poor financial performance seem to concentrate on downsizing as the preferred method for restoring competitiveness. Before contemplating an outsourcing contract, managers need to go back to first principles. Why do they want to transfer this activity to someone else, how will it benefit the company, and are they sure that they are not depriving themselves of key skills that the company might need in the future?

FURTHER READING

Bragg, Steven M. *Outsourcing: A Guide to Selecting the Correct Business Unit; Negotiating the Contract; Maintaining Control of the Process.* New York: John Wiley & Sons, 1998.

Davenport, Thomas. "The Coming Commoditization of Processes." *Harvard Business Review,* June 2005, 101–108.

De Ramos, Abe. "The Future of Outsourcing." *CFO Magazine,* June 15, 2005, http://www.cfo.com/article.cfm/3860276.

Greaver, Maurice. *Strategic Outsourcing: A Structured Approach to Outsourcing Decisions and Initiatives.* New York: AMACOM, 1999.

Klepper, Robert, and Wendell O. Jones. *Outsourcing Information Technology, Systems and Services.* Upper Saddle River, NJ: Prentice Hall Press, 1997.

Milgate, Michael. *Alliances, Outsourcing, and the Lean Organization.* Westport, CT: Quorum Books, 2001.

Moran, Nuala. "Looking for Savings on Distant Horizons." *Financial Times IT Review,* July 2003.

Nelson-Nesvig, Carleen, Eric Norton, and Mary Jane Eder. *Outsourcing Solutions: Workforce Strategies That Improve Profitability.* Travers City, MI: Rhodes & Easton, 1997.

The Outsourcing Institute. www.outsourcing.com.

Quinn, James Brian. "Outsourcing Innovation: The New Engine of Growth." *Sloan Management Review,* Summer 2000, 13–28.

Quinn, James Brian. "Strategic Outsourcing: Leveraging Knowledge Capabilities." *Sloan Management Review,* Summer 1999, 9–21.

Useem, Michael, and Joseph Harder. "Leading Laterally in Company Outsourcing." *Sloan Management Review,* Winter 2000, 9–36.

28

INVESTMENT (PORTFOLIO) MANAGEMENT

What is this practice and how effective is it?

Every large organization uses investment (portfolio) management in some form or other to track and optimize its portfolio of investment projects. But few scrutinize their project portfolios well, and even fewer track the progress of projects and take action to improve their performance. We will look at the latest ideas for managing portfolios of investments and how best to maximize their value.

Alternative names and related topics: portfolio management; corporate portfolio management; investment optimization system (IOS); options theory; capital planning; capital budgeting

Few companies have control over their investment portfolios, which can include hundreds of initiatives with an aggregate cost of millions of dollars. Few have clearly defined processes for reviewing project proposals. Bad projects squeeze out good ones, and there is little visibility or transparency throughout the organization. An AMR Research report contends that as many as 75 percent of IT organizations have little oversight of their project portfolios and employ nonrepeatable, chaotic planning processes.[1]

Portfolio management begins with gathering a detailed inventory of all the projects in your company, ideally in a single database, including name, length, estimated cost, business objective, ROI, and business benefits. Excellent portfolio management processes can save companies huge amounts. Dennis S. Callahan, CIO of Guardian Insurance, and Rick Omartian, CFO of Guardian's

IT group and chief of staff, claim that portfolio management has reduced their companies' overall IT applications expenditures by 20 percent and that, within that spending reduction, maintenance costs have gone from 30 percent to 18 percent. AMR Research says that companies doing portfolio management report saving 2 percent to 5 percent annually in their IT budgets.[2]

Some organizations are using "options theory" to give them more flexibility in making decisions under conditions of risk and uncertainty. John Browne, former CEO of BP, believed in buying the right options "that will give us a shot at competing in the future—that will give us the right to play if we decide we want to when it becomes clearer what the game is about."[3] According to author Steve Morlidge, it is worthwhile to explore the principles that underpin this theory because they demonstrate exactly why a more flexible approach to management is not only intuitively appealing but also necessary in order to maximize value creation.[4] Morlidge starts by looking at the two investments, shown in figure 28-1. These could be potential investments in projects or businesses. What they show is that while they share the same expected rate of return, they have very different risk profiles. The conventional wisdom says that project A (the lower-risk project) has a higher value than project B. Thus, we would give project B a higher hurdle rate to reflect its high-risk profile. However, this decision is only valid if we assume that it is an "all or nothing" decision, that is, that there is no opportunity to defer the

FIGURE 28-1

Risk and value

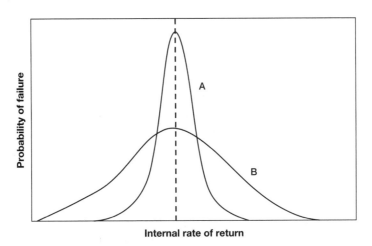

Internal rate of return

Source: The discussion of options theory and related illustrations are from the authors' discussions with Steve Morlidge. For more information, see Steve Morlidge and Steve Player, *Future Ready: How to Master Business Forecasting* (Chichester, UK: John Wiley & Sons, 2010), 151–178.

decision or to stagger the investment. However, if we *can* defer or stagger the investment, then the risk profile of B changes.

We can illustrate this apparent paradox by looking at the choice between two alternative share purchases (see figure 28-2). Suppose A represented a low-risk stock such as a water utility and B a high-risk stock such as a telecommunications company. If this were a straightforward either-or share purchase, we would probably opt for A because there is no extra reward for the additional risk we would be taking if we purchased B. If, however, A and B were *options to purchase shares*, and all other things were equal, we would opt for B. The reason is that an option is a *right but not an obligation*. In this case, it is a right to share in the rewards of above expected performance but not an obligation to share in the costs of failure. We only exercise options if we are "in the money."

In effect, for an investor in an option, the risk profile of option B has shifted to the right because the downside tail is eliminated. Options theory— the famous Black-Scholes formula—values this shift. The value of an option is a function of two things. The first is our ability to get valuable information about the nature of the risk in capital markets where history is a reasonable guide. The second is our ability to respond to this new information, that is, the amount of flexibility we have to exercise the option. In capital markets, this is represented by the amount of time you have before you need to exercise the option. But in practice, options theory can be complicated and even dangerous.

FIGURE 28-2

Project B: The real risk profile

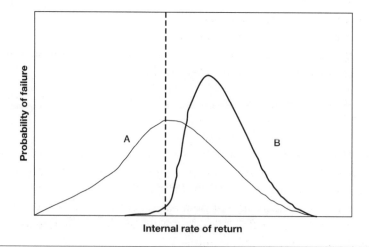

The biggest implication, according to Morlidge, comes from the recognition that in business, most decisions are more like options than straightforward share purchases. We usually have the option to defer a decision, and we usually have tremendous scope to structure proposals to change their risk profile and to give us flexibility to change course midstream.

This approach is in stark contrast with the conventional wisdom that says that projects are conceived as complete proposals that are considered and authorized at the same time. Alternatives are seen as inferior options to reject, rather than opportunities to exploit. This has two sets of implications. First, it demonstrates the value of having a performance management system that is flexible and responsive, rather than one that aims to fix plans based on a prediction. In a conventional management system through the use of fixed targets, fixed resources, and so on, we are constraining flexibility—literally closing down options—and therefore destroying value. Second, it provides a basis for constantly reviewing investments as we react flexibly to new information, restructure projects, and reallocate resources. There is also a need to delay the point of commitment so that as much information as possible is available to the decision maker.

Portfolios need to be actively managed. Steven Wheelwright and Kim Clark suggest eight steps for managing a project portfolio for new product development.[5] The same principles can be applied to more general business projects:

- "Define project types as either breakthrough, platform, R&D, or partnered projects.
- Identify existing projects and classify by project type.
- Estimate the average time and resources needed for each project type based on past experience.
- Identify existing resource capacity.
- Determine the desired mix of projects.
- Estimate the number of projects that existing resources can support.
- Work to improve development capabilities."[6]

The performance review is essentially about reacting to unusual or exceptional information. Is the project veering off track? What is the cause? Can it be corrected by a few minor adjustments, or have the very core assumptions on which the strategy was based become untenable? With an effective online project management system, managers can constantly monitor progress and adjust plans according to actual events and competitive actions. In other words, such a system can benefit from what Chris Argyris calls "double-loop learning," that is, feedback that links cause and effect and can lead to effective action through a process of learning.

Building an investment optimization system at American Express

In the typical company, around 20 percent to 30 percent of spending is discretionary, that is, it is not essential to the maintenance of the business. Spending promotes growth and improves profitability. A number of years ago, American Express neither knew how much of its discretionary spending was on worthwhile projects nor if it was optimizing risk across its portfolio. It monitored its investments on thousands of spreadsheets, but no one could collate the whole picture. With around seven thousand investment initiatives in play at any one time and total spending of $5 billion (representing around 30 percent of the operating expense base), the potential for waste in the system was huge.[a]

The problem was that business units didn't use the same methods to calculate returns. "It was every group for itself," says Anand Sanwal, director of corporate finance at American Express. "There were guidelines, but it was so easy to change things inadvertently or on purpose."

The international payment services group was the first unit to take the initiative and built a prototype for what would eventually become the parent company's investment optimization system (IOS). The company now easily evaluates a project's worth based on projected profits and fit with its overall strategy. It can also compare initiatives within units and company-wide. "People are starting to embrace what is right for the enterprise," Sanwal says.[b]

[a] Elizabeth Bennett and Briana Hallstrom, "The Baseline 2005 ROI Leadership Awards; Great Gains," *Baseline*, July 2005, 29.
[b] Ibid.

What is the performance potential of this practice?

- **To improve decision making and accountability.** The aim is to reduce waste by aligning investments with strategy and to make teams accountable for their results.
- **To allocate funds to the best current opportunities.** The aim is to break free from the annual budgeting window and enable investment funds to support the best current opportunities anywhere in the business.
- **To track investment performance and reallocate funds as necessary.** By tracking the performance of individual projects and the portfolio as a whole, leaders can track performance and reallocate funds to optimize risk and return as appropriate.

What actions do you need to take to maximize the potential of this practice?

ACTIONS TO AVOID

✖ **Be wary of the complexity of options theory.** While the theory is fine, there are many problems in practice. Options theory is complicated and ambiguous. While in one survey, 27 percent of four thousand CFOs said they used "some sort of options approach," another survey of 451 senior executives who had tried the real options approach concluded that fully a third had given up using it in the same year.[7] What is perhaps more serious is that most stock options holders fail to act optimally. As Tom Copeland and Peter Tufano note, "at times, holders are too trigger-happy, exercising too soon; at other times, they fall asleep at the switch. If holders of financial options don't always behave optimally, we can hardly expect holders of far more complex real options to behave any better."[8]

ACTIONS TO TAKE

✓ **Set up a team with the necessary capabilities.** Leading organizations manage each chosen initiative not only individually but also as part of an integrated portfolio. To achieve this, they establish a multifunctional team with the requisite skills. This might be the executive board itself or a specialized team. Thus, there are likely to be two levels of team—the portfolio team and the individual project team—and both need to appoint a leader who can direct matters in accordance with the agreed-on rules of engagement. Individual project teams need to agree on targets, time scales, milestone measures, and the frequency of reporting (and who is in the reporting loop). The information system and the network through which it is disseminated also need to be agreed on. The portfolio team needs to ensure that underperforming projects are terminated, thus releasing resources for other projects that fulfill the current criteria.

✓ **Do a project inventory.** When Rod Kifer joined DHL Americas as vice president of program management in 2001, one of his first tasks was getting control of project portfolio activities. He created an inventory, put that into a master project schedule, gained an understanding of the resource requirements of all the projects, then did a reconciliation of the projects, and reduced the schedule to a manageable level. Creating a project portfolio inventory can be painstaking but is well worth the effort. For many companies, it may be their first holistic view of the entire IT portfolio and any redundancies. A good inventory is the foundation for developing the projects that best meet strategic objectives.[9]

✓ **Identify projects that match strategic objectives.** In the 1990s, "U.S. bank Wells Fargo developed a balanced ranking model for its online financial services (OFS) business. The executive team had identified three strategic platforms: (1) attract and retain high-potential-value customers, (2) increase revenue per customer, and (3) reduce cost per customer. The initiative identification process started by sorting initiatives into two categories: 'strategic' and 'business as usual.' The team developed three criteria for strategic initiatives: helps OFS achieve a strategic objective (as listed on the balanced scorecard); builds a competitive advantage; and builds a sustainable point of differentiation. To qualify as strategic, an initiative had to score high on each criterion. (Initiatives that were rated medium to high were considered to be 'major' projects; initiatives that rated medium to low were considered to be 'minor' projects; and initiatives that rated low were considered only as 'activities.') Once past the initial screen process, the team then segmented them into two groups: those that were function-specific and shorter term, and those that were cross-functional, relatively expensive, and longer term. The team used three questions in this segmentation process: Does the initiative reallocate resources within other functional units? Does the initiative cost more than $500,000? Does the initiative take more than three months to implement? Only those initiatives that received a yes to *any one* of these questions would pass through this screen to the initiative ranking model. Of the complete list of over one hundred initiatives, only eleven survived the first two screens. At this stage, the proponents of each project would be asked to prepare a more detailed business case proposal."[10]

✓ **Prioritize projects by scoring and categorizing them.** After evaluating projects, most companies will still have more than they can actually fund. The beauty of portfolio management is that ultimately the prioritization process will allow you to fund the projects that most closely align with your company's strategic objectives.

✓ **Distinguish between growth and maintenance spending.** When looking at capital expenditure, it is important to distinguish between the element that supports "asset maintenance" and the element that supports "growth." When looking at a business unit, for example, a fast-growing unit might be pouring its cash flow into expansion, while another is spending on "business as usual." This is particularly important when looking at "free cash flows." There ought to be some way to distinguish a cement company that has no free cash because it consumes all its cash replacing worn-out machinery, from a retailer gobbling all its cash on new locations. According to Jack Gage, there is no perfect way to do this because companies do not report—and often don't know—how much of

Distinguish between project risk and portfolio risk

If we put all our investments in one basket, the risks will be greater than if we spread them around, and the greater the spread, the lower the risk. This view also applies to new ventures. The risk that any new venture will fail is quite high (say, six or seven out of ten). But venture capital companies look for the one that pays off. In other words, they look for a huge upside of, say, 100 to 1 or even 1,000 to 1.

Gary Hamel makes an important point here regarding new investments within large organizations. "Risk is the product of investment multiplied by the probability of failure," says Hamel. "A $100,000 experiment with an 80 percent chance of failing is substantially less risky than a $100 million investment with a 1 percent chance of failure . . . Yet which would be quicker to win funding in your company? Most companies fail to grasp this simple arithmetic. If they did, they'd be doing fewer big mergers, for example, and would instead be spawning dozens upon dozens of radical low-cost, low-risk experiments."[a]

Hamel's style is designed to make executives uncomfortable, and rightly so. We have seen billions of dollars poured down the drain in the name of shareholder value creation based on forecasting models with pages of numbers that prove what the project sponsors want to hear, but without stressing the risks involved.

[a] Gary Hamel, *Leading the Revolution* (Boston: Harvard Business School Press, 2000), 266.

their capital spending generates growth and how much merely maintains the status quo. "As a rough measure of how much cap-ex is growth-related," notes Gage, "we look at growth in revenue and at the historical relationship between revenue and fixed assets. If $1 of property, plant and equipment supports $3 of revenue, then a $300 million revenue gain calls for $100 million of new plant, property and equipment. This part of cap-ex is growth cap-ex. Anything else is (we presume) maintenance cap-ex. Only the maintenance cap-ex is subtracted from cash flow to get 'adjusted free cash flow.'"[11]

✓ **Actively manage the portfolio.** The essence of portfolio management is to continually reexamine the balance of risk. This active management insures that every project remains worth pursuing. Releasing resources locked into poorly performing projects is a key part of this review process. Adaptive organizations tend to have a high-level review team that meets, say, monthly or quarterly to perform this task, as American

Express does. A top-notch evaluation and prioritization process is emasculated rather quickly if the portfolio is not actively managed following approval of the project list. Doing that involves monitoring projects at frequent intervals, at least quarterly. At Blue Cross Blue Shield of Massachusetts, a project management office has that responsibility. Once or twice a month, the office gets financial and work progress perspective updates from project leaders. That information goes into a database, and the CIO reports to the entire company monthly, giving the project inventory and its status. He assigns project status—green (good), yellow (caution), or red (help!)—and includes an explanation of the key driver causing a yellow or red condition. The IT steering committee meets once a month to make decisions to continue or stop initiatives, assess funding levels, and resolve resource issues.[12]

Conclusions

Most organizations are fixated on negotiating and meeting budgets. They pay less attention to the quality of spending and whether it truly adds value. Effective management of the investment portfolio should be (but rarely is) high on the management agenda. Portfolio management is not difficult, though in large organizations with hundreds of initiatives, well-designed systems are a great help.

FURTHER READING

Datz, Todd. "Portfolio Management—How to Do It Right." *CIO Magazine*, May 1, 2003, 56–68.

Morlidge, Steve, and Steve Player. *Future Ready: How to Master Business Forecasting.* Chichester, UK: John Wiley & Sons, 2010.

Sanwal, Anand. *Optimizing Corporate Portfolio Management.* Hoboken, NJ: John Wiley & Sons, 2007.

29

EXPENSE MANAGEMENT

What is this practice and how effective is it?

Expense management focuses on overhead costs such as marketing, travel, and IT that represent a significant proportion of expenditures. Too many of these costs just increase each year with the annual "last year plus 5 percent" budget round. But some companies are looking at expense management in more innovative ways and making huge reductions. We will examine these ideas.

Alternative names and related topics: cost driver analysis; discretionary cost analysis; spend management; value-added analysis

"According to a recent McKinsey survey, 79 percent of all companies have cut costs in response to the recent economic crisis, but only 53 percent of executives think that doing so has helped their companies weather it."[1] In another recent survey of 401 top financial executives, 80 percent said "they would decrease spending on 'discretionary' activities like marketing and R&D to meet short-term goals."[2] But how discretionary can such spending be, given that cutbacks in these areas can have substantial negative effects on future performance? It's true that this kind of shortsightedness may temporarily fool the stock market by giving the appearance of improved prospects. However, in a study following the financial performance of 2,859 companies over five years, "firms that appeared to make short-term expense adjustments to inflate earnings when they issued equity ended up losing profits in the long run, causing their market value to drop by more than 20 percent four years out."[3]

The trouble is that most organizations cut the wrong costs when using the blunt instrument of budget reductions. It is the "hidden" costs that are the real opportunity, and their extent can be huge. In 2005 General Electric CEO Jeff Immelt lamented that "40 percent of GE consists of unproductive administration and back-office work and [he] wants to halve it in five years."[4] In the 2010

GE letter to shareholders Immelt noted "our productivity, measured by revenue per employee, has expanded by 50% since 2000."[5] That gives you an idea of scale of waste in one of the best-managed companies in the world.

When forced to make cuts in operating costs—as many companies now are—most leaders have little choice but to cut budgets. "Your budget has been cut by 15 percent" is a common directive in many companies today, and managers spend many tense and exhausting days with their spreadsheets, trying to understand what this means for their businesses and departments. They inspect hundreds of account codes and cost centers to see where they can make cuts. But this type of action is based on accounting numbers rather than deeper knowledge about the root causes of costs. It is like trying to improve your game by manipulating the scoreboard.

In 2005, McKinsey looked at 230 companies that had launched cost-reduction programs and discovered that only 10 percent were able to sustain the initiative beyond the end of the second year. It noted four reasons. First, cost reductions dampen morale. Second, managers want to expand the business, not cut it. Third, most cost reductions are born in the downswing in the economic cycle, and as soon as the upswing starts, they end. And fourth, managers pay more attention to operating costs than overhead expenses.[6]

But there are other hidden drivers of expense growth. One is that the root causes of costs fail to appear on the management radar screen and get lost in major account headings such as "wages," "transport," "production," and "administration." The reality is that costs are caused by the work that people do, usually within work processes such as handling an order, paying a supplier, or launching a marketing campaign.

Line managers are well known for including contingencies in their budget estimates. These amounts will vary according to the level of uncertainty, ranging from 10 percent to 20 percent up to 50 percent to 70 percent or even more. Contingencies protect against unpredictable outcomes. The greater the uncertainty, the larger and more likely managers are to pad their budgets for these contingencies. The result is funding that is not available for the rest of the organization to spend (by definition, it's hidden). Suppose that the contingency amount is 50 percent and the probability of it not being met is 40 percent. This means that 20 percent of the budgeted amount is excess *and will probably be spent toward the end of the year to protect the budget for the following year.* The typical game is that accountants know this goes on, so they try to cut the budgets back. Managers work to preempt this tactic by increasing the contingency amount and hiding it in hard to find places. Whatever the outcome, the result is wasted expenditure in one part of the business, while other parts that desperately need funding may go without. This is a classic problem of traditional budgeting and is particularly prevalent in the public sector.

Some organizations have taken discretionary spending away from business units and held these funds at a higher level. This avoids placing spending on autopilot, whereby budgets for expenses such as marketing, consulting, and training are spent mindlessly just because they are there. The major benefit is that "sandbagging" disappears.

One approach to dealing with the annual budget problem is to split costs between "core" (those essential for running the business) and "discretionary" (those support costs that are nonessential). From 2000 to 2003, Sydney Water Corporation deemed around 6 percent of expenses to be discretionary, and without any redundancies, it was able to meet its cost-reduction targets.

Another approach is that, instead of managing costs through hundreds of account codes in the general ledger, managers focus on understanding the root causes of costs (the cost drivers) that they can only see through a transaction or process lens. While revenues are driven by customer orders, costs are driven by activities and transactions and the work that people do to fulfill

---

How Cisco Systems cut travel expenses

One way to tackle expenses in general and travel in particular is to change how you describe expenses so that people can distinguish between those that add value and those that don't. In 2008, Cisco Systems cut travel expenses from around $750 million per year to approximately $350 million. While "travel and meetings for sales, new business, and customer opportunities continued unaffected, internal travel and meetings are now redirected to Cisco's various virtual meeting technologies." Cisco found that 49 percent of travel was for internal reasons. But leaders wanted more. "So, Cisco bumped the exception approval to the executive level. Now when you click on internal meetings as a reason for a trip in the self-booking tool, you stop. The system won't let you go further. Only a senior vice president can approve internal travel." said Cisco's global travel manager, Jane Garner. "Cisco also moved more of its training to Web-based classes, identified only a few classes for which travel is allowed, and mandated that other travel for training purposes 'must be approved by the senior vice president of human resources in conjunction with the CFO,'" explained Garner. Cisco believes that a lot of the expenses will never come back.[a]

[a] Mary Ann McNulty, "Cisco Virtually Eliminates Internal Travel," *The Transnational*, February 11, 2009, http://www.thetransnational.travel/news.php?cid=Cisco-virtual-meeting-telepresence.Feb-09.11.

them. Many bad transactions such as defects, returns, or repeat phone calls are caused by errors and work not done right the first time. But costs can also be reduced by cutting the number of good transactions such as those driven by purchase and customer orders, sales invoices, and check payments. Cutting the volume of transactions and reducing unnecessary work are the real opportunities for cost reduction. Table 29-1 shows more examples of cost drivers. One idea is to do an inventory of the cost drivers and work out a plan for eliminating those that add no value.

One area of spending that needs new thinking is travel and entertaining (T&E). T&E represents an organization's largest discretionary spending, consuming 1.6 percent of revenues for the average organization (or $5,019,500 annually for each five hundred business-traveling employees, or an annual cost of $10,039 per traveler).[7]

The lesson is that categorizing expenses by the typical chart of account headings such as car rental, air fares, entertaining, and so forth gives people

TABLE 29-1

Examples of cost drivers

Reduce number of:	Eliminate number of:
Purchase orders	Production defects
Sales orders and order lines	Warranty returns
Machine setups	Stockouts
SKUs	Supplier late deliveries
Schedule changes	Supplier defects
Inspections	Accounts payable errors
Credit inquiries	Order entry errors
Invoices processed	Customer claims
Customer inquiries	Refunds
Checks processed	Customer returns
Cost center postings	Customer complaints
Measures, reports, and spreadsheets	Repeat telephone calls
Reconciliations and journals	Late payments
Management tools and IT systems	Unnecessary e-mails and meetings

few clues about whether they add value or not. The Cisco approach is interesting and powerful because for the first time, people can understand the value of their decisions. How much more could organizations save if finance managers had the time and inclination to walk people through the profit-and-loss statement and explain the key cost drivers, instead of being fixated on budgets and targets?

What is the performance potential of this practice?

- **To understand the root causes of costs (the drivers) and thus how to reduce them.** Accounting numbers show costs by charting account categories such as salaries and depreciation. They fail to show the causes of costs. Identifying the cost drivers such as the number of purchase orders handled or credit checks made is the first step to understanding costs and therefore reducing them.
- **To provide real performance insights that help managers cut unnecessary work.** Managers need to see what work and which costs add value to customers and which don't.

What actions do you need to take to maximize the potential of this practice?

ACTIONS TO AVOID

✘ **Avoid budget negotiations and sandbagging.** Most managers add provisions into their cost budgets just in case they need them. The trouble is that whether they need them or not, they will spend them in order to protect next year's budget. These provisions, also known as sandbagging, can amount to huge hidden sums that represent waste within the accounting system.

ACTIONS TO TAKE

✓ **Consider splitting operating costs into core and discretionary spending.** Hold discretionary spending at a higher level; don't allocate to local budgets. Enable teams to access these funds based on standard decision criteria—below an agreed-on threshold—and to bid for higher-value funding; the peer group should make these decisions.
✓ **Cut detail and complexity that lead to unnecessary transaction volumes.** Take an axe to the number of general ledger accounts, cost centers, and budget lines. Aim for no more than 50 accounts in the general ledger and even fewer in the budget or forecast. Cut the number of reports by around 50 percent and the number of spreadsheets by even more.
✓ **Use bigger cost buckets to give managers more responsibility for managing costs.** Keep cost controls at a higher level and agree with managers to

"reduce costs by 30 percent over three years" or "keep increases to zero or 2 percent."

✓ **Focus on managing processes rather than budgets.** Controlling costs through hundreds or even thousands of cost-center budgets provides little value. A better approach is to identify a number of key processes, such as "purchase to pay," "order to cash," and "record to report," and appoint process owners who are accountable for continuously improving these processes.

✓ **Do an inventory of good and bad cost drivers.** Good cost drivers reflect what we should be doing to satisfy customer needs. Bad cost drivers are usually caused by doing either something wrong or something we don't need to do at all. These drivers need eliminating. Costs on accounting statements are *results*. They do not show their causes or drivers. Most costs are driven by pieces of work, such as "issuing a purchase order" or "inspecting a product." It is at this level of knowledge that costs can be understood and managed. Do an inventory of cost drivers and work out a plan for (1) reducing transaction volumes and (2) eliminating drivers caused by system failures or errors. Set waste-reduction goals at or even beyond industry best-practice levels.

✓ **Reduce central services.** One idea is to charge for services, for instance, requiring business units to pay for reports from a shared market research function. Often, that reduces use. More importantly, it creates a market mechanism that favors the most efficient, high-quality services. Another option is to redesign support services. The key is to focus on the most essential processes—financial reporting in finance, for instance, or recruiting in HR—eliminating steps that add little or no value. Yet another approach is to open support services to bids from external providers. Travel management, cleaning and maintenance services, and IT help-desk services are all candidates.

✓ **Build expense forecasts from cost drivers and revenue drivers.** Much knowledge is overlooked when cost budgets are based on last year's numbers. Building expense forecasts from cost and revenue drivers is a better approach. Higher numbers of satisfied customers (a revenue driver) translates into fewer complaints (a cost driver) and fewer people required in customer support (a financial forecast). Over 50 percent of expenses vary with customer demand. So we need to find our key revenue drivers before we can determine our key cost drivers and finally translate these drivers into a financial forecast.

✓ **Give frontline teams full profit-and-loss accountability.** Who managers perceive to own the resources is critical to how they think and behave. If they see expenses as belonging to "corporate," they are more likely to spend them, whether justified or not. But if they see them as their own, they are likely to be more careful. When Handelsbanken gave branch managers decision-making authority over staffing levels and even salaries, senior executives thought that expenses would increase. Instead, the opposite happened. Because the bank measured managers on two key metrics—cost-to-income ratio and profit-per-employee— they wanted to take every action to reduce costs. In the old budget model, they would hang onto staff in a down period, knowing it would be hard to get them back when better times came along. In the new model, they act like business owners always trying to match resources to prevailing demand. The lesson is to give managers more accountability for spending but measure their performance relentlessly against peers and benchmarks. But giving teams full profit accountability only works if they can clearly understand their cost drivers and spend most of their time improving the business rather than preparing irrelevant reports and attending useless meetings.

✓ **Use benchmarks and peer pressure to drive the right behavior.** At Handelsbanken, every region and every branch—and even the whole bank—knows how it is performing against its peers. There are no fixed budgets. Peer pressure is a powerful driver of low costs. But how it's done is important. Structured league tables (which use key performance indicators to compare units) show the rankings comparing each branch's relative performance within its region as well as how their region compares to the rest of the organization. However, these tables *are not* accompanied by senior management analysis (of who's done well and who's done badly). At Handelsbanken, the reason the system works so well and has lasted for decades is because it is low key. It is the transparency in the system that makes it so powerful. Each team knows who it should be beating and it can draw its own conclusions. There is no need for management judgments. Managers provide their own motivation. No manager wants to attend a meeting of his peers and be a consistent underperformer.

✓ **Make expenses open and transparent.** Recent evidence suggests that if expenses are open and transparent for everyone to see, employees are more responsible and the level of expenses will fall. Roche Pharmaceuticals experimented with this in 2009 (more explanation is given in chapter 36).[8]

✓ **Educate people on basic financial numbers.** Finance managers can do the organization a great service by spending more time teaching their business colleagues what drives costs and value rather than controlling their performance from the corporate center.

Conclusions

Despite many years of cost-reduction programs, most organizations still operate with much higher levels of cost than is warranted by their size, scale, or profit potential. The annual budgeting process has much to answer for in this regard. The budget negotiation process almost guarantees that costs and capital will increase over the previous period, and that by the end of the year, all the money allocated in the budget will be spent, whether justified or not. Finance people should spend less time on budgets and more time teaching people to understand their costs and how to reduce them.

FURTHER READING

Heywood, Suzanne, Dennis Layton, and Risto Penttinen. "A Better Way to Cut Costs." *McKinsey Quarterly* no. 1 (2010): 64–65.
Nimocks, Suzanne P., Robert L. Rosiello, and Oliver Wright. "Managing Overhead Costs." *McKinsey Quarterly* no. 2 (2005): 106–117.

Part IV

Performance Measurement

30

ENTERPRISE RESOURCE PLANNING (ERP) SYSTEMS

What is this practice and how effective is it?

Enterprise resource planning (ERP) systems have cost large organizations huge sums of money over recent years, but few have delivered the promised benefits. Some of this is due to overhyped expectations, and some to poor implementation. But the main problem is that too few leaders have prepared their organizations to move to a process-driven structure. Consequently, many ERP systems simply automated the old practices. However, as we will show, some companies have derived real value from their ERP investments, and there are many lessons we can learn.

Alternative names and related topics: enterprisewide information systems; materials requirements planning (MRP); manufacturing resources planning (MRP II)

In the past fifteen years or so, companies such as SAP and Oracle have experienced explosive growth selling enterprise resource planning (or ERP) systems that enable large corporations to integrate their functions, such as order processing, production, sales, and accounting. Now a salesperson can tell a customer where an order is in the system and when she is likely to receive it. For the uninitiated, until quite recently, most companies bought an order-processing and manufacturing system from one vendor, a sales management system from another, and an accounting system from yet another, and then spent countless hours and millions of dollars trying to get them to communicate with each other.

The ultimate goal is to have one unified system—one database—for the whole organization to increase speed and reduce complexity and costs. One immediate advantage is the time saved in rekeying data and reducing the need for huge numbers of month-end journals. The Hackett Group reports that companies that have just one ERP platform *and* embrace consistent technology and data standards incur 23 percent lower costs than those that don't.[1] Integration can reduce costs by 30 percent, according to Gartner.[2]

While most mid- to large-sized organizations have now implemented ERP systems, many have simply automated their old, inefficient, and ineffective processes. They have lost the potential gains. Various surveys over the past ten years tell a familiar story. Only around half of the systems are successful. Many take about twice as long and cost twice as much as originally planned, and a significant number (30 percent in one survey) were canceled before completion. Boeing, Dell, Hershey, and Nike, all had botched implementations.[3] The result is that few companies have realized their vision of totally integrated systems (only 2 percent of systems are fully integrated, 69 percent partly integrated, and 29 percent are not integrated at all).[4] The level of wasted investment has been huge.

Does it matter which vendor you choose?

A few years ago, the Hackett Group astounded the IT industry by announcing that it doesn't matter which ERP vendor an organization used, at least as far as the finance applications were concerned. ERP systems from SAP, PeopleSoft, and Oracle were used at more than 80 percent of the 2,500 organizations in Hackett's database, as well as at over 92 percent of all companies that achieve what Hackett describes as "world-class" performance levels in finance (i.e., the top 25 percent in the peer group). But no single vendor was used more frequently than any other, and all the ERP vendors supported similar best practices in finance.

Where the differences did matter was in consistency and standardization. What Hackett found was that world-class finance organizations that embraced data and technology consistency spent 31 percent less than their peers on finance, completed their monthly financial reporting cycles more quickly, and operated with about one-half the staff. These organizations also embraced simplicity in other forms. For example, they relied on a single chart of accounts, used half the bank accounts of typical companies, and did fewer budget iterations.[a]

[a] Stephen Swoyer, "Why ERP Does Matter," *Enterprise Systems*, August 16, 2005, www.esj.com/Enterprise/article.aspx?EditorialsID=1476.

To address these problems, vendors created clunky, proprietary methods of connecting their systems with others, which rather defeated the point of systemwide integration. So IT departments built complex integration links from enterprise software to other systems to keep the business running. Or they built dozens or even hundreds of unique installations of the same enterprise software to meet the needs of individual departments or businesses that all had to be linked together. Gradually, ERP vendors came to realize that to serve customers better, they needed to break up their suites into application components and create complex ways to link to them over the Internet so that customers would not have to rewrite connections to pieces of the suite, such as financials, which didn't change much.

ERP systems are aimed at efficiency and control. Their roots are in manufacturing (MRP) systems that aimed to apply linear programming to control every activity through the production process. They were never designed for flexibility and responsiveness, features that organizations desperately need in the new competitive environment. The vision of efficiency and control has proved to be an illusion as firms constantly change strategies, business models, products, and partners as they respond to a fast-changing environment.

This is not to say that ERP systems aren't valuable to the companies that bought them. Despite the initial problems, most of the systems work well. The happiest customers are those who used enterprise software to create new capabilities and processes that they could not express in software with their old systems.

What is the performance potential of this practice?

- **To support business processes.** ERP systems could simply replicate the paper trails and hierarchical accounting systems of old, but this would be a major mistake. Companies should see them as opportunities to become process-driven organizations.
- **To integrate financial information and provide more reliable information.** As the CEO tries to understand the company's overall performance, he or she may find many different versions of the truth. Finance has its own set of revenue numbers, and sales has another version. ERP creates a single version of the truth that cannot be questioned, because everyone is using the same system.
- **To integrate customer order information.** ERP systems are where the customer order lives from when it is received until it is shipped and paid for. By having this information in one system, companies can track orders more easily and coordinate manufacturing, inventory, and shipping among many different locations simultaneously.

- **To standardize and speed up manufacturing processes.** Manufacturing companies often find that multiple business units across the company make the same widget using different methods and computer systems. ERP systems come with standard methods for automating some steps of a manufacturing process. Standardizing those processes and using a single, integrated computer system can save time, increase productivity, and reduce head count.

What actions do you need to take to maximize the potential of this practice?

ACTIONS TO AVOID

- ✖ **Avoid customization and complexity.** "Companies that work with a small number of ERP vendors and reduce the amount of customization in their projects reap greater value from the applications, according to the Hackett Group. Hackett also noted that companies using the so-called best-of-breed approach in their ERP plans will struggle to keep costs down, as that approach leads a company to use a different vendor for each function. Businesses that engage in deep application customization may also struggle with costs."[5] "Standards and complexity are not mutually exclusive," notes David Hebert, an analyst at the Hackett Group. "You can still get efficiencies from eliminating steps and simplifying and standardizing your systems. The problem is that complexity will build itself right back up again. If you acquire another business, you get new complexity overnight. You have to get rid of it where it doesn't create an advantage."[6]
- ✖ **Be aware of the costs of data conversion.** Moving corporate information, such as customer and supplier records, product design data, and so forth from the old system to the new ERP system can take time and cost a lot. Also, most users discover that most of the data in their legacy systems is of little use. Companies often deny their data is dirty until they actually have to move it to the new client-server setups that popular ERP packages require. Consequently, those companies are more likely to underestimate the cost of the move. But even clean data may demand some overhaul to match the process modifications necessitated—or inspired—by the ERP implementation.[7]
- ✖ **Avoid setting unrealistic time scales.** If you are going to move from a traditional (vertical) hierarchical organization to a (horizontal) process-based organization, allow plenty of time for the design work. Getting it right the first time will save huge amounts of time and cost later on. It will also save time and money in customizing systems. But installing an ERP system is rarely straightforward. Stories about three- or six-month

average implementation times are exceptional and invariably apply to a small part of a business or finance only. A full-blown ERP implementation can take a few years, especially if it involves process changes. The important point is not to focus on how long it will take, but rather to understand how you will use it to improve your business.

ACTIONS TO TAKE

✓ **Align the ERP system with your strategy.** Investing in a new ERP system is an opportunity to align operating and accounting systems with business strategy. So find out what information managers need and when they need it. Don't squander this opportunity by copying old charts of accounts and reproducing dysfunctional systems. Rethink your systems to fit your strategy.

✓ **Let business processes drive the system.** ERP systems are intended to integrate processes *horizontally* as value is created for internal and external customers. But to do this, horizontal processes must exist in practice as well as in theory. The main work prior to acquiring a new system should be in process design and development. Assigning processes to teams and teams to processes and establishing a clear sense of ownership and accountability are crucial to success.

✓ **Eliminate redundant processes.** When mapping core and subprocesses, there is a golden opportunity to stop doing activities and tasks that are only necessary because of how work was done before. For example, there's an opportunity to rethink the accounts payable process by using digital connections with suppliers, thus cutting out lots of document handling and all the errors and rework it involves. Be brutal. Cut these and give the new system space to breathe and mature.

✓ **Involve the right people.** Include not just ERP specialists but also business process owners. Only process teams can understand what systems they require to fulfill their objectives of satisfying customer needs and make decisions on the scope, time scale, investment, and measurements necessary. Software and process people together can set realistic goals and milestones for developing the system. They can better see the key technology integration points where one process meets the next, and they can develop key performance indicators that provide process owners with the performance insights they need. Create joint teams that work together in the same location and take ownership of the development process.

✓ **Invest in training and education as people change the way they work.** New ERP systems have a dramatic impact on how people in different parts of the organization do their work. In the past, the paper trail was simple to understand. "Finance did its job, the warehouse did its job, and if anything went wrong outside the department's walls, it was somebody else's problem. ERP systems changed all this. The customer service representatives are no longer just entering someone's name into a computer and hitting the return key. The ERP screen turns them into businesspeople. It flickers with the customer's credit rating from the finance department and the product inventory levels from the warehouse. Did the customer pay for the last order yet? Will we be able to ship the new order on time? These are decisions that customer service representatives have never had to make before, and the answers affect the customer and every other department in the company . . . People don't like change, and ERP asks them to change how they do their jobs. If you use ERP systems to improve the ways your people perform their work, you will see value from the software."[8] Otherwise the new software could slow you down by simply replacing the older software that colleagues were accustomed to with entirely new software that no one is familiar with.

✓ **Focus on one technology platform and data consistency.** Hackett researchers found that 61 percent of world-class organizations are more likely than their peers to have a single ERP system, and 20 percent are more likely to rely on common data definitions. As if that's not enough, Hackett reports, such companies cut costs by another 21 percent over companies that focus on just these two elements. U.K. bank Barclays reduced finance costs by approximately £30 million and pared its head count from 1,650 to 1,150 by moving from thirty-seven different general ledger systems to just one. The bank now spends less time gathering and processing data and more time on analysis and business advisory services.[9]

✓ **Operate with one companywide database.** A single ERP and database platform enables significant cost reductions as well as advantages in terms of speed and efficiency. Operating with one profit-and-loss account is also a distinct advantage. Cisco provides a good example. It operates *one global profit-and-loss account* that it updates daily. Despite a structure involving three market-oriented divisions (large enterprises, service providers, and small and medium-sized businesses) and a number of central support functions, the company feels and acts as one seamless business.

✓ **Set up disaster recovery procedures.** If the system is down for a short time, a company needs a way to continue operating. The procedure should include not just an IT contingency plan but plans for any risk to the operation, for example, being able to ship and send out bills without a computer system.

✓ **Look to the future.** Many IT industry observers believe that cloud computing will replace in-house systems and revolutionize corporate computing. Cloud computing comes into play only when you think about what IT always needs: a way to increase capacity or add capabilities on the fly without investing in new infrastructure, training new personnel, or licensing new software. Cloud computing encompasses any subscription-based or pay-per-use service that, in real time over the Internet, extends IT's existing capabilities.[10]

Conclusions

Most mid- to large organizations have implemented some form of ERP systems. The best implementation examples can be found in a single unified system that increases speed and reduces complexity and costs for the whole organization. However, many have merely automated old, inefficient, and ineffective processes, which negates the benefits that could have been achieved. To be successful, organizations should be designed to support business processes and integrate financial, operational, and customer information. This should speed up the management process.

FURTHER READING

Davenport, Thomas H. *Mission Critical: Realizing the Promise of Enterprise Systems.* Boston: Harvard Business School Press, 2000.

Koch, Christopher. "The ABCs of ERP." Framingham, MA: CIO Magazine Research Center, 2006.

Koch, Christopher. "Integration's New Strategy." *CIO Magazine*, September 15, 2005, 38–48.

31

BUSINESS INTELLIGENCE

What is this practice and how effective is it?

Business intelligence systems offer organizations an integrated enterprisewide information system that enables all managers to be on the same page at the same time. Their planning, forecasting, and scorecard capabilities enable an organization to make fast, well-informed decisions at every level. But managers often use them to tighten control rather than to empower people. We will show how organizations can derive more benefits from them.

Alternative names and related topics: corporate performance management (CPM); business performance management; enterprise performance management

A company's survival often depends on a manager's ability to use intelligent IT systems to sense what's happening in the marketplace earlier than competitors and respond faster to unpredictable change. Strategy must be highly adaptable and in the hands of local managers who use a continuous stream of new knowledge, together with other leading indicators, to make fast decisions on markets, customers, products, prices, new business ventures, and so forth.

The term for managing a business in this way is *managing by wire*—an expression meant to draw an analogy to modern aviation's fly-by-wire systems. As author Stephan Haeckel explains,

> When jet engine technology arrived, airplanes became so fast that unassisted human pilots could no longer sense, interpret, and act on information quickly enough to fly them. So computer systems were developed to present pilots with concise displays of essential information and then translate pilot responses into the myriad actions needed to

execute the pilot's decisions. This technology mediated and accelerated the pilot's adaptive loop, making it possible to fly a plane traveling at several times the speed of sound. Managers needing to "fly" modern, fast-moving businesses will increasingly find similar systems both technically feasible and necessary.[1]

But "fly by wire" is a long way from where most organizations are today. In a 2007 survey, only 10 percent of executives reported that the information to make a decision is usually there when they need it, while more than one-third admitted it is available only after a long delay or not at all.[2] When author Ken McGee asked a number of *Fortune* 1,000 executives: "Is there information that would help you run your company far better if you had it in real time, and, if so, what is it?" the answer was always yes to the first part, and then the executives reeled off two or three key indicators. Dave Doman of AT&T said he wanted real-time customer transaction information, such as contract renewals and cancellations. Rick Wagoner at General Motors wanted real-time progress reports on new vehicle development. Dick Notebaert at Qwest wanted customer satisfaction numbers.[3] But none of these executives or others McGee interviewed could get what they wanted. Their information systems were just not up to the task.

The poor levels of IT integration—even after one or more ERP systems—mean that managers at every level have to rely on hundreds of spreadsheets to link one system with another and prepare plans and forecasts. While spreadsheets are fine for local requirements, spreadsheets cause problems when organizations need to aggregate them, as different units use different assumptions and algorithms and often work on different versions of the system, making it difficult to combine and consolidate plans and forecasts.

The time spent on keying data from one system to another leads to many errors and corrections. According to one expert, between 10 percent and 30 percent of recorded data is inaccurate, inconsistent, incorrectly formatted, or entered in the wrong field.[4] The result is that valuable days at the end of the month are spent rekeying data from one system to another and then posting thousands of journal entries to tie everything together. "You've got people customizing and formatting spreadsheets for the majority of the day rather than providing insights into business performance," notes Cody Chenault, finance practice leader at the Hackett Group.[5] Given the money poured into IT over the past ten years, this is a wretched state to be in.

The IT community thinks that the answer to many of these problems is "business intelligence," better known as "BI." BI describes the ability to organize, access, and analyze information in order to learn and understand the business.[6] Data warehousing and data mining have been around for many years.

More recently, online analytical processing (OLAP) and service-oriented architecture (SOA) have enabled a synthesis of various strands of management information technology to provide a single, enterprisewide view of information so that anyone, anywhere, anytime can find the information he or she needs to support a decision problem. Many of the leading IT vendors, including SAP (Business Objects), IBM (Cognos), and Oracle (Hyperion), now offer BI "stacks" that provide planning, budgeting, forecasting, scorecards, and consolidation platforms as well as sophisticated online reporting systems. BI and analytics have been the top priorities for CIOs on Gartner surveys since 2006.[7]

While BI might sound a bit like the executive information system of the 1980s, what makes it different is the closed-loop nature of its design, in which data doesn't just flow toward a decision maker but through a company, allowing decisions at all levels to be driven by strategy and, when needed, to alter that strategy. In a sense, BI is to performance data what ERP is to transactional data: a broad embrace of all relevant information, fully integrated and thus providing a single view, tailored, in this case, to the needs of finance and operations executives.

These integrated systems enable senior executives to see where their company is now, what the trends look like, and what they need to do differently to improve performance. The systems also enable more effective controls (a big advantage in the Sarbanes-Oxley world) and pave the way for more radical decentralization of decision making. Another advantage is that finance can use integrated platforms to build business rules and structures, then modify systems as their business evolves, easily accommodating changes such as extra locations, new or discontinued product lines, or restructured cost centers. Many have powerful modeling capabilities that enable teams to flexibly devise, compare, and assess alternative business scenarios. Such systems allow teams to build models in days rather than months. They also enable the building of cross-functional models.

American Express experienced huge problems after 9/11 when the travel business collapsed and most managers were paralyzed into inaction.[8] Determined never to be in this position again, the CEO challenged the organization to design a new management system that would enable more adaptive planning. The team outlined six guiding principles:

1. **Increased focus on analysis:** more value-added activities and financial analysis.
2. **More frequent updates:** conduct high-level monthly risk assessments to increase visibility in non-quarter months; allow for continuous resource-allocation reviews based on current information.
3. **Driver-based methodology:** focus on the impact of key drivers of business results to the bottom line.

> ## Welcome to the world of business intelligence
>
> A CFO at a computer software vendor provides an example of how the BI
> system is enabling fast decisions and how real-time control works:
>
> > I come in every morning, turn on my computer, and go straight to my BI
> > environment where I see five different reports. The first report tells me
> > every deal that we've closed in the last 24 hours. The second report tells
> > me about any deals in the pipeline that have changed in the last 24 hours
> > with some threshold. The third report tells me about any deals that have
> > slipped from one quarter to the next. The fourth report tells me about all
> > the big deals that we are tracking in a quarter so I know to whom we're
> > selling on an ongoing basis. And the fifth report is a summary that basi-
> > cally tells me where we are from a revenue point of view. That takes me
> > only 10–15 minutes because when you're used to the reporting frame-
> > work you're just looking for the changes and the exceptions.[a]
>
> [a] Jeremy Hope, *Reinventing the CFO: How Financial Managers Can Transform Their
> Roles and Add Greater Value* (Boston: Harvard Business School Press, 2006), 70.

4. **Standardization:** create consistent driver-based methodologies among similar products; implement standard calendars for corporate and business units.
5. **Increased continuous planning:** produce rolling forecasts with a minimum five-quarter visibility.
6. **Reduced cycle time:** reduce time by moving away from a detailed bottom-up process.[9]

The key to providing this new process was a fast, Web-based BI system using a single enterprisewide database. To verify that the BI system was truly user friendly and would have all the functionalities needed, one business unit built its own planning model. At the same time, another group was struggling to employ the legacy planning tools. The consumer card group grappled with an accounts receivable model that had to plan for changing rates on balance transfers when the 2 percent promotional rate reverted to the full consumer rate. It was a very detailed, robust model that the group was trying to keep afloat on spreadsheets. When the interest rate changed, the spreadsheet had twenty different locations that needed manual adjusting. The BI system proved its case by easily handling this problem without needing the manual adjustments or wasting a lot of time and human resources.

American Express replaced the annual budget with rolling forecasts in 2005. It improved planning by switching from annual budgets to continuous planning, driver-based rolling forecasts, and fast consolidations. This enabled more visibility, faster response, and more effective decision making. It improved resource management, enabling the constant prioritization of resources, leading to better risk management and the ability to fund the best current investment opportunities. And it implemented more effective controls through fast KPIs, rolling forecasts, relative measures, investment tracking, and transparent systems.

This example describes the real value of a BI system. To be effective, BI requires a change in thinking about the value of information inside the organization. For the system to enable all employees to improve their work, they need access to a wide array of information and not have it dictated to them. Open access also has implications for decentralization and control. One of the primary controls in the decentralized organization is the transparency and openness of the information itself. Everyone should be able to see the performance of everyone else. This can only happen in an integrated system and leads to an immediate sharing of problems and alerts key people to the dangers of not acting quickly. BI systems running on a common platform facilitate this process since all users work from a single data warehouse. They also tend to let information flow more freely within the organization, breaking down the silos that departments and divisions set up to protect their data from others.

What is the performance potential of this practice?

- **To deliver fast, relevant information to key decision makers.** Most management information systems are slow and provide a list of standard reports that vary in relevance. In some cases, managers don't know the month-end position until the third week of the following month. Receiving fast, relevant information at Internet speed puts managers in a strong position to respond rapidly to changing events and make decisions with the latest and best information possible.

- **To provide more time for the finance team to add value to their business partners.** Fragmented information systems demand huge amounts of time to key and rekey data into the system. Needless to say, this work adds little value and prevents finance managers from supporting the needs of hard-pressed line managers. A fast BI system saves huge amounts of low-value-adding time and enables finance managers to add real value in terms of decision support.

- **To reduce costs through fewer errors and less reworking.** Overcoming "spreadsheet mania" is a real challenge. That's why implementing BI systems is a key step in enabling managers to save significant maintenance costs.

- **To enable the organization to adapt to change.** Acquiring new businesses or divesting old ones is invariably a nightmare for most finance departments as they have to disentangle general ledgers, budgets, and reporting systems. With BI systems, it is easier for managers to absorb change and preserve the integrity of the consolidated system. By maintaining common standards and coding systems, managers are better able to produce consistently high-quality results.
- **To provide more effective compliance and control.** A common factor in many corporate governance scandals over the past ten years was the disconnection between group general ledgers and business unit systems. Thus, managers were not able to see the flow of transactional traffic between businesses and groups. Real control comes from transparent systems, and this is difficult to implement without completely integrated systems.
- **To enhance the effectiveness of decentralized decision making.** Many leaders want to decentralize decision making, but without fast consolidation systems, they could weaken control and expose the organization to fraud. Fast, integrated information systems are a prerequisite for the radical devolution of decision making to frontline teams. They enable the corporate center to monitor patterns and trends across the wider organization and focus where necessary on abnormalities.

What actions do you need to take to maximize the potential of this practice?

ACTIONS TO AVOID

- ✖ **Avoid multivendor systems.** Gartner advises users to cover multiple management processes, including, for example, planning, budgeting, forecasting, consolidation, scorecards, and reporting, all sitting on top of one database. Otherwise, the value of your investment that comes from integration will fail to meet its potential. A single, integrated suite means one installation, one interface to learn, one application to maintain and upgrade, and no requirement to perform complex mapping between independent applications sitting on different database technologies. It ensures that all information users are accessing all information from one common source. It means a shorter delay before adopting additional performance management components, since you already own and are trained on the technology. Integrating all these applications under one umbrella makes them fast. As one director of finance put it: "Before, you'd submit it before lunch and when you came back in the middle of the afternoon, your report would be ready. Running a simple report out of an ERP system that had to go through multiple departments and multiple time periods could take several hours and be a batch process. Now, the reports run in seconds."[10]

ACTIONS TO TAKE

✓ **Look for BI to provide new performance insights.** BI is not about a better budgeting system. Research shows that the top two reasons CFOs choose BI is to better see current results and better understand future performance trends.[11] BI is about gaining new performance insights and responding to them.

✓ **Involve as many users as possible.** Capturing and reacting to feedback is important for keeping the interest of participants. This was the case at American Express. Every single business unit had representation on the

---

Avoid using BI to micromanage people

BI can be seen either as a liberating tool of empowerment or as a tool of tighter micromanagement. If micromanagement wins out, then decentralized decision making will be stillborn. Facilitating "drill downs" to minute levels of detail or building information "cockpits" to better enable central control are just two of the features that many information systems vendors boast about. Information system designers often assume that it is the speed and power of data analysis that users value, hence the notion of the information cockpit, with a few senior executives pulling levers and pressing keys to make decisions that are, more often than not, far better done by frontline managers. The problem is that such systems appear to offer better controls, but this is a fallacy. If used in the right way, integrated systems enhance the effectiveness of decentralized decision making. Real control comes from transparent systems, and this is difficult to implement without completely integrated systems. While the corporate center can see patterns, trends, and exceptions, executives only need to interfere when they see movements that trigger a dialogue. This leaves local managers free to spend all their time developing the business rather than dancing to the tune of top-down control systems such as budgets and variances. The CFO needs to ensure that the systems design delivers what managers need, that is, fast, relevant information.[a]

[a] Jeremy Hope and Robin Fraser, "Beyond Budgeting Questions and Answers," Beyond Budgeting Round Table, CAM-I, October 2001, http://www.hpartner.com/pdf/Beyond_Budgeting.pdf.

planning transformation team. They all had a voice and were helping to manage the change. "There was a lot of psychology to all of this," according to project leader, Jamie Croake. "We felt it was important for managing the culture changes to make people feel empowered, that it was their process."[12]

✓ **Ensure that new systems eliminate the need for linking spreadsheets.** One of the benefits of using BI should be the elimination of multiple spreadsheets. According to Gary Crittenden, former CFO of American Express, "spreadsheets are great for individual productivity work but they cause problems when there is a lot of sharing and aggregation going on. Using driver-based forecasts together with dedicated systems and Web technology enables hundreds of managers to work on forecasts together and aggregate the outcomes to the highest level, thus providing more control than ever to the board. The new approach has enabled us to standardize on a single methodology and align key assumptions and algorithms across the organization."[13]

✓ **Look for a user-friendly front end.** The idea of BI is to get hundreds and, in some cases, thousands of people analyzing and interpreting information. But users across the organization are unlikely to embrace the new system if it has an unfriendly interface and requires extensive training. The user interface needs to be intuitive and look and feel as much like a spreadsheet as possible, but without all the problems inherent in popular spreadsheets.

✓ **Keep systems simple.** Some IT people are addicted to complexity. It seems that the more complex systems are, the more people will need their knowledge and support. But most organizations don't need sophisticated solutions. The goal is to maximize performance while minimizing complexity and confusion. Avoid customization and go for a one-vendor solution. Start with bite-sized chunks and grow the system over time, rather than trying to do everything at once.

✓ **Create structures and rules that enable scalability.** Acquiring new businesses or divesting old ones is invariably a nightmare for most finance departments as they have to disentangle general ledgers, budgets, and reporting systems. With BI, it is easier for managers to absorb change and preserve the integrity of the consolidated system. By maintaining common standards and coding systems, managers are better able to produce consistently high-quality results. Also plan for increasing numbers of users. The whole point of a Web-based BI system is to empower people by enabling them to access whatever information they think will be useful to them.

✓ **Make sure the data is clean.** Data is the most fundamental component of any BI system. It provides the building blocks for insight. Companies have to get their data stores and data warehouses in good working order before they can begin extracting and acting on insights. If not, they'll be operating on flawed information.

✓ **Ensure that data provides "one truth" throughout the organization.** Unlike fragmented ERP systems, the same data flowing through a BI system is used for planning, forecasting, and reporting, so everyone is on the same page at the same time. This is a "big win" for BI, and systems designers must not let users down. Another benefit is meeting Sarbanes-Oxley requirements. "Compliance demands are prompting organizations to look at the financial-consolidation applications as the financial-reporting system of record," says Kathleen Wilhide, director of corporate-governance solutions, compliance applications, and business process management (BPM) software at research firm IDC. In the quest for a "single view of the truth," companies are replacing or augmenting stand-alone software products and spreadsheets with integrated BI implementations. CareFusion (formerly Viasys Healthcare) stumbled onto the value of BI as part of its effort to make the company's data more consistent. "We didn't realize how important for compliance it would be, but we wanted a closed loop between our underlying general ledger, our ERP systems, and our financial-management system," says John Imperato, corporate vice president of finance at Viasys/CareFusion.[14]

✓ **Provide open access to information.** BI requires a change in thinking about the value of information inside the organization. To be effective, management teams need to open information access. This approach empowers users to drive greater value.

✓ **Provide self-service reporting tools.** BI gives local teams their own reporting capabilities unfettered by restrictions and conventional wisdom about which reports are useful. Providing online reports—often sent direct to mobile devices—also reduces the dependency on closing the books quickly at the end of the month or quarter.

✓ **Use BI to support business processes.** The latest versions of BI are not only helping senior managers to respond more rapidly, but also helping operating people improve their business processes, which is a huge new opportunity for BI to add value. In a computer systems manufacturer, one particular activity that IT sought to understand and make easier for salespeople was their preparation for quarterly meetings with customers. When IT people sat down with sales leaders to learn what went into the quarterly reviews, they quickly realized that while the sales leaders traditionally created their reports individually, they all incorporated the same information (customer profitability, number of orders booked and billed, percentage of on-time deliveries and so on). So the IT people wrote a program that automatically populates a standard PowerPoint template that all salespeople now use to prepare for the quarterly business reviews. Because they no longer have to build the review from scratch, salespeople can meet with more customers each quarter. And they no longer have to hunt down the information themselves. Now that the BI system matches up with the way the company conducts its business, improving those processes and sharing the improvements is that much easier, as was the case with the PowerPoint template and the quarterly reviews.[15]

Conclusions

BI is dealing the aspiring adaptive and transparent organization a new deck of cards. It will become the primary enabling tool of any business that wants to devolve decision making to frontline people and take fast action to meet new threats and opportunities. But everything depends on how companies use it. If they see it as another weapon in the command-and-control armory, they will lose the opportunity and their investment returns will be disappointing. If they use it as a tool of empowerment, they will spread management capability around the organization and greatly add to its intellectual capital. Another major benefit is that a well-implemented BI system can provide a stunning return on investment. According to data research company IDC, you can achieve a return of 430 percent over a five-year period.[16]

FURTHER READING

Axson, David A. J. *Best Practices in Planning and Management Reporting.* Hoboken, NJ: John Wiley & Sons, NJ, 2003.

Banham, Russ. "Quantum Loop." *CFO Magazine*, March 17, 2003, 20–26.

Brown, Mark Graham. *Beyond the Balanced Scorecard.* New York: Productivity Press, 2007.

Davenport, Thomas H. *Competing on Analytics: The New Science of Winning.* Boston: Harvard Business School Press, 2007.

Davenport, Thomas H., Jeanne G. Harris, and Robert Morison. *Analytics at Work: Smarter Decisions, Better Results.* Boston: Harvard Business School Press, 2010.

Hope, Jeremy. *Reinventing the CFO: How Financial Managers Can Transform Their Roles and Add Greater Value.* Boston: Harvard Business School Press, 2006.

Hope, Jeremy, and Robin Fraser. *Beyond Budgeting: How Managers Can Break Free from the Annual Performance Trap.* Boston: Harvard Business School Press, 2003.

Levinson, Meredith. "The Brain Behind the Big, Bad Burger and Other Tales of Business Intelligence." *CIO Magazine*, March 15, 2005, 49–58.

"A Practical Framework for Business Intelligence and Planning in Midsize Companies." Armonk, NY: IBM, August 2010.

32

KEY PERFORMANCE INDICATORS

What is this practice and how effective is it?

Key performance indicators (KPIs) enable managers to continuously learn and improve. Organizations often spend months trying to determine their KPIs. The result is too many measures that lead to the wrong behavior. We will look at what constitutes an effective KPI and how managers can find and use them to best effect.

Alternative names and related topics: performance measurement; leading indicators; strategic monitoring

"Drowning in data and thirsting for knowledge" is one of the pithier aphorisms sometimes used to describe what's wrong with performance measurement today. Think about how most corporate measurement systems work. Each month, most managers receive accounting reports that tell them how the business is performing and whether they need to take any action to meet the predetermined budget. If they want more information, they can drill down into lower levels of detail and find out what's going on by division, department, or cost center. They can see reports that tell them how many blue pens were purchased in location X or Y compared with this year's budget and last year's actuals. They can tell whether twenty or more types of travel and entertaining expenses are within budget. They can analyze every detail about product sales and whether each product has met its gross profit target and kept within its estimated standard cost.

But it is what these reports *don't* tell managers that's important. For example, they don't tell them whether they are gaining or losing the best customers, whether they are attracting and keeping the best people, or whether key operating processes—like production—are achieving best-practice standards.

The problem is that accounting numbers show only a one-dimensional view of performance. Like an iceberg, most reports show managers only the one-tenth of information that is visible above the water. The real performance insights—the other nine-tenths—remain below the surface. You need to use a lot more imagination as well as good systems to find and report on them. In other words, financial numbers tell you the score but don't help you to play and win the game.

Leading organizations place teams at the center of the management and measurement system. Most teams have a reasonable idea of which measures are critical to their success. If they are given the scope and authority to find these measures, they often approach the task with enthusiasm and imagination. Trial and error is part of the process. They will develop complex, multi-variant formulas that might work for awhile, but get superseded by other

Which measures are important?

To start the process of what to measure and report on, each team needs to agree on its success criteria. Think of a frontline value center team, such as the branch of a bank. This team might want to know: How well are we improving our financials? KPIs might include cost-to-income ratio and profit per employee. How well are we satisfying our customers? KPIs might include customer profitability, customer retention, customer satisfaction, and customer complaints. How well are we managing our operations? KPIs might include staff productivity and branch efficiency, based on the actual hours worked compared with total available hours. And how well are we managing our people? KPIs might include employee satisfaction, absenteeism levels, and recruitment rating (how graduates rate us as a potential employer compared with our peers).

Some organizations use balanced scorecards to perform this analysis. At Norwegian oil company Statoil, for example, each team has its own "ambition-to-action" (its version of the balanced scorecard) that it uses to set ambitious goals for the team, agree on how it will measure progress, and set action plans to improve performance. But KPIs are not passive. They are "pressure tested" to check that they provide a true and fair view of the performance picture with the benefit of hindsight. In other words, when other factors are taken into account, did a team's result truly reflect extraordinary effort or was it just fortunate to gain advantage from market growth?[a]

[a] See Bjarte Bogsnes, *Implementing Beyond Budgeting* (Hoboken, NJ: John Wiley & Sons, 2009).

more useful variants. And so the process goes on, until it settles down. But the point is that *the team* owns these measures. The measures have not been imposed on the team by a higher authority.

Individual KPIs are important, but they rarely capture enough knowledge about what's happening to tell managers whether one or another success factor is being achieved. You wouldn't know, for example, if customer relationships were in good or bad shape just from looking at customer complaints (many unhappy customers don't complain—they just never return or repurchase). This KPI would give you some clues, but it would not tell the full story. So you likely need a minimum of three KPIs to support each success factor.

Take customer relationships again. How many metrics would you need to be confident that you know whether these are strong and improving or weak and deteriorating? You might want to start by breaking down customer relationships into three key issues: (1) How good are we at attracting new customers? (2) How good are we at satisfying our existing customers? (3) How good are we at improving the profitability of our customers? Think of the metrics you might use for the first issue—attracting new customers. You might think about the number of seminars, one-on-one contacts, demonstrations, brochures, leads, prospects, proposals, and percentage of proposals that are closed. These are all quantifiable factors that you can count, and some might provide a useful correlation with actual sales. You can then move on to customer satisfaction and customer profitability and think of another ten to twenty possible metrics. You could easily end up with over fifty metrics that in one way or another help you to measure customer relationships.

The aim is to choose only three to five KPIs for each success factor. As far as customer relationship management is concerned, some managers might choose "willingness to recommend," "number of complaints," and "customer retention." What managers are looking for is a triangulation effect. In other words, do all KPIs relating to one success factor tell the same story? If so, the confidence level that the story is right—and therefore any action plan based on it will also be right—will be much higher.

The primary role of traditional measurement systems is to pull good information up so that senior managers can make good decisions that flow down. However, information is much more relevant if it is available in real time, and the team doing the work can take action immediately. This is the role of KPIs. They enable frontline teams to regulate their own performance and thus continuously improve.

What is the performance potential of this practice?

- **To enable managers to continuously learn and improve.** If managers can clearly define the purpose of a process, they can derive KPIs that tell them if they are improving their performance and moving toward perfection.

- **To provide managers with a radar screen to take fast, corrective action.** Most measures are too slow to enable fast action. Daily or weekly KPIs enable managers to react quickly to emerging events and take action that will avoid problems or maximize opportunities.

- **To enable process managers to measure progress toward strategic goals.** Most measurement systems are financial, making it difficult for managers to monitor their progress toward strategic goals. KPIs enable managers to continuously monitor their strategic progress and take corrective action where appropriate.

What actions do you need to take to maximize the potential of this practice?

ACTIONS TO AVOID

✖ **Avoid turning KPIs into fixed targets.** If measures are aimed at evaluating performance against predetermined targets, people will focus on meeting those targets rather than meeting the needs of the customer. Improving a KPI usually takes more than twelve months. The team should set its own improvement goals over a two- to five-year period and continuously monitor how well it is progressing toward those goals. Goals should be informed by benchmarks and best practices.

✖ **Don't try to link operating KPIs with financial performance.** This is the holy grail of measurement, but despite many attempts, it is difficult to achieve. Linking KPIs to measurable process improvement should be good enough.

ACTIONS TO TAKE

✓ **Base KPIs on teams.** Focus KPIs on three types of team: the executive team, the support services team, and the value center (or business unit) team. The aim is to find those KPIs that reflect the performance of the whole team, *not its individual members.* We have been involved with teams that have produced hundreds of metrics on the basis that everyone's contribution needs measuring. This overwhelms the system and leads to information overload.

✓ **Start the process of what to measure and report on by agreeing on the success criteria for each team.** Perhaps the most important principle of an effective KPI is that it is derived from the purpose or strategy of the team. When the purpose becomes "serve the customer" instead of "meet this activity target," measurement and management attention are completely transformed. Doctors and nurses can focus on treating patients, and the police department can focus on preventing crime. Measures should focus on flow—the end-to-end customer delivery cycle—rather than how much of any activity has been completed. The result is that everyone focuses on improving the work by applying his or her own and other people's knowledge.

✓ **Use a balanced scorecard.** One way to derive KPIs is to use the strategic framework provided by a well-designed balanced scorecard. The various perspectives of the scorecard help KPI designers to choose those that most closely relate to the team's strategy.

✓ **Brainstorm potential KPIs.** Get teams together and brainstorm potential KPIs for each success factor that reflects its performance over time. Choose the metrics that have high data integrity to help managers to learn and improve.

✓ **Include both leading and lagging indicators.** In your choice of three to five KPIs for each perspective, try to select a mix of leading (predictive) and lagging (results) indicators.

✓ **Limit the number of KPIs to three to five for each success factor, such as customer relationships.** One truck manufacturer we visited showed us a book containing hundreds of KPIs on just about everything you could think of concerning performance—and it employed sixty people producing them. But when we looked at the measures more deeply, there were few concerning customers and even fewer concerning employees. Finding the right number and balance of measures is not easy. A single measure is invariably too simplistic, while a wide range of measures is likely to lead to contradiction and confusion and make it difficult to prioritize what's important. Managers at any level shouldn't need more than six or seven measures. Harvard professor Robert Simons's rule of thumb for accountability systems is that individuals should be accountable for no more measures than they can remember—usually about seven.[1]

✓ **Choose KPIs that provide clear direction and guidance about what's important.** KPIs send signals to people about what leaders think is important. Think of an oil rig. What is more important, profit or safety? While profit is, of course, ultimately important, safety is absolutely critical in the short term, as BP leaders have discovered to their cost. So ensure that your chosen KPIs send the right messages.

✓ **Choose KPIs that encourage the right behavior.** There is little doubt that "what you measure is what you get," so think about the behavior you want before deciding on the KPI. Consider what happened at a printer manufacturer that was competing in a market where time to market was *the* critical success factor, but its existing measurement systems were sending conflicting messages. Based on assumptions of 20 percent market growth,

12 percent annual price decline, and a five-year product life cycle, a study showed that if the company met its budgetary targets but is six months late to market with the product, the cumulative profit decline (over the five-year life) is 31.5 percent. If the company overruns its cost budget by as much as 30 percent but gets to market on time, the decline in profitability is minimal—only 2.3 percent. The study offers clear evidence of managers reacting to the wrong performance measures. The same program managers who know to the penny what an engineer will cost, and what profits will be lost if cost targets are missed, cannot begin to quantify the losses associated with a six-month slip in the development process. They willingly slow down the development process to contain the project budget or to hit the cost targets.[2] Think about traffic wardens. Do you want them to maximize their income from issuing tickets, or do you want them to improve the flow of traffic? The measurement system should reflect the behavior you want to encourage.

✓ **Choose KPIs that reflect the whole process.** A classic measurement pitfall is when a company measures one team in a way that undermines the performance of another, downstream team. For example, consider a sales order processing team whose KPIs were primarily focused on the accuracy of order entry. It spent so much time checking orders before entering them into the system that the delivery and installation teams were unable to meet their KPIs and customer satisfaction—an important KPI for many other teams—was affected. Leaders must realize that teams are part of an interdependent network that must connect and combine to deliver products and services to customers. The whole interconnected process needs to be measured.

✓ **Choose KPIs that are understandable.** Employees must know what's being measured, how it's being calculated, and, more importantly, what they should do (and shouldn't do) to positively affect the KPI. It is not enough to simply publish a scorecard; you must train individuals whose performance you are tracking and follow up with regular reviews to ensure they understand and are acting accordingly.

✓ **Choose KPIs that lead to fast action if the trend line changes.** The true test of a worthwhile KPI is that managers take action based on it if the trend line changes. Few KPIs pass this test.

✓ **Report KPIs daily and weekly.** Becoming a truly adaptive organization requires fast, relevant and frequent information, especially the effective use of a few KPIs at every level. They represent the critical indicators for the adaptive organization.

✓ **Keep testing KPIs.** Finding the right KPIs is not always straightforward or intuitive. All too often, the tendency is to grab the easiest, most readily available measures, missing the more important ones that may be crucial to delivering high value to your customers. For example, customer retention levels are thought to be effective KPIs, but new research shows that the difference between "promoters" (those that score a five on a typical customer satisfaction survey) and "detractors" (those that score a one) is a better leading indicator of growth and profitability. Also, the most appropriate KPIs can change over time.

✓ **Share KPI performance widely.** The best organizations provide open access to KPI data. They show goals and results on Web sites and bulletin boards, and report them frequently in newsletters. In this way, all employees become involved and can see the impact they are having on performance. Open access also encourages them to come forward with suggestions for improvement.

Conclusions

Many organizations have completely overhauled their management information systems so they know where they are every day, week, or month and put themselves in a better position to forecast the short-term future. This combination of fast, relevant information and good short-term visibility is the very essence of control in an unpredictable world.

FURTHER READING

Axson, David A. J. *Best Practices in Planning and Management Reporting.* Hoboken, NJ: John Wiley & Sons, 2003.

Brown, Mark Graham. *Beyond the Balanced Scorecard.* New York: Productivity Press, 2007.

Davenport, Thomas H. *Competing on Analytics: The New Science of Winning.* Boston: Harvard Business School Press, 2007.

Hope, Jeremy. *Reinventing the CFO: How Financial Managers Can Transform Their Roles and Add Greater Value.* Boston: Harvard Business School Press, 2006.

Hope, Jeremy, and Robin Fraser. *Beyond Budgeting: How Managers Can Break Free from the Annual Performance Trap.* Boston: Harvard Business School Press, 2003.

Parmenter, David. *Key Performance Indicators.* Hoboken, NJ: John Wiley & Sons, 2007.

33

ROLLING FORECASTS

What is this practice and how effective is it?

Rolling forecasts enable managers to anticipate short-term outcomes and therefore influence them. Forecasts are a quantum leap from annual budgets that act as a barrier to fast response. On the one hand, budgets and their periodic revisions focus on the forthcoming year-end; managers use them to take whatever action is required to achieve the agreed-on targets. On the other hand, rolling forecasts provide managers with a moving window of the future that will help them to make strategic decisions, manage cash flows, and set shareholder expectations. But there are many implementation pitfalls that can distort these forecasts and put managers in a worse position than before. We will examine these issues and provide some guidelines that enable managers to place rolling forecasts at the center of the management system.

Alternative names and related topics: rolling financial reforecasts; driver-based forecasting; continuous planning

Most organizations not only spend months preparing annual budgets, but also spend many more weeks and months revising the budget or preparing forecasts to give senior executives a view of the likely year-end position. Many organizations suffer from using limited forecasts that are geared to the fiscal year-end and aimed at helping managers to keep on track. Often known as "3+9," "6+6," and "9+3," the first number represents months of actual results completed while the second number represents the months remaining until the accounting year-end. In some firms, this approach amounts to four budget recompilations per year and thus adds a huge extra burden to already hard-pressed finance staff. The forecasts are invariably confined to asking the question, "Are we on track to meet our targets and, if not, what action do we need to take?" The resulting action often ruptures carefully crafted strategies designed to create long-term value.

But using the rearview mirror of budgets and variances to manage performance when the market is changing so rapidly is a recipe for disaster. Managers need early warning of changes that affect their business, particularly if the changes spell trouble ahead. But most organizations are poor at forecasting. Not only do they have a lack of foresight, but they have an inherent fear of taking positions that go against the grain of conventional wisdom. At one global company, there were seventy-five levels of review and consolidation, and it took a huge amount of time and effort to produce a forecast. Such was the detail involved that one business unit alone spent 585 people days over eight weeks to produce a forecast that was immediately out of date. Not only do forecasts take too long, but also their quality leaves a lot to be desired.

Most managers know that their operations don't switch off on December 31 each year and start again on January 1. They deal with these problems by moving to monthly or, more commonly, quarterly *rolling forecasts* (see figure 33-1). Let's assume we are just approaching the end of quarter one. The management team gets the rough figures for that quarter and starts to review the next five quarters ahead. Four of those quarters are already in the previous forecast, so they just need updating. The team needs to add a further quarter, however. It should spend more time on the earlier quarters than the later ones, using as much relevant knowledge and business intelligence as it can gather. By definition, the fiscal year-end is always on the twelve- or eighteen-month rolling forecast radar screen.

FIGURE 33-1

A five-quarter rolling forecast

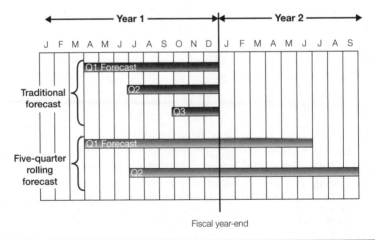

The more practice managers have at preparing forecasts, the better they become. But while adopting rolling forecasts is a major step forward, *how these forecasts are prepared* is crucial to success. Forecasts must be seen as a tool for strategic management and learning, not for control. Such a process must therefore be quick and impartial, and paint a moving picture of the factors that create financial outcomes. To be quick, the process must only focus on the key performance drivers and involve a few people. To be impartial, forecasts must

Bias is a major problem

Too many forecasts are prone to bias. Many companies, for example, rely far too heavily on the opinions of salespeople and managers, rather than use hard data. These opinions tend to distort results because people confuse targets (hope) with forecasts (reality). They also tend to produce forecasts for their own functions and mistrust forecasts from other areas, overestimate the effect of marketing campaigns and other revenue-management actions, and use forecasts that differ from those used in other parts of the company. For example, financial, manufacturing, and sales functions may produce forecasts independently, but none monitor the changes in the others' projections or revise their own to reflect these changes.

Researchers Rogelio Oliva and Noel Watson interviewed twenty-five people in the sales forecasting process at a California-based electronics firm. They found that the company's planning process had, historically, been driven largely by the sales function. Sales directors responsible for regional markets made initial forecasts, which they then passed on to operations and finance. The process was ad hoc, with important communication as likely to take place in hallways as in formal meetings. Armed with these forecasts, the finance department created plans and monitored results. Finance tended to pressure the sales team to hike up its forecasts so that the company could meet its financial goals. Meanwhile, because people in the operations group were generally skeptical of the forecasts from the sales team, they made their own forecasts to put the best light on potential inventory shortages for which they might be blamed. Similarly, the marketing director took the forecasts from sales and factored in the possible effects of promotions and other activities. This flawed system eventually contributed to an inventory write-off equaling about 10 percent of revenues and the recruitment of a new CEO and executive group.[a]

[a] Rogelio Oliva and Noel Watson, "Managing Functional Biases in Organizational Forecasts: A Case Study of Consensus Forecasting in Supply Chain Planning," working paper 07-024, Harvard Business School, Boston, 2007.

be an independent process disconnected from targets, performance evaluation, and rewards; only in this way will senior managers obtain unbiased forecasts that truly reflect what operating managers expect to happen. And to paint a moving picture of future financial outcomes, forecasts must constantly look a year or more ahead, thus giving managers time to influence the outcomes.

"Most organizations suffer because they can't access the data they need quickly. Leading organizations use proprietary calculation engines that enable them to evaluate models and test assumptions in minutes. They avoid unproductive activities like tracking down numbers, fixing broken links, and debugging macros. They enable driver-based forecasting and the rapid recompilation of multidimensional models. They also go to great lengths to ensure that their forecasting models, together with key assumptions and algorithms, are consistent across the group. This is essential if multiple users are working on forecasts at the same time and sharing information."[1] Companies that successfully implement a unified forecasting process can expect revenue gains of at least 10 percent, according to the Gartner Group.[2]

At one U.K. manufacturer, managers used to produce what was called a financial digest that was due on the eighth working day following the month-end. It was geared to explaining variances from budget and whether any further action was needed to meet the agreed-on year-end targets. While six-quarter rolling forecasts were part of this process, they were not taken seriously beyond the fiscal year-end. They were also the last thing to be done during the monthly closing process, and the finance people usually did the forecasts. In recent years, this has changed radically. The forecasting process is now the key management tool for managing the business at every level.

While the manufacturer still has an annual strategy formulation process in which it discusses the big issues, action planning is now a quarterly event. These quarterly business reviews together with supporting six-quarter rolling forecasts are completed around three weeks after the quarter end. The company has separated forecasts from targets and performance measurement, thus taking much of the bias out of the forecasting process. The annual financial plan is simply the four quarterly forecasts that fall within the fiscal year.

Another important element of the forecasting process is the monthly "flash" forecast. The manufacturer now prepares these forecasts in the middle of each month, when there is more time available, and looks to the end of the current month and a further two months ahead. So senior managers now receive monthly results and short-term forecasts for the following two months, the current quarter, and the full year, four working days prior to the month-end. Given that average organizations take six days to close the books, a further eleven days to finalize reports, and fifteen days (concurrently) to prepare forecasts, this is a real breakthrough in information management.

Rolling forecasts, if well prepared, form the backbone of a new and much more useful information system that connects all the pieces of the organization together and gives senior management a continuous picture of both the current position and the short-term outlook. In effect, they are the aggregate of business-as-usual forecasts (extrapolations of existing trends), all the action plans in progress, and all plans in the pipeline. In other words, forecasts should be baseline, plus anticipated events, with the effort being focused on events. An honest view has no bias, so managers should expect to see half of their forecasts on the high side of actual outcomes and half on the low side. The ideal forecast has clean data that enables managers to improve decision making. Forecasts must not be seen as commitments, otherwise bias and distortion—dirty data—will be inevitable. That's why implementing rolling forecasts under the umbrella of fixed targets rarely works.

What is the performance potential of this practice?

- **To improve decision making.** A well-prepared forecast provides an excellent decision-making framework for management (e.g., deciding on how much capacity is needed).
- **To support regular strategic performance reviews by identifying future performance gaps.** Rolling forecasts enable managers to focus on the medium-term outlook and encourage managers to take actions that close gaps against peers or benchmarks rather than this year's target.
- **To enable senior executives to manage performance expectations and avoid shock profit warnings.** With little future visibility, leaders are always vulnerable to the shock profit warning that is the nightmare scenario for any board of directors. With rolling forecasts that are quickly consolidated throughout the group, leaders can anticipate sharp changes in performance. Whether they are able to influence these swings is one question, but they should be in a better position to manage expectations and give the impression that they are in control of events rather than driven by them.

What actions do you need to take to maximize the potential of this practice?

ACTIONS TO AVOID

- ✖ **Understand that the purpose of forecasting is not to predict the future but to influence it.** The mistake that many organizations make is assuming that forecasts are about predicting and controlling future outcomes. The only certainty about a forecast is that it will be wrong. The only question is by how much. Narrowing that variation comes from learning, experience, and decent information systems. The purpose of a forecast is not so much to provide an accurate view of the future but to provide some insights about how strategic options and future events will combine to produce the financial outcomes that you want.

✖ **Avoid linking forecasts to targets, measures, and rewards.** Most unbiased forecasts are not the ones leaders want to see. If you ask managers to forecast within a budget- or target-based system, don't be surprised when their forecasts magically meet the agreed-on budget or target. Managers know that their leaders don't want to be told bad news nor do they want to go to difficult meetings to explain why the new forecast is worse than the previous one. This is why forecasting needs to be divorced from target setting, measurement, and rewards. When Danish petrochemicals company Borealis implemented rolling forecasts, it found that accuracy improved when it separated forecasting from targets and rewards. The initial response of managers was to include—indeed inflate—their capital expenditure commitments, thinking it would influence their approval ratings, but when they realized that this had no effect—these investment decisions were taken over by a quarterly review committee—they gradually adjusted their forecasts to reflect a more realistic view of essential project expenditure.

✖ **Avoid turning forecasts into contracts and commitments.** For the same reasons as the previous point, you must avoid turning forecasts into contracts and commitments. This caveat not only applies explicitly but also implicitly; even if you don't intend such a result, managers may still interpret the forecast as a commitment to deliver the agreed-on outcomes.

✖ **Don't allow forecasts to be changed without consultation.** While higher-level management can challenge the assumptions on which a forecast is based, and therefore its outcomes, it cannot unilaterally change the forecast. Otherwise all credibility in the bottom-up process will evaporate.

✖ **Stop forecasting to the wall.** Rolling forecasts almost always roll beyond the fiscal year-end. Just updating the annual target and budget is *not* a rolling forecast.

ACTIONS TO TAKE

✓ **Base forecasts on rolling periods of twelve months or more.** The purpose of forecasts is to provide a more useful framework for decision making. So they should be done regularly and cover a period that enables leaders to effectively steer the business. Almost inevitably, rolling forecasts go past the next fiscal year-end, thus providing leaders with more visibility.

✓ **Make forecasts a light-touch process; base forecasts on a few key drivers, not masses of detail.** Most forecasts are recompilations of budgets. We've often heard managers complain, "These rolling forecasts are a great idea, but it means we are doing four full budgets a year. It's four times the workload. It is intolerable." Compiling forecasts from hundreds of lines of detail is the wrong approach. In most businesses, few numbers change much from period to period. It therefore makes more sense to focus on the key drivers of sales and costs. Many finance people believe that greater forecasting detail equals greater accuracy. But this is not rational. Given that each forecast is prone to error, the more forecasts you combine, the greater will be the error, as one mistaken assumption affects another. In other words, the distortion impact is exponential because errant assumptions have a multiplier effect. The experience at Borealis bears this out, as financial controller Thomas Boesen explains:

> Just because forecasts include a thorough bottom-up approach including a review of all budget line items does not mean that the result will be greater accuracy. In fact, just the opposite is more likely to be the case. By concentrating on a few key variables such as orders, sales, costs, and capital, managers can project the major performance variables without imposing a heavy workload on participants. The essential point is that they can see the "big picture" and not get too involved in discussing the detail. You get a far better result from the minimum of effort, provided of course that forecasts are not caught up in the measurement process.[3]

✓ **Choose the right forecasting horizon.** The forecasting intervals and time taken should reflect the needs of the business. In a financial services business, for example, with no physical supply chain and inventories to manage, forecasts should take no longer than a few days. However, in a fast-changing, capital-intensive business, which uses forecasts to make key decisions about capacity requirements often involving significant capital sums, forecasts can take longer. There is no precise answer to the question of the length of the forecasting horizon. It depends on how long a company takes to make key decisions about operations, capacity, and capital spending. In other words, if the company takes two years to bring new facilities on stream, this might be a reasonable guide. In a fast-moving consumer products business, forecasting should reflect lead times. If the business takes three months to change supply contracts or adjust marketing programs, there is no point in preparing forecasts for less than this period. The horizon also depends on the speed of change. For an airline, changes are happening at lightning speed, and revising forecasts each month would be advisable. In a public-sector organization, quarterly forecasts would be sufficient. Most leading organizations spend more time and effort on near-term periods and less on the long-term ones.

✓ **Recognize that forecasts are more accurate at higher levels of aggregation.** Some organization use risk-pooling techniques to reduce demand and supply risks. In the late 1990s, Cadillac changed its distribution strategy in Florida, one of its largest markets. Instead of allowing dealers to order the cars it assumed customers wanted, Cadillac sent only demonstration vehicles. When a customer placed an order, Cadillac delivered the car overnight from its distribution center. This enabled Cadillac to pool its demand forecasts from its Florida dealers, rather than respond to individual dealers' forecasts. The aggregate forecast was much more accurate than the individual dealers' forecasts and resulted in vastly improved customer service.[4]

✓ **Set common standards and rules.** Create clear methods of standardizing inputs to the sales-forecasting process. If all your salespeople adhere to the same rules in classifying opportunities, the forecast model is at least based on similar data standards each time it's run. Standardizing requires implementing rules for classifying sales opportunities. First, define the stages in your sales cycle. Then, define the type of progress required to move up a stage. Finally, assign probabilities of closure based on standard rules. In general, you should base inputs on facts rather than opinions.

✓ **Ensure that forecasting models are consistent and aligned.** Most forecasting processes use simple spreadsheets. While this is fine for small, local requirements, spreadsheets can cause problems when they need to be aggregated across and up the organization. In large organizations, different units use different assumptions, algorithms, and software, which makes it difficult to combine and consolidate forecasts. The IT industry is now offering sophisticated models to enable large organizations to prepare forecasts quickly and consolidate reports. Teams can build business rules and structures, then modify the model as their business evolves, easily accommodating changes such as added locations, new or discontinued product lines, or restructured cost centers. Many systems have powerful modeling capabilities that enable teams to flexibly devise, compare, and assess alternative business scenarios. Such systems allow teams to build models in days rather than months. They can import data definitions from other sources like ERP and general ledger systems. They also enable teams to build cross-functional models.

✓ **Reduce business lead times.** Forecasting what will happen tomorrow is much easier than what will happen in six or twelve months. So the shorter the lead time to introduce new products or strategies, the more accurate and useful the forecasting process will be. Fast response is the real aim. Beyond Budgeting Round Table member chairman Steve Morlidge learned this at Unilever, where he moved from controller of the Best Foods Group to lead Unilever's implementation of Beyond Budgeting. "The only reason you forecast is because you can't react fast enough and if you're given a choice of improving your speed of reaction or improving your capacity to forecast, you should always choose speed of reaction. If you're a boxer, which would you prefer—better forecasts or faster reflexes? There's just no debate because any forecast by its nature is flawed. It's always going to be wrong. So if you can react more quickly, then that's the best option," notes Morlidge.[5]

✓ **Dovetail one forecasting cycle into another.** One manufacturer uses multiple interlocking cycles to build medium-term forecasts. One-month flash forecasts look one quarter ahead; quarterly rolling forecasts look one year ahead; one-year rolling forecasts look four years ahead, and an annual strategic planning process looks ten years ahead. One forecast dovetails into another like cogs in a wheel. These forecasts form the core

Spend the most time on the sales forecast

The basic building block of any forecast is the sales or income line. Most other variables are related to sales. But obtaining an unbiased sales forecast is no easy task. A well-prepared sales forecast should take account of marketing and promotion and new product launches. It should consider market share, production capacity, and competitive actions. And it should examine customer behavior patterns. Forecasts will also vary depending on the knowledge available. For example, in some businesses—such as those that work on government contracts—customers will enable managers to prepare reasonably accurate forecasts. Other businesses will give blanket sales orders that they will draw down as required. Companies that rely on only a few customers can ask those customers for an order forecast for the forthcoming period. This, together with some probability adjustment, should provide a reasonable forecast. Companies that make a wide range of standard products that are sold to large numbers of customers can use statistical forecasting methods to predict demand based on history and prevailing trends. However, companies geared to meeting exact customer needs have no such forecasting method available. Reading the competitive climate and good judgment are probably all that they can reasonably do.

information for the monthly meetings, the development programs, and the strategy reviews. Managers build competence in "sketching the future," and within that future lie the opportunities and threats that traditional budget-driven processes fail to see until it's too late.

✓ **Match the model to the requirement.** A model is a simplified representation of the world to use to form a prediction. There are three types of models. Statistical models extrapolate from history to generate a prediction, based on the assumption that "the future will be a continuation of the past." This model is often used to forecast revenue lines, including consumer spending and product sales. Mathematical models attempt to understand and model the relationship between various elements of the business to produce a prediction. Many cost forecasts, of course, vary with revenues. Judgmental models are in the head of the person producing the forecast. Although forecasting based on judgment seems simplistic, human beings are capable of modeling in very sophisticated ways. The aim is to use the most appropriate model for each part of the forecast.

✓ **Use range forecasting.** Most organizations prepare forecasts on the basis of single-point estimates of future outcomes. The forecasts are usually simple extrapolations of existing trends. Executives often demand a number, which implies certainty in the forecast and invariably ends up being the average of past periods. The trouble is that averages are usually wrong. And averages added to averages are even more wrong, especially if other assumptions depend on them. Instead of aiming for a single-demand forecast that is invariably wrong, leading organizations forecast a range of potential outcomes. In this way, the organization becomes used to—and is better able to deal with—uncertain outcomes.

✓ **Allow for random variation, but eliminate bias.** The greatest forecasting challenge is to produce a forecast that is genuinely objective, that is, with no errors. Forecast error is made up of *variation* based on external volatility and *bias*, or consistent, internal systematic error. The problem is that many people confuse bias with variation. They can't avoid variation. By definition, it is beyond anyone's control. Variation is caused by, for example, volatile markets and unpredictable events and is almost impossible to correct. However, managers can estimate the degree of volatility and provide control or tolerance ranges that, if exceeded, will alert them to investigate whether there is bias in the system. Bias is the real enemy of effective forecasting and is endemic in many companies. The most common problem is second-guessing that can lead to shock profit warnings, as forecasts repeatedly tell senior executives what they want to hear rather than the unpleasant reality. Once a forecast becomes a target or a commitment, it ceases to be an effective forecast. That's the nub of the problem. Managers avoid attention if they provide forecasts that fit prevailing expectations. This, of course, means that they are less likely to be objective and give their best guess on forecast outcomes. In other words, the *system* drives chronic bias. Whether intended or not, the prevailing culture is one of providing forecasts that are treated as fixed targets or commitments. If these forecasts change, explanations are necessary and can sometimes lead to unpleasant confrontations. Needless to say, few managers want to go through this ordeal, at least not more than once a year. *The lesson is that implementing rolling forecasts within an existing regime of fixed targets often leads to spurious outcomes and a devalued process.*

✓ **Carry out postmortems on forecasts to learn how to improve their quality.** Managers should learn from their forecasting experience. Borealis always carries out postmortems on its forecasts. The purpose is not to attribute blame but to learn if forecast accuracy is improving and how to improve it further. Forecasting inaccuracy can be seen in the same light as process variability. Teams therefore need to better understand the causes of that variability and work to reduce them.

✓ **Transfer ownership to the frontline team.** Leading organizations are placing rolling forecasts at the center of their management processes. Managers prepare the forecasts first and foremost for themselves, rather than for corporate, because the forecasts enable them to take the right actions that influence future outcomes. If management and corporate needs align in this way, the data entering the forecasting process is likely to be unbiased and more useful.

Conclusions

A number of companies are adopting rolling forecasts in an effort to anticipate change, but most fail to reap the benefits because the forecasts are distorted by the gaming that invariably occurs when supervisors ask managers for their expected performance figures. If senior executives use forecasts to micromanage or demand immediate action, trust and confidence will rapidly evaporate. The only time they can fairly ask such questions is if forecasts show a significant change and managers have not explained the change beforehand. Managers should be responsible for dealing with problems and reflecting any corrective actions they have taken in their revised forecasts.

Effective forecasting only works in a culture underpinned by transparency and trust. If well implemented, rolling forecasts perform a number of useful roles. They help senior executives to manage shareholder expectations; they enable accountants to consolidate and manage cash requirements; and they help operational managers to make decisions. Fast strategic actions that either create—or take advantage of—market opportunities or counter threats can thus be tested within a dynamic rolling planning and forecasting process.

FURTHER READING

Axson, David A. J. *Best Practices in Planning and Management Reporting.* Hoboken, NJ: John Wiley & Sons, 2003.

Bligh, Philip, Darius Vaskelis, and John Kelleher. "Take the Frenzy out of Forecasting." *Optimize Magazine* 17 (March 2003).

Hope, Jeremy. *Reinventing the CFO: How Financial Managers Can Transform Their Roles and Add Greater Value.* Boston: Harvard Business School Press, 2006.

Hope, Jeremy, and Robin Fraser. *Beyond Budgeting: How Managers Can Break Free from the Annual Performance Trap.* Boston: Harvard Business School Press, 2003.

Morlidge, Steve, and Steve Player. *Future Ready.* Chichester, UK: John Wiley, 2009.

34

BUSINESS ANALYTICS

What is this practice and how effective is it?

Business analytics take "dumb" KPIs and turn them into "intelligent" analytics. While KPIs, like accounting numbers, tell managers what has happened, they are unable to tell them *why* it happened. Business analytics provide managers with both a high-level view of a process or the whole organization *and* the ability to drill down to find the reasons performance trends are moving up or down. But, as we will show, analytics takes some time to implement and even more time for people to get used to.

Alternative names and related topics: KPI analysis; performance dashboards; drill-down analysis

Despite all the time, effort, and investment that has gone into developing and implementing KPIs in recent years, most still lack clarity, context, and understanding. In their efforts to follow so-called best practice, most scorecard leaders have kept KPIs to a small number to avoid confusing busy managers, but the chosen KPIs have not provided enough breadth of analysis or depth of knowledge to help them understand the root causes of problems and thus take the right actions when the trend line changes. Managers have recognized that they need to find a better way to achieve both simplicity and depth, which is leading to the emergence of what is becoming known as "business analytics." Professor Thomas Davenport has described analytics as the extensive use of data, statistical and quantitative analysis, explanatory and predictive models, and fact-based management to drive decisions and actions.[1]

To understand how analytics work, consider how you measure your health. You might think of a number of key measures such as body weight, blood pressure, exercise level, sleep, and so forth. You can probably think of ten to fifteen important measures. But wouldn't just a few measures and one

> ## Most standard KPI reporting systems suffer from problems
>
> - Measures are usually single point, with no ranges or trends. Too many measures can easily be manipulated to meet agreed-on targets; for example, surveys show that working capital ratios fall significantly at corporate year-end but rise rapidly in the first few months of the following year.
> - There are too many financial and lagging measures; managers don't know where the company is now, what the trends are, and what went right or wrong.
> - The only context for good or bad performance is the annual target that is negotiated and fixed; there is no relative context and no rate of improvement.
> - Measurement bases are varied; for example, some are in dollars, some in absolute numbers, some in percentages, and some come from surveys.
> - There is no weighting that reflects the relative importance of different measures.
> - There are rarely any measures related to ethics, risk, or external—for example, environmental—factors.

composite index be helpful? You might think of three distinct measurement categories, including lifestyle, body fitness, and medical history. Then you might consider the relative importance of each one. While most people are aware of their diet, exercise, and sleep patterns, they are not usually good at measuring them accurately. On the other hand, blood pressure, cholesterol, and weight are precise measures that professional medical people often consider. Rating your own medical history is also an exercise in judgment rather than precise measurement. Thus, you might want to give body fitness a much higher weighting in the overall health index than the other two. By converting all the measures of health into one common scale (score out of 100) and forming one health index, underpinned by ten to fifteen KPIs, you can more easily monitor whether your overall health is improving or declining.

An analytic focuses on a particular aspect of performance, not just more detail. Each team should have three to six high-level analytics, each with two to three subanalytics—each with around three KPIs attached—to measure its performance. The result will be around thirty to fifty individual KPIs, but you only need to drill down to them when there is a problem.

Analytics are always shown as scores out of 100, a scale that everyone understands and allows the combination of unlike units of measurement. For example, customer complaints are an absolute number, customer retention is a ratio, and customer satisfaction is usually a survey. Using software to convert these different measurement bases into a common index simplifies understanding and enables KPIs to be combined into a higher analytic. Analytics should be weighted according to importance, data integrity, and credibility. Analytics-based reports are usually produced directly from a BI data system and thus no longer require spreadsheets and PowerPoint slides as presentation tools. In this way, people can monitor performance on a daily basis.

Analytics are, more often than not, clusters of KPIs. Analytics provide the high-level alerts (the breadth), while KPIs provide the detail metrics (the depth). The first step in designing an analytics-based reporting system is to agree on the success criteria for each team and then agree on five or six high-level metrics (financial, customer, operations, people management, risk, and so forth). The next step is to brainstorm the KPIs that will underpin each analytic. Take operations within a call center, for example. Many potential KPIs spring to mind, including call-handling time, talk time, after-call work time, first-contact resolution rate, Interactive Voice Response completion rate, and percent of calls transferred.

Let's assume that a call center team has decided on two subanalytics for operations—quality and call handling (see figure 34-1). The team has also decided they are equally important and thus have equal weightings. It has

FIGURE 34-1

Using analytics to monitor performance

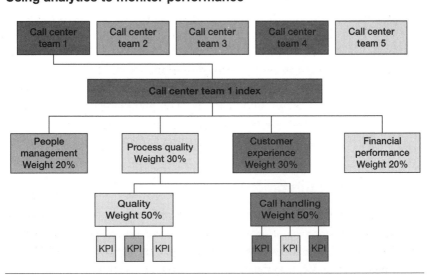

also chosen three KPIs for each subanalytic. In this way, managers can control the metrics they track and respond to, but also have the ability to drill down to lower levels if the higher-level indicators suggest a reason to do so.

A well-designed analytics system enables managers to monitor performance every day, week, and month. Unlike most balanced scorecard or KPI reports, analytics enable managers not only to monitor performance in real time but also to find out what is happening and *why*. The *why* is the critical advantage and allows managers to act swiftly to deal with problems before they become major issues that affect the bottom line.

Despite analytics' obvious appeal, managers may take some time becoming comfortable with analytics-based reports. It's rather like learning a new measurement system. For the past twenty years, the United Kingdom has been switching temperature readings from Fahrenheit to centigrade and from imperial measures to the metric system (e.g., pounds to kilos). But for people educated in the traditional measures, the change has been a struggle. For the same reasons, many people may take longer to adapt to the new measurement formats of analytics.

Management is about exercising judgment to make decisions. Measures are just the evidence. But, as in a criminal trial, much of the evidence is circumstantial and needs to be treated carefully. With powerful IT systems, too many managers see opportunities for more metrics and less judgment. They "always want to uproot the radishes to see how they're growing" is one way of putting it. W. Edwards Deming was a skeptic who believed that answering the question, "How do you know?" is crucial. People would talk about performance in terms of numbers, and he would ask, "How do you know? How can you possibly assess things with the minuscule little elements you're looking at here? How do you know?"[2] This question is disturbing to all those involved in performance measurement.

What is the performance potential of this practice?

- **To provide managers with an early warning system.** Analytics give managers fast, relevant reports that alert them to potential problems and enable them to respond rapidly to problems and opportunities.
- **To pinpoint the root causes of problems.** If problems arise, analytics can help to highlight them and guide managers to take the right actions.

What actions do you need to take to maximize the potential of this practice?

ACTIONS TO AVOID

- ✖ **Avoid the management cockpit view of control through numbers.** A number of years ago, a major software vendor ran an advertising campaign based on the idea of a management cockpit. The image was of a few executives in a central office controlling every part of their business through a crescent-shaped bank of screens, rather like a traffic control system. The executives were able to react immediately to any variances from the plan or target and send instructions to the relevant team telling them what to do to change course. This view of measurement over management is wrong-headed. Information systems are designed to serve and support people. How measures are analyzed, interpreted, and used is the key to success. If we allow information systems to dictate actions, then we are all in trouble.

✖ **Avoid basing alerts and dashboards on short-term fixed targets.** Many systems designers send alerts and provide dashboards to managers, often through mobile devices. While there is nothing wrong with this approach, managers should be careful when using fixed targets as the performance benchmark. Fixed targets are often annual and negotiated and are usually wrong, in many cases, disastrously wrong. They also drive management behavior, and, again, this behavior can and often is the opposite of that intended. A better benchmark would be to compare performance against best practice, which is neither negotiated nor fixed. It engages managers in a relentless march toward continuous improvement.

ACTIONS TO TAKE

✓ **Base analytics scorecards on teams.** Design an analytics-based scorecard for each of three teams: the executive team, the support services team, and the value center team.

✓ **List all current metrics and brainstorm possible metrics to track.** Think of past, present, and future metrics, and also consider the integrity of the data. Narrow the list to a few vital metrics.

✓ **Assign weights to the submetrics that will make up the analytic.** Give the more important metrics and those that have higher credibility a higher weighting.

✓ **Complete data-definition sheets for each KPI.** For example, what is the purpose of this KPI (what behavior is it expected to drive)? What is the definition of this KPI (for example, how do you define customer referrals or employee satisfaction)? What type of KPI is this (single measure, analytic or index, ratio)? What is the unit of measure and expected scale (convert the natural unit of measurement into a scale of 100)? What is the formula for calculating this KPI? How often will data be collected (will you survey customers or employees once or twice a year, or perhaps sample them monthly)? What data collection method will you use (e.g., surveys)? Does the data exist on this KPI (can you look at an existing trend)? Who is the owner of this KPI? Who is responsible for collecting the KPI on this metric? What is the desired polarity (is higher better or is lower better)?[3]

✓ **Establish red, yellow, and green targets or ranges.** Establish values for the expected range of performance on all submetrics. You might need to convert raw data into indexes and decide on the scale. For each metric, you need to decide what is zero performance, 10 percent, 20 percent, and so on, up to 100 percent. Take customer complaints. Maybe you are running at 5,000 per month, and you decide that best practice is only 250 per month. So you might set the scale at 0 = 10,000, 50 percent = 5,000, and 100 percent = 50 complaints. So cutting complaints to 2,500 would raise your score to 75 percent.

✓ **Phase analytics in over a reasonable period of time.** A scorecard can include analytics and single metrics. Analytics take time to master and trust, so phase them in over time. Analytics can include many of your existing metrics, so all the work you have done over recent years is put to good use.

✓ **Use dedicated software.** A real-time monitoring system requires effective software. Spending time transferring data into spreadsheets and PowerPoint presentations is a thing of the past.

Conclusions

KPIs and scorecards have evolved over the past twenty years. Since the concept of the balanced scorecard was first discussed in 1992, it has been refined so that it now helps managers to align metrics with strategy and thus enables them to take action if performance is veering off track. In the first phase, managers thought that the more KPIs they had, the more control they had, but they discovered that too many metrics often led to confusion and lack of control. Now the aim is to balance simplicity and depth through the use of analytics. The real power of analytics is that they enable managers to find out quickly not only if something is changing but also *why*. It is the "why" that enables them to take the right action quickly.

FURTHER READING

Axson, David A. J. *Best Practices in Planning and Management Reporting.* Hoboken, NJ: John Wiley & Sons, 2003.

Brown, Mark Graham. *Beyond the Balanced Scorecard.* New York: Productivity Press, 2007.

Davenport, Thomas H. *Competing on Analytics: The New Science of Winning.* Boston: Harvard Business School Press, 2007.

Davenport, Thomas H., Jeanne G. Harris, and Robert Morison. *Analytics at Work: Smarter Decisions, Better Results.* Boston: Harvard Business Review Press, 2010.

Hope, Jeremy. *Reinventing the CFO: How Financial Managers Can Transform Their Roles and Add Greater Value.* Boston: Harvard Business School Press, 2006.

Levinson, Meredith. "The Brain Behind the Big, Bad Burger and Other Tales of Business Intelligence." *CIO Magazine,* March 2005, 49–58.

35

BEST-PRACTICE REPORTING

What is this practice and how effective is it?

Best-practice reporting challenges the historic, detailed, and slow reporting systems that most large organizations have grown up with. Some organizations are encouraging people to fit their reports on one page and provide online reports as performance unfolds. This forces managers to be brief and ensure they get the key points across in a well-organized way. Done well, these concise reports help managers respond rapidly to changes in performance. We will show how best-practice reports are prepared and used in practice.

Alternative names and related topics: one page management; business analytics; management by exception

Managers can only respond to the information they receive. If information is slow and unhelpful, they are unlikely to be able to assess the situation and take the right actions. If, however, it is fast, frequent, and insightful, they will likely respond rapidly with the right decisions. How reports are prepared and presented is critical to success, but this part of management improvement has been neglected for too long.

Relevance is the most important attribute of any report. In other words, if a report shows a significant variation from the trend line, it should indicate that some action is required either to correct the deviation or to rethink the strategy or purpose. But nine of ten reports are focused on accounting cycles, rather than strategic demands or management needs.[1] Most organizations have twice as many reports as they need. Many should be either consolidated or eliminated. What remains should be those reports that provide real insight. Just as the fuel gauge in a car forewarns drivers that they have only thirty to forty miles to go before they run out, so management indicators should act as early warning systems that tell managers to sit up and take action. But contrary to providing more control, most reporting systems are a primary cause of why companies are *out of control*.

As we learned in chapter 34, business analytics enable organizations to switch from many detailed and disconnected metrics and reports to fast, frequent, and relevant reports that are available directly on a manager's desktop or even mobile device. Figure 35-1 shows how an executive team might design a comprehensive reporting system for the whole organization.

But how should each analytic and individual KPI be presented? Managers can drill down from each analytic into its component KPIs. An important principle is, where possible, to use only one page for a report (see figure 35-2). The person preparing the report is forced to be brief yet capture the key pieces of information. Further depth is accessible, if required.

There are five features of a particular report that give managers the information to make a reasonable assessment of what is happening and what (if any) action to take.

1. **Context.** Reports should give *context*; for a report to be meaningful, the user needs to know how the organization defines success. Do we compare results with fixed targets or relative goals based on, for example, peers, best practices, or prior periods? Many organizations now realize that external benchmarks provide a better context for success than internal targets. Not only do they not need to be negotiated each year, but they are also more inspiring and motivational.

FIGURE 35-1

Examples of analytics-based reports

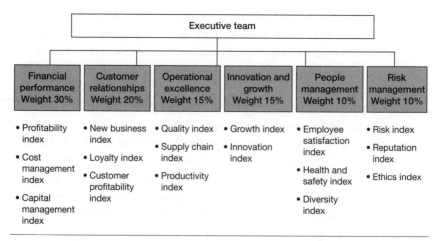

FIGURE 35-2

Report on a page

Level (What is going on today?)

Failure calls this week

		# Calls	% Failure
Agent	1	270	60%
Agent	2	220	45%
Agent	3	280	62%
Agent	4	300	40%
Agent	5	240	30%
Agent	6	190	70%
Agent	7	310	35%
Average		259	49%

Trend (What will future outcomes be?)

Analysis (Why is trend moving up/down?)

Despite previous actions, failure calls continue to run at unacceptable levels. We need to urgently rethink how we tackle these problems as our costs remain at far higher levels than best-practice competitors.

Action (What action, if any, should we take?)

Goal: To reduce failure calls by 80% over 2 years.

Action: To engage a lean consultant to investigate the problem and recommend improvements.

2. **Level.** What is going on today, and is there cause for review? Reports should monitor KPIs on a daily or weekly basis. An effective KPI has a knock-on effect in that it spurs action. Improving quality, for example, lowers defect rates, speeds up inventory turns, and ultimately increases profitability. However, too many organizations fall into the trap of using KPI dashboards with dials and graphs that show how this or that indicator is performing against a short-term target. As soon as a KPI becomes a target, management behavior changes to "meet the target" rather than "make the right decision." Any set of metrics only tells part of the story. They should support management judgment, not replace it.

3. **Trend.** What is the trend and what will be the outcomes over the next six to twelve months? Patterns and trends provide many more insights than columns of figures. Trends can be adjusted for seasonal fluctuations and show, for examples, moving averages. The time horizon depends on the business. Monitoring the performance of a call center, for example, might look at a moving window of thirteen weeks, with longer trend lines tracking a few years also available. All trend reports should show a benchmark to give the user some indication of whether performance is good or bad. In this example, a call center's failure calls—calls that should not be made in the first place—are still running at unacceptable levels.

4. **Analysis.** Why is the trend moving up or down? The analysis part of the report gives the user some essential background information on why the

trend line is moving up or down and whether further action is required. It should be short and succinct.

5. **Action.** What action (if any) should we take? The action plan tells the user whether or not the organization needs to take action and provides a summary of what that action is. The user can then consider the whole report and decide whether the local manager is in control of the situation or a senior manager needs to intervene. Reading and evaluating this report takes only a few minutes and might solicit an e-mail or phone call to gather more information to challenge the analysis or action plans.

The aim is to create a real-time, forward-looking organization. Most companies will tell you it takes months—even a year—to get an up-to-date, full view of their business. But in today's tough, dynamic environment, managers need fast, high-quality actual numbers and equally fast and high-quality forecasts. Then they will be in control and can make fast, effective decisions. Teams learn as they go and improve their work processes when appropriate.

What is the performance potential of this practice?

- **To tell teams where they are today and where they're going in the near term.** Fast, frequent, relevant reporting is the key to successful management. But it should focus less on the past and more on the present and future.
- **To tell teams when to take action and what action to take.** Effective reports help managers to make the right decisions.
- **To communicate performance.** Best-practice reports are the way that leading companies communicate performance to their people.

What actions do you need to take to maximize the potential of this practice?

ACTIONS TO AVOID

- ✖ **Eliminate unnecessary reports.** Most organizations produce about twice as many reports as they need. Have your finance team prepare a list of all the reports your company produces each week, month, and year. Then test to see if they are useful or not. If the trend line on the key numbers on the report changes, does anything happen? In other words, does anyone take any action? If the answer is no, just eliminate the report. Do not consult anyone, because managers will instinctively look for reasons why they need the report. Just wait and see what happens. We can almost guarantee that nothing will happen, and you will have saved the finance team many days and weeks of unnecessary work. "So what?" you might say. You may think these reports cost little to prepare, but studies suggest differently. When you take into account the time spent gathering and analyzing data, coding and entering it into the system, and preparing budgets and reports, you can begin to see how much time and money is spent. This low-hanging fruit in terms of performance improvement should not be overlooked.

ACTIONS TO TAKE

- ✓ **Make reports fast, online, frequent, and relevant.** Avoid producing long, detailed reports. Send reports directly to electronic devices and make them available electronically directly from the system. One benefit is that no one has the opportunity to manipulate the numbers.
- ✓ **Keep most reports to one page showing level, trend, analysis, and action.** Break the page into four quadrants—one each for level, trend, analysis, and action. The person will be forced to be brief yet capture the key pieces of information. Toyota is a great believer in this principle.

Base the context for good or bad performance on relative performance rather than fixed targets

How does the user of a report know if performance is good, bad, or indifferent, and therefore whether he or she needs to take any action? Most reports show current performance against an agreed-on budget or target, but fixed targets are often a poor way to drive performance improvement. They need to be reset every year, which can take months. Whether they are achievable is often based on assumptions about the economy that are often wrong, and they can lead to unethical reporting as managers strive and strain to meet them.

An alternative is to opt for relative goals and measures. The aim is not to have endless negotiations about targets with all the time-wasting and dysfunctional behavior involved. Instead, a common KPI is picked to evaluate performance and each team's performance is posted on a league table, which ranks where they actually perform. Each team can compare its performance against any other team. The power in the system is in the peer pressure that results from comparisons, which can be achieved only if all similar teams share common KPIs. The need for economic assumptions is filtered out as each team is compared based on the actual conditions faced by that team. The league table allows everyone to see who is moving up and who is moving down. The comparison can be extended from internal measures all the way to the external marketplace where the organization is judged against its true competition.

✓ **Be careful with peer comparisons.** Peer comparisons can be powerful motivators, but how they are used is crucial to their effectiveness. Svenska Handelsbanken uses such comparisons extensively to drive performance. It uses only a few KPIs that, while not perfect, are good enough. Every month, each branch or region can see where it is compared to other branches or regions. Branches have just two main KPIs—cost-to-income ratio and profit per employee. Regions use cost-to-income ratio and return on equity. The head office does not tell low performers what to do; instead, it says that "you are closest to the customer, and you have the necessary authority to do what has to be done." There are no excuses. If the team doesn't improve, the branch takes action to change the manager or other members of the team. What's important is that league tables provide a ranked listing of performance. They do not have any reports that "name and shame" underperformers. Rather, the bank just publishes the results. The power comes from the pride, passion, and peer pressure that teams feel. Each team knows who it compares itself with.

✓ **Maintain the highest ethical standards.** Anyone who misuses the system should clearly understand that this abuse is a firing offence.

✓ **Create a Web portal for delivery of standard reports.** When information is consolidated, report it on a Web site so that users of the information can view it online and make quick decisions if appropriate. This access is particularly critical for large, multinational companies that operate in countries across different time zones.

✓ **Enable self-service reporting.** Leading organizations are moving toward self-service reporting, that is, managers generating their own reports rather than bringing in IT or other accounting personnel. In this way, individual managers can analyze and interpret information in ways that they think will provide insights that weren't available before. But managers need some help in designing reports so they deliver precisely the right information and maximize the possibility of the user making the most informed decision possible.

Conclusions

Management reporting is radically transforming from slow, month-end procedures to instant, online availability. But while the technology is advancing rapidly, the ability and willingness of managers to change their thinking and redesign their reports is moving more slowly. That pace is picking up speed.

FURTHER READING

Axson, David A. J. *Best Practices in Planning and Management Reporting.* Hoboken, NJ: John Wiley & Sons, 2003.

Brown, Mark Graham. *Beyond the Balanced Scorecard.* New York: Productivity Press, 2007.

Hope, Jeremy. *Reinventing the CFO: How Financial Managers Can Transform Their Roles and Add Greater Value.* Boston: Harvard Business School Press, 2006.

Hope, Jeremy, and Robin Fraser. *Beyond Budgeting: How Managers Can Break from the Annual Performance Trap.* Boston: Harvard Business School Press, 2003.

Parmenter, David. *Key Performance Indicators.* Hoboken, NJ: John Wiley & Sons, 2007.

36

OPEN BOOK MANAGEMENT

What is this practice and how effective is it?

Open book management means that leaders make information accessible and transparent. Most organizations work on the assumption that the corporate center can dictate and direct information—that people only need to see "what they needed to know." This command-and-control assumption must be tossed aside if leaders really want to move to a more empowered and adaptive organization. As we will explain, true transparency is potentially the best control system an organization can devise. But implementing it needs some courage.

Alternative names and related topics: business transparency; open, integrated systems; collaborative systems

Too many organizations operate behind a cloak of secrecy and obfuscation. Just because leaders have the authority to make decisions, they think they have the right to neither explain the reasons nor accept the consequences. This poor communication and decision making creates opportunities for misrepresentation and fraud. Dictating and directing information so that people only see "what they need to know" denies them the insights to see the bigger picture and prevents them from raising tough questions about their peers' performance. "The risks of having a completely open system would be too great," some leaders say. "Anyhow, how can we trust people with sensitive information? It would reach our competitors in no time at all." Such a culture restricts information, and with only one interpreter of that information, the potential richness is lost and creativity is stifled. The synthesis of information in often unique ways leads to insight and discovery. By denying this opportunity, command-and-control leaders do their best to destroy innovation.

Open, transparent information is the glue that holds the decentralized organization together. The Internet offers a fast and effective way to capture and distribute information. It has the capability to provide frontline managers with the information to make quick, well-informed decisions, to effectively manage project-based strategic initiatives, and to bounce ideas around with colleagues across the company before making important decisions. It enables support services managers to keep up to date with best practices. It enables divisional managers to see trends, patterns, and "breaks in the curve" long before their competitors and thus make crucial decisions regarding products and markets. And it enables senior executives to ask important questions concerning strategic assumptions and risks, while ensuring that operating units remain within acceptable performance parameters. Perhaps, above all, it helps to share knowledge throughout the company so that strategic changes can be made quickly and potential problems solved before they fester and grow.

The Internet is making it easier to share information. Such words as *freedom* and *autonomy* define the World Wide Web. All attempts to "control" the Web have come undone. But the Web itself has moved on. If Web 1.0 was about the Web as an information source, then Web 2.0 is about the Web as a platform for

Five key features of real transparency

1. **Everyone can see the organization's and the team's goals, strategies, and plans.** Every team member can understand goals, strategies, and so on and has every opportunity to engage in and contribute to these important processes.
2. **Everyone sees complete financial statements—except for group forecasts—as well as KPIs, trends, and peer-to-peer comparisons.** Everyone can see how his or her own team and the whole business are performing.
3. **Everyone can see every employee's salary, bonus, and peer review.** Salaries, bonus differentials, and performance appraisals—especially peer reviews—are a source of much employee dissatisfaction. One option is to open them to everyone.
4. **Everyone can see everyone's expenses.** Again, open the books so everyone's expense account is available for scrutiny, which will probably cut expenses by 20 percent to 30 percent.
5. **Everyone can see the minutes of key meetings.** Open the decision-making process so everyone can see how decisions were made, including which options were considered but discarded—and why.

participation and connectivity that includes such social networking sites as wikis and blogs that aim to facilitate creativity, collaboration, and sharing among users. Information is open, transparent, and accessible in an instant. Like Web 2.0, management in today's organizations should be about linking—but not controlling—people and releasing their energies and capabilities across an enterprise for the benefit of all stakeholders.

Consider what Roche—a $50 billion Swiss pharmaceutical business—did to test an open book system. In April 2009, six Roche managers from different parts of the group met to discuss their perception that red tape was absorbing too much energy. "We needed to think of something to tackle bureaucracy that we as a group felt was getting a bit out of control," noted one manager. After considering a number of options, the team chose to examine travel expenses—Roche spends $430 million a year on travel and entertaining—to see what a change of management control might achieve. So they set up two pairs of matched groups of fifty people each—one group in Germany and one at the head office in Basel, Switzerland. In one group in each place, there was no change in the travel policy, but the other group was told that its travel would no longer require any prior approval, provided it abided by the company's policies, *but* its expenses would be available to everyone on the intranet.

The experiment was designed to test three things. Would people be more motivated by removal of the bureaucratic process of preauthorization? Was the new process simpler than before? And what would be the consequences for costs? The answer to the first question was that 45 percent were more motivated and 46 percent were neutral. Ninety-four percent were comfortable with full transparency and 83 percent said the new process was more in tune with Roche's values and wanted it to become permanent. On the second question, around 80 percent found the system to be more efficient. But the real surprise was the answer to the third question. While costs in the control groups remained the same, they went down in both groups operating under the new system—in one group, substantially.[1]

Transparency offers new opportunities for enterprisewide control systems. Think about the time and cost spent administering travel and entertaining expenses. How many account codes and cost centers do you use and how many transactions take place? Think about the impact of opening these expenses to scrutiny by others. The evidence suggests that people will think twice before booking travel that is not for a valid business reason.

Despite these developments, too many organizations continue to operate in a gray area between what's right or wrong and too often step over the wrong side of the ethical line. But in a world of constant digital surveillance, twenty-four-hour, seven-day-a-week media, and Web-based social networks, any of which can turn an error of judgment or hidden truth into a reputation meltdown in an instant, operating in the twilight world of balancing cost or profit against what's ethically right or wrong makes no sense at all. The ethical decision is the only one to make.

Strong evidence suggests that "transparent" organizations, while possibly sacrificing a few short-term opportunities, attract the best people, customers, and investors as well as perform better and endure longer than their rivals.[2] And because they trust people with information and give them more scope and authority to make decisions, they don't need many layers of management and the costs they incur. They also recover more quickly from economic downturns and other setbacks. Building and sustaining organizations that place transparency at the center of their management model is fast becoming a key success factor in the digital age and *the* litmus test of leadership quality.

But total transparency is a step change from where most companies are today. It requires leaders to change how they think about information and how the measurement and control system works. Information systems should provide frontline managers with the capability they need to "run their own business," to effectively manage project-based strategic initiatives, and to share knowledge and best practices with colleagues across the company before making important decisions.

Transparent information gives leaders confidence that every team will make effective, consistent decisions. It also breeds a collegiate, collaborative culture within which people immediately share and deal with problems before they get out of hand and lead to serious damage.

What is the performance potential of this practice?

- **To avoid reputational damage.** While a few dodgy deals here and there might increase short-term profits, the risk of detection is high and can lead to catastrophic consequences for both the bottom line and the share price. And in an age of constant media attention and instant sharing of bad news across the Internet, organizations should never contemplate such risks.
- **To provide more confidence in decision making.** If everyone knows that ethical decisions are paramount, leaders and managers will have more confidence in each other that the right decision will always be made.
- **To provide more control.** Opening up the information system to more scrutiny represents a powerful system of checks and balances that is hard to match even by expensive internal control and risk management systems.
- **To improve employee satisfaction and engagement.** Employees who are trusted with information are more satisfied and motivated.

What actions do you need to take to maximize the potential of this practice?

ACTIONS TO AVOID

✖ If left unchecked, the management control bureaucracy will continue to impose a huge administrative burden on value center's and process teams. You need to remove the top-down control system. For example, cut the chart of accounts to a minimal number (fewer than fifty), including ten to twenty main headings with four to five lines of subanalysis. Do an inventory of currently used account codes, measures, reports, spreadsheets, and so on. Agree on relevant criteria and reduce detail and complexity. Keep detailed analysis at a local level; do not aggregate it up the organization through budgeting and reporting systems.

✖ Avoid information overload. An open information system does not mean that managers will get many more reports and have to attend many more meetings. It means just the opposite. In a devolved management model, there are fewer budgets, reports, and meetings. In one organization, leaders were proud to claim that they had given managers their time back. So instead of spending 20 percent to 30 percent of their time on budgeting and reporting, they have more time to learn, adapt, and improve.

✖ Remove the barriers to collaboration and sharing. Though most senior executives want to create an organization without boundaries in which everyone shares knowledge, resources, and best practices, the "I win, you lose" management culture means that people fiercely protect their own parts of the business. Teams maintain their own closely guarded information systems. This parochial attitude means that people hide both good news and (far worse) bad news. Calamitous results such as defective products, disaffected customers, or environmental disasters fester and grow as local people try to cover up their problems. How a company rewards people is a primary cause of this behavior. Recent research from the executive recruiting industry showed that "people rewarded for individual performance shared the least information those rewarded for team performance shared more; and those rewarded for company performance shared the most."[3] Leaders of transparent organizations know that building communities of people who positively want to share information and collaborate with each other is important. But they also know that sharing and collaboration will not happen without transparency and trust, built on shared goals and values and supported by open information systems. In this collaborative culture, people will go out of their way to help and support others. But before this can happen, systemic barriers—such as individual targets and rewards—to sharing knowledge and best practice need to be dismantled.

✖ **Stop people from hiding or manipulating information.** Hiding or manipulating information is endemic in many large bureaucracies. An organization that truly believes in its core values must consider this a firing offence. On the other hand, no one should ever get fired for telling the truth, no matter how unpalatable it might be. Norwegian oil company Statoil has business ethics high on the agenda. Statoil is ruthless about policy violations, which usually lead to dismissal. It has a simple ethics test so that people know whether or not their action is acceptable. They just need to ask themselves this question: is it acceptable if the results of my action appear on the front page of the newspaper? If yes, go ahead. If no, don't do it."[4]

ACTIONS TO TAKE

✓ **Make information open and transparent.** Google CEO Eric Schmidt believes that in the future, corporations won't be able to be as controlling as they are now. As Schmidt explains, "they will need to let information out. So a more transparent company is a better organization. There is also a lot of evidence that groups make better decisions than individuals, especially when they are selected from among the smartest and most interesting people. The 'wisdom of crowds' argument is that you can operate a company by consensus, which is, indeed, how Google operates. The role of a leader, in this case, is not to force an outcome, but to force execution—literally, by having a deadline. Either by having a real crisis or creating a crisis. You also need dissent. If you don't have dissent then you have a king."[5]

✓ **Ensure that data is clean and accurate.** Operating with fast, transparent information is a laudable aim, but it will be a waste of time if the data in the system is unreliable. Dirty data is endemic to most management information systems and represents an increasing cost. Data, the most fundamental component of any information system, provides the building blocks for analysis and insight. Companies have to get their data stores and data warehouses in good working order before they can begin extracting and acting on insights. If not, they'll be operating on flawed information. The problem is that data quality quickly degenerates over time. Experts say 2 percent of records in a customer file become obsolete in one month because customers die, divorce, marry, and move. In addition, data entry errors, systems migrations, and changes to source systems, among other things, generate bucket loads of errors. More perniciously, as organizations fragment into different divisions and units, interpretations of data elements mutate to meet the local business needs. A data element that one individual finds valuable may be nonsense to someone in a different group.[6]

✓ **Treat data as a strategic asset.** Data quality needs to be part of everyone's job. It should be included in each job description. For appropriate people, it should be a part of the performance evaluation and incentive package. Too many such systems focus on completeness (i.e., fill in the form), rather than accuracy (i.e., fill in the form with correct information), so data quality will continue to remain a serious problem.

✓ **Operate with "one version of the truth."** Many organizations have to deal with a patchwork quilt of legacy information systems that are difficult to stitch together, a primary cause of slow information. They also keep parallel sets of books, sometimes including one for cost accounting, one for management accounting, and one for financial accounting. Some have yet another that is information suitable for regulators. Most managers don't know what happened last month until the second half of the following month. They typically spend the first few weeks joining their systems together, often rekeying information into spreadsheets to show leaders a complete picture. In a fast-changing market or in the first months of a new product launch, these information delays block the feedback loop and can mean the difference between making the right and wrong decisions that, in turn, can have a major impact on the bottom line.

✓ **Use Web portals to provide fast access to key information that supports strategy, planning, forecasting, and decision making.** Many believe that too much transparency will stop people from responding rapidly and taking risks. This is a valid objection *if decision making and risk remain the prerogative of a few senior executives.* By contrast, organizations that are open and transparent offer the opportunity for faster decision making and risk taking to many more people. For the first time, these people will have the information they need to make the right decision and experiment with new ideas. Transparency builds confidence at every level.

✓ **Use one integrated information system.** Trust and transparency depend on everyone being able to see the same information at the same time. This, in turn, depends on an integrated, enterprisewide information system.

✓ **Teach people to analyze, interpret, and use information.** Just allowing information to roam freely around the organization is insufficient. Leaders—especially in finance—need to educate people on the meaning of the information and how they can use it. Part of the new role for finance is to act more like teachers than controllers.

Conclusions

Leading organizations have advanced information flows to new levels of openness and transparency. They have given their people access to the sort of strategic, competitive, and market-based information that was once the preserve of senior executives. And they have understood that all the numbers should stick to "one truth" and be transparent. Everyone should see the numbers in their raw state, without misleading alterations. Then everyone will have confidence in the numbers and support devolved decision making.

FURTHER READING

Case, John. *Open-Book Management: The Coming Business Revolution.* New York: Harper Business, 1995.

Hope, Jeremy. *Reinventing the CFO: How Financial Managers Can Transform Their Roles and Add Greater Value.* Boston: Harvard Business School Press, 2006.

Hope, Jeremy, and Robin Fraser. *Beyond Budgeting: How Managers Can Break Free from the Annual Performance Trap.* Boston: Harvard Business School Press, 2003.

Nayar, Vineet. *Employees First, Customers Second: Turning Conventional Management Upside Down.* Boston: Harvard Business Press, 2010.

Stack, Jack, and Bo Burlingham. *The Great Games of Business: Unlocking the Power and Profitability of Open-Book Management.* New York: Currency Doubleday, 1992.

Stack, Jack, and Bo Burlingham. *A Stake in the Outcome: Building a Culture for the Long-term Success of Your Business.* New York: Currency Doubleday, 2002.

Part V

Performance Evaluation

37

PERFORMANCE APPRAISALS

What is this practice and how effective is it?

People deeply dislike performance appraisals and think they are fundamentally flawed, yet they are ingrained management processes in most organizations. While many leaders—including within human resources—would like to abandon them, few know what to do differently and even fewer can summon the courage to act. We examine the evidence for and against performance appraisals and provide some guidelines that will help leaders to think more seriously about abandonment.

Alternative names and related topics: performance management; performance evaluation; peer review analysis

Next to firing an employee, managers cite the annual performance appraisal as the task they hate the most. Given that the typical performance appraisal is fundamentally flawed, this attitude is understandable. Appraisals are incongruent with the values-based, devolved, and participative work environments many leading organizations favor. They are a direct descendent of Frederick W. Taylor's principles of scientific management in which he said, "each employee should receive every day clear-cut, definite instructions as to just what he is to do and how he is to do it, and these instructions should be exactly carried out, whether they are right or wrong."[1]

In a classic HBR article in 1970, Harry Levinson launched a scathing attack on performance appraisal systems. One comment stands out: "No matter how detailed the job description, it is essentially static—that is, a series of statements. However, the more complex the task and the more flexible an employee must be in it, the less any fixed statement of job elements will fit

Be wary of "forced rankings"

Despite the evidence that appraisals are flawed, performance appraisals have become even more severe. In some organizations, "forced ranking" or "rank and yank" (as it has become known) has spread to around 20 percent of U.S. companies, including GE, Ford, Microsoft, and Conoco (now ConocoPhillips). Sun Microsystems ranks its forty-three thousand employees into three groups. The top 20 percent are rated as "superior"; the next 70 percent as "standard." At the bottom is a 10 percent band of "underperformers." The company frankly tells underperformers that they must improve and gives them one-on-one coaches. It offers underperformers who fail to improve a "prompt exit" package. If they decline it, they face a bleak future in which further incidents of poor performance could lead to dismissal. Advocates believe that such rankings force managers and supervisors to make the tough decisions that otherwise they would avoid as being too difficult or unpleasant. Some organizations view the forced ranking approach as a way to create a continuously improving workforce.

The primary problems with forced ranking is that someone must always fall into the lower or underperforming category, even if everyone has performed at a satisfactory or better level. It is possible that those rated as poor performers in highly productive departments may contribute more to the overall progress of the organization than those rated as good performers in other departments. Forced ranking can also weaken teamwork. It can encourage unhealthy levels of internal competition, leading to a decline in team values as individuals seek to protect their own position at the expense of their coworkers. As one employee said about the impact of forced ranking in his organization, "all the relationships instantly become strained."[a]

One of the leading practitioners of forced ranking was Enron. It is sobering to reflect that commentators had, in the months preceding its demise, held up the once highly profitable company as proof that rank and yank was the way of the future for all performance appraisals. Some said that rank and yank had produced in Enron "a hotbed of overachievers"—bold rhetoric that now seems a little embarrassing, to say the least.

[a] John Greenwald, "Rank and Fire," *Time,* June 11 and June 18, 2001.

what that person does. Thus, the higher the person rises in an organization and the more varied and subtle the work, the more difficult it is to pin down objectives that represent more than a fraction of his or her effort."[2]

Most employee appraisals are scored in the range of three to four (out of five). Years ago, an American psychologist gave a group of personnel managers a well-established personality test. But instead of giving them the actual results, he gave each of them bogus feedback in the form of thirteen statements derived from horoscopes and graphological analyses. He then asked each manager to read the feedback—supposedly derived from the scientific tests—and comment on how accurate it was by marking each statement as: (a) amazingly accurate, (b) rather good, (c) about half and half, (d) more wrong than right, and (e) almost entirely wrong. Over half felt their profile was an amazingly accurate description, while 40 percent thought it was rather good. Almost none thought it to be very wrong.[3]

According to research done by McKinsey, only 16 percent of the 13,000 executives it interviewed believed their companies could tell high performers from low performers.[4] After analyzing 180,000 records in the U.K. civil service in 2001, a study found that there was extensive discrimination against ethnic minorities and disabled people.[5] These are damning indictments of the effectiveness of performance appraisals.

U.K. occupational psychologist John Seddon makes an important point about whether managers can tell whether people's performance is caused by their personal qualities or by the system that governs their work. He gives the example of a customer services manager for a large retail bank who had to leave the organization because of stress. In her last year, she had been given five targets, of which she succeeded on three and failed on two. Her appraisal meeting focused on the two she had failed. She was perplexed because she was unable to say why she had failed on two targets and was also unable to account for the three "successes."[6]

Seddon's point is that all performance is subject to variation. A study of measures used to judge the bank manager's performance revealed that all had been subject to normal variation. A pass or fail had been just as probable on all five measures. Yet the employee had believed, as her manager did, that she was responsible. Focusing performance on the individual rather than the system can lead to a poor understanding of problems and to the wrong solutions. Unfortunately, the appraisal system leads inevitably to these mistakes.

W. Edwards Deming believed that annual ratings and management by objectives were usually management by fear. In his view, it "leaves people bitter, crushed, bruised, battered, desolate, despondent, dejected, feeling inferior, some even depressed, unfit for work for weeks after receipt of rating, unable to comprehend why they are inferior."[7]

There is little doubt that performance appraisals, as conducted at most organizations, damage workplace trust, undermine productivity and harmony, create emotional anguish, and generally fail to get the best out of people. Also, the costs are huge. When you take into account preparing appraisals; setting goals and objectives; conducting interim and annual performance reviews; reviewing at higher levels the appraisals written at lower levels;

Using peer reviews at HCL Technologies

HCL Technologies is one organization that uses open peer reviews to great effect. CEO Vineet Nayar knew that the traditional approach wasn't working. Employees were often reluctant to criticize their managers for fear of retaliation, and the whole process was conducted within vertical silos. "Today, HCLT employees are able to rate the performance of *any* manager whose decisions affect their work lives, and to do so anonymously. These ratings are published online and can be viewed by anyone who has submitted a review. This visibility challenges managers to be more responsive and exercise their authority judiciously. The number and organizational scope of the reviews a manager receives are also a good indicator of an individual's zone of influence—is he or she adding value across a wide swath of the company, or only within a narrow sphere? Importantly, this "feed-forward" process isn't connected to compensation and promotion decisions. It is purely developmental. Nevertheless, there aren't many hiding places left at HCLT for mediocre managers."[a]

[a] Gary Hamel, "HCL: Extreme Management Makeover," Wall Street Journal blog, July 6, 2010, http://blogs.wsj.com/management/2010/07/06/hcl-extreme-management-makeover/tab/print/.

---

designing, printing, copying, filing, and distributing appraisal forms; designing and communicating the appraisal process; training supervisors, managers, and executives in the appraisal process; and handling postappraisal appeals, grievances, and lawsuits, the costs can be well over $2,000 per person.[8] In a large organization, that can amount to hundreds of millions of dollars. So is it worth it? What should organizations do instead?

The One Minute Manager by Kenneth Blanchard and Spencer Johnson, one of the best-selling business books of all time, had three simple messages: use one-minute goals, one-minute praisings, and one-minute reprimands. Though setting one-minute goals might be too simplistic, their points on praising and reprimands hold up well. The authors recommend that managers tell people up front that they are going to let them know how they are doing. Then they suggest emphasizing three main things in praisings. First, be immediate. Don't save praisings for a holiday. Second, be specific. Just saying to someone, "Good job," is nice, but it is not very helpful because he does not know specifically what is good so that he can do it again. Third, share feelings about his work. With one-minute reprimands, the authors also recommend that a manager tell people beforehand that they are going to let them know how they are doing and then reprimand them immediately. Managers should tell the employee exactly how they feel about what he did wrong. But at the same time, the manager should remind him how much he is valued. And realize that when the reprimand is over, it's over.[9]

If you prefer an annual process, open peer reviews appear to be the new approach. Unlike the rank-and-yank approach, open reviews don't rely on one person's views but encompass twenty or more peer reviews.

Annual performance reviews are a classic relic from the bureaucratic command-and-control organization. Of course, people need to know what the organization thinks about them. Open peer reviews are the way forward. The more people involved in this assessment and the more transparent it is, the more people learn and improve.

What is the performance potential of this practice?

- **To give employees relevant feedback to improve their performance.** People need to know what others think of their performance and what they need to do to improve.
- **To provide a framework for employee development and training.** People need to know what further development and training they need to improve their knowledge and performance.
- **To provide a basis for promotions and rewards.** Senior people need a framework for evaluating and rewarding both teams and individuals.

What actions do you need to take to maximize the potential of this practice?

ACTIONS TO AVOID

- ✖ **Stop spending so much time on annual performance appraisals.** Instead of saving up performance reviews for the annual process, give feedback—whether positive or negative—when it is due so that people can relate the advice to their (recent) actions and learn from the experience.
- ✖ **Be wary of forced rankings.** A survey of more than two hundred human resource professionals from companies employing more than twenty-five hundred people found that even though half of the companies used forced ranking, the respondents reported that it resulted in lower productivity, inequity, and skepticism, negative effects on employee engagement, reduced collaboration, damage to morale, and mistrust of leadership.[10]
- ✖ **Don't assume that people cause most of the problems.** Deming famously said that 94 percent of business problems are concerned with systems rather than people.[11] His message was "act *on* the system" rather than *in*

the system. "In the Toyota Production System, there is nothing recognizable as performance appraisal. Every operation in the system has an associated measure. The measure has been worked out between the operators and their manager. In every case the measure is related to the purpose of the work. That measure is the basis of feedback to the manager and worker alike."[12] Information and decision making are integrated with the work. "If there is a problem with performance, it is immediately reflected in the measure. The manager and operator seek the causes and turn them to seeds for improving the method."[13] In this way, Toyota deals with immediate problems. "Both managers and workers are psychologically safe in the knowledge that it is the system—not the worker—that is the primary influence on performance. It is management's responsibility to ensure that workers operate in a system that enables them to perform."[14]

ACTIONS TO TAKE

✓ **Use open peer reviews to hold people accountable.** As W. L. Gore's CEO Terri Kelly puts it:

> We don't need a bureaucratic system to hold people accountable. We don't need time cards, because we don't care when the person comes or leaves—we just care about their contribution. So you can deconstruct a lot of the typical bureaucratic processes that are typically used to measure and control performance. We've also found that by not having hard and fast metrics of performance we can avoid a lot of unintended consequences. You get a lot of negative behavior when you have narrow metrics that really don't represent the complexity of the business. Instead, we ask our associates to view performance holistically, in terms of someone's total impact, versus focusing on a few specific variables.[15]

✓ **Focus on process performance and learning over results.** When Toyota evaluates managers, it usually emphasizes process performance and learning over results. The company looks at how managers achieved their goals, how they handled issues, how they fostered organizational skills, and how they developed, motivated, and empowered people. The company uses five kinds of criteria, all of which are fuzzy and subjective. For instance, one category it employs is personal magnetism (*jinbo*), which captures how much trust and respect the manager has earned from others. Jinbo is a vague criterion that is open to interpretation and impossible to quantify; you can evaluate people on it only if you have worked closely with them. Another quintessentially Toyota measure of manager performance is persistence or resilience. The company sees this as part of its DNA, describing it as *nebari*.[16]

✓ **Manage at the level of the team rather than the individual.** Except for people who are engaged in routine, repetitive work, expectations and goals change on a regular basis. Expectations should be set at the level of the team, and each team member should know his or her expected contribution. Clarity emerges as a result of a continuing dialogue, not a one-time discussion. The frequency of such discussions must match the rate of change in the work itself. To rely on annual or even quarterly performance reviews as the mechanism for conveying expectations will lead to a rigid approach. Also, most people work on multiple tasks, so it is difficult to tie their performance to one or two.

✓ **Provide development advice and training through continuous assessments.** If you operate with a continuous appraisal process, at which point do you review training and development needs? The short answer is "when appropriate." In a team-based organization, the team leader provides continuous feedback to each member. HR is involved indirectly, until a job change is required. This gives the team leaders a huge responsibility, but something they are paid to do. How can the organization protect itself against lawsuits for wrongful dismissal or discrimination? It should train team leaders in the legal aspects of this process. Little or no evidence indicates that performance appraisal systems discourage lawsuits and quite a bit suggests that performance appraisal systems backfire in court. The best protection against lawsuits for discrimination is, of course, not to discriminate and to show that the effects of discrimination are not widespread in the organization.

Conclusions

Performance appraisals urgently need rethinking. One approach is to make team leaders responsible for providing continuous feedback to their people. Another is to use open peer reviews similar to those at W.L. Gore and HCL Technologies.

FURTHER READING

Blanchard, Kenneth, and Spencer Johnson. *The One Minute Manager.* New York: William Morrow, 1982.

Deming, W. Edwards. *Out of Crisis.* Cambridge, MA: MIT, 1982; 26th ed., 1998.

Nayar, Vineet. *Employees First, Customers Second.* Boston: Harvard Business Press, 2010.

Pfeffer, Jeffrey, and Robert I. Sutton. *Hard Facts, Dangerous Half-Truths and Total Nonsense.* Boston: Harvard Business School Press, 2006.

38

RECOGNITION AND REWARDS

What is this practice and how effective is it?

Recognition and rewards are a minefield of ideology and misinformation. Most leaders believe in incentive compensation as a key driver of higher levels of performance. However, the evidence that financial incentives motivate people is hard to find, and there is plenty of evidence for the opposite view that incentives do more harm than good. So what is the alternative? We will examine the evidence and look at alternative approaches.

Alternative names and related topics: incentive compensation; management rewards; recognition systems

To many people, motivation and rewards go together like peaches and cream. They are inseparable. But if we just revisit Motivation 101 for a moment, we will recall that all the great social scientists of the past were careful to avoid this connection. If anything, there was almost a negative correlation. Frederick Herzberg's most telling point is often forgotten. He argued that the opposite of job dissatisfaction is *not job satisfaction*. In other words, if an employee is unhappy because of problems with pay, status, or working conditions, he will not suddenly be motivated to greater effort and productivity by removing these problems. Motivation is intrinsic to the job. It is about responsibility, recognition, achievement, and personal development, and no amount of pay on its own will drive a person to higher levels of achievement. In one of Herzberg's most telling metaphors, he said that, whereas a motivated person is self-powered by a generator, an unmotivated person is powered by a battery that needs constantly recharging.[1]

Incentive compensation is almost without exception dysfunctional to some degree or another. A study by consultants at William Mercer concluded that most individual merit or performance-based pay plans share two attributes: they absorb vast amounts of management time and resources, and they make everybody unhappy.[2] But, given that most organizations have little choice but to do their best with them, there are ways of minimizing the damage by raising rewards to the level of teams. In some cases, these "teams" are the whole division or company. Leaders in these companies don't talk about "incentives" for reaching a target; they talk about rewarding employees for achieving an exceptional result—more akin to a dividend on their "human capital" that ranks along with the dividend paid to the shareholders.

Most social scientists criticize incentives as applied to *individuals*. They are less concerned about teams. Indeed, the view that enlightened leaders take is that results are invariably due to the combined efforts of many people and teams. Even taking the example of a salesperson "winning" a major order, can anyone really say that she achieved that on her own? In most cases, this is doubtful. There are usually back-up support teams involved in managing brands, designing solutions, preparing quotations, providing demonstrations, doing cooperative marketing, and so forth.

Many people agree with team-based rewards in principle but reject the idea because of what's known as the "free-rider" problem. In other words, they object to someone benefiting from the team's achievements who has not made a full contribution. One way to deal with this problem is to ensure that individual performance appraisals are handled within the team and not by the HR department. This exerts huge pressure on individuals to raise their game or face exclusion.

An extreme version of this approach occurs at Whole Foods, where teams vote on the acceptance of a new recruit after six-months' employment. Another approach is to operate with 360-degree peer reviews and then post all reviews on the firm's intranet. At HCL Technologies, the CEO's 360-degree feedback is open to all fifty-five thousand employees to see on the internal Web. All thirty-eight hundred managers participate in an open 360-degree peer review, and the results—which are anonymous so that people are candid—are available on the internal Web for those who gave feedback to see. Anyone who has had interaction with any manager can post a peer review. This makes a person's boss less powerful in the process, which is independently audited to ensure fair play. It forces managers who get a low score to look at their own performance and learn how they can improve or face dismissal.[3]

The impact on the behavior of frontline people must not be underestimated. It can lead to what Harvard professor Chris Argyris calls "internal commitment." The hidden problem, according to Argyris, is that people have to deal with two types of commitment. First, there is *external commitment*, which, by and large, leads people to fulfill contractual obligations specified by others, and in which performance goals are top down. Second, there is *internal commitment*, which allows individuals to define their own plans and the tasks required to fulfill them, and which is participatory, comes from within the individual, and leads to people taking risks and accepting responsibility for their actions.[4] The relative improvement contract seeks to encourage this behavior. The rhetoric of leaders does not produce internal commitment any more than it leads to effective empowerment or personal responsibility. Such changes require a fundamental change in the process that determines the behavioral context.

While this approach can be universally applied, it needs to be tailored to fit the company and the team. Table 38-1 shows an example of an evaluation scorecard for a value center team. The performance criteria cover the key elements of performance outcomes on which management will be evaluated. Column a enables these criteria to be weighted to place greater emphasis on some criteria over others. Column b is the assessment score. Column a × b reflects the weighted score; that score enables the company to pay rewards based on the percentage score achieved. This percentage can relate, for example,

TABLE 38-1

Value center team evaluation scorecard

Performance criteria	Weighting	Score (out of 100)	Weighted average score
	a	b	a × b
How well are we doing relative to peers?	30%	60	18.0
How well are we managing our strategic investment portfolio?	10%	50	5.0
How well are we innovating?	20%	60	12.0
How well are we managing our resources?	10%	60	6.0
How well are we satisfying our customers?	30%	80	24.0
Total	100%		65%

to base salary—the whole year, three months, or whatever the chosen 100 percent benchmark is.

The performance criteria for the scorecards vary by type of team. For example, a support services team will emphasize partner satisfaction and costs as well as cycle times, quality, cost, and customer satisfaction. Underpinning each chosen evaluation criterion are a number of points that judges consider. These points provide some consistency among judges.

Evaluating teams based on relative improvement focuses managers on maximizing value at all times, rather than playing games with the numbers because there are no fixed targets that lead to irrational behavior. Performance is judged after the event, rather than being based on a fixed target. The logic is that only after the event can you judge whether performance is good in the context of actual market conditions. What was the inflation rate? What impact did the floods have? What was the impact of our biggest customer going bankrupt? Only after the event can you determine whether your performance is acceptable or not. However, even though managers are evaluated and rewarded in hindsight, there is still a performance contract based on some form of relative result. The benefits are that the process is fast, and because the performance bar is always being raised, it is more likely to maximize performance potential.

Leaders should not overlook the power of recognition—as opposed to rewards—which is one of the most potent tools in the manager's toolbox, but rarely used to maximum effect. Going out of your way to praise someone's effort or performance can make his day. A birthday card, some flowers, or a book coupon says that your work has been recognized. These are all simple expressions that say thank you. And they're inexpensive.

The important issue is not so much the financial payout but the recognition of the contribution that employees make to the organization's success. Many leaders reject the idea that financial incentives are necessary to reinforce performance improvement. Jan Wallander, former CEO at Handelsbanken, sums up the point: "Why do people need cash incentives to fulfill their work obligations to colleagues and customers? It is recognition of effort that is important. Managers will only strive to achieve ambitious stretch targets if they know that their 'best efforts' will be recognized and not punished if they fail to get all the way."[5]

What is the performance potential of this practice?

- **To attract, keep, and motivate people.** There is a long-running debate on whether rewards send the right motivational messages, but, in any case, rewards do need to be competitive within the industry to ensure that you attract the most talented people.

- **To provide a fairer rewards system.** The number-one complaint about all reward systems is that they are unfair. So ensuring that fairness is a key aim of the rewards system is crucial to success.
- **To encourage more sharing.** Teams focusing on their own vested interests is one of the greatest barriers to knowledge sharing. Well-designed recognition and team-based rewards systems help to remove these barriers, enabling much greater collaboration across the organization.
- **To build pride and passion.** People either bring pride and passion to work every day or they don't, depending whether the right performance drivers are switched on or off. Recognition and rewards have a major influence on their decisions at work.

What actions do you need to take to maximize the potential of this practice?

ACTIONS TO AVOID

- ✖ **Avoid linking rewards to short-term fixed targets.** Fixed targets lead to lazy thinking about who is accountable for what. In most organizations, accountability is attached to the target itself. If you meet your target, you have done your job. But as most managers quickly discover, there are ways to meet the financial target that leave other stakeholders feeling dissatisfied. You can consider these three cases which were discussed in earlier chapters. Think of a purchasing manager with a target of reducing cost who orders in bulk or pays suppliers late but feels no accountability for the poor quality of the products bought, the costs of high inventories, or the deteriorating relationships with suppliers. Think of a pension salesperson who sells products that give her the highest commissions but who is not accountable for providing her client with funds that best fit their needs. And think of a mortgage broker who ignores risk controls and sells mortgages to people who can't afford them to achieve his maximum bonus. In all these cases, the manager or salesperson has met his obligations (to meet the target), but he has left the customer and the shareholder out in the cold. Additional examples include the manufacturing plant that overproduces to reach a monthly manufacturing efficiency target, a sales executive who gives extra discounts to pull a large order into this accounting period, and executives who cancel and rebook orders to keep shipping targets from slipping.
- ✖ **Avoid basing rewards on individual performance.** Robert Simons believes it is impossible to separate the marginal contributions of individuals. He asks the questions, "When Ford launches a successful new automobile, how can senior managers calibrate the relative contribution of the design

team that created the concept, the engineering team that developed and applied the new technologies, the marketing team that launched the product, and the division president who oversaw the entire effort? How do we measure the contribution of a single violin player in relation to the successful season enjoyed by a symphony orchestra?"[6] Jeffrey Pfeffer made a similar point when he said that, "individual incentive pay in reality undermines performance of both the individual and the organization. Many studies strongly suggest that this form of reward undermines teamwork, encourages a short-term focus, and leads people to believe that pay is not related to performance at all but to having the 'right' relationships and an ingratiating personality."[7] Base rewards on teams.

✖ **Don't be persuaded by the free-rider argument.** Many people like the idea of team-based rewards but think again when someone points out that the underperformers get a free ride. While undoubtedly unfair to the top performers, there is plenty of evidence to suggest it is not a major problem, provided the team leader has the scope and authority to deal with it. Poor performers must either improve their contribution or face dismissal from the team. When peer reviews are used, free riders become even more obvious. As one comprehensive review reported, "under conditions described by the theory as leading to free riding, people often cooperated instead."[8]

ACTIONS TO TAKE

✓ **Persuade the executive team and the HR community to change the basis of recognition and rewards at every level to support relative improvement.** Use the language of teams and rewards rather than of individuals and incentives. The language an organization uses to talk about rewards sets the tone for how people understand and internalize them.

✓ **Choose whether you want to implement a groupwide profit-sharing scheme or a team-based rewards scheme—or a combination of both—at each level.** In either case, demonstrate to people what the effects of the new scheme would have been in the previous three years, and if applicable, compare these effects with the existing incentives payout. Sell the scheme on the basis of everyone sharing in the exceptional performance of the company or team.

✓ **Make rewards fair, consistent, and inclusive.** The number-one factor on most employees' list of pay-related issues is *fairness*. Fairness in this context is about differentials between one level and another and between employees on the same team. However, achieving fairness is a difficult task, as each person may have a different view. One hallmark of fairness is inclusiveness. Having different schemes for different levels with significant differences in the size and opportunity of payout can spell disaster for any rewards scheme. All permanent employees should share in one way or another.

✓ **Encourage people to spend their bonuses on gifts or charitable donations.** Research shows that how people spend their bonuses affects their happiness. Professors Michael Norton and Elizabeth Dunn found that people get no meaningful boost in happiness by spending money on things like new clothes, TVs, and iPods. But they do tend to feel better if they spend even a small portion of a windfall on others. They surveyed more than six hundred Americans and found that the more money people spent on gifts for others and on charitable donations, the likelier they were to report being happy with their lives in general.[9]

Think about how to use the power of recognition systems

In a *McKinsey Quarterly* survey, respondents viewed three noncash motivators—praise from immediate managers, leadership attention (for example, one-on-one conversations), and a chance to lead projects or task forces—as no less or even more effective motivators than the three highest-rated financial incentives: cash bonuses, increased base pay, and stock or stock options. The survey's top-three nonfinancial motivators play critical roles in making employees feel that their companies value them, take their well-being seriously, and strive to create opportunities for career growth. These themes recur constantly in most studies on ways to motivate and engage employees.[a]

Southwest Airlines takes employee recognition seriously. If you walk around its head office in Dallas, you will see thousands of photographs and certificates on the walls of employees and teams and what they have done for the organization. Chairman Herb Kelleher has never believed that compensation was the primary motivator. "If somebody was working just to be compensated," he says, "we probably didn't want them at Southwest Airlines. We wanted them working in order to do something in an excellent way. And to serve people. So we said to [employees]: This is a cause, this is a crusade. This isn't just an ordinary corporation, and you're doing a lot of good for everybody. We're proud of you, and we want you to have psychic satisfaction when you come to work. We get people who take a 25 percent cut in pay because they say: We just want to enjoy what we're doing."[b]

[a] Martin Dewhurst, Matthew Guthridge, and Elizabeth Mohr, "Motivating People: Getting Beyond Money," *McKinsey Quarterly* no. 1 (2010): 12.

[b] "Herb Kelleher on the Record, Part 2," *Businessweek.com.* December 23, 2003. http://www.businessweek.com/bwdaily/dnflash/dec2003/nf20031223_5702_db062.htm

✓ **Include everyone.** Everyone on the team should participate in the reward payout. All must agree on how the formula works, for example, everyone gets the same or based on pro rata base salaries.

Conclusions

Performance evaluation and incentive compensation stir deep emotions in people. Most managers will accept that they should be held accountable for their performance if they see the evaluation process as fair and transparent. But if we set self-interest aside, we must be skeptical about the link between rewards and motivation and wonder whether pay for performance is worth the effort. Perhaps the last word should be left to Frederick Herzberg, who once said that "if you want someone to do a good job, then give them a good job to do."[10]

FURTHER READING

Argyris, Chris. "Empowerment: The Emperor's New Clothes." *Harvard Business Review*, May–June 1998, 98–105.

Hope, Jeremy. *Reinventing the CFO*. Boston: Harvard Business School Press, 2006.

Hope, Jeremy, and Robin Fraser. *Beyond Budgeting*. Boston: Harvard Business School Press, 2003.

Nayar, Vineet. *Employees First, Customers Second*. Boston: Harvard Business Press, 2010.

Pfeffer, Jeffrey. *The Human Equation: Building Profits by Putting People First*. Boston: Harvard Business School Press, 1998.

Pfeffer, Jeffrey. "Six Dangerous Myths About Pay." *Harvard Business Review*, May–June 1998, 109–119.

Pfeffer, Jeffrey, and Robert I. Sutton. "Evidence-Based Management," *Harvard Business Review*, January 2006, 62–74.

Pfeffer, Jeffrey, and Robert I. Sutton. *Hard Facts, Dangerous Half-Truths and Total Nonsense*. Boston: Harvard Business School Press, 2006.

39

EXECUTIVE COMPENSATION

What is this practice and how effective is it?

A board that uses an executive compensation plan assumes that it can motivate senior executives by well-designed compensation packages that include some element of pay for performance. The underlying assumption is that the plans align the interests of executives with those of shareholders. But the evidence is tenuous at best. However, as we will show, there are a number of ways that boards can design schemes that reward long-term performance while minimizing the toxic effects of these schemes.

Alternative names and related topics: executive incentives; share options; compensation committees

The mean salary plus bonus for CEOs, adjusted for inflation, grew by 58 percent from 1993 to 2005, and the mean total compensation, which included stock and stock options, increased by 116 percent. Meanwhile, over the same period, mean annual compensation in the United States overall rose by only 15 percent.[1]

What drives CEO pay to such high levels? According to Edgar Woolard, former CEO of DuPont, the primary cause is that most boards want their CEO to be in the top half of the CEO peer group because they think it makes the company look strong. "So when Tom, Dick and Harry receive compensation increases in 2002, I get one too, even if I've had a bad year. We stopped doing that at DuPont in 1990 . . . Instead, we use the pay of the senior vice presidents—the people that actually run the businesses—as a benchmark and then decide how much more the CEO ought to get," notes Woolard.[2]

Scrap executive bonuses, says Henry Mintzberg

Management guru Henry Mintzberg believes that executive bonuses should be scrapped altogether. "This may sound extreme," he notes, "but when you look at the way the compensation game is played—and the assumptions that are made by those who want to reform it—you can come to no other conclusion. The system simply can't be fixed. Executive bonuses—especially in the form of stock and option grants—represent the most prominent form of legal corruption that has been undermining our large corporations and bringing down the global economy. Get rid of them and we will all be better off for it."[a]

[a] Henry Mintzberg, "No More Executive Bonuses," *Sloan Management Review,* Winter 2009, http://sloanreview.mit.edu/business-insight/articles/2009/5/5151/no-moreexecutive-bonuses/.

Woolard's view is reinforced by recent research that finds that compensation benchmarking accounts for at least half the increase in executive pay. A standard practice in many industries, benchmarking occurs when compensation committees use peer executives at rival firms to establish a fair market wage. The problem is that each year, some CEOs leapfrog others by raking in huge bonuses or raises that are unrelated to their company's performance. Other companies then use these inflated salaries to set their compensation levels; over time, the snowball effect makes CEOs' salaries swell dramatically.[3]

Many boards tie executive pay to performance, which usually takes the form of financial bonuses, share options, and restricted shares that can only be sold within agreed parameters. How aggressive these contracts are is often a strong signal that the board is encouraging excessive risk taking. The process can also seduce the board into setting unrealistic goals and believing that high growth is possible every year.

Pär Boman, chief executive of Handelsbanken, agrees with Mintzberg. Handelsbanken's executives receive the same profit share as all other employees. In an interview, Boman said that bonuses risked creating a "mismatch" between short-term incentives and long-term performance. While many bank executives have acknowledged the need for pay restraint and a shift toward long-term incentives, few have gone as far as Boman in rejecting the business case for bonuses. Handelsbanken, the second-largest Nordic bank by market capitalization, was skeptical of bonuses long before the financial crisis and paid most of

---

Do financial incentives motivate leaders to improve the value of the business?

According to Jeroen van der Veer, former CEO of the giant Shell Oil Company, financial incentives do not motivate leaders to improve the value of their businesses. Van der Veer was criticized by shareholders for receiving a € 1.36 million bonus, even though the company failed to meet its performance targets. At a recent conference, he talked about his performance: "You have to realize, if I had been paid 50 percent more, I would not have done it better. If I had been paid 50 percent less, then I would not have done it any worse."[a]

That just about sums up the problem with financial incentives within large corporations.

[a] Carola Hoyos and Michael Steen, "Outgoing Shell Chief Calls for Reform of Salaries," *Financial Times,* June 9, 2009, 1.

---

its employees, including senior management, only a fixed salary. "It doesn't make sense to pay bonuses in good times and then in bad times tell [employees] they have to work harder for 30 percent less money," said Boman.[4]

Many boards, like Shell's, assume a correlation between executive incentives and financial results. But this correlation is tenuous at best and downright misleading at worst. In a recent study, Harvard professor B. V. Krishnamurthy suggested that "there is growing evidence to show that firm performance and top management compensation are inversely related. In a study of three hundred listed companies, we have found that the total compensation of top management in the top 5 percent of the companies measured by a variety of criteria (ROI, growth, market share, efficiency, and innovation) was less than that in the bottom 5 percent of the companies measured along the same set of criteria."[5] A U.K. study of the top three hundred fifty firms concluded that there was no evidence that executives' long-term incentive plans had any positive impact on total shareholder returns but have a significant financial cost to shareholders.[6]

Do share options offer a better alternative? There is one huge snag with fixed-price options. Around 70 percent of the stock price of individual companies is driven by market and industry factors, and only 30 percent by individual company performance.[7] This means that executives could easily get a free ride when the market is improving and similarly suffer unfairly when the market is declining. Alfred Rappaport, one of the founding fathers of value-based management, believes this is wrong. "Fixed priced options reward executives for any increase in the share price—even if the increase is well below that realized by competitors or by the market as a whole," he notes. He believes in the power of shareholder value measures to evaluate and reward executive performance, provided that such measures are based on returns equal to or better than those earned by the company's peer group or by broader market indexes.[8] Erik Stern of Stern Stewart also believes fixed options are flawed. He favors three types of relative measure. The first is beating peers based on exceeding the cost of capital. The second is based on an industry league table (which shows how a firm performed in comparison to its competitors). And the third is based on a country league table (which is similar to an industry league table but uses the country to define the participants in the league). "The stellar performers are those that rank highly in all three over a five-year period," notes Stern.[9]

The basic idea of share options is that they align the interests of executives with shareholders and help to offset the tendency of executives to avoid risky but potentially profitable investments. But it turns out that the conclusions were based more on optimistic theories than actual data. Recent analysis provides some disturbing results. It appears that really big options grants make it more likely that companies will fudge their numbers and that companies with such grants will more likely go broke. One study by Jared Harris, a doctoral candidate, and Philip Bromley, a management professor at the University of Minnesota, compared 435 companies that were forced to restate their financial statements with similar companies that did not have such problems. The report found that the higher the proportion of the boss's pay in stock options, the more likely the company was to be forced to restate profits. For companies where bosses got 92 percent or more of their pay in options, about a fifth ended up faking their books within five years.[10] Another study that shows the dangers of excessive options comes from Moody's, the bond-rating service. The study's authors, Kenneth A. Bertsch and Christopher Mann, found that companies with the highest-paid bosses, adjusted for things like company size and performance, were far more likely to default on debt or to suffer major cuts in bond ratings.[11]

American Express is one company that has learned the lessons on executive pay. In early 2008, the Amex board gave CEO Ken Chenault options on 2.75 million shares—a mega-grant by any definition. However, to receive the full grant, he must achieve several goals over the next six years, an unusually distant time horizon. These include:

- Earnings per share must grow at least 15 percent a year on average.
- Revenues must grow at least 10 percent a year.

- Return on equity must average at least 36 percent per year.
- Total return to shareholders must beat the S&P 500 average by at least 2.5 percent a year.[12]

There are no simple answers to the questions concerning executive pay for performance. Boards and compensation committees will continue to argue that they need to pay the market rate to get the best people. The trouble is that if the next CEO is more interested in the pay than the job, you have to wonder if he or she is the right person.

What is the performance potential of this practice?

- **To focus leaders on long-term performance improvement.** The practice should reward leaders for achieving sustainable long-term growth.
- **To reward success.** Rewards should not be paid to executives who fail to achieve relative performance improvement.
- **To send the right messages to employees.** Employees should be able to see that the executive scheme is fair and reasonable and aligned with the best interests of all stakeholders.

What actions do you need to take to maximize the potential of this practice?

ACTIONS TO AVOID

- ✖ **Don't assume that the compensation committee adds value.** Companies that use compensation consultants often award their CEOs higher salaries than those that don't. Using a sample of more than two thousand firms and examining total annual CEO compensation data from each company's most recent fiscal year that ended on or after December 31, 2006, the authors of a study found that the problem has less to do with the fact that consultants were hired than with underlying governance problems at the companies themselves. Companies with weak boards of directors and overpaid executives often hire compensation consultants who are unwilling or unable to correct the overpayment, even if it is what's best for the company. The authors also examined whether consulting firms recommended higher salaries when they provided additional services unrelated to compensation, but found no evidence that this was the case. Although compensation consultants don't necessarily encourage excessive pay, they are often hired by companies with deficient corporate governance, and rarely prevent the boards of such companies from overpaying their executives.[13] Another problem is that compensation committees sometimes act to strengthen incentives by increasing

Focus on the person not the pay

According to Claudio Fernández-Aráoz of Egon Zehnder International, the real aim should be not just to avoid public frustration and excess, but to aim for a much more ambitious objective—to ensure that CEOs and other leaders make the greatest potential contribution toward building lasting greatness. Whom you pay is much more important than how much you pay, and even how you pay. He makes the point that people are very different when it comes to how they perform in complex jobs. Research shows that the difference in performance grows exponentially with the complexity of the job.[a] While a star blue-collar worker on a traditional assembly line would be 40 percent more productive than a typical worker, that performance advantage can be 240 percent for a star insurance salesman, and more than 1,000 percent for star workers in more complex jobs, such as a computer programmer or an account manager of a professional service firm. Thus, a CEO's performance, given the complexity of the job, will have a huge spread. Therefore, the key debate should not be about how much and how to pay to the CEO, but rather about how to make sure that the best CEO is in place, and boards should focus much more, and much better, on that question.

Fernández-Aráoz concludes that clearly companies need to pay reasonably well in order to attract and retain the right people in the first place. However, he believes that the purpose of compensation is not to "motivate" the right behaviors from the wrong people. Compensation should be reasonable because it is part of human nature to expect fair treatment when it comes to compensation, which should be somehow proportional to our efforts and/or results.[b]

[a] Claudio Fernández-Aráoz, "Whom to Pay Is More Important Than How Much or How," http://blogs.hbr.org/hbr/how-to-fix-executive-pay/2009/07/whom-to-pay-is-more-important-than-how-much-or-how.html.
[b] Ibid.

share option grants after a year of strong stock-price performance or decreasing them after a bad year. On the surface, this appears to be good news. But such moves have little overall impact because directors tend to reverse their actions the following year. According to consultant Stephen O'Byrne and Insead professor David Young, an option grant that rewards good performance or penalizes poor performance is followed almost half the time by a grant that penalizes good performance or rewards poor performance. On balance, therefore, ad hoc adjustments by boards contribute almost nothing to wealth leverage.[14]

✖ **Avoid basing large payouts on short-term performance.** Some organizations use, for example, "bonus banks" that pay rewards based on performance over a number of years, tying performance not to fixed targets but to results compared with peers, and forcing executives to hold stock for longer periods of time. Essentially, each executive's bonus is "banked" and paid out over a number of years. For example, only a third or a half of the bonus bank can be paid out in any year. Clearly, a company cannot pay a bonus one year and take it back the next. The bonus bank ensures that performance is sustained or the payment made is significantly reduced. Companies such as Diageo and Eli Lilly use this type of plan.

ACTIONS TO TAKE

✓ **Consider limiting executive pay to a certain number times the average employee's salary. (Somewhere between fifteen and twenty-five times average salary seems to be par.)** Executives need to be more aware of their levels of earnings compared with their employees. One idea is to limit executive pay to a multiple of average earnings. Whole Foods CEO John Mackey bemoans the trend in which a Fortune 500 CEO made about twenty-five times the average worker pay; now that has climbed to three hundred times average employee pay. Mackey says this violates the principle of "internal equity—what your leadership is getting paid relative to everyone else in the organization."[15] In 2006, the Whole Foods board of directors voted to raise the salary cap from fourteen times the average pay to nineteen times the average pay. Mackey explained that the reason was to make the compensation to his executives more competitive in the marketplace. "Everyone on the Whole Foods leadership team (except for me) has been approached multiple times by 'headhunters' with job offers to leave Whole Foods and go to work for our competitors. Raising the salary cap has become necessary to help ensure the retention of our key leadership . . . This increase to 19 times the average pay remains far, far below what the typical *Fortune* 500 company pays its executives."[16]

✓ **Base rewards on relative performance.** For its most senior executives, Diageo, one of the world's leading consumer goods companies, has a long-term incentive program (LTIP). The LTIP establishes a global peer group of sixteen companies, including direct competitors—such as Kellogg, Nestlé, Unilever, and McDonald's—and the best-performing consumer goods companies—such as Coca-Cola, Gillette, and Procter & Gamble.

In order to maximize their bonuses under the LTIP scheme, Diageo executives must put the company at the top of that peer group over three years. Coming in fifth wins them 100 percent of the agreed-on bonus; fourth, 125 percent; and first, second, or third, 150 percent. Between fifth and tenth, they operate on a sliding scale, but if Diageo fails to make the top ten, its executives get nothing. This order is tough, but one that 90 percent of shareholders approved at the annual general meeting. The performance shares awarded in 2005 vested at 35 percent of the initial award in September 2008, based on a relative total shareholder return (TSR) ranking of ninth position (median) in the peer group. Share options granted in 2005 vested in full in September 2008 after exceeding the required performance condition of adjusted earnings-per-share growth of Retail Price Index plus 15 percentage points.[17]

✓ **Be wary of share options and restricted stock grants.** There is nothing wrong with executives owning shares in the organizations they run; it should be encouraged. But providing shares—in the form of options or restricted stock—as "benefits" should be examined very closely, because such benefits can lead to dysfunctional behavior (e.g., short-term actions aimed at influencing the share price). For example, there is evidence that accounting restatements are linked to the use of share options. Also, if options are to be used, they should be spread widely among the management team.

✓ **Compel directors to hold their stock for the long term.** Stock ownership guidelines that set ownership targets as a dollar value that equals a multiple of base salary are still the most common model. (It was used by 82 percent of companies, in a recent report.) Other companies use a fixed number of shares (13 percent of the Fortune 250 companies), and some use a combination of both. Five times the base salary for the CEO "was and is still the norm."[18] Some boards insist that directors hold their stocks for longer than the usual three-year period. Exxon Mobil top executives can't sell half of their restricted stock grants for five years and must hold the other half for ten years or until retirement. In another positive trend, many companies require that their executives hold between five and eight times their annual salary in shares. At JPMorgan Chase, CEO Jamie Dimon has senior executives retain 75 percent of stock awards until they leave the company.[19] Extending the length of time that executives hold stock negates many of the toxic effects of short-term actions that affect the short-term share price but damage future wealth creation.

✓ **Include values in performance evaluations.** "A board should explicitly base a defined portion of the CEO's cash compensation and equity grants on his or her success in handling the foundational task of fusing high performance with high integrity at all levels of the company. The board can do that by judging whether the CEO has established company-wide performance-with-integrity *principles* for which the firm's leaders are responsible and accountable. Examples of these include demonstrating committed and consistent integrity leadership; managing performance with integrity as a business process; using early-warning systems to stay ahead of global trends; providing timely, risk-assessed training; and giving employees a voice. Has integrity permeated every aspect of the corporate *culture*? One vital tool for assessing that is an annual, anonymous employee survey across all businesses and regions that asks, 'Is integrity compromised by business pressures?' and 'Are the leaders' verbal commitments to integrity reflected in action?' The board can also have outside HR experts periodically conduct 360-degree assessments of the CEO and top executives that explore such questions."[20]

Conclusions

Today's leaders face an overwhelming task of restoring confidence and respect in both leadership and in business, while guiding their organizations through times of turbulence and uncertainty. A different type of leadership is called for, one that is less about being a high-profile public figure and more about being focused on operating performance and business fundamentals. Making that change successfully largely depends on compensating boards—and especially the CEO—fairly, but not excessively. Compensation committees and boards should look at their executive incentive proposals in the light of the most optimistic and the most pessimistic outcomes and consider that if these occurred, would the outcomes from their compensation plans be both reasonable and acceptable? They should also ensure that rewards even out over the performance cycle. Finally, they should consider this: how many CEOs have turned down a board's offer because the compensation is too low? Not many, is the answer.

FURTHER READING

Colvin, Geoff. "AmEx Gets CEO Pay Right." *Fortune,* January 21, 2008, 22–24.
Elson, Charles. "What's Wrong with Executive Compensation." *Harvard Business Review,* January 2003, 68–77.
Mintzberg, Henry. "No More Executive Bonuses." *Sloan Management Review,* Winter 2009.
Nayar, Vineet. *Employees First, Customers Second.* Boston: Harvard Business Press, 2010.
Pfeffer, Jeffrey. *The Human Equation: Building Profits by Putting People First.* Boston: Harvard Business School Press, 1998.
Pfeffer, Jeffrey. "Six Dangerous Myths About Pay." *Harvard Business Review,* May–June 1998, 109–119.

Pfeffer, Jeffrey, and Robert I. Sutton. "Evidence-Based Management." *Harvard Business Review,* January 2006, 62–74.

Pfeffer, Jeffrey, and Robert I. Sutton. *Hard Facts, Dangerous Half-Truths and Total Nonsense.* Boston: Harvard Business School Press, 2006.

Rappaport, Alfred, and Thomas Nodine. "New Thinking on How to Link Executive Pay with Performance." *Harvard Business Review,* March-April 1999, 91–101.

40

PROFIT-SHARING SCHEMES

What is this practice and how effective is it?

Many organizations use profit sharing to provide a fairer approach to recognizing and rewarding managers and employees. But most programs fail to survive a bad year in which profits fall and employees receive little or no bonus. This "entitlement creep" problem—bonuses are soon built into an individual's expectations—suddenly becomes a crisis, and the scheme is abandoned. We will examine how a few smart organizations have found ways around these problems.

Alternative names and related topics: gainsharing; fair compensation; team-based rewards

Most social scientists criticize financial incentives when they are applied to *individuals* but are less concerned about teams. Indeed, the alternative view is that teams are the right focus for rewards. In this context, rewards are seen as a share of success (like a dividend on intellectual capital) rather than a "do this, get that" type of incentive linked to a target. MIT professor Edgar Schein, an acknowledged expert in the field of corporate culture, puts the problem of changing the incentive mind-set down to the sacred cow of individual accountability. "No matter how much team-work is touted in theory," he notes, "it does not exist in practice until accountability itself is assigned to the whole team and until group pay and reward systems are instituted."[1]

What constitutes a "team" is this context? The answer is any group that represents an interdependent value-delivery network. Anything less than this, to some degree or other, is likely to be divisive. Rewarding the success of the business unit or firm as a whole is not intended to manipulate behavior, but to

Groupwide profit sharing at Handelsbanken and Southwest Airlines

Every year since 1973, Handelsbanken has allocated part of its profit to a profit-sharing system for employees. The formula for allocating profits to the bonus pool is linked to the extent to which the Handelsbanken Group has a higher return on equity after standard tax than the average for other peer group banks. All employees receive the same allocated amount. The profit-sharing system can only be understood in the context of its purpose. It is not intended to be an incentive for individuals to pursue financial targets; rather, it is intended as a reward for their collective efforts and competitive success. It might be called a "dividend" on its human capital.

Handelsbanken executives believe that its groupwide profit-sharing scheme is an important element in removing the cellular or "defend your own turf" mentality that pervades many organizations. It avoids the problem of rewards becoming entitlements that, if not received, lead to a disaffected and, in some cases, a demoralized workforce. Since abandoning fixed targets in the 1970s, Handelsbanken has produced outstanding returns for shareholders, consistently beating its rivals in Europe on the key ratios of cost to income and costs to total assets.

The profit-sharing plan at Southwest started in 1973 and is at the heart of its compensation and benefits program. All employees qualify on the January 1 following the commencement of their employment. Fifteen percent of pretax profits are paid into the profit-sharing pool, which is shared across all employees according to base salary. The payments go into a retirement fund for individual employees. While employees are free to increase that amount, 25 percent of the profit-sharing fund is used to purchase Southwest shares. Pilots and flight attendants have other stock option plans. There are no incentive schemes based on achieving annual fixed targets.

demonstrate that everyone is in the same boat, all rowing in the same direction, all dependent on each other. At Handelsbanken and Southwest Airlines, the team is the whole company. At Tomkins and Ahlsell, the team is a business unit.

How the scheme is designed matters. In 1990, DuPont pulled the plug on one of the most ambitious and closely watched incentive pay programs in American history—a plan in which the company's twenty thousand fibers-division employees had a portion of their pay increases at risk. Employees received bigger increases if DuPont exceeded its profit goals, but smaller payouts or none at all if goals weren't met. Two years into a three-year trial, DuPont canceled the plan, partly in response to plummeting employee morale: the 1990 recession had made it almost certain that for the first time, the company wouldn't reach its goals.[2] The problem is that when employees get rewards, they feel good, but the moment the rewards stop, they feel resentful. This phenomenon, often known as entitlement creep, is a common problem with pay-for-performance schemes. A typical response from an employee would be "In a recent quarter, I got 96 percent of the maximum bonus. Why was I docked the 4 percent?"

The profit-sharing approach relies more on peer pressure than on direct incentives. No self-respecting manager would want to go to a meeting of his or her peers knowing that they have underperformed and let down the whole team and possibly drained the bonus pool. Internal and external league tables enable a framework for performance evaluation that provides a powerful force for continuous improvement, as one business unit strives to improve its position against its rivals.

Peer pressure can be either positive or negative. Negative peer pressure leads to a fortress mentality. Local vested interests are paramount, as managers seek to gain the maximum advantage (e.g., the most resources) from the corporate center. Other similar business units are seen as the enemy. Positive peer pressure is about improving faster than rivals but within a climate of cooperation and sharing. Achieving a balance between competition and cooperation needs to be carefully managed. The defining difference is the rewards system. If rewards are at the whole business level, then individual units have little need to act with a fortress mentality.

Southwest's Herb Kelleher has no doubt of the success of profit sharing. "The profit sharing is an expense we'd like to be as big as possible so our people get a greater reward," he notes.[3] When the first Gulf war broke out, the cost of jet fuel rocketed. So Kelleher wrote a memo to his pilots saying that fuel needed to be cut back. He continued, "And in one week our costs went down, just like that. Now let me contrast that with the consultant who wanted to set up an incentive program whereby pilots' pay would be increased to the extent they conserved fuel. I kept telling the guy we didn't need to do that. Our pilots just did it on their own."[4]

What is the performance potential of this practice?

- **Create sustainable performance improvement relative to peers.** Negotiating a target and meeting it is unlikely to maximize performance potential. But this can be achieved, if all managers aim to be the best, that is, the best organization, division, business unit, plant, sales team, and so forth in their peer group. Group profit sharing supports this relative view of performance evaluation.

- **Build a high-performance culture.** Individual bonuses often reward the best political negotiators rather than the best performers. They discourage cooperation and sharing. These factors work against a high-performance culture. Group reward schemes eliminate these problems. Managers can thus create a climate of ambition and continuous improvement that encourages teams at every level to push the boundaries and not just accept a result that can be excused as "up to industry standards."
- **Provide a clear and fair framework for evaluating and rewarding performance.** Most incentive schemes are seen to be unfair. For every individual winner, there are many disgruntled losers. Group- or team-based schemes are seen to be fairer, because most people understand that the whole team creates good or bad results.

What actions do you need to take to maximize the potential of this practice?

ACTIONS TO AVOID

✖ **Avoid the entitlement problem.** Most profit-sharing schemes hit the rocks when the first bad year comes around. (Profit shares either fall or disappear altogether.) The result is collapsing employee morale and intense dissatisfaction with senior management, which is seen to have caused the problem. Senior executives don't want to go through this pain again, so they scrap the scheme. The problem is one of design. Neither Handelsbanken nor Southwest Airlines pay employee profit shares immediately in cash. They pay the shares into a pension plan that the employee can take when he or she leaves or retires. In this way, the bad year is less of a problem because employees see it as a low (or nil) contribution year, but the value of the fund still does reasonably well.

ACTIONS TO TAKE

✓ **Create teams at the highest level of interdependence.** Profit shares can apply to a team within a business or the whole group. Most organizations choose the whole group. U.K. retailer John Lewis Partnership is a good example. In 2010, it handed more than seventy thousand staff a bonus equal to nearly eight weeks' pay after the department store and Waitrose supermarket chain posted a near 10 percent rise in profits. The payout was equal to 15 percent of salary, and all permanent staff, from the mailroom to the chairman, got the same level of reward.[5]

✓ **Choose your profit-sharing formula and make it clear and transparent.** Some organizations, like Southwest and John Lewis, use a profit-sharing formula based on actual profits. Handelsbanken uses a formula based on results that are relative to peer group banks.

✓ **Get employees to buy into the plan.** The key to buy-in is to get employees engaged. Handelsbanken involved trade unions, which took a great deal of convincing. The development team should include a cross-section of employees that represent the total organization.

✓ **Include everyone.** One hallmark of fairness is inclusiveness. Having different schemes for different levels with significant differences in the size and opportunity of payout can spell disaster for any rewards plan. All permanent employees should share in one way or another. Include new hires the first day they join the organization. Some organizations also include temporary or contract employees.

✓ **Communicate the plan clearly.** Communication requires listening. If an organization shares profits, employees will start asking more questions. If management fails to listen and respond and fails to act on employee ideas and suggestions, the whole system will collapse.

✓ **If you choose relative performance, don't set the bar too high.** Handelsbanken pays out once the company's return on equity is equal to or greater than the average of its peer group. Why average? Because it's not hard to beat and avoids the bad-year syndrome. President Arne Mårtensson, said, "Relative measures mean that managers can keep the same goal for a long time as the average keeps improving. You can of course argue that it is based on continuous improvement rather than radical change, but it is consistency of performance that we believe is the most important factor." This telling comment goes to the core of how success is measured. Stretch targets on their own can encourage the roller-coaster boom-and-bust approach to strategy, whereas relative targets support the steady-improvement approach. This, indeed, describes Handelsbanken's success story over the past thirty years.

Conclusions

Companies such as Handelsbanken, Southwest, and John Lewis have given all their employees a stake in success through their profit-sharing schemes. They send a clear message that all employees are valued for their contribution. But how a company designs and implements these schemes matters greatly. Once the schemes become an entitlement and are built into people's spending plans, when a bad year comes, there will be little or nothing to pay out. That's why the deferral idea works best.

FURTHER READING

Hope, Jeremy. *Reinventing the CFO*. Boston: Harvard Business School Press, 2006.

Hope, Jeremy, and Robin Fraser. *Beyond Budgeting*. Boston: Harvard Business School Press, 2003.

Nayar, Vineet. *Employees First, Customers Second*. Boston: Harvard Business Press, 2010.

Pfeffer, Jeffrey. *The Human Equation: Building Profits by Putting People First*. Boston: Harvard Business School Press, 1998.

Pfeffer, Jeffrey. "Six Dangerous Myths About Pay." *Harvard Business Review*, May–June 1998, 109–119.

Pfeffer, Jeffrey, and Robert I. Sutton. "Evidence-Based Management." *Harvard Business Review*, January 2006, 62–74.

Pfeffer, Jeffrey, and Robert I. Sutton. *Hard Facts, Dangerous Half-Truths and Total Nonsense*. Boston: Harvard Business School Press, 2006.

11. Lawrence M. Fisher, "An Interview with John Seely Brown," *Strategy + Business*, 4th quarter, 1999, 85–95.

12. Kevin Freiberg and Jackie Freiberg, *Nuts! Southwest Airlines' Crazy Recipe for Business and Personal Success* (New York: Broadway Books, 1998), 66.

13. Mackey, "Creating the High Trust Organization."

14. Bragdon, *Profit for Life*, 130–131.

15. Tim Stevens, "Follow the Leader," *Industry Week*, November 18, 1996.

16. Lisa L. Shu, Francesca Gino, and Max H. Bazerman, "Dishonest Deed, Clear Conscience: Self-Preservation Through Moral Disengagement and Motivated Forgetting," working paper 09-078, Harvard Business School, February 2009.

Chapter 2

1. Stephan Haeckel, *Adaptive Enterprise: Creating and Leading Sense-and-Respond Organizations* (Boston: Harvard Business School Press, 1999), 39.

2. Christopher A. Bartlett and Sumantra Ghoshal, "Beyond the M-Form: Toward a Managerial Theory of the Firm," www.gsia.cmu.edu/bosch/bart.html.

3. James Brian Quinn, *Strategies for Change: Logical Incrementalism* (Homewood, IL: Irwin, 1980), 122.

4. Herb Kelleher, "A Culture of Commitment," *Leader to Leader*, Spring 1997.

5. "Speed, Simplicity, Self-Confidence: An Interview with Jack Welch," *Harvard Business Review*, September–October 1989, 112–120.

6. Charles Handy, "Balancing Corporate Power: A New Federalist Paper," *Harvard Business Review*, November–December 1992, 59–67.

7. Kevin Freiberg and Jackie Freiberg, *Nuts! Southwest Airlines' Crazy Recipe for Business and Personal Success* (New York: Broadway Books, 1998), 86.

Chapter 3

1. Marshall Loeb, "Jack Welch: Let's Fly on Budgets, Bonuses, and Buddy Boards," *Fortune*, May 29, 1995, 145–147.

2. Hirotaka Takeuchi, Emi Osono, and Norihiko Shimizu, "The Contradictions That Drive Toyota's Success," *Harvard Business Review*, June 2008, 96–104.

Chapter 4

1. "Ask The Source," *CIO Magazine*, September 19, 2002, www2.cio.com/ask/source/2002/session27.html.

Chapter 5

1. Gary Hamel, "Bringing Silicon Valley Inside," *Harvard Business Review*, September–October 1999, 76.

2. Todd Datz, "Portfolio Management—How to Do It Right," *CIO Magazine*, May 1, 2003, www.cio.com/archive/050103/portfolio.html.

3. Judith Samuelson, "A Critical Mass for the Long Term," *Harvard Business Review*, February 2006, 62–63.

4. Massimo Giordano and Felix Wenger, "Organizing for Value," *McKinsey Quarterly*, July 2008, www.mckinseyquarterly.com/Corporate_Finance/Capital_Management/Organizing_for_value_2171.

5. Steve Player, "BBRT Case Reports," Beyond Budgeting Roundtable Dallas, TX, January 19, 2005.

6. "Strategic Decisions: When Can You Trust Your Gut? Nobel Laureate Daniel Kahneman and Psychologist Gary Klein Debate the Power and Perils of Intuition for Senior Executives," *McKinsey Quarterly*, February 2010, 58–69.

7. Gary Hamel, *Leading the Revolution* (Boston: Harvard Business School Press, 2000), 266.

8. Only 30 percent of acquisitions have added value for the acquiring company's shareholders, according to a 2001 KPMG survey, quoted in "Enterprise Governance—A Report," by International Federation of Accountants, 2003.

Notes

Introduction

1. Scott Keller and Carolyn Aiken, "The Inconvenient Truth About Change Management," *McKinsey Quarterly*, April 2009, www.mckinsey.com/clientservice/organizationleadership/The_Inconvenient_Truth_About_Change_Management.pdf.

2. Peter Drucker, "A Meeting of Minds," *CIO Magazine*, September 15, 1997, www.cio.com/archive/091597_interview.html.

3. Darrell Rigby and Barbara Bilodeau, "Management Tools and Trends 2009," Bain & Co., www.bain.com/bainweb/PDFs/cms/Public/Management_Tools_2009.pdf.

4. Ibid.

5. Ibid.

6. In 1991, Xerox conducted a detailed analysis of the purchasing habits of customers who gave Xerox scores of 4 and 5 on satisfaction and found that customers giving 5s (i.e., very satisfied customers) were six times as likely to repurchase Xerox products as those who gave 4s (i.e., quite satisfied). These conclusions led to Xerox's descriptions of customers as *apostles*—they were so delighted that they persuaded their friends to buy from Xerox—and *terrorists*—they were so dissatisfied that they told their friends to have nothing to do with the company. See James L. Heskett, Thomas O. Jones, Gary W. Loveman, W. Earl Sasser Jr., and Leonard A. Schlesinger, "Putting the Service-Profit Chain to Work," *Harvard Business Review*, March-April 1994, 164–174.

7. Rigby and Bilodeau, "Management Tools and Trends 2009."

8. Darrell Rigby and Barbara Bilodeau, "Management Tools and Trends 2005," Bain & Co., www.bain.com/management_tools/Management_Tools_and_Trends_2005.pdf.

9. Rigby and Bilodeau, "Management Tools and Trends 2009."

Chapter 1

1. Vivek Kaul, "Profit Can't Be Primary Goal of Business," *DNA India*, June 19, 2010, www.dnaindia.com/opinion/interview_profit-can-t-be-primary-goal-of-business_1398327.

2. Heather Stewart, "Shareholders and Targets Won't Do the Business," *The Observer*, March 14, 2010, www.guardian.co.uk/business/2010/mar/14/shareholder-value-comment.

3. Ibid.

4. Stefan Stern, "Unilever Warning on 'Shareholder Value,'" *Financial Times*, April 4, 2010, www.ft.com/cms/s/0/72d68b60-4009-11df-8d23-00144feabdc0.html.

5. Herb Kelleher, "A Culture of Commitment," *Leader to Leader*, Spring 1997, 20–24.

6. In a 2003 survey of more than eight hundred people with MBA degrees from eleven leading North American and European business schools, 97 percent said they would take a 14 percent pay cut to work for an "ethical" company, and intellectual challenge topped the list as the most important attribute in their job-choice decision. The financial package was only 80 percent as important as intellectual challenge. See Joseph H. Bragdon, *Profit for Life* (Cambridge, MA: Society for Organizational Learning, 2006), 170.

7. Jeffrey Abrahams, *The Mission Statement Book—301 Corporate Mission Statements from America's Top Companies* (Berkeley, CA: Ten Speed Press, 1999).

8. http://investor.google.com/corporate/faq.html#mission.

9. Kaul, "Profit Can't Be Primary Goal of Business."

10. John Mackey, "Creating the High Trust Organization," Whole Foods Market CEO Blog, March 9, 2010, http://www2.wholefoodsmarket.com/blogs/jmackey/2010/03/09/creating-the-high-trust-organization/#more-155.

9. Dan Lovallo and Olivier Sibony, "Taking the Bias out of Meetings," *McKinsey Quarterly,* February 2010, 58–69.

10. Dan Lovallo and Olivier Sibony, "The Case for Behavioral Strategy," *McKinsey Quarterly,* February 2010, 41–43.

11. "Strategic Decisions: When Can You Trust Your Gut?"

12. Michael Schrage, "Daniel Kahneman: The Thought Leader Interview," *Strategy + Business,* Winter 2003, 125.

Chapter 6

1. Don Durfee, "Strategic Risk Management—A Report" (prepared by CFO Research Services, New York, NY, 2002).

2. "The Future of Business Risk Management" (prepared by CFO Research Services, conference, 2002).

3. Ibid.

4. Michael Power, *The Risk Management of Everything: Rethinking the Politics of Uncertainty* (London, UK: Demos, 2004), http://www.demos.co.uk/files/riskmanagementofeverything.pdf? 1240939425.

5. Ibid.

6. Matthew Leitch, "Control of Decentralized Risk Taking Using 'Risk Appetite' Rules," white paper, Beyond Budgeting Round Table, June 12, 2008.

7. James E. Hunton and Jacob M. Rose, "Effects of Anonymous Whistle-Blowing and Perceived Reputation Threats on Investigations of Whistle-Blowing Allegations by Audit Committee Members," *Strategy + Business,* February 2010, www.strategy-business.com/article/re00107.

8. Bruce Caplain, "Risk Management: Why It Failed, How to Fix It," *Internal Auditor,* http://www.theiia.org/intAuditor/free-feature/2008/risk-management-why-it-failed-how-to-fix-it-ii/.

9. Michael Schrage, "Boards of Prevention," *Strategy + Business,* June 2010, http://www.strategy-business.com/article/00037?gko=67f92.

10. Ibid.

11. Denton Collins, Adi Masli, Austin L. Reitenga, and Juan Manuel Sanchez, "Earnings Restatements, the Sarbanes-Oxley Act, and the Disciplining of Chief Financial Officers" *Journal of Accounting, Auditing and Finance* 24, no. 1 (2009): 1–34.

12. Robert Simons, "How Risky Is Your Company?" *Harvard Business Review,* May–June 1999, 85–94.

Chapter 7

1. Cyril Brookes, "Gaining Competitive Advantage Through Knowledge Management," http://www.gvt.com/kmpap2us.htm.

2. Peter F. Drucker, *Managing in a Time of Great Change* (Oxford: Butterworth-Heinemann, 1995), 12.

3. Brookes, "Gaining Competitive Advantage Through Knowledge Management."

4. W. Edwards Deming, *Out of Crisis* (Cambridge, MA: MIT, 1982; 26th ed., 1998), 19.

5. Charles G. Sieloff, "If Only HP Knew What HP Knows: The Roots of Knowledge Management at Hewlett-Packard," *Journal of Knowledge Management* 3, no. 1 (1999): 47–53.

6. John Seely Brown and Estee Solomon Gray, "The People Are the Company," http//www.com/fastco/issues/first/people.htm.

7. http://www.egonzehnder.com/global/ourfirm/aboutus.

8. James Manyika, "McKinsey Conversations with Global Leaders: John Chambers of Cisco," *McKinsey Quarterly,* April 2009, 80–87.

9. Jeffrey A. Martin and Kathleen M. Eisenhardt, "Rewiring: Cross-Business-Unit Collaborations and Performance in Multi-Business Organizations," *Academy of Management Journal* 53, no. 2 (2010): 265–301.

10. Edgar H. Schein, "Organizational Learning: What Is New?" MIT School of Management, http://learning.mit.edu/res/wp/10012.html.

11. Joseph L. Bower, "Jack Welch: General Electric's Revolutionary," Case 9-394-065 (Boston: Harvard Business School, April 1994).

12. Jack Welch, speech to shareholders, GE annual meeting, April 27, 1988.

13. Alan M. Webber, "What's So New About the New Economy?" *Harvard Business Review,* January–February 1993, 28.

14. Thomas A. Stewart, "The Invisible Key to Success," *Fortune,* August 5, 1996, 125.

15. Alice Dragoon, "Less for Success," *CIO Magazine,* October 15, 2004, www.cio.com/archive/101504/km.html.

16. Ibid.

17. Don Cohen, "What's Your Return on Knowledge?" *Harvard Business Review,* April 2007, 28.

Chapter 8

1. Noel M. Tichy and Ram Charan, "The CEO as Coach: An Interview with Allied Signal's Lawrence A. Bossidy," *Harvard Business Review,* March–April 1995, 69–78.

2. Joseph L. Bower, "Jack Welch: General Electric's Revolutionary," Case 9-394-065 (Boston: Harvard Business School, April 1994).

3. Ibid.

4. Julian Birkinshaw, *Reinventing Management* (Chichester: John Wiley, 2010), 257.

5. Jeffrey Pfeffer and Robert I. Sutton, *Hard Facts, Dangerous Half-Truths, and Total Nonsense: Profiting from Evidence-Based Management* (Boston: Harvard Business School Press, 2006), 6–7.

6. The editors of *BusinessWeek* with Cynthia Green, *A Business Week Guide: The Quality Imperative* (New York: McGraw-Hill, 1994), 11.

7. Eric Krell, "Why Benchmarking Doesn't Always Lead to Best Practices," *Business Finance,* October 2003, www.businessfinancemag.com/magazine/archives/article.html?articleID=14008.

Chapter 9

1. Joseph H. Bragdon, *Profit for Life* (Cambridge, MA: Society for Organizational Learning, 2006), 144.

2. Georg Kell and Peter Lacy, "Study: Sustainability a Priority for CEOs," *BusinessWeek,* June 25, 2010, www.businessweek.com/managing/content/jun2010/ca20100624_678038.htm.

3. Peter A. Soyka and Mark E. Bateman, "The Road Not Yet Taken: The State of U.S. Corporate Environmental Policy and Management" (Vienna, VA: Sustainable Enterprise Institute, 2009), 10.

4. Sheila Bonini and Hans-Werner Kaas, "Building a Sustainable Ford Motor Company: An Interview with Bill Ford," *McKinsey Quarterly,* January 2010, 92–93.

5. Bragdon, *Profit for Life,* 12.

6. Russ Banham, "How Green Is My Company?" CFO.com, October 18, 2004, www.cfo.com/article.cfm/3304849/c_3214842?f=insidecfo.

7. Ibid.

8. Bragdon, *Profit for Life,* 127.

9. Ibid., 20.

10. Ibid., 157.

11. Ibid., 115.

12. Banham, "How Green Is My Company?"

13. H. Thomas Johnson, "Confronting the Tyranny of Management by Numbers," *Reflections: The SoL Journal on Knowledge, Learning and Change* 5, no. 4 (2004): 1–11.

14. Bonini and Kaas, "Building a Sustainable Ford Motor Company."

15. Bragdon, *Profit for Life,* 144.

16. Ibid., 145.

17. Joshua D. Margolis and Hillary Anger Elfenbein, "Do Well by Doing Good? Don't Count on It," *Harvard Business Review,* January 2008, 19–20.

Chapter 10

1. Denise Caruso, "The Real Value of Intangibles," *Strategy + Business,* Autumn 2008, www.strategy-business.com/article/08302?pg=all.

2. Ibid.

3. Juergen Daum, "Interview with Baruch Lev: Accounting, Reporting and Intangible Assets," *The New New Economy Analyst Report,* March 06, 2002, www.juergendaum.com/news/03_06_2002.htm.

4. Leif Edvinnson and Michael S. Malone, *Intellectual Capital* (New York: HarperBusiness, 1997), 35–36.

5. Interbrand Group, *Best Global Brands 2010* (New York: Interbrand Group, 2010).

6. Heather Baukney, "Intangible Assets—An interview with Baruch Lev," IT World.com, http://www.itworld.com/Man/2817/CIO010315lev/pfindex.html.

7. Lowell Bryan, "The New Metrics of Corporate Performance: Profit per Employee," *McKinsey Quarterly,* February 2007, https://www.mckinseyquarterly.com/Strategy/Strategic_Thinking/The_new_metrics_of_corporate_performance_Profit_per_employee_1924.

8. Christopher W. Hart, "Beating the Market with Customer Satisfaction," *Harvard Business Review,* March 2007, 30–32.

9. Caruso, "The Real Value of Intangibles."

10. Baukney, "Intangible Assets."

11. Bryan, "The New Metrics of Corporate Performance."

Chapter 11

1. Bill Birchard and Alix Nyberg Stuart, "On Further Reflection: Do EVA and Other Value Metrics Still Offer a Good Mirror of Company Performance?" *CFO Magazine,* March 2001, www.cfo.com/article.cfm/2991941.

2. John McGrath, "Tracking Down Value," *Financial Times Mastering Management Review,* December 1998; and www.sternstewart.com/action/diageo.php.

3. Ibid.

4. Ibid.

5. Mark Graham Brown, *Beyond the Balanced Scorecard* (New York: Productivity Press, 2007), 25–26.

6. Ken Lever, interview with author, March 2005.

7. Regina Fazio Maruca, "The Cost of Capital," *Harvard Business Review,* September–October 1996, 9–10.

Chapter 12

1. Alfred Rappaport, "Ten Ways to Create Shareholder Value," *Harvard Business Review,* September 2006, 66–77.

2. John D. Martin and J. William Petty, *Value Based Management: The Corporate Response to the Shareholder Revolution* (Boston: Harvard Business School Press, 2000), 100.

3. Thomas A. Stewart, "Marakon Runners," *Fortune,* September 28, 1998, 153–158.

4. Ken Chenault, speech, New York, NY, June 3, 2004, http://library.corporate-ir.net/library/64/644/64467/items/173911/040603_text.pdf.

5. Steve Player, "BBRT Case Report," Beyond Budgeting Roundtable, Dallas, TX, January 19, 2005.

6. From Timothy Koller, "What Is Value-Based Management?" *McKinsey Quarterly,* March 1994, 87–101.

7. Christopher Null, "The Check Is in the Car: Complaints Are Down and Profits Are Up Since Progressive Insurance Put Its Reps on the Road," *Business 2.0,* July 2003.

8. Rappaport, "Ten Ways to Create Shareholder Value," 68–69.

9. Ibid.

Chapter 13

1. Thomas A. Stewart, "Growth as a Process: An Interview with Jeff Immelt," *Harvard Business Review,* June 2006, 60–70.

2. Ibid.

3. Ibid.

4. Adrian Slywotzky, Richard Wise, and Karl Weber, *How to Grow When Markets Don't: Discovering the New Drivers of Growth* (New York: Warner Books, 2003).

5. Jim Bramante, Gregor Pillen, and Doug Simpson, "CFO Survey: Current State and Future Direction," IBM Business Consulting Services, 2003.

6. Joseph McCafferty, "Testing the Top Line," *CFO Magazine*, October 1, 2004, 89–91, www.cfo.com/printable/article.cfm/3219980.

7. Michael Treacy and Jim Sims, "Take Command of Your Growth," *Harvard Business Review*, April 2004, 127–133.

8. Stewart, "Growth as a Process."

9. Jim Geisman and John Maruskin, "A Case for Discount Discipline," *Harvard Business Review*, November 2006, 30–32.

10. Ken Iverson, *Plain Talk* (New York: John Wiley, 1998), 179.

11. Treacy and Sims, "Take Command of Your Growth."

12. Geisman and Maruskin, "A Case for Discount Discipline."

13. Michael Treacy, *Double-Digit Growth: How Great Companies Achieve It—No Matter What* (New York: Penguin, 2003), 59.

14. "An Interview with Adrian Slywotzky, Co-Author of *How to Grow When Markets Don't*," April 2008, http://www.asme.org/NewsPublicPolicy/Newsletters/METoday/Articles/isDemand_Innovation. cfm.

15. Treacy, *Double-Digit Growth,* 18.

Chapter 14

1. For more on the value proposition, see Arnoldo C. Hax and Dean L. Wilde II, "The Delta Model: Adaptive Management for a Changing Model," *Sloan Management Review*, Winter 1999, 11–28.

2. Michael E. Porter, "What Is Strategy?" *Harvard Business Review*, November–December 1996, 62.

Chapter 15

1. Theodore Levitt, "Marketing Myopia," *Harvard Business Review*, September–October 1975, 26–28, 33–34, 38–39, 44, 173–183.

2. Michael Treacy and Fred Wiersema, *The Discipline of Market Leaders* (Reading, MA: Addison-Wesley, 1996), 38.

3. Michael Krigsman, "CRM Failure Rates: 2001–2009," August 3, 2009, http://www.zdnet.com/blog/projectfailures/crm-failure-rates-2001-2009/4967.

4. "The 10 Biggest CRM Mistakes," *Sales & Marketing Management*, December 2005, www.salesandmarketing.com/smm/magazine/article_display.jsp?vnu_content_id=1001526253.

5. Alice Dragoon, "CRM Wake-Up Call," *CIO Magazine*, July 15, 2005, www.cio.com/archive/071505/call_center.html.

6. Ibid.

7. Ulla K. Bunz and Jeanne D. Maes, "Learning Excellence: Southwest Airlines' Approach," *Managing Service Quality* 8, no. 3 (1998): 165.

8. Kevin Freiberg and Jackie Freiberg, *Nuts! Southwest Airlines' Crazy Recipe for Business and Personal Success* (Austin, TX: Bard Press Inc., 1996), 295.

Chapter 16

1. Frederick F. Reichheld and W. Earl Sasser Jr., "Zero Defections: Quality Comes to Services," *Harvard Business Review*, September–October 1990, 105–111.

2. Robert Kaplan, "A Balanced Scorecard Approach to Measure Customer Profitability," HBS Working Knowledge, August 5, 2005, http://hbswk.hbs.edu/item/4938.html.

3. John O. Whitney, "Strategic Renewal for Business Units," *Harvard Business Review*, July–August 1996, 89–90.

4. Tom Peters, *Thriving on Chaos* (London: Macmillan, 1987), 98.

5. Paul M. Dholkia, "The Hazards of Hounding," *Harvard Business Review*, October 2005, 20–24.

6. Robin Bellis-Jones, "Customer Profitability Analysis," *Management Accounting*, February 1989, 26–28.

7. Jeffrey Pfeffer and Robert I. Sutton, *Hard Facts, Dangerous Half-Truths, and Total Nonsense: Profiting from Evidence-Based Management* (Boston: Harvard Business School Press, 2006), 16.

8. Rita McGrath, "A Better Way to Cut Costs," Harvard Business Review Blog, March 9, 2009, http://blogs.hbr.org/hbr/mcgrath/2009/03/a-better-way-to-cut-costs.html.

Chapter 17

1. Rahul Jacob, "Why Some Customers Are More Equal Than Others," *Fortune,* September 19, 1994, 215–221.

2. Stephen Hall, "Loyalty—It's Worth More Than You Think," *Resource,* June 2003, www.loma.org/res-06-03-loyalty.asp.

3. Frederick F. Reichheld, "The One Number You Need to Grow," *Harvard Business Review,* December 2003, 47–54.

4. Mark Graham Brown, *Beyond the Balanced Scorecard* (New York: Productivity Press, 2007), 75.

5. Grahame R. Dowling and Mark Uncles, "Do Customer Loyalty Programs Really Work?" *Sloan Management Review,* Summer 1997, http://sloanreview.mit.edu/the-magazine/articles/1997/summer/3846/do-customer-loyalty-programs-really-work/.

6. Ibid.

7. Michael Treacy, *Double-Digit Growth* (New York: Penguin, 2003), 96–98.

8. Ibid.

9. Joseph C. Nunes and Xavier Drèze, "Your Loyalty Program Is Betraying You," *Harvard Business Review,* April 2006, 150.

10. Reichheld, "The One Number You Need to Grow."

11. Brown, *Beyond the Balanced Scorecard,* 75.

12. Hall, "Loyalty—It's Worth More than You Think."

13. Ibid.

Chapter 18

1. These principles are set out in W. Edwards Deming, *Out of Crisis* (Cambridge, MA: MIT Press, 1982; 26th ed., 1998).

2. John Seddon, "A Brief History of ISO 9000—Where Did We Go Wrong?" www.lean-service.com/6.asp.

3. Seddon, "A Brief History of ISO 9000."

4. Deming, *Out of Crisis,* 75.

5. Jim P. Womack, Daniel T. Jones, and Daniel Roos, *The Machine That Changed the World* (New York: HarperCollins, 1990), 90–91.

6. Deming, *Out of Crisis,* 29.

7. Ibid., 65.

8. Ibid., 66.

9. Ibid., 69.

10. John Seddon, "The Case Against ISO 9000," www.uwe.ac.uk/bbs/trr/Issue2/Is2-1_1.htm.

11. Teruyuki Minoura, "The 'Thinking' Production System: TPS as a Winning Strategy for Developing People in the Global Manufacturing Environment," June 18, 2003, http://www.toyota.co.jp/en/special/tps/tps.html.

12. H. Thomas Johnson and Anders Bröms, *Profit Beyond Measure* (London: Nicholas Brealey Publishing, 2000), 102.

13. John Seddon, "Death to ISO9000—An Economic Disease," www.lean-service.com/6-22.asp.

Chapter 19

1. Peter F. Drucker, "Managing for Business Effectiveness," *Harvard Business Review,* May–June 1963, 53–60.

2. See Tony Hope and Jeremy Hope, *Transforming the Bottom Line* (London: Nicholas Brealey Publishing, 1995), chapter 3.

3. Robin Cooper and Robert S. Kaplan, "Profit Priorities of Activity-Based Costing," *Harvard Business Review,* May–June 1991, 130–135.

4. Robin Cooper and Robert S. Kaplan, *Cost and Effect: Using Integrated Cost Systems to Drive Profitability and Performance* (Boston: Harvard Business School Press, 1997), 81–82.

5. Robin Cooper and Robert S. Kaplan, "Activity-Based Systems: Measuring the Costs of Resource Usage," *Accounting Horizons,* September 1992, 1–8.

6. H. Thomas Johnson, "It's Time to Stop Overselling Activity-Based Concepts," *Management Accounting,* September 1992, 26–35.

7. H. Thomas Johnson, *Relevance Regained* (New York: Free Press, 1992), 149.

8. Elliot B. Ross, "Making Money with Proactive Pricing," *Harvard Business Review,* November–December 1984, 145.

Chapter 20

1. Quoted in Thomas Davenport, Sirkka L. Jarvenpaa, and Michael C. Beers, "Improving Knowledge Work Processes," *Sloan Management Review,* Summer 1996, 54.

2. James P. Womack and Daniel T. Jones, "From Lean Production to the Lean Enterprise," *Harvard Business Review,* March–April 1994, 93–103.

3. Thomas H. Davenport, "The Fad That People Forgot," http://fastcompany.com/fastco/Issues/First/Reengin.html.

4. Ibid.

5. John Seely Brown and Estee Solomon Gray, "The People Are the Company," http://www.fastcompany.com/fastco/issues/first/people.htm.

6. John Seely Brown and Paul Duguid, "Practice Makes Process," *CIO Magazine,* March 2001, www.cio.com/archive/030100/process.html.

7. Ibid.

8. Michael Hammer, "Hammer Responds: Process Makes PRACTICE Better," *IT World,* March 2001, http://www.itworld.com/CIO030100_reply_content.

9. Howard Gleckman, John Carey, Russell Mitchell, Tim Smart, and Chris Roush, "The Technology Payoff," *BusinessWeek,* June 14, 1993, 39.

10. Frank Ostroff and Douglas Smith, "The Horizontal Organization," *McKinsey Quarterly,* January 1992, 148–168.

Chapter 21

1. Teruyuki Minoura quoted in Toyota Georgetown Web site report, "The 'Thinking' Production System: TPS as a Winning Strategy for Developing People in the Global Manufacturing Environment," regarding his remark made at the 2003 Automation Parts System Solution Fair on June 18, 2003, and compiled and published on October 3, 2003, by the Public Affairs Division of Toyota Motor Company, http://www.toyotageorgetown.com/tps.asp.

2. H. Thomas Johnson and Anders Bröms, *Profit Beyond Measure* (London: Nicholas Brealey Publishing, 2000), 102.

3. Jeffrey K. Liker, *The Toyota Way* (London: McGraw-Hill, 2004), 10–11.

4. Johnson and Bröms, *Profit Beyond Measure,* 3.

5. W. Edwards Deming, *The New Economics* (Cambridge, MA: MIT Press, 2000), 31–33.

6. Taiichi Ohno, *Toyota Production System* (New York: Productivity Press, 1988), 30.

7. Quoted in Jeffrey K. Liker, *The Toyota Way* (New York: McGraw-Hill, 2004), 144–145; and P. S. Adler, "Building Better Bureaucracies," *Academy of Management Executive* 13, no. 4 (1999): 36–47.

8. Steven J. Spear, "Learning to Lead at Toyota," *Harvard Business Review,* May 2004, 78–86.

9. Liker, *The Toyota Way,* 192–193.

10. Based on an article by Rajan R. Kamath and Jeffrey K. Liker, "A Second Look at Japanese Product Development," *Harvard Business Review,* November–December 1994, 154–170.

11. Ohno, *Toyota Production System,* 45.

12. Teruyuki Minoura quoted in Toyota Georgetown Web site report, "The 'Thinking' Production System."

13. Liker, *The Toyota Way,* 198.

14. "Catching Up with Uncle Sam: The EEF Final Report on U.S. and U.K. Manufacturing Productivity," Engineering Employers Federation, December 2001, 4–41.

Chapter 22

1. James P. Womack and Daniel T. Jones, "Lean Consumption," *Harvard Business Review,* March 2005, 58–68.

2. John Seddon, *Freedom from Command and Control—A Better Way to Make the Work Work* (Buckingham, England: Vanguard Education Limited, 2003), 13.

3. John Seddon, "Watch Out for the Toolheads!" http://www.triarchypress.com/pages/articles/Understanding-the-Variety-of-Demand.pdf.

4. Ibid.

5. W. Edwards Deming, *Out of Crisis,* 26th ed. (Cambridge, MA: MIT Press, 1998), 333.

6. Ibid., 334.

7. John Seddon, "Measurement and Management," www.lean-service.com/measurement.asp.

8. Simon Caulkin, "The Quality of Mersey," *Observer,* April 17, 2005, 9.

Chapter 23

1. Bob Gilbert, "Sick Sigma?" www.contextmag.com/archives/200208/Feature2SickSigma.asp.

2. Ibid.

3. www.ge.com/sixsigma/makingcustomers.htm.

4. Ibid.

5. Jeffrey K. Liker, *The Toyota Way* (New York: McGraw-Hill, 2004), 297.

6. Jim Parke, telephone interview with author, March 2005.

7. http://www.vaneekhoutconsulting.nl/wp-content/uploads/2010/08/Six-sigma-risks.pdf.

8. Gilbert, "Sick Sigma?"

9. Ibid.

10. Ibid.

11. Ibid.

12. Ibid.

Chapter 24

1. Jeffrey K. Liker, *The Toyota Way* (New York: McGraw-Hill, 2004), 130.

2. Robin Cooper, *When Lean Enterprises Collide: Competing Through Confrontation* (Boston: Harvard Business School Press, 1995), 135.

3. John Templeman, "Daimler's New Driver Won't Be Making Sharp Turns," *BusinessWeek,* July 4, 1994, 48.

4. M. Bromwich and A. Bhimani, *Management Accounting Pathways to Progress* (Burlington, MA: CIMA, 1994), 177.

5. Cooper, *When Lean Enterprises Collide,* 141.

6. Based on an article by Rajan R. Kamath and Jeffrey K. Liker, "A Second Look at Japanese Product Development," *Harvard Business Review,* November–December 1994, 154–170.

7. Cooper, *When Lean Enterprises Collide,* 164.

8. Kamath and Liker, "A Second Look at Japanese Product Development."

9. Ibid.

10. Cooper, *When Lean Enterprises Collide,* 185.

11. Quoted in Willard L. Zangwill, *Lightning Strategies for Innovation* (New York: Lexington Books, 1993), 287.

12. Cooper, *When Lean Enterprises Collide,* 147.

13. Ibid., 143.

Chapter 25

1. Tony Hope and Jeremy Hope, *Transforming the Bottom Line: Managing Performance with the Real Numbers* (Boston: Harvard Business School Press, 1996), 114.

2. Ibid, 115.

3. Brian Maskell and Bruce Baggaley. *Practical Lean Accounting*. Montvale, NJ: Productivity Press, 2004, 2.

4. Karen M. Kroll, "The Lowdown on Lean Accounting," *Harvard Business Review,* July 2004, 69–76.

5. Bruce Baggaley, "Costing by Value Stream," *Journal of Cost Management,* May/June 2003, 24–30.

6. Brian Maskell, "Do We Need to Simplify Financial Reporting?" www.maskell.com.

Chapter 26

1. Mark Krueger, "Best Practices in Cost Rationalization," *Answerthink Report,* 2004.

2. Ibid.

3. "CFOs: Driving Finance Transformation for the 21st Century 2002," *CFO Magazine* Research Series, www.cfoenterprises.com/research.shtml, 21.

4. A.T. Kearney, "Success Through Shared Services 2003," www.atkearney.com/main.taf?p=5,3,1,74.

5. Karen M. Kroll, "Sharing the Wealth," IndustryWeek.com, October 1, 2005, www.industryweek.com/ReadArticle.aspx?ArticleID=10729.

Chapter 27

1. Thomas H. Davenport and Jeanne G. Harris, *Competing on Analytics: The New Science of Winning* (Boston: Harvard Business School Press, 2007), 147.

2. www.ebstrategy.com/Outsourcing/cases/failures.htm.

3. "Reining in Outsourcing Risk," *Strategy + Business,* November 30, 2005.

4. Michael Bloch, Dejan Boskovic, and Allen Weinberg, "How Innovators Are Changing IT Offshoring," *McKinsey Quarterly,* January 2010, 21.

5. Arjun Sethi and Olivier Aries, "The End of Outsourcing (As We Know It)," *BusinessWeek,* August 10, 2010, www.businessweek.com/print/technology/content/aug2010/tc20100810_440259. htm.

6. Ibid.

7. Pete Engardio, Michael Arndt, and Dean Foust, "The Future of Outsourcing," *BusinessWeek,* January 30, 2006, www.businessweek.com/magazine/content/06_05/b3969401.htm.

8. Ibid.

9. Joseph H. Bragdon, *Profit for Life* (Cambridge, MA: Society for Organizational Learning, 2006), 140.

10. Jeffrey Pfeffer, "Six Dangerous Myths About Pay," *Harvard Business Review,* May–June 1998, 112.

11. Ibid., 114

12. John Kavanagh, "Outsourcing: What's the Pay-off?" ComputerWeekly.com, February 20, 2006, www.computerweekly.com/Articles/2005/05/09/209860/OutsourcingWhat'sthepay-off.htm.

13. Engardio et al., "The Future of Outsourcing.

14. Bloch et al., "How Innovators Are Changing IT Offshoring," 22.

15. Engardio et al., "The Future of Outsourcing."

16. Carrie Mathews, "How to Improve Outsourcer Relationships," *CIO Magazine,* July 1, 2005, www.cio.com/archive/070105/forum.htm.

17. Anne Stuart, "Same Caller, New Message," *CFO Magazine,* February 22, 2005, www.cfo.com/article.cfm/3665064/2/c_3686543.

Chapter 28

1. Todd Datz, "Portfolio Management—How to Do It Right," *CIO Magazine,* May 1, 2003, www.cio.com/archive/050103/portfolio.html.

2. Ibid.

3. Steven E. Prokesch, "Unleashing the Power of Learning: An Interview with British Petroleum's John Browne," *Harvard Business Review*, September–October 1997, 147–168.

4. The discussion of options theory and related illustrations are from the authors' discussions with Steve Morlidge. For more information, see Steve Morlidge and Steve Player, *Future Ready: How to Master Business Forecasting* (Chichester, UK: John Wiley & Sons, 2010), 151–178.

5. Steven C. Wheelwright and Kim B. Clark, "Creating Project Plans to Focus Product Development," *Harvard Business Review*, March–April 1992, 2–14.

6. Ibid.

7. Tom Copeland and Peter Tufano, "A Real-World Way to Manage Real Options," *Harvard Business Review*, March 2004, 90.

8. Ibid., 91.

9. Datz, "Portfolio Management."

10. Robert S. Kaplan and Nicole Tempest, "Wells Fargo Online Financial Services (B)," Case 9-199-019 (Boston: Harvard Business School Publishing, 1998); and Jeremy Hope, *Reinventing the CFO: How Managers Can Transform Their Roles and Add Greater Value* (Boston: Harvard Business School Press, 2006), 141, 142.

11. Jack Gage, "Good Cap-Ex, Bad Cap-Ex," Forbes.com, May 5, 2005, www.forbes.com/business/forbes/2005/0905/083.html.

12. Todd Datz, "Portfolio Management Done Right," http://www.corporateportfoliomanagement.org/article-29-Portfolio-Management-Done-Right.

Chapter 29

1. Suzanne Heywood, Dennis Layton, and Risto Penttinen, "A Better Way to Cut Costs," *McKinsey Quarterly* no. 1 (2010): 65.

2. Ibid.

3. Natalie Mizik and Robert Jacobson, "The Cost of Myopic Management," *Harvard Business Review*, August 2007, 22.

4. Simon Caulkin, "Bloated Firms Not Watching Their Waste," *Observer Business*, October 23, 2005, 10.

5. Jeff Immelt, 2010 General Electric Annual Report in the Letter to the Shareowners.

6. Suzanne P. Nimocks, Robert L. Rosiello, and Oliver Wright, "Managing Overhead Costs," *McKinsey Quarterly* no. 2 (2005): 110–111.

7. "Total Employee Mobility Benchmarking Report" (Waterford, WI : Runzheimer International, October 8, 2009).

8. Simon Caulkin, "Roche: From Oversight to Insight," MLab Notes, London Business School, July 16, 2010, http://www.managementlab.org/files/site/publications/labnotes/mlab-labnotes-016.pdf.

Chapter 30

1. Cited in Stephen Swoyer, "Why ERP Does Matter," *Enterprise Systems*, August 16, 2005, www.esj.com/Enterprise/article.aspx?EditorialsID=1476.

2. Christopher Koch, "IT Integration's New Strategy," *CIO Magazine*, September 15, 2005, www.cio.com/archive/091505/integration.html.

3. Jeffrey Pfeffer and Robert I. Sutton, *Hard Facts, Dangerous Half-Truths, and Total Nonsense* (Boston: Harvard Business School Press, 2006), 182.

4. "CFOs: Driving Finance Transformation for the 21st Century 2002," *CFO Magazine* Research Series, www.cfoenterprises.com/research.shtml, 13.

5. Matt Hines, "Customization, Complexity Still Dog ERP Efforts," CNET News.com, July 19, 2005, www.news.zdnet.com/2100-3513_22-5795115.html.

6. Information Week Q&A, "In Search of the Sophisticated Infrastructure," InformationWeek Web site (September 13, 2005), http://www.informationweek.com/news/170702244.

7. Christopher Koch, "The ABCs of ERP," *CIO Magazine* Research Center, www.cio.com/research/erp/edit/erpbasics.html.

8. Jagan Nathan Vaman, *ERP in Practice* (New York: McGraw-Hill, 2007), 35–36.

9. Vinay Couto, Irmgard Heinz, and Mark J. Moran, "Not Your Father's CFO," *Strategy + Business*, February 15, 2005, 1–10.

10. Eric Knorr and Galen Gruman, "What Cloud Computing Really Means," July 19, 2010, http://www.infoworld.com/d/cloud-computing/what-cloud-computing-really-means-031.

Chapter 31

1. Stephan Haeckel, *Adaptive Enterprise: Creating and Leading Sense-and-Respond Organizations* (Boston: Harvard Business School Press, 1999), 20.

2. "Business Objects and EIU Study 2007," quoted in "Improving Decision-making in Organisations—Unlocking Business Intelligence," Chartered Institute of Management Accountants, September 2008.

3. Ken McGee, "Give Me That Real-Time Information," *Harvard Business Review*, April 2004, 26.

4. John Goff, "Drowning in Data," CFO.com, www.cfo.com/printable/article.cfm/3010723.

5. John Goff, "In the Fast Lane," *CFO Magazine*, December 2004, www.cfo.com/printable/article.cfm/3419652.

6. "A Practical Framework for Business Intelligence and Planning in Midsize Companies" (Armonk, NY: IBM), August 2010, http://public.dhe.ibm.com/software/data/sw-library/cognos/pdfs/analystreports/ar_a_practical_bi_and_planning_framework_for_midsize_companies.pdf.

7. Ibid.

8. Steve Player, "Beyond Budgeting Round Table (BBRT) Case Report: American Express: Using Rolling Forecasts to Become More Adaptive," September 12, 2005, 6.

9. Ibid.

10. Eric Laursen, "How CPM Software Empowers Users," *CFO Magazine*, February 15, 2005, www.cfo.com/printable/article.cfm/3621246.

11. Russ Banham, "Quantum Loop," *CFO Magazine*, March 17, 2003, www.cfo.com/printable/article.cfm/3008650.

12. Player, BBRT Case Report.

13. Gary Crittenden, interview by author, February 14, 2005.

14. Connie Winkler, "Getting a Grip on Performance," *CFO Magazine*, November 15, 2004, www.cio.com/research/erp/edit/erpbasics.html.

15. Meredith Levinson, "Business Intelligence: Not Just for Bosses Anymore," *CIO Magazine*, January 15, 2006, www.cio.com/archive/011506/business_intelligence.html.

16. Meredith Levinson, "The Brain Behind the Big, Bad Burger and Other Tales of Business Intelligence," *CIO Magazine*, March 15, 2005, www.cio.com/archive/031505/intelligence.html.

Chapter 32

1. Robert Simons, *Levers of Organizational Design: How Managers Use Accountability Systems for Greater Performance* (Boston: Harvard Business School Press, 2005), 104.

2. "A Smarter Way to Manufacture," *BusinessWeek*, April 30, 1990, 110–117.

Chapter 33

1. Jeremy Hope, "Planning and Forecasting: Use Continuous Planning and Rolling Forecasts to Support Adaptive Management" (Ottawa: Cognos Innovation Center, 2006), 8–9.

2. Philip Bligh, Darius Vaskelis, and John Kelleher, "Take the Frenzy out of Forecasting," *Optimize Magazine* 17 (March 2003), www.optimizemag.com/issue/017/financial.htm.

3. Thomas Boesen, "Borealis Case Study" presentation (Denver, CO: BBRT North America Annual Conference), March 2002.

4. Yossi Sheffi, "A Demand for Steady Supply," *Financial Times*, August 22, 2005, 10.

5. Steve Morlidge discussion with the authors, London, March 2009.

Chapter 34

1. Thomas H. Davenport, *Competing on Analytics: The New Science of Winning* (Boston: Harvard Business School Press, 2007), 7.
2. "Assessment for Learning Research Initiative: Report of the First Research Forum," Society for Organizational Learning, January 14, 1998, http://www.solonline.org/com/AR98/index.html.
3. Mark Graham Brown, *Beyond the Balanced Scorecard* (New York: Productivity Press, 2007), 53.

Chapter 35

1. David A. J. Axson, *Best Practices in Planning and Management Reporting* (Hoboken, NJ: John Wiley & Sons, 2003), 59.

Chapter 36

1. Simon Caulkin, "Roche: From Oversight to Insight," MLab Notes, London Business School, July 16, 2010, http://www.managementlab.org/files/site/publications/labnotes/mlab-labnotes-016.pdf.
2. Kim Cameron, "Ethics, Virtuousness and Constant Change," in *The Ethical Challenge*, eds. Noel Tichy and Andrew R. McGill (San Francisco: Jossey Bass, 2003), 85–94, http://64.233.183.104/search?q=cache:Z5r8tcM9EF0J:www.competingvalues.com/pdf/ethics.pdf+kim+cameron+vituous&hl=en&ct=clnk&cd=1.
3. Marshall W. Van Alstyne, "Create Colleagues, Not Competitors," *Harvard Business Review*, September 2005, 24.
4. Jeremy Hope and Peter Bunce, "Beyond Budgeting Round Table (BBRT) Case Report on Statoil," November 2007.
5. Eric Schmidt, "Collaborate or Perish," McKinseyDigital.com, February 26, 2009, http://whatmatters.mckinseydigital.com/organization/collaborate-or-perish.
6. "Executive Summary," TDWI Data Quality Report, http://www.webdedication.com/perfect-data/NewFiles/articles.html.

Chapter 37

1. Quoted in Jonathan D. Day and James C. Wendler, "The New Economics of Organization," *McKinsey Quarterly* no. 1 (1998): 4–17.
2. Harry Levinson, "Management by Whose Objectives?" *Harvard Business Review*, January 2003, 108.
3. Quoted in Adrian Furnham, *Management and Myths* (New York: Palgrave McMillan, 2004), 26.
4. Quoted in Stephen Overell, "Let's Have a Little Chat About Work Shall We?" *Financial Times*, March 6, 2003, 13.
5. Ibid.
6. John Seddon, "Performance Without Appraisal," www.lean-service.com/6-14.asp.
7. W. Edwards Deming, *Out of Crisis* (Cambridge, MA: MIT, 1982; 26th ed., 1998), 102.
8. Fred Nickols, "Don't Redesign Your Company's Performance Appraisal System, Scrap It!" http://home.att.net/~nickols/scrap_it.htm.
9. Kenneth Blanchard and Spencer Johnson, *The One Minute Manager* (New York: William Morrow, 1982).
10. Quoted in Jeffrey Pfeffer and Robert I. Sutton, *Hard Facts, Dangerous Half-Truths and Total Nonsense* (Boston: Harvard Business School Press, 2006), 107.
11. Deming, *Out of Crisis,* 315.
12. Seddon, "Performance Without Appraisal."
13. Ibid.
14. Ibid.
15. Gary Hamel, "W.L. Gore: Lessons from a Management Revolutionary," Wall Street Journal blog, April 2, 2010, http://blogs.wsj.com/management/2010/04/02/wl-gore-lessons-from-a-management-revolutionary-part-2/.

16. Hirotaka Takeuchi, Emi Osono, and Norihiko Shimizu, "The Contradictions That Drive Toyota's Success," *Harvard Business Review,* June 2008, 96–104.

Chapter 38

1. Frederick Herzberg, "One More Time: How Do You Motivate Employees?" (Boston: Harvard Business Review Business Classics, 2008), 13–22.

2. Jeffrey Pfeffer, "Six Dangerous Myths About Pay," *Harvard Business Review,* May–June 1998, 109–119.

3. Gary Hamel, "HCL: Extreme Management Makeover," Wall Street Journal blog, July 6, 2010, http://blogs.wsj.com/management/2010/07/06/hcl-extreme-management-makeover/tab/print/.

4. Chris Argyris, "Empowerment: The Emperor's New Clothes," *Harvard Business Review,* May–June 1998, 100.

5. Jeremy Hope, *Beyond Budgeting* (Boston: Harvard Business School Press, 2003), 62.

6. Robert Simons, "Control in an Age of Empowerment," *Harvard Business Review,* March–April 1995, 80.

7. Pfeffer, "Six Dangerous Myths About Pay."

8. Ibid., 115.

9. Michael I. Norton and Elizabeth W. Dunn, "Help Employees Give Away Some of That Bonus," *Harvard Business Review,* July–August 2008, 27.

10. Frederick Herzberg, "Workers' Needs: The Same Around the World," *Industry Week,* September 21, 1987, 30.

Chapter 39

1. Thomas A. DiPrete, Greg Eirich, and Matthew Pittinsky, "Compensation Benchmarking, Leapfrogs, and the Surge in Executive Pay," *American Journal of Sociology* 115, no. 6 (May 2010): 1671–1712.

2. Charles Elson, "What's Wrong with Executive Compensation," *Harvard Business Review,* January 2003, 68–77.

3. DiPrete et al., "Compensation Benchmarking, Leapfrogs, and the Surge in Executive Pay."

4. Andrew Ward and Patrick Jenkins, "Bank chief champions case for fixed pay," *Financial Times,* February 17, 2010, http://www.ft.com/cms/s/0/d0a6a32c-1be9-11df-a5e1-00144feab49a.html.

5. Quoted in James Haskett, "Has Managerial Capitalism Peaked?" HBS Working Knowledge, October 4, 2007, http://hbswk.hbs.edu/item/5794.html#original.

6. Francesco Guerrera, "Executive Shares Fail to Raise Value," *Financial Times,* May 14, 2001, 1.

7. J. C. De Swann and Neil W. C. Harper, "Getting What You Pay for With Stock Options," *McKinsey Quarterly* no. 1 (2003): 152–155.

8. Alfred Rappaport, "How to Link Executive Pay with Performance," *Harvard Business Review,* March–April 1999, 93.

9. Erik Stern, "Putting the Boss's Achievements into Context," *Financial Times,* March 6, 2001, 16.

10. Floyd Norris, "Stock Options: Do They Make Bosses Cheat?" *New York Times,* August 23, 2010, http://query.nytimes.com/gst/fullpage.html?res=9E05E7DF163EF936A3575BC0A9639C8B63.

11. Ibid.

12. Geoff Colvin, "Amex Gets CEO Pay Right," *Fortune,* January 6, 2008, http://money.cnn.com/magazines/fortune/fortune_archive/2008/01/21/102659595/index.htm.

13. Chris Armstrong, Christopher D. Ittner, and David F. Larcker, "Consultants Are No Help in Preventing High CEO Salaries," Strategy + Business.com, August 21, 2008, http://www.strategy-business.com/article/re00036.

14. Stephen F. O'Byrne and S. David Young, "Why Executive Pay Is Failing," *Harvard Business Review,* June 2006, 28.

15. Stephen Moore, "The Conscience of a Capitalist," http://online.wsj.com/article/SB100014240527487044715045744471140588870676.html.

16. John Mackey, "Compensation at Whole Foods Market," *The CEO Blog,* Wholefoods.com, November 2, 2006, http://www2.wholefoodsmarket.com/blogs/jmackey/2006/11/02/compensation-at-whole-foods-market/#more-16.

17. Diageo, 2009 Annual Report, http://annualreport2009.diageoreports.com/governance/directors-remuneration-report.aspx.

18. Melissa Klein Aguilar, "Few Best Practices on Equity Ownership Plans," *Compliance Week,* August 10, 2010, www.complianceweek.com/article/6101/few-best-practices-on-equity-ownership-plans.

19. Shawn Tully, "Five Commandments for Paying the Boss," *Fortune,* July 10, 2006, 51–53.

20. Ben W. Heineman Jr., "The Fatal Flaw in Pay for Performance," *Harvard Business Review,* June 2008, 31–34.

Chapter 40

1. Edgar Schein, *Corporate Culture* (San Francisco: Jossey-Bass, 1999), 53.

2. Lynn Brenner, "The Myth of Incentive Pay," *CFO Magazine,* July 1995, 26–31.

3. Kevin Freiberg and Jackie Freiberg, *Nuts!* (Austin, TX: Bard Press, 1996), 100.

4. Ibid., 102.

5. Julia Finch and Zoe Wood, Guardian.co.uk, March 11, 2010, http://www.guardian.co.uk/business/2010/mar/11/john-lewis-staff-share-151m-in-bonuses.

6. Jeremy Hope, "Performance Evaluation: Base Accountability on Team Performance with Hindsight," IBM Cognos' Innovation Series, April 2009, http://www.scribd.com/doc/38524271/Jeremy-Hope-Performance-Evaluation.

Acknowledgments

We want to acknowledge and thank the many people who helped make this book possible. There are far more than we could list, but we thankfully acknowledge our many clients and members of the Beyond Budgeting Round Table (BBRT) for providing real companies in which we could see how performance management tools work on the front lines of business. We especially thank the volunteer BBRT membership chairmen, Steve Morlidge of Unilever and Bjarte Bogsnes of Statoil, for their support and diligent efforts in building the Round Table. We also thank our fellow BBRT directors, Peter Bunce and Franz Röösli, who have helped in the development of the ideas in this book and who share the load and make our time together more enjoyable. We would also like to thank retired director Robin Fraser, but he probably doesn't want his name in a book about tools.

We greatly appreciate the encouragement, friendship, and leadership of our academic advisor, Charles Horngren. Even though he has recently passed away, his guidance has permanently shaped our view of the world.

Our back office support team keeps us going wherever we are in the world, so special thanks to the North America team of Robin Baumgartner, Heather Bryce, Sandy Wilson, Melissa Rosandich, Pierre Guillaume, Ron Bradley, John Miller and Cynthia Thomas. We also want to thank those thought leaders who have helped shape our views, especially Mark Graham Brown and Stephen M.R. Covey.

We have been blessed with a great publishing team at Harvard Business Review Press. This includes Tim Sullivan, Kevin Evers, Allison Peter, and Jen Waring. We also want to thank our excellent research assistants, our sons Oliver Hope and Dave Player, who helped us at times when no one else could.

Our travels in pursuit of information for this book have taken us around the globe many times. The strength to make these journeys comes from the support of our families, who stand behind us and support us wherever we go. So our most heartfelt thanks go to Dot, Ben, Vicky, and Oliver Hope, and to Lydia, Dave, Emily, and Michael (Cole) Player, and also to Tony Hope and Ray and Lynnette Player. Your love sustains us.

—Jeremy Hope and Steve Player

About the Authors

Jeremy Hope (1948–2011) served as research director of the Beyond Budgeting Round Table, a collaborative that offers shared learning, performance management research, and consulting support. Jeremy authored, coauthored, and edited six books, including *The Leader's Dilemma: How to Build an Empowered and Adaptive Organization Without Losing Control, Reinventing the CFO,* and *Beyond Budgeting: How Managers Can Break Free from the Annual Performance Trap*. This book is produced and presented in his memory.

Steve Player, founder and managing director of The Player Group, has coauthored and edited five industry-leading cost and performance management books. He is program director for the Beyond Budgeting Round Table in North America. Previously, he served as the managing partner of the Advanced Cost Management Team of a global accounting firm. He is a top-ranked speaker and consultant, helping clients implement leading edge practices. He also writes a monthly column on Finance Transformation.

Contact the authors by email at: steve@theplayergroup.com
Web: www.bbrt.org
Web: www.theplayergroup.com